THE PLANTING OF CHRISTIANITY IN AFRICA

LONDON
Lutterworth Press, 4 Bouverie Street, E.C.4

AUSTRALIA and NEW ZEALAND
J. H. Morgan, Lane Centre, 325 Flinders Lane, Melbourne

CANADA
G. R. Welch Co. Ltd., 222 Evans Avenue, Toronto

CARIBBEAN
K. Jackson Marshall, P.O. Box 420, Barbados, British West Indies

FAR EAST
M. Graham Brash & Son, Prinsep House, 36c Prinsep Street, Singapore 7
M. Graham Brash & Son, F-1, 12th floor, Mirador Mansions, 58 Nathan Rd,
Kowloon, Hong Kong

INDIA
Christian Literature Society, P.O. Box 501, Park Town, Madras; Tract and
Book Society, South Street, Bangalore; Wesley Press and Publishing House,
Mysore

S. AFRICA
J. R. and D. L. Dorman, P.O. Box 5532, Johannesburg

ZAMBIA
United Society for Christian Literature, 3 Cairo Road, Lusaka, N. Rhodesia
and P.O. Box 274, Kitwe, Zambia

THE PLANTING OF
CHRISTIANITY IN
AFRICA

By
C. P. GROVES
*Formerly Professor of Missions in the Selly Oak Colleges
Birmingham*

VOLUME ONE to 1840

LONDON
LUTTERWORTH PRESS

PRINTED IN THE NETHERLANDS BY DRUKKERIJ HOLLAND N.V., AMSTERDAM

Wherefore he who would learn wisdom from the complex experience of history, must question closely all its phenomena, must notice that which is less obvious as well as that which is most palpable; must judge not peremptorily or sweepingly, but with reserves and exceptions; not as lightly overrunning a wide region of truth, but thankful if after much pains he has advanced his landmarks only a little.

THOMAS ARNOLD, *Christian Life*

1. By end of 2nd Century in both Egypt and North Africa a strong Church.

2. Christian Church not appeared in Abyssinia and there in Nubia.

3. In North African Church no Missionary activity among pagan tribes beyond Roman frontier.

4. In 7th Century came Arab Armies & spread of Islam from Red Sea.

PREFACE

IT is the purpose of this history to present in perspective within the limits of a single narrative the various attempts to plant Christianity in Africa. It has been usual to treat Africa south of the Sahara as the unit for purposes of missionary history. This has involved beginning the story in the fifteenth century, unless indeed it has been limited to the work of the Protestant Missionary Societies, when the beginning has been made at the end of the eighteenth. The present study takes the continent as the unit concerned, and thus begins with the early Church in Egypt and North Africa. The northern shores need not be surrendered on the ground that they are also part of the Mediterranean world. Such modern ethnological surveys as Professor C. G. Seligman's *Races of Africa* or the comprehensive research project of the International African Institute are fully continental in scope. Moreover, such a range is necessitated by the advance of Islam, a development that, in relation to Christian Missions, has profoundly modified much of Africa south of the Sahara, and an outline of which has accordingly been included. Madagascar, on the other hand, is not comprised in the present history, since here the ethnological associations are in the main Malayo-Polynesian and the story of missions on the island is not bound up at all intimately with current events in Africa.

The method of presentation is chronological rather than regional, taking the whole story forward stage by stage rather than dealing completely with one region at a time, which latter has been the method followed, for example, by Dr. Julius Richter in his *Geschichte der evangelischen Mission in Afrika* and by Dr. Du Plessis in his *Evangelisation of Pagan Africa*.

One result of such a scope and method is to throw into relief the fact that the present Christian missionary activity represents the third opportunity of Christianity in Africa. The first entry belongs to the early Christian centuries. By the end of the second century there is both in Egypt and North Africa a strong Christian Church. In lands to the south of Egypt there appeared Christian kingdoms, first in Abyssinia, then in Nubia. In the case of the North African Church, however, no missionary activity among pagan tribes beyond the Roman frontier is recorded. Then came, in the seventh century, the conquering Arab armies and the spread of Islam from the Red Sea to the

Atlantic coast. In Egypt the Coptic Church has survived to our own day, much diminished in numbers and influence; a Christian Church has also lived on, in enfeebling isolation, in Abyssinia. But these two Christian communities alone remain of the planting of the early Church. In Nubia the Christian Church held on tenaciously for wellnigh a thousand years before it finally succumbed to Islam. In North Africa the once influential Church of a region that has been described as a second Italy in time totally disappeared. And so the first opportunity came and went. And it was not repeated. The chance to enter Africa from the north was not given again. That the opportunity was a real one, despite the physical obstacles, is shown by the advance of Islam into the heart of Africa from this very vantage-ground.

Seven centuries passed after the entry of Islam before the next opportunity was presented. A door into Africa swung open a second time when the Portuguese adventurers, under the inspiration of the great leader Prince Henry, crept farther and farther along the African coast until at length they reached the eastern seas and crossed to India. Though when this was done the Portuguese found their dominating interest in the Indies, they did nevertheless establish themselves at three points in particular on the immense coastline of the Africa they had skirted—on the Guinea Coast, at the Congo estuary and in Angola, and on the Lower Zambezi. They took their Christian religion with them, and chiefs and people were won to the faith. For two hundred years the Christian missions were sustained and Africans admitted to the Orders and the priesthood. Then came the decadence of Portuguese power, and the Christianity that had been introduced along with it faded away. Thus came and passed the second opportunity.

The third is that of our own modern age, which in its effective beginnings appeared only in the closing decade of the eighteenth century. For fifty years, struggling heroically against heavy odds—the dread malaria in the west, recurrent frontier wars in the south, and over all the still flourishing slave-trade and persisting slave-owner mind—the pioneers held on. Yet by 1840 there was little more than a precarious foothold in the west outside Sierra Leone, while in the south the Zambezi was not even in sight and the pouring out from the British Colony of the disgruntled Boer trekkers to establish independent republics was scarcely propitious for missionary advance. It is to this point that the present volume takes the story.

The authorities upon which I have relied are sufficiently indicated in the course of the narrative itself. These consist almost entirely of already published material, though in many cases the books are not easy of access to the ordinary reader.

The spelling of proper names has presented difficulties. Arabic names for the most part follow the *Encyclopaedia of Islam*. In the case of African tribal names the spelling adopted by the International African Institute has been used with few exceptions; where certain forms have long been familiarized by usage (as Bechuana for the more accurate Tswana) these have still been employed. Strict consistency has therefore yielded to custom on occasion. In the case of South African place names where alternatives in Afrikaans and English have both been current, one has usually become established and is then the one used. In passages quoted the spelling of the author has naturally been preserved.

I have been helped by many friends. To three in particular who have read the entire MS. I am under obligation. Dr. Edwin W. Smith, to whom I have for many years been indebted for much encouragement in African studies, has provided valuable comment and searching criticism from his extensive learning in the African field. In particular, he has generously placed at my disposal the MS. of his *Life and Times of Daniel Lindley*, thus enabling me to refer in advance of publication to what will rank as a first-hand authority on its period, based as it is on the original Lindley papers not hitherto available. My colleagues at Selly Oak, Professor John Foster and Professor Godfrey E. Phillips, who first proposed the undertaking of the work, have offered valued criticism and suggestion on many points. For such defects as remain I am alone responsible.

Mr. Leonard Jolley, the Librarian of the Selly Oak Colleges Library, has been unfailingly helpful and has made available for me a number of books not easily procurable. Miss Jean East has kindly prepared the maps. Dr. R. Dunkerley has generously given his expert help in the reading of the proofs. To these friends I owe my thanks.

It is due to the generosity of Dr. Edward Cadbury in endowing missionary research at Selly Oak that the work was first undertaken. The grant of a bursary from the Missionary Research Fund of the Selly Oak Colleges enabled me to devote time to it while on the staff of Kingsmead College.

To my wife I owe that constant help and encouragement

which have carried me over difficult periods in a task that proved far more exacting than I imagined when, rather light-heartedly perhaps, I undertook it.

C. P. GROVES

SELLY OAK
February 1946

CONTENTS

xi

CHAPTER 7
THE ENTERPRISE RENEWED

CHAPTER 8
A PERIOD OF PAUSE

CHAPTER 9
ASSAULT ON SLAVERY

CHAPTER 10
THE MISSIONARY AWAKENING

CHAPTER 11
SOUTH AFRICAN DEVELOPMENTS

CHAPTER 12
WEST AFRICAN HOPES

LIST OF MAPS

ABBREVIATIONS USED

D.C.B.	Dictionary of Christian Biography.
D.N.B.	Dictionary of National Biography.
E.R.E.	Encyclopaedia of Religion and Ethics.
H.D.B.	Hastings' Dictionary of the Bible.
I.R.M.	International Review of Missions.
J.(R.)A.S.	Journal of the (Royal) African Society.
M.R.W.	Missionary Review of the World.
O.E.D.	Oxford English Dictionary.

CHAPTER I

THE LAND

THE continent of Africa is seen to best advantage on a globe, where the other continents do not receive that artificial extension which Mercator's projection gives them. It lies fully astride the Equator with a length north to south of some 5,000 miles, and a width in its northern section of about 4,600. It is the paradox of this vast continent that while sharing in the earliest history of the human race, it was yet not opened up until late in the nineteenth century. In this seclusion from the rest of mankind the physical environment played a vital part.

In sharp contrast with the generous size of Africa is the sparseness of its population. This is estimated at approximately 145 millions, though it may be as high as 163 or as low as 138 millions.[1] While historical causes, such as the slave-trade, have operated to reduce population, yet its low density appears mainly attributable to the physical environment.[2]

Equally, therefore, to understand the life of those who live in Africa, as to appreciate the task of those who have sought to enter it from without, some consideration of the physical environment, in the two principal aspects of land configuration and climatic influence, is necessary.

(1) *Configuration and its Effects.*

The configuration of the continent is the result of vast changes which geologists believe they are able to trace, in outline at least. There was a time when Africa as Africa did not exist. It was merged in a much larger land area extending from Brazil to Australia, when the Europe of to-day, for the most part, lay under water. To this early continent the name Gondwanaland has been given.[3] Through the disintegration of Gondwanaland Africa appeared as a distinct continent. There are two principal theories as to how this came about. That associated with the name of Professor J. W. Gregory assumes the occurrence of faultings on a gigantic scale in this extensive land area, as a result of which certain blocks sank below the original level

---

[1] Hailey, *An African Survey* (1938), 107. It is interesting to note that a century and a half ago, with the then limited knowledge of the continent, the conjectural estimate was 150 millions—*First Report of the African Institution* (1807), 9, note. [2] Hailey, *op. cit.*, 2.
[3] The name, derived from Gondwana in India (part of this original land mass), was given by the Austrian geologist, Suess.

while others remained at that level. These sinkings produced the Indian and South Atlantic Oceans. In due course the massive plateau, which is the characteristic feature of Africa, became entirely isolated. It has as a foundation primitive (or Archean) rock, and extends from the Guinea Coast to Somaliland and from Egypt to South Africa. This is the continental core. Successive invasions and recessions of the sea finally left the continent as we know it. These events extended, in geological time, from the Carboniferous era to the Pliocene.[1]

An alternative theory of the disintegration of Gondwanaland is that of continental displacement or drift, propounded by Professor Wegener. He assumes that the continents are actually floating land masses in a heavier, though at times more liquid, material. When, through internal heat, the greater liquidity occurs, the floating land masses tend to slip from their moorings. Owing to the rotation of the earth, this movement is to the west, and results in due course in a tearing apart at points that are least resistant. Thus South America has drifted away from Africa (there is a striking correspondence of coastline), and Africa has in turn moved from its eastern neighbours.

Associated with these events (on whichever theory) was intense subterranean disturbance with results that made deep marks upon the face of Africa. On Gregory's view, the foundering of the land which is the floor of the Indian Ocean, led to volcanic outbreaks on a colossal scale. On the African side eruptions occurred from Abyssinia to Nyasaland. Mounts Kilimanjaro (19,320 feet) and Kenya (17,040 feet), the highest peaks in Africa, were then built up. Mt. Kenya originally held pride of place, being 3,000 feet higher than to-day. Further, as a consequence of this foundering there appeared one of the most remarkable features of the earth's surface, the Great Rift Valley as Gregory has named it. He says of it: "The Great Rift Valley extends from Lebanon to the Sabi River, and its branches reach eastward to the mouth of the Gulf of Aden, and westward through Tanganyika to the rift valleys of the Central Congo. It is no local fracture, and its length is more than one-sixth of the circumference of the earth. It must have had a deep-seated, world-wide cause."[2] The gigantic arch which had

[1] A map showing the successive stages in the growth of land masses will be found in the *Cambridge Ancient History*, I, 16.

[2] J. W. Gregory: *The Rift Valleys and Geology of East Africa* (1921), 23. On Wegener's view, the Great Rift Valley is explained as a pulling apart through a drift westwards, so that we now see the beginning of the disruption of East Africa where a sub-continent may in due course appear. An interesting account is given in Julian Huxley's *Africa View*, XXVI.

been formed by earlier compression in East Africa had its eastern support weakened by the sinking that produced the Indian Ocean, with the result that the keystones along the top of the arch fell in, these forming the floor of the trough which steadily deepened.

It is in the Great Rift Valley and its main Western Branch that, with one exception, the great lakes of Central Africa are found, with the result that they are long and narrow with steep rocky margins. The southernmost is Lake Nyasa, accessible from the Zambezi up the Shiré Valley, and discovered along that route by Livingstone and Kirk in 1859. The second of the great lakes to be discovered, it was the first to be explored. With a length of 360 miles, it is only some 15 to 20 miles wide. "That the trough of Lake Nyasa was formed by a rift valley seems indisputable. The lake is bounded by steep, high cliffs. The lake basin is obviously due to the subsidence of the block which once occupied it."[1] It was the first of the great lakes to have missions established around it, owing to its accessibility and the circumstances of its discovery by Livingstone. At the northern end of the main valley lies Lake Rudolf on the confines of Abyssinia. The Western Branch of the valley leaves it just above Lake Nyasa, and strikes northwards in a crescent-shaped course until it reaches the headwaters of the Nile. Lake Tanganyika is the southernmost lake in this valley, the first of the Central African lakes to be discovered, having been reached by Burton and Speke in 1858. It is the largest of all the Rift Valley lakes, with a length of 400 miles, and is the second deepest lake in the world (4,708 feet). Farther north in the same valley lie Lake Kivu, Lake Edward, and Lake Albert, which last Sir Samuel Baker showed to belong to the course of the Nile. The one exception to the Rift Valley origin of the great Central African lakes is Lake Victoria. This lies in a vast depression between the main and western Rift Valleys to the north of Lake Tanganyika. It is the largest lake in the Old World, with an area of some 25,000 square miles and a shore line of 3,000 miles. Compared with the Rift Valley lakes it is shallow, the greatest depth varying from 270 to 280 feet.[2] By contrast with the steep escarpments bordering Nyasa and Tanganyika, Lake Victoria has gradually shelving shores which favour extensive settlement. It is therefore not surprising that

[1] Gregory, *op. cit.*, 301.
[2] An interesting description of the lake is given in Sir J. Bland-Sutton, *Men and Creatures in Uganda* (1933), III and IV.

3

a dense population throngs its borderlands. On its northern shore lies Uganda, a kingdom that contributes a dramatic chapter to African mission history. South-west of the lake, between it and Lakes Kivu and Tanganyika, lie the kingdoms of Ruanda and Urundi, with a population dense for Africa. Roman missions have witnessed spectacular advances among the three millions of this small territory of 20,000 square miles since it became a Belgian Mandate.

One further result of the earth turmoil accompanying the disintegration of Gondwanaland remains to be noticed. The volcanic activity that built up Mounts Kilimanjaro and Kenya has been mentioned; the eruptions were on a colossal scale. "They deluged the country under floods of molten lava. The size of the area buried under volcanic material, the vast bulk of the ejecta, the variety of the lavas, and the prolonged duration of the eruptions make East Africa one of the great volcanic regions of the world."[1] The extensive lava-plains of East Africa, treeless but grass-covered, amount in area to some 7,500 square miles, and are the home of herds of game. The volcanic uplands, on the other hand, show country dissected by deep valleys, where the rocks have decomposed into thick layers of rich soil, and provide the most valuable agricultural land in the interior of East Africa.[2] This fertility has attracted not only African population, but also in the present century considerable European settlement. This has had important reactions on missionary work in the area.

The only comparable region on the west coast is that of the Cameroons highlands, an ancient range heightened by lava deposits, with Cameroons Mountain as the highest peak (13,350 feet), a volcano still intermittently active. The neighbouring islands of Fernando Po, San Thomé, Principe and Annobon belong to the same series.

Turning now to the great plateau that constitutes the bulk of the continent, this makes the contour of Africa rather like that of an upturned plate—the central tableland bounded by a rim or escarpment, beyond which is the drop to the sea over narrow coastlands. The plateau, however, lies at two different levels in the north and the south. The Sahara and the Sudan which constitute in the main the northern section range from 1,000 to 1,500 feet, isolated plateaux running to twice that height or even more. The southern section stands some 1,500 feet higher than the northern. Over this vast tableland no folded

[1] Gregory, *op. cit.*, 96.   [2] *Ibid.*, 99, 101.

4

mountains occur (formed by the crumpling up of rocks), which are so marked a feature of the other continents. Indeed, the only folded mountain chains in Africa are those of the Atlas range, skirting the plateau on the north-west, and of the Cape in the extreme south. Again, the extent of the plateau, often running up close to the very coast, excludes any great alluvial plains such as other continents enjoy, and which constitute such an agricultural asset.[1] The great rivers of Africa arise within the plateau, its varying levels providing depressions which serve as basins for these river systems.[2] The Congo basin was at one time a vast inland lake, until a gorge was eventually cut through the bounding escarpment, thus permitting release of the waters through the present Congo estuary to the sea. This directs attention to yet a further feature of the continent, due to the nature of the central plateau. The great rivers have at some point to find their way from the plateau across the encircling escarpment to the sea. Where they do so, the various ledges of descent render the fine, broad waterways impossible for navigation. The Nile has its series of cataracts, the Niger its various rapids. Livingstone was frustrated in his plans to open up the Zambezi valley because of the Kebrabasa Rapids above Tete. Stanley's first task in 1879 was to construct a road from the Congo estuary to Stanley Pool, flanking the cataract region of the river, where to-day a railway runs for some 250 miles.[3] There is then uninterrupted navigation on the Middle Congo for a thousand miles.

In addition to the barrier presented by the plateau escarpment, and the block to navigation on Africa's broad rivers where they cross it, there is the shortness of the coastline in relation to the area of the continent. This is due to absence of deep indentations of the sea which in the case of the other continents facilitate entry to the interior, a point to which Livingstone directed attention.[4] The great scarcity of natural harbours has been yet a further difficulty.

These geographical features, resulting from the configuration of the continent, were among the conditions that combined to lock up the interior of Africa from the outside world until the middle of the nineteenth century.

[1] "In no other continent does the area of plain below 600 feet represent so small a proportion of the total area."—W. Fitzgerald, *Africa* (2nd ed. 1936), 11.
[2] Fitzgerald distinguishes twelve of these.—*Ibid.*, 13.
[3] From Matadi to Léopoldville, 400 km., begun in the 'nineties and completed in 1929.—Hailey, *op. cit.*, 1592.
[4] Sedgwick and Monk, *Dr. Livingstone's Cambridge Lectures* (1858), 1.

(2) *Climate and its Influence.*

Prevailing climate is nowhere a more significant factor in the physical environment than in Africa. It has reacted deeply on nature and on man. The cardinal point from which any consideration of climate must start in the case of this continent is that the great bulk of it lies within the tropics. It is bisected by the Equator. From almost the first cataract on the Nile to the northern Transvaal the sun is directly overhead twice during the year. No other comparable land mass receives so much direct solar radiation. The effect of this on climate is largely determined by the configuration of the continent and its water boundaries. The wide northern section with its adjacent land frontiers south and east and only an inland sea separating it from Europe on the north, experiences in the interior the so-called continental variety of climate. The narrower southern section exposed to ocean influences on three sides, and with its greater height averaging 3,000 feet and over, has even its interior climate modified towards the oceanic type.

Of the different elements constituting climate—light and direct solar radiation, wind, temperature and moisture—information for Africa is not equally available. The effect of radiation in the tropics is a field as yet largely unsurveyed.[1] It is known that even in the absence of direct sunlight in tropical Africa the light intensity may be very high, so that on cloudy days adequate head protection is still required for those coming from a temperate climate. The elements of temperature and moisture are more obvious and more readily measurable so that records are available for a reasonably reliable description of climate in these terms.[2]

The only regions congenial to a white population bred in the temperate zone are at the extreme north and south of the continent. Even so it is not a temperate but a sub-tropical climate that is enjoyed. Northern Africa, as part of the ancient Mediterranean world, was open to all the influences of Graeco-Roman civilization, and South Africa from the seventeenth century onwards has been colonized by peoples of European stock. The only other area in the continent attempted for

---

[1] "It is significant that medical science has not yet decided what kind of radiation is responsible for the sunstroke from which Europeans so frequently suffer in tropical Africa; some attribute this to ultra-violet radiation, others to infra-red." E. B. Worthington, *Science in Africa* (1938), 121.

[2] Egypt and the Union of South Africa have the most adequate records. For the rest, meteorological stations are of comparatively recent development and unequally distributed. See Worthington, *op. cit.*, 92–109.

European settlement is in the highlands of East Africa where, in sections ranging from 5,000 to 8,000 feet, it is held that altitude may compensate for some of the effects of equatorial latitude.[1]

Moving towards the Equator from these two favourable zones we enter the tropics, and meet first of all with desert. This is the extensive Sahara in the north. Interior temperatures are high though the heavy fall at night offers a daily range of 50° F. Rainfall is practically non-existent. These conditions are, of course, modified near the coasts. The absence of rainfall does not necessarily mean absence of vegetation. Where subterranean water supplies are available, oases occur, and these have made trans-Saharan travel a possibility. In the south there is but a strip of corresponding true desert, bordering the western coast. The Kalahari to the east of this, despite its one-time description as "the Southern Sahara"[2] is not extreme desert, for with a rainfall of from five to ten inches there is some scanty growth of vegetation. Farther east more favourable conditions appear. Beyond the deserts, still moving toward the equatorial belt, are regions of greater rainfall and so of more active vegetation. South of the Sahara this is the 600-mile-deep belt of the Sudan. Temperatures are high, and rainfall ranges from eight inches on the desert fringe to fifty in the south. Vegetation is of open savannah type, from scrub-country adjoining the desert to full forest. Similar conditions prevail below the Equator, though modified by the higher plateau and proximity of the sea.

Astride the Equator itself is the equatorial zone of climate from approximately 7° N. to 5° S. lat.[3] It is characterized by heat throughout the year, combined with a high atmospheric humidity; rainfall which is heavy may be well distributed or precipitated in a "rainy season" extending over the greater part of the year. The annual range of temperature is small. Nowhere on the Guinea Coast or in the Congo Basin is there recorded a lower monthly mean than 70° F., and in the Congo Basin it is nearer 80° F. This constant heat, combined with a high degree of humidity, makes the climate a particularly trying one for Europeans. On the Guinea Coast a slight respite is afforded by the blowing of a north-east seasonal wind from the Sahara, known locally as the Harmattan. It is a dry wind

---

[1] But not of course for the direct incidence of solar radiation.
[2] John Campbell, *Travels in South Africa: A Second Journey* (1822), II, 104, 113; Robert Moffat, *Missionary Labours and Scenes in Southern Africa* (1842), 141; and map at page 18.   [3] Fitzgerald, *op. cit.*, 33, note.

and so, though not cold, it has a cooling effect by assisting body evaporation. Rainfall on the Guinea Coast reaches high levels; stations at sea-level have recorded 174 inches (Freetown), 144 inches (Akassa in the Niger Delta), and 159 inches (Duala in Cameroons). The Congo average of precipitation is between 50 and 60 inches.[1] The characteristic vegetation in these areas is tropical rain-forest. It extends along the Guinea coast from Sierra Leone to the Ivory Coast, and along the coast of Nigeria, reaching 100 miles or more inland in its widest sections. It then continues through the southern Cameroons and southern French Equatorial Africa into the Belgian Congo, covering about half of the last-named territory. The explorers of the River Congo and its tributaries, finding dense forest everywhere along the rivers, were under the impression that it covered the whole of the Congo Basin. Actually the areas between the rivers are less densely forested. Bordering the tropical rain-forest both north and south, wherever the rainfall is below fifty inches, the vegetation thins out into savannah forest.

The East African highlands already mentioned fall within the equatorial belt, but with a climate modified by altitude have a rainfall, on the Kenya highlands, for example, of 40 inches. Vegetation is consequently of savannah type, and so here comes a break in the dense forest of the equatorial zone. This region has thus provided a route for migrating tribes, circumventing the tropical rain-forest, and so has been a factor of importance in the history of the continent.[2]

The effect of climate as an obstacle to European penetration of Africa has been twofold in relation both to vegetation and to health. In its effect on vegetation it has been active in producing two barriers to progress, the desert and the forest. Outstanding in the story of Africa has been the Sahara desert. When the Ice Age occurred in Europe and rainbearing winds from the Atlantic were deflected to the south over Africa, the Sahara was for the most part grassland, and even boasted, it is claimed, its own forests. Some still survive where underground water supplies exist at a sufficiently high level.[3] Crocodiles

[1] Fitzgerald, *op. cit.*, 36, 38, on whose account this section is based.
[2] "The East African savanna provides the critical connecting link between the two vast belts of tropical grass-land that border the equatorial forest on its northern and southern sides respectively. Not only has it provided a home for pastoral peoples, it has also offered the only easy route which migrating pastoral tribes, moving north or south, might follow so as to skirt the barrier of the selva."—*Ibid.*, 46–7.
[3] Lavauden quoted by Stebbing, "The Threat of the Sahara", Supplement to *J.R.A.S.*, May, 1937, 7–9.

have been found and other fauna characteristic of a humid region—isolated survivors testifying to a decisive change of climate.[1] The final retreat of the glaciers in Europe deprived the Saharan region of its rainfall, and desiccation set in long before historical times. The desert existed for Phoenicians, Greeks and Romans as a formidable natural barrier to the south of the Mediterranean lands. To-day, save for the valley of the Nile, it extends 3,600 miles from the Atlantic to the Red Sea (the Libyan desert is only a local name), and has an average width of 800 miles from north to south. There is evidence that desiccation is still extending, or, as it is more dramatically put, that the Sahara is advancing. Was, then, the Sahara less extensive for the ancients than it is to-day? E. W. Bovill shows the significance of the question: "The Sahara dominates the whole of the history of the interior of northern Africa. A slight increase in the aridity of this immense desert would produce far-reaching political consequences. It would drive the wild desert tribes into the settled uplands and plains of Barbary and the Sudan, and it would so extend the waterless stages that the caravan routes would become impassable to camels and therefore to men. A correspondingly slight increase in rainfall would quickly multiply the water-holes and desert pastures, render man independent of the now necessary camel, and, by making his life more endurable, tame the nomad. Whether there has been any material change in the climate of the Sahara in historical times is therefore a question of great importance to the student of history."[2] Impressive evidence has been marshalled to prove the affirmative: in North Africa, the disappearance of a fauna (notably the lion and the elephant) numerous in Roman times; stories of water failure in well and spring; ruins of once populous Roman cities that now have to be excavated from the sand. On the southern side, the existence to-day of desert west of the Niger Bend, where the empire of Ghana flourished 1,000 years ago; the plight of Timbuktu, once one of the most famous centres of the Sudan, where sand-dunes now enter the city; the desert east of Gao on the Niger which can scarcely have existed in the time of the Songhay

---

[1] Stebbing, *op. cit.*, 17; E. W. Bovill, *Caravans of the Old Sahara* (1933), p. 8. It is generally recognized that the change from grassland to desert occurred more than once in Saharan history. A summary of the relation of pluvial periods in Africa to glacial periods in Europe according to three recent authorities is given by Dr. E. W. Smith in his Presidential Address, *Journal of the Royal Anthropological Institute*, LXV (1935), 16.

[2] E. W. Bovill, *op. cit.*, 1–2.

empire; and the alleged general southerly movement of the population.[1] Bovill concludes for North Africa, after a careful weighing of the evidence, that the case for a general modification of climate there in historical times has not been made out, and quotes the French authority Gsell to the effect that while rainfall may have been slightly more abundant in Roman times, any climatic change has been extremely slight. On the southern side the spread of desiccation is not denied, but the effective cause, it is often contended, is to be found not so much in a change of climate as in the human factor. Man's interference with the equilibrium of nature has produced more desert. Protective forest ·has been cleared for agricultural purposes, and the annual firing practised in many areas is also destructive. The African practice of shifting cultivation is blamed for this state of affairs. When the cleared areas are no longer able to support the usual crops, they become pasture areas for cattle, and with progressive deterioration sheep and goats replace the cattle, until the final stage is reached when man moves out and sand-dunes sweep in like an advancing tide. It is important for the future to determine how far climatic change and how far human activity account for this. Meanwhile some extension of the desert in historical times is undeniable.

In the corresponding zone south of the Equator desert conditions are much less extensive. They are limited to the western side of a much narrower land area, and extend from the Bechuanaland Protectorate to the Atlantic coast. The region known as the Kalahari is not such complete desert as the land farther west between it and the sea. Whereas in the Sahara it was the coming of the camel that provided the most efficient transport for the desert crossing,[2] ox-waggons were the regular means used in the Kalahari. Nevertheless the difficulties of crossing it were great, and it was a formidable barrier to those seeking Central Africa from the south, and desiring to avoid both the warrior Zulu tribes and the lands of the Boers farther east.

The equatorial forest is a physical obstacle of a different type, due to the opposite condition of abundant rainfall. It stands sentinel still over the Guinea Coast and the waterways of west Central Africa. It is a survival from primeval times. The forests

[1] E. W. Bovill, *op. cit.*, 1; E. P. Stebbing, "The Threat of the Sahara"; "The Man-made Desert in Africa", Supplements to *J.R.A.S.*, May 1937; January 1938; E. B. Worthington, *op. cit.*, 111–18.
[2] Horses and oxen were used at an earlier date.—H. R. Palmer in *J.A.S.*, XXXI, 158.

of Europe, by contrast, are of recent origin. "Primeval forests", writes M. Louis Lavauden, the French authority on forestry, "are closed formations, that is to say, formations in biological equilibrium, in which no space is available for the invasion of foreign species. Their almost infinite complexity safeguards them against the majority of natural calamities such as epidemics of insect or fungal pests. The prevalent moist conditions prevent the spread of fire. The density of the forest, its several storeys, the variety of its components, the flexible stems and foliage of the palms and the anchoring leaves make the whole forest proof against the most violent storms: the primeval forest does not contain within itself the seeds of its own decay."[1] Stanley offers some vivid descriptions of travel through the Congo forest, with all the strain on mind and body it involved. But the equatorial forest in Africa is receding. Lavauden, for example, declares, "though the retrogression of the equatorial forest in Africa goes far back in geological time, there is no doubt that at the beginning of *historical* time this forest was infinitely more extensive than it is to-day".[2] It would seem that in the time of Pliny, for instance, the equatorial forest reached to the neighbourhood of Khartoum, whereas it has now receded some ten degrees farther south. Further recessions can be measured within recent centuries.[3] There has been measurable retreat since Stanley's journeys.

These two extremes of African vegetation, the desert and the rain-forest, though in such sharp contrast, have each served as barriers to the penetration of Africa, and have restricted human migration and development within the continent itself.[4] The second effect of climate to be noticed is its reaction on man. There are two aspects of it, the direct effect of tropical conditions on the human organism, and the prevalence of tropical disease. Native Africans as well as immigrant Europeans have been subject to both. H. J. Fleure has pointed out how the skin of African races shows adaptation to heat dispersion, with generous development of blood vessels and large sweat glands promoting rapid evaporation. While he admits a certain amount of brown pigment could be understood as protective

[1] Lavauden, "The Equatorial Forest of Africa: Its Past, Present and Future", Supplement to *J.R.A.S.*, April 1937, 3–4.   [2] *Ibid.*, 5.
[3] *Ibid.*, 6–7. "In Ruanda, forest now occupies only one-twentieth of the country, yet there is reasonable certainty, from native evidence, that seven generations (about two centuries) ago twelve-twentieths of the region were under forest."
[4] Plate II in E. B. Worthington, *op. cit.*, 158, presents the contrast.

against the chemically active solar radiation, yet the association elsewhere of colour darkening with poor health may indicate, he suggests, that its excess is "an expression of the difficulty and incompleteness of the adaptation of the human constitution to torrid conditions."[1] If in these and other ways the African has become to some extent adapted to the direct effects of climate, the outsider from the temperate zone has no such protection. He enters tropical Africa subject to the strain of an unusually difficult climate, to which the nervous system seems to be particularly exposed. He soon discovers that coupled with this there is a warfare to be waged with tropical disease.

Many of the diseases of tropical Africa, among which malaria in its various forms is the most notable, are spread, not by direct contact with an infected patient, but through the bite of an insect which conveys the parasite. It was not until 1897, however, that Sir Ronald Ross made his revolutionary discovery that part of the malaria parasite's life cycle is passed in the *Anopheles* mosquito. This opened up an entirely new approach to malaria control, through protection from mosquitoes, and where possible attempted control of their breeding-places. In this and other cases—the parasite of sleeping sickness, for example, is conveyed by a species of tsetse fly—control of the insect vector would mean control of the disease. This, however, is more easily planned than executed under African tropical conditions that favour a prolific development of insect life. Since such procedure is more feasible in urban than in rural areas, an improvement in standard of living, and so of the powers of resistance, remains the chief remedy in the case of the bulk of the African population. The immigrant European, however, has enjoyed a protection in the twentieth century which was entirely unknown to his predecessors. The heavy mortality from tropical disease, malaria in particular—described as "the African fever"—all too often decided the fate of an enterprise. Indeed, the ravages of disease were so serious from the time of the Portuguese pioneers to the discovery of Ross that Sierra Leone, the first area on the West Coast to be opened up to sustained missionary work in the nineteenth century, was called "The White Man's Grave", a name it held for a century.[2] Tropical disease, it has been claimed, was the most effective of all the natural barriers that kept Africa a closed continent for

[1] H. J. Fleure, *The Races of Mankind* (1927), 26–9.
[2] H. H. Johnston, *Britain Across the Seas: Africa*, 278. The name came to be loosely applied to the Guinea Coast in general.

so long. "The diseases of Africa", writes Dr. Norman Leys, "explain the fate of its invaders, and provide the key to the history and present condition of the African race."[1] As this statement indicates, there is not merely the direct heavy mortality due to disease—a tragic record among the early missions as we shall have cause to see, to which no other continent can present a parallel—but also the steady deterioration in health of those who survive, limiting seriously individual energy and enterprise and often not without a lamentable corroding effect on personal relationships.

Such are some of the features of a remarkable physical environment that are significant for the enterprise that is to be surveyed.

---

[1] Norman Leys, *Kenya* (2nd ed., 1925), 19. The author proceeds to draw a striking contrast between the epidemic and endemic diseases of Africa and Europe, *ibid*, 19–21.

CHAPTER 2

THE PEOPLE

DIFFICULT for human life as the survey of the physical environment shows Africa to be, it has nevertheless had a human history commensurate with that of Europe and Asia. Some indeed are inclined to think it was in Africa *homo sapiens* first appeared.[1] Africa has been very late in being penetrated by visitors from other continents, but man in Africa has had a hoary history.

(1) *The Antiquity of Man in Africa.*

Direct evidence for the antiquity of man in Africa comes both from stone implements and from fossil remains. Stone implements of recognizable stages of human culture have been found both north and south of the Equator. In Tunis and Algiers the same stone cultures have been found as in prehistoric Europe. If there was at one time a land-bridge to Europe, of which Sicily and Malta were part, say some 12,000 years ago, the cultures would appear to antedate that event. Sir Arthur Keith remarks: "We cannot tell as yet whether any or all of these ancient cultures were invented in Africa and then spread to Europe or if matters fell out in an opposite way.[2] It is sufficient for us to note that in ancient times, as to-day, the frontiers of Europe extended to what is now desert. The Sahara is a great racial frontier; north of it we find men of the European type, south of it men of the true African or negro type."[3] The same ancient stone cultures are found some 1,500 miles east of Tunis and Algiers, in the Nile Valley at Thebes; and again, some 1,500 miles from Thebes, in Somaliland. Uganda has yielded stone implements dated as early as neo-Palaeolithic.[4] Dr. L. S. B. Leakey has made discoveries of early implements in Kenya.[5] At so many places in South

[1] Charles Darwin was inclined to regard Africa as the original home of man, but rather as an auxiliary to his evolutionary theory than from any direct evidence available in his time.—*The Descent of Man* (2nd ed., 1894), 155.
[2] There is, of course, a further possibility of a common source, in Asia, with streams diverging north and south to Europe and Africa.
[3] Keith, *Antiquity of Man* (1925), I, 351.   [4] *Ibid.* I, 344–52.
[5] Reported in *The Times*, Aug. 8, 1928, March 7, 1929. See also his *Adam's Ancestors* (1934) and *Stone Age Africa* (1936).

Africa have implements of ancient stone cultures been found that Sir Arthur Keith can say: "We know now that South Africa almost rivals Europe in the richness of its ancient stone cultures. . . . Stone implements are so abundant in the gravels of South Africa that Major E. R. Collins was able to gather an extensive collection from trenches dug during the Boer War."[1] There is thus abundant evidence available for the existence of ancient stone cultures in Africa which for Europe have been provisionally placed 15,000 to 120,000 B.C. The correlation in time of the cultures in the two areas is, however, so debatable a territory that it would seem no useful inference as to the African time-table can be derived from it.

We can, however, appreciate the fact that man in Africa and man in Europe shared a common culture in the first dim dawn of human achievement. "We are apt to think of Africa as the dark continent, as a land which became open to European influences for the first time in our day, but here we have evidence of penetration of culture at the very dawn of man's Stone Age."[2]

The first discovery of fossil man in Africa was made in 1913 near Boskop in the Transvaal and at Oldaway in the then German East Africa. In 1921 further fossil remains were discovered about 100 miles to the west of Port Elizabeth. In the same year the famous skull of "Rhodesian man" was unearthed at Broken Hill in Northern Rhodesia, described by Sir Arthur Keith as "the most complete and important document that has yet lain on the anthropologist's table."[3]

There followed, in 1927, the discovery of a skeleton at Asselar in the Sahara of a man of *homo sapiens* species, who apparently lived when that part of the Sahara was fertile.[4] In 1928 and 1929 skeletons were found in Kenya in connexion with the expedition conducted by Dr. Leakey. The scientific debate is necessarily a protracted one, but whatever the precise conclusions, the antiquity of man in Africa remains undisputed.

Dr. Edwin W. Smith has graphically sketched the changes in the African scene which man has witnessed: "He has seen Victoria Nyanza grow from a marsh into a lake covering over 26,000 square miles. He has witnessed its breaking a way through over the Falls which, seventy-three years ago (July

---

[1] Keith, *op: cit.*, I, 361–2.   [2] *Ibid.*, I, 352–3.
[3] *Ibid.* II, 382. See further for suggested placing, 416–17.
[4] E. W. Smith, Presidential Address, *Journal of the Royal Anthropological Institute*, LXV (1935), 30–1.

28th, 1862), Speke was (so far as we know) the first European to see. He has seen the eruption of mighty subterranean forces, the uprising of great volcanoes, the later stages in the formation of the greatest wound on the earth's surface—the Rift Valley system. He has seen, and assisted in, the disappearance of much of Africa's primeval forest. He has seen vast tracts of well-watered land degenerate into sandy desert. He has seen the Nile eating its way through sandstone hills. He has seen the Niger deflected from its ancient course and find a way to the sea. . . . He has seen the Zambezi wearing its way through the Tertiary basalt to a depth of 500 feet ten miles back to the present lip of the Victoria Falls. He has seen—but why continue? The African has lived to see, in our own day, the Saharan desert crossed by the white man's motor car, his lands penetrated from all directions by the white man's iron road, and the white man's flying machines making regular scheduled journeys across the once Dark Continent, north, south, east and west.''[1]

(2) *The Inhabitants in Historic Times*.

Linking up with the later Stone Age cultures are the Bushmen of South Africa, now a disappearing race.

At one time, as rock paintings and other evidence bear witness, they covered almost the whole region south of the Zambezi. They were steadily pressed back by later invading peoples on the north and east, and in the seventeenth and eighteenth centuries by European colonists from the south. To-day, found mainly in the Central and Northern Kalahari Desert and the north of South-West Africa, they are estimated to number some 17,500. It is agreed they are not continuous with men of the earlier stone cultures of South Africa, but entered the country from the north, having previously occupied tropical East and East Central Africa. Tanganyika and Uganda have both yielded evidence of Bushman culture. They are nomads, leading a hunting and collecting life. They are grouped in small hunting bands, each of which has its own territory, recognized as such by the other bands. The band might be only half a dozen individuals, and rarely larger than thirty. The pressure upon them of invading peoples resulted in a hostile attitude to others. It is not surprising under these conditions that the early missionaries at the Cape found work among them extremely difficult, and eventually in many cases impossible to pursue.

16

[1] *Ibid.*, 18.

Closely related to the Bushmen are the Hottentots. Indeed, Bushmen and Hottentots are known collectively as the Khoisan peoples.[1] The name Hottentot is usually derived from the Dutch *Hüttentüt* (= stammerer) presumably applied by the early colonists on account of the "clicks" characteristic of this people's speech.[2] The Hottentots are held to be the result of racial intermixture, the Bushman strain being crossed by Hamite blood. The mixed race probably appeared in the region of the Great Lakes. They too migrated south after the Bushmen, passing towards the west coast. They reached the Cape and settled from Table Bay as far east as the Kei River. The Hottentots were in possession of the Cape territory when the first Dutch settlers arrived in 1652, and groups were found as far north as the Orange River. They thus occupied the western half of South Africa. It was among them that the earliest missionary work was done by the Moravians and the London Missionary Society. It has been estimated that when the Dutch first settled at the Cape, the Hottentots in the Cape Peninsula alone numbered some 45,000 to 50,000 persons.[3] Largely through miscegenation with the white race they have now disappeared as a pure-blooded group, and are to-day merged in the "Coloured People" of South Africa.[4] The Koranna and Namaqua sections, lying to the north, were also the object of early missionary effort. To-day, like the Bushmen, they are a disappearing people.

Before noticing the major race groups it is appropriate to mention the Negritos or Pygmy people of the equatorial forest. As Dr. Seligman reminds us: "There is no human group of whom less is known", though as far back as the third millennium B.C. the Pharaohs were sending to tropical Africa for Pygmy dancers.[5] Their existence was also known to Homer, Herodotus, Aristotle, Pliny and other ancient writers.[6] Informed opinion tends to regard them as an early human type rather than a degeneration from a taller stock. Dr. Paul Schebesta, who has

[1] Khoisan is an ethnologist's term made up from the name *Khoi-khoin* (men of men) by which the Hottentots referred to themselves, and *San* by which they referred to the Bushmen. The Bushmen are said to be without a group name of their own.—I. Schapera, *The Khoisan Peoples of South Africa* (1930), 31, 44.   [2] *Ibid.*, 44, but cf. *J.R.A.S.*, XLVI, 163–5.   [3] *Ibid.*, 45.
[4] "Some half a million people of many varying shades, the descendants of Hottentots, Malays, negro slaves, and many others, with a strong admixture of European blood, are comprehensively spoken of as 'the Coloured People'." —W. M. Macmillan, *The Cape Colour Question* (1927), 266.
[5] C. G. Seligman, *Races of Africa* (1930), 48.
[6] A. de Quatrefages, *The Pygmies* (1895), 1–6; *E.R.E.*, V, 123.

spent much time among them, says the Negroes always insisted on the racial difference between themselves and the Pygmies.[1] As the original home of the Bushmen is placed in the equatorial region, the question has been raised whether they are related to the Pygmy stock. The answer would seem to be: only in so far as they may share a common ancestry. When Dr. Seligman wrote his survey of the races of Africa he was able to say of the Pygmies: "No one has yet been able to discover whether they have a language of their own, all recorded vocabularies belonging to the speech of their negro neighbours." This statement must now be altered. An African pastor of the Church Missionary Society in Uganda became a pioneer missionary among the Pygmies of the Ituri. He made a translation of St. Mark's Gospel into their language. This came into the hands of Dr. E. W. Smith, who declares that a native language of the Pygmies has at last been identified.[2]

The largest racial group in Africa, and one of the oldest stocks, is the Negro. Evidence of the existence of typical Negroes goes back to the third millennium B.C.[3] They now occupy the continent south of a line drawn from the mouth of the River Senegal on the Atlantic coast to the Niger Bend and thence to Khartoum, continuing along the western border of Abyssinia to the Indian Ocean at the mouth of the River Juba. They have been modified both in blood and culture by Hamitic influence, and on this basis three major divisions are distinguished by Dr. Seligman, the true Negro, the Bantu, and the Half-Hamites.[4]

The true Negro shows the least Hamitic influence. His home is in West Africa, between the Guinea Coast and the Sahara. The many languages spoken by these peoples are now known to be sufficiently related to be called the Sudanic family, though their scientific classification still presents great difficulties.[5] The Negro type is a characteristic one, with its dark brown skin, woolly hair, and a stature taller than the Bushman's. The prevailing occupation is agriculture and the people therefore live in settled village communities. Arts and crafts have been well developed, from weaving and wood and ivory carving to smithing and bronze casting.[6] These were the peoples supplying

[1] Schebesta, *Revisiting My Pigmy Hosts* (1936), 76–7.
[2] E. W. Smith, "The Language of Pygmies of the Ituri", *J.R.A.S.*, XXXVII (1938), 464–70. Dr. Smith says it shows affinities with some Sudanic languages.
[3] Seligman, *op. cit.*, 52–3.   [4] *Ibid.*, 53.
[5] Hailey, *An African Survey*, 76.
[6] See Sadler, *Arts of West Africa* (1935).

for the most part the cargoes of slaves shipped to the West Indies and the American colonies. They were the peoples met by the pioneer missionaries along the Guinea Coast.

Before proceeding to the Negro groups that have been modified by Hamite influence, it will be well to notice the Hamites themselves. Ethnologists agree that Hamites and Semites are to be regarded as having stemmed from a common stock. That their differentiation is not very ancient is held to be shown by common cultural elements, by linguistic evidence and by obvious physical relationship. The Hamites are therefore regarded as deriving from Asia (Southern Arabia has been suggested), though a claim has been entered for the eastern-most horn of Africa behind Cape Guardafui. The two main branches are the Eastern and Northern Hamites. The Eastern include the Egyptians, ancient and modern, most Abyssinians, the Galla, Somali and minor tribes. The Northern Hamites include the Berbers of North Africa, the Tuareg (the veiled people of the desert), the Fula of Nigeria and others. The Hamites are important not only as a distinct racial group but for the influence they have had upon the other peoples of Africa, which has been profound. The Hottentots, appearing as the result of the mixture of Bushman and Hamite blood, have already been noticed. A similar mingling of Negro and Hamite blood has produced the large and important section of African population, called Bantu,[1] as well as such groups as the Half-Hamites and Nilotes. The Hamites were the invaders of Negroland, and the stimulating factor, through racial admixture and cultural contact, in the development of her peoples. Dr. Seligman is emphatic on this point: "The civiliza-tions of Africa are the civilizations of the Hamites, its history the record of these peoples and their interaction with the two more primitive African stocks, the Negro and the Bushman, whether this influence was exerted by highly civilized Egyptians or by such wilder pastoralists as are represented at the present day by the Beja and the Somali."[2]

As might be anticipated from this account of racial affairs, the mixed stocks of Negro and Hamite will tend to show a heavier Hamitic strain in the east and north, and a lighter in

[1] The term Bantu strictly denotes a language family, but is also used ethnologically of the peoples speaking these languages.

[2] Seligman, *op. cit.*, 96. On the other hand Dr. E. W. Smith writes: "It seems to me that some writers tend to exaggerate the importance of 'Hamitic blood'." Presidential Address, *J.R.A.I.*, LXV (1935), 58. See his further remarks *ad loc.*

the west and south, though migration resulting from population pressure as well as from enterprise frequently modifies the situation.

In Seligman's account the primary divisions of the Negro modified by Hamite influence are three—the Half-Hamites, the Nilotes, and the Bantu. The Half-Hamites are to be found in East and East-Central Africa, occupying much of Kenya, northern Tanganyika and northern Uganda. Tribes typical of this group are the Masai, Nandi, and Suk. The Nilotes are Negroes in whom the Hamitic element is the weaker strain, and who inhabit the Nile Basin mainly in the south of the Anglo-Egyptian Sudan. The Shilluk and Dinka are representative tribes.

The Bantu constitute the largest division of Negroes modified by Hamitic influence. They occupy the whole of central and southern Africa, save for those groups already noticed. They are classified on the basis of language. Stated at its simplest, the Bantu group includes those who use the root *ntu* to signify human being, thus: *muntu* = a man, *bantu* = the men, *ubuntu* = the quality of manhood. Dr. A. Werner notes as the main peculiarities of Bantu languages: (1) inflexion by means of prefixes ("principiation instead of declension") illustrated above, (2) absence of grammatical gender, (3) the alliterative concord.[1] The Eastern Bantu, east of the Great Rift Valley, and the Southern Bantu, south of the Zambezi and Cunene Rivers, reveal a stronger Hamitic strain than the Western Bantu, lying between the Rift Valley and the Atlantic coast. The linguistic affinity, however, overrides any such variations among the Bantu. Thus one of Vasco da Gama's men, in 1498, found he could understand the talk of the people in the neighbourhood of the Limpopo, through what he had learned on the west coast, which would be Angola or the Congo.[2]

It was the Southern Bantu with whom Dutch colonists came into contact when they moved eastwards beyond the Hottentot domain, and who were called "Kaffirs" well on into the nineteenth century.[3] When the first Dutch settlement was made at the Cape in the seventeenth century, the Bantu tribes were still moving south and west. How long before this they had arrived in Africa south of the Zambezi it is impossible to

[1] A. Werner, *Language Families of Africa* (1915), 21.
[2] A. Werner, *Myths and Legends of the Bantu* (1933), 28.
[3] The term is of Arabic origin (*kafir*=unbeliever, infidel) and was applied by Muslims to the pagan tribes. It was taken over by the Portuguese and so passed into general currency as a specific name.

say. Certainly the Portuguese in the sixteenth century found the Makalanga already long established in the Southern Rhodesia of to-day. The particular Bantu tribe with whom Europeans made contact over the colonial frontier was the Xhosas. These are the "Kaffirs" of the early Kaffir Wars. Tembus, Fingoes and others lay behind, while in the present Natal the strong Zulu people were established. These vigorous warriors, under military leaders of renown, sent out return waves of migration to the north. Thus arose the Matebele between the Limpopo and Zambezi, and the Ngoni west of Lake Nyasa. The Eastern Bantu include peoples built up into strong kingdoms bordering on Lake Victoria, among which that of Uganda is the most famous. By contrast with the agricultural West Coast, cattle constitute the economic wealth of many tribes in the east and south wherever the absence of tsetse makes this possible. The pastoral life indicates a sparser population, through the necessity of a larger territory for feeding-grounds than the agriculturist requires for farms. We are supplied with a number of scientific monographs of the front rank on Bantu tribes of the east and south.[1]

The tribes of the Western Bantu with whom European contact was first made were those of the Lower Congo. In the so-called "Kingdom of Congo" the first serious attempt was made to establish Portuguese influence; it extended southwards into Angola, but never seems to have penetrated far inland. At the time of Livingstone's pioneer journey to the west coast, he found the Portuguese outposts only some 300 miles from the sea.[2] Knowledge of the Western Bantu is still comparatively meagre, though scientific studies of the Congo peoples have been made under the sponsorship of the Belgian Government.

The Semites complete the list of peoples by race who inhabit Africa. They include Phoenicians, Jews and Arabs. The Phoenicians established colonies on the North African coasts, of which Carthage was the most renowned. Their influence was effective only on this coastal strip between the Sahara and the sea, though some colonies were planted on the Atlantic coast of Morocco. They have become absorbed into the Northern Hamites.

---

[1] The first three of outstanding note to appear, all by missionaries, were: *The Baganda* (1911), by James Roscoe; *The Life of a South African Tribe* (1912, second ed. 1927), by Henri A. Junod; and *The Ila-Speaking Peoples of Northern Rhodesia* (1920), by Edwin W. Smith and A. Murray Dale, for the greater part of which the missionary co-author, Dr. Smith, was responsible.

[2] Livingstone, *Missionary Travels and Researches in South Africa* (1857), 375.

Jews have entered Africa at various periods, even sharing, it has been suggested, in Phoenician commercial enterprise. Certainly colonies of Jews were early found on the North African littoral, from Alexandria to Morocco. They maintained themselves after the Arab invasion longer than the Christians, though the subsequent story was one of steady decline.[1] The Falashas, or so-called "black Jews" of Abyssinia, a separate community of some one hundred to one hundred and fifty thousand, are classified by Seligman as Hamites, though they profess a Jewish faith.[2] It has also been argued that Jewish influence is to be seen in peoples on the Guinea Coast, notably the Ashanti and the Yoruba.[3]

It is, however, the Arabs who constitute the most marked Semitic element in Africa. Their effective invasions coincided with the rise of Islam, when Egypt and North Africa fell under their control; and from settlements along the East African coast whence commerce eventually took them inland to the Great Lakes and beyond. Yet so much intermarriage has occurred that "Arab" in Africa may be more an indication of religion and culture than of race, so that Dr. Seligman can say: "It is obvious that in Africa the term Arab may be applied to any people professing Islam, however much Negro or other foreign blood may run in their veins, so that while the term has a cultural value it is of little ethnic significance and often is frankly misleading."[4] The purer Arab strain is to be found in the north and east.

(3) The Social Pattern.

For the most part the peoples of Africa live in communities characterized by a definite social pattern. Individuals are securely woven into it, so that any response to a religious message that involves new forms of behaviour will be correspondingly difficult to secure with sincerity. While each group must be studied separately for its own detailed social pattern, yet there are certain features found in common that may be usefully set down here.

The family is the starting-point. The family as a simple social group is the same everywhere—father, mother and children. But a more complex group may appear. The practice

[1] J. W. Parkes, *The Jew and his Neighbour* (1930), 63–5.
[2] Seligman, *op. cit.*, 120–21, 247.
[3] See J. J. Williams, *Hebrewisms in West Africa* (1930).
[4] Seligman, *op. cit.*, 234.

of polygyny modifies it in this way. It is customary for each wife to have her own hut or place in the compound, and her own piece of land to farm. She will take her turn in preparing the husband's food. Thus there is not joint domesticity so much as a "multiple monogamy" (Malinowski) or a "number of families with a common factor, the father and husband" (Rivers). Polygyny as a social institution is bound up, among other things, with hospitality. The woman is the food producer to a large extent, and entirely the food preparer. A man of position, wishing to offer hospitality to clan brother or travelling stranger, would be unable to do so without several women to prepare the food. One wife would be overburdened. The chief, upon whom the obligation of hospitality normally falls, is therefore in the old order invariably a polygamist. The more wives, the more cultivated lands, the more children (it is hoped), and the greater the affluence of the man concerned. More will have to be said in a later chapter about the relation of the Christian Mission to this particular social institution. Meanwhile it can be noted as the greatest obstacle, on the social side, to the acceptance of Christianity in Africa.

The family of father, mother and children will not live in isolation. At one end of the scale they may be accompanied by other members of the family, as, for example, among the Pondos of South Africa, where the *umzi* or group of huts inhabited by the family may include the man's mother, his brothers and sisters and others. Neighbouring *imzi* will be scattered over the hillsides, thus constituting a little settlement. Then, in primarily agricultural communities, come settled villages with streets, set in a belt of farmlands, through which the traveller must wend his way to reach the village. At the other extreme are considerable towns, usually the capital of a paramount chief or ruler of a kingdom. The tribe will include as many of these settlements as speak a common language, recognize the validity of customary law among themselves, and band together for defence against aggressors or for attack upon others. There will be a paramount chief as supreme ruler, who may vary from a "chief-in-council" to a despot, upon the strength and wisdom of whose personal rule the integrity and vigour of the tribe will largely depend. In any disturbed state of the country an able and powerful chief will have people seeking his protection upon condition of acknowledging his rule; while one who neglects his people and is unduly oppressive may lose them piecemeal to others. Livingstone discovered cases of both kinds in recent history on his pioneer travels in Central Africa.[1] Moshesh of Basutoland was an outstanding example of the chief of character receiving refugees and welding them into a people under his personal rule.

Social cohesion in these societies is strong. Adolescence is often marked by initiation rites held in seclusion, that seek to prepare the individual for life within the community. Severe physical endurance tests may be imposed on the boys, for they must be found fit to take their part in the life of the tribe, facing danger with courage and enduring fatigue and strain without collapse. Direct instruction in social behaviour is imparted and respect for elders is inculcated under conditions that ensure the lesson is learned once for all. Preparation for marriage, assumed to be a universal social obligation, is included, and this is the heart of the matter in rites for girls. The individual who comes successfully through this period has secured status as a man. He is entitled to privileges, and is bound by reciprocal obligations. In particular, he has been brought into relation with the departed ancestors, upon whose favour and continued guidance and help the well-being of the community is believed still to depend. Thus kinship duties within the family, coupled with communal dependence beyond it, bind the individual to the group with hoops of steel. His very survival depends in the last resort upon his acceptance of the network of reciprocal obligations through which he himself receives as well as gives. It would thus not be difficult for a member of such a society to confess a strange creed if that were all that were required; but if such confession is to mean at the same time a reform in social conduct, then it will go hard with him when he declines to discharge the recognized obligations involved in kinship ties and community membership.

Nor is the situation much modified in the case of the chief himself. True, he has a liberty of action denied to his subjects, but only in so far as he acts for their welfare. If chief of a tribe, for example, in a region subject to drought, where action as rain-maker might be the chief's function, then his conversion to a faith that no longer permitted its exercise would imperil his hold upon his people. James Backhouse, when visiting Moshesh in 1839, reports a controversy between the chief and his people over the burial of a wife of his own. Though Moshesh was not himself a confessed Christian, he desired the wife to be buried in the new Christian way. No one of the conservative opposition

[1] Livingstone, *op. cit.*, 247, 323.

was willing to challenge his argument, but Backhouse reports there was talk of secession from the tribe.[1]

Thus even in these simple societies the hold of the group upon its members is tenacious, and will tend to restrain any save those of strong personality from accepting a faith that means cutting loose from various social responsibilities as authorized by tradition. The way of security is the way of the ancestors. All the force of conservatism through respect for the past therefore confronts the would-be innovator.

(4) *The Mystic Environment.*

Each child, as he grows to maturity, discovers that as well as belonging to a family with its kinship obligations, he enjoys birthright membership in a wider group, the clan. This is reckoned through one parent, usually the father. It is then styled patrilineal. Cases where descent is matrilineal occur, and even various combinations for the different purposes of descent, succession and inheritance. Through the clan the boy is linked up with his ancestors. Now the clan extends into the unseen; there is one community of the living and the dead. This exists at two levels. There are the family ancestors that concern the family group and no one else; and there are the chief's ancestors, who are not only his family forebears, but also, as past rulers of the community, its present guardians in the unseen. Not only is there recourse to these unseen helpers in seasons of distress—illness or personal misfortune in the family, drought or epidemic in the community—but their guidance may be sought before enterprises of importance are undertaken. They were the living elders in their day and have but moved up in status; they have power to help or harm, but are also dependent upon the living here. But more, in areas where the conception of their function is clearest, they are regarded as intermediaries between the living and the Supreme. An African from Nyasaland (of mixed Ngoni and Senga blood) has written: "Our regard for the spirits of our ancestors does not make them gods; they are merely media between us and the God-spirit, and they can exercise that authority which was given them during their earthly life towards relatives who are still alive, and under Him they can punish as do our Resident or Governor under King George. The punishment

[1] *Extracts from the Journal of James Backhouse*, South Africa, Part IX (1841), 17–23.

comes from the God-spirit, but to reach us it can only pass through and be known to the ancestral spirit."[1]

That such is not an isolated interpretation by an educated African is evidenced by similar testimony over a wide area. Thus a young Nigerian of the Oron people who, speaking of his sister's successful passage of the poison ordeal when accused of witchcraft, said of her thanksgiving to the ancestor: "She reported herself to our great ancestor because of the help she had received from God through the appeal of our ancestor."[2]

The vital traffic with persons in the unseen world is thus with the ancestors, though there is a wide range of practice between regular remembrance and forgetting them until some illness or calamity occurs. Likewise for most peoples there is evidence of belief in a Supreme Being or Power, often thought of as Creator, though now remote from the world of men. At its weakest it is rather a vague belief, even in an impersonal power. Thus Junod has reported for the Thongas that the name *Tilo* (which he translates "Heaven") seems to indicate pre-eminently a place. One of the most intelligent women in the congregation at Lourenço Marques, who was also said to be best acquainted with ancient Thonga custom, said one day: "Before you came to teach us that there is an All-Good Being, a Father in Heaven, we already knew there was a Heaven, but did not know there was anyone in it." Yet *Tilo* is not merely a place, because it is spoken of as a power: "It is sometimes called *Hosi*, Lord." Junod doubts whether *Tilo* can be thought of as personal; it is rather, he suggests, a personification of Nature, since the power is associated with certain great cosmic phenomena.[3] Among the Southern Bantu generally the belief in a Supreme Being is less precise than it is farther north. Among the Ila-speaking peoples *Leza* is the Lord of all. While the name is associated with those natural phenomena that are so marked in a tropical climate, yet the myths testify that *Leza* is regarded as personal. Epithets used of him describe him as the Originator and the Moulder of things, and also as their undisputed Owner with a reference here to the decrees of fate that determine human lives. There are occasions of emergency when prayers may be offered to him.[4] The Nyaruanda, an East African Bantu tribe, think of *Imana* as Creator, Master and

[1] "The Religion of my Fathers", in *I.R.M.*, XIX (1930), 365.
[2] Personally communicated, 1922.
[3] Junod, *Life of a South African Tribe* (2nd ed. 1927), II, 429–33.
[4] Smith and Dale, *The Ila-Speaking Peoples of Northern Rhodesia* (1920), II, 197–212.

Giver. The name is used in blessings, as *"Imana* be with you". There are also proverbs and myths about him. Direct prayer is to the ancestral spirits alone, but *Imana* may be remembered in the expression of wish.[1] Among the Western Bantu there is also a name. Jean Kenyon Mackenzie, writing of the Bulu, says: *"Nzambi, Nzam, Anzam*—in our neighbourhood it is called *Zambe.* Other forms has the Name among other tribes, but of it you will be told—'Our Fathers knew this name—it is the name of Him-who-created-us'." There are sayings in which his name occurs among the Bulu; the commonest, says Miss Mackenzie, is *"Zambe,* having created us, forgot us". Yet of one who has experienced a remarkable deliverance it may be said: *"Zambe* has saved him, he is a son of *Zambe."*[2]

More precise and richer in content are the conceptions of the Supreme among the great peoples of the Guinea Coast, as that of *Onyame* among the Ashanti, or of *Olorun* among the Yorubas. A number of Ashanti proverbs name *Onyame* and reveal something of the thought about him as the sky-god. Offering and prayer are made to him on ceremonial occasions, and at other times. The altar to him is the forked branch of a certain tree, on which Rattray comments: "Beside these rude altars are to be found, hidden away in remote corners of the older palaces, beautifully designed temples to the Sky-God."[3] *Olorun* is the name by which the Supreme is generally known among the Yorubas. Farrow, who lived in Yorubaland before the British Government had extended its rule to include it, says that one morning, when visiting in a village where there was no Christian, he inquired: Who created us? Who preserves us? Who gives us food? Who sends us rain and sunshine? To each question came the answer, *Olorun ni* (= It is God). This, he says, was the usual experience. Occasionally a person might say, "We do not know", or name his own idol, but these were rare exceptions. *Olorun* is also exalted in his attributes. Some titles are used of him alone, others he shares with lesser spirits or *orishas* of whom there are many in the Yoruba pantheon from nature spirits to deified ancestors.[4]

In view of the more precise conception of the Supreme, his attributes and his activities, among these peoples, it is legitimate

---

[1] E. Johanssen, "The Idea of God in the Myths and Proverbs of Some East African Bantu Tribes", *I.R.M.*, XX (1931), 345–55, 534–46.

[2] Jean Kenyon Mackenzie, *An African Trail* (1917), 80, 86.

[3] R. S. Rattray, *Ashanti Proverbs* (1916), 17–28; *Ashanti* (1923), 139–44.

[4] S. S. Farrow, *Faith, Fancies and Fetich* (1926), 21–67; O. Johnson, *The History of the Yorubas* (1921), 26–38.

to ask whether the conception as reported is due to Christian or Muslim influences, for both faiths are found on the Guinea Coast, Christian influence advancing from the coast northwards, and Islam from the Sudan southwards. Both Rattray and Farrow regard the conception of the Supreme as anterior to the appearance of either of these religions in West Africa.[1] Thus there is generally found in Negro and Bantu Africa a belief in a Supreme Being as evidenced by a name for him, and while prayer and offering to him direct are of rare occurrence, they are not unknown. David Livingstone wrote in 1860, after twenty years' experience of South and Central Africa, of an area where he was the pioneer: "The idea of praying direct to the Supreme Being, though not quite new to all seems to strike their minds so forcibly that it will not be forgotten. Sinamane [a Batoka chief on the lower Zambezi] said that he prayed to God, Morungo, and made drink-offerings to him."[2] The belief would appear to be a fading one among the Southern Bantu. The Hottentots believed in a powerful being mainly venerated as a rain-god.[3] The Bushman's belief, though not untouched by foreign influences, has included a great being who made all things and to whom prayer could be made.[4]

This spiritual hierarchy—the Supreme Being or Power, lesser gods (where they exist), and the ancestral spirits—does not exhaust the mystic environment. There are minor spiritual forces, inherent in certain plants for example, which may be tapped and through appropriate vehicles be made to render service. Such are "charms", which may be worn on the person for protection, or placed in house or garden for defence, or used offensively. In Ashanti where the name *suman* is given to such sacred objects, Rattray says he made inquiries as to the difference between an *obosom* (lesser god) and a *suman*, and one man ("a very remarkable Ashanti") replied: "*Obosom* and *suman* are like the white man's cannon and lesser guns. He cannot take big guns everywhere."[5] That would seem to express admirably the African view. As a result of careful investigation on the point in this one area, Rattray offers the following definition of *suman*, using the term "fetish" under

[1] R. S. Rattray, *Ashanti Proverbs*, 17–19; S. S. Farrow, *op. cit.*, 32. Both writers correct A. B. Ellis, whose statement is to the contrary, but whose knowledge of the vernacular, as both writers point out, was inadequate to enable him to give a reliable verdict.

[2] D. and C. Livingstone, *The Zambesi and its Tributaries* (1865), 319.

[3] I. Schapera, *The Khoisan Peoples of South Africa* (1930), 376–84.

[4] *Ibid.*, 181.

[5] R. S. Rattray, *Religion and Art in Ashanti* (1927), 22.

protest: "A fetish (*suman*) is an object which is the potential dwelling-place of a spirit or spirits of an inferior status, generally belonging to the vegetable kingdom; this object is also closely associated with the control of the powers of evil or black magic, for personal ends, but not necessarily to assist the owner to work evil, since it is used as much for defensive as for offensive purposes."[1] Here we cross, some would say, from the realm of religion to that of magic, while others find a terminological escape from the difficulty of definition by speaking of the magico-religious sphere. The distinction often made, that in religion man prays and in magic he commands, is a useful one, but subject to qualification.[2] Magical beliefs and practices have ramifications as extensive as the feeling of insecurity in African life. Because material media are used, they are often the first element in the realm of belief to strike the observer. The surrender of the objects concerned has been a usual demand upon Christian conversion.

More sinister is belief in witchcraft in the restricted sense in which Dr. Evans-Pritchard has now taught us to use the term. It is believed to be a psychic activity of a malignant personality within the community, and is distinguished from sorcery or black magic by the absence of material medium, spell and rite.[3] This has been truly described as "the shadow over Africa". Misfortunes, from failing crops to fatal illness, will all be attributed to witchcraft, and the current means of identification be adopted, usually by a poison ordeal. The witch-doctor functions here as a witch-finder. Indeed, this is strictly the only function to be associated with the name. In other activities he functions as medicine-man or as diviner.

Here is a world of belief where a stranger may blunder in all innocence and forfeit not only his welcome but his life. Two missionaries in Central Africa entered a native village after night-fall. One, interested as a builder in the construction of the village, drew a plan of it on the ground with his stick. The men

---

[1] R. S. Rattray, *Religion and Art in Ashanti* (1927), 23. On the objections to perpetuating the terms "fetish" and "fetishism", see the same, 9–24, also *Ashanti*, 86–91. There has been no clear agreement as to what the term signifies. The confusion involved is seen in such a usage as Mary Kingsley's: "I mean by fetish the religion of the natives of the Western Coast of Africa." —*West African Studies* (1899), 113. Here fetish either includes belief in a supreme being and lesser gods, and then the term is entirely misleading, or it implies these elements are absent from West African religion, which is untrue.

[2] See Raymond Firth, *Human Types* (1938), 165.

[3] Evans-Pritchard, *Witchcraft, Oracles and Magic among the Azande* (1937), 21, 33–7.

were seen and their action reported. We are told that "next morning there was great excitement and the villagers were barely restrained from throwing the two men into the Zambezi to be devoured by crocodiles". Not only had they been guilty of a serious breach of conduct in entering the village by night, but one had acted the part of a sorcerer, for his marking on the ground was the action of one seeking the chief's death, who would in anticipation mark out the places for the funeral fires and so prophesy the event itself.[1] With such a conception of personality being constantly exposed to unseen and unpredictable perils, the development of an excessive caution, not to say suspicion, in the African character is not surprising. Of witchcraft in the strict use of the term he would not suspect a stranger, but sorcery is another matter. Father Gonzalo da Silveira, the pioneer Jesuit missionary to the Makalanga in the Zambezi country, was accused by his Muslim enemies of being a mighty sorcerer acting as an advance spy for the Portuguese; this so aroused the fears of the court that Silveira became the first Christian martyr in South Africa.[2]

There would appear to be a relation between religious belief and practice in certain particulars and the physical environment. Thus in drought-afflicted areas of South Africa, for both Bushman and Hottentot a rain god held pre-eminence. Moreover, the passage from open country to equatorial forest brings its changes, as Livingstone frequently observed on his pioneer journey from Linyanti to Loanda: "In the deep, dark forests near each village, you see idols intended to represent the human head or a lion, or a crooked stick smeared with medicine, or simply a small pot of medicine in a little shed, or miniature huts with little mounds of earth in them. But in the darker recesses we meet with human faces cut in the bark of trees. Frequent cuts are made on the trees all along the paths, and offerings of small pieces of manioc-roots, or ears of maize, are placed on branches. . . . It seems as if their minds were ever in doubt and dread in these gloomy recesses of the forest, and that they were striving to propitiate, by their offerings, some superior beings residing there."[3] It will be found very largely true that the darker pictures of African religion come from the heavy forest areas on the Guinea Coast and in west Central Africa, while accounts with less repellent features derive from more open lands.

[1] Reported by E. W. Smith in *I.R.M.*, XIII (1924), 522.
[2] G. M. Theal, *History of South Africa before 1795*, I (1907), 311–12.
[3] Livingstone, *Missionary Travels and Researches in South Africa*, 304–5.

CHAPTER 3

THE ENTERPRISE BEGUN
(A) EGYPT

ONLY part of the continent and only some of its peoples were known to the ancient world. It is well to see what these limits were before commencing to trace the Christian story, for they indicate what could reasonably be regarded as the available field for any missionary effort at that time.

(1) *Ancient Knowledge of Africa.*

The two African lands most familiar to the ancients were Egypt and the portion of North Africa that lay across the straits from Italy and Sicily, at the heart of which was the Africa Proconsularis of the Romans.

Egypt had intimate ties from the second millennium B.C. with Palestine and Syria, clay tablets of the period in cuneiform from Egyptian governors in those countries having come to light in Egypt. From then onwards Egypt was more or less intimately involved in the politics of the Near East until the conquests of Alexander the Great, and later the eastward march of Rome, refashioned the map of that part of the world.

The North African coast west of the Libyan desert and the Gulf of Syrtis was colonized by enterprising Phoenicians. Utica was founded about 1100 B.C., and Carthage, the most famous of their settlements, some three centuries later. With the development of the Roman power in the Italian peninsula, there came the historic clash between Roman and Punic arms.

In both these lands the fertile area was a comparatively narrow strip; in Egypt the actual Nile valley, a north to south irrigation of a strip of the desert, and in the case of North Africa a coastal territory of highlands, plateaux and border ranges with a mean width of some 200 miles, bounded on the north by water and on the south by sand. These were the two vantage-points in Africa held by the civilized peoples of the ancient world. What was known of Africa beyond these limits?

Egyptian voyages were early made down the east coast to Somaliland in the neighbourhood of Cape Guardafui and beyond. Herodotus states that Necho, king of Egypt at the beginning of the sixth century B.C., commissioned an expedition of Phoenicians to sail round Africa, and that this was successfully accomplished from east to west. There are difficulties, however, in accepting this story, so that as one historian puts it: "It is safer to believe merely that in Necho's reign Phoenician navigators sailed down the coast of East Africa into the southern hemisphere; and, for the rest, to keep an open mind."[1] There is historical evidence, however, for regular sailings down the east coast south of Cape Guardafui in the Greek and Roman periods. This is supplied by the *Periplus of the Erythraean Sea* (or Indian Ocean), a pilot's guide written in the second half of the first century A.D.[2] In the manner of such a work, it enumerates features of interest to the navigator and trader. It describes the eastern coast in this way between Guardafui and Zanzibar. The slave-trade was already active in those days.[3]

It was the Carthaginians who bore the palm for exploration of the West African coast. During the sixth century B.C. they were trading along the Atlantic coast of the present Morocco, and apparently had discovered Madeira. The grand enterprise, however, was that of Hanno in the early decades of the fifth century. Setting out from Carthage with a fleet of sixty ships he was commissioned to found colonies along the West African coast, designed to trade with friendly tribes where they were to be found. Much of the coast was apparently more favourable then for habitation than it is to-day. A detailed record of the geographical features and of the colonies established has survived. This shows that Hanno passed Cape Verde and the estuary of the Gambia, and even reached Sierra Leone and Sherbro Sound. This would take him some 3,000 miles from home.[4] His great enterprise was not emulated and the southern-

[1] Warmington in *Cambridge History of the British Empire*, VIII (1936), 56.
[2] *The Periplus of the Erythraean Sea:* Travel and Trade in the Indian Ocean by a Merchant of the First Century. Translated from the Greek and annotated by Wilfred H. Schoff (1912).
[3] R. Coupland, *East Africa and its Invaders* (1938), 16–18. Marinus of Tyre, who wrote at the beginning of the second century A.D., gathered information from Greek merchants trading in East Africa. It seems that they had penetrated as far south as Cape Delgado, and knew at least by hearsay of the island of Madagascar. Again, whether by first-hand knowledge or by report, they knew of the White and Blue Niles and spoke of them as flowing from two lakes, and of a mountain range, the "mountains of the Moon", not far away.—Warmington, *op. cit.*, 65–8.
[4] Warmington, *op. cit.*, 57–8; W. Bovill, *Caravans of the Old Sahara*, 14-16. The record of Hanno's expedition survives in his own words in a Greek translation from the Punic (in which the original was probably written). The identifications of places mentioned confirm quite remarkably the trustworthiness of the record. One of the latest of these was by the late Professor Schwarz in a letter to *The Times*, March 21, 1929. See also issue of March 25.

most settlements in due course disappeared. Then came the conquest of Carthage, when Rome fell heir to her maritime possessions. But the interest of Rome beyond the straits lay to the north, in Gaul and Britain, and direct knowledge of the Atlantic coast of Africa slipped away.

Explorers overland had to face greater obstacles still than those of the maritime adventurers. The Nile might seem to offer an arterial highway into the heart of the continent. Apart, however, from the cataracts, which effectually prevented through navigation, the impenetrable masses of sudd[1] in the upper reaches of the river barred the way by water to the interior. Khartoum was apparently the limit of knowledge toward the south. There remained the possibility of desert transit, whether from Egypt or North Africa, to make contact with the Sudan. It would seem that in Carthaginian times there was commercial intercourse along the route from Tripoli to Chad, running through the settlements of the Garamantes, a desert people lying midway on this route. These people may, it is surmised, have acted as middlemen so that there was through transit for goods but not for merchants. This has been characteristic elsewhere of trade with the interior.[2] In Roman times two distant expeditions are recorded to the south along this route. A Roman officer made a three months' journey beyond Garama to "the land of the Ethiopians", and a citizen of Leptis went for four months beyond, and reached "the assembling place of the rhinoceros", presumably Lake Chad.[3] With the help of the camel, first introduced into Africa in the period of the Roman occupation, desert transport was greatly facilitated. Indeed, the coming of the camel marked an epoch in the relations between North Africa and the Sudan. New routes could be opened up, new oases brought into service, and the desert journey be undertaken with a new confidence.[4]

Two ancient geographers sought to co-ordinate the material available to them, and deduce the form and extent of the continent. Eratosthenes (c. 200 B.C.) believed in a very restricted Africa, with the Atlantic coast swinging south-east and then sweeping across to join the east coast wholly north of the

[1] Drifting vegetation torn from its place where the Nile makes its way through extensive swamps of papyrus and reeds, and carried down-stream. It has given its name to this region of the Nile. Cf. Fitzgerald, *Africa*, 410–12. An illustration showing how massive is the obstruction occurs in J. Yardley, *Parergon* (1931), 64.

[2] E. W. Bovill, *op. cit.*, 17.

[3] R. Syme in *Cambridge Ancient History*, XI (1936), 145.

[4] E. W. Bovill, *op. cit.*, 20–2.

Equator.[1] Mainly through Gaius Julius Solinus (c. A.D. 250) the Africa of Eratosthenes became the popularly accepted conception. The geographer Ptolemy (c. A.D. 150) was more cautious in delimiting the unknown to the south, and assigned no definite frontier. On the west, he offered no speculation of what lay beyond the coast actually visited. On the east, however, beyond the land of the "anthropophagi" he conceived of the coast swinging across to China, as a southern land frontier of the Indian Ocean.[2] The view of Ptolemy was less known than that of Eratosthenes and did not displace it in popular estimation. These two incompatible accounts of the form and extent of Africa are sufficient testimony to the ignorance in the ancient world of what lay to the south of the great desert. Such, then, was the limited Africa which could be regarded as a field of enterprise by the earliest Christian missionaries.

(2) Christianity in Africa in the Apostolic Age.

We have no record in the New Testament of any missionary activity in Africa. Various contacts, however, are indicated. The easy accessibility of Africa from Palestine is shown by the story of the flight into Egypt of Joseph and Mary with the infant Jesus (Matt. 2: 13-15). African Christians are glad to think that their continent provided a refuge for the Lord in time of need.

Simon of Cyrene, who bore the cross, came from northern Africa (Luke 23: 26). He was apparently a Jewish settler in a Greek settlement lying in the Barca district of modern Tripoli. Other Cyrenian Jews are referred to in the Book of Acts (2: 20; 6: 9; 11: 20; 13: 1). In one place (6: 9) the Alexandrians are coupled with them. An Alexandrian Christian, Apollos, appears in Corinth and Ephesus as a missionary preacher, but when and where he became a Christian is unknown (Acts 18: 24-19: 1).

One dramatic passage, however, gives the first definite record of an African becoming a Christian convert (Acts 8: 26-40). The Ethiopian in the story came, not from Abyssinia, but the region of the Nile between Aswan and Khartoum. From the sixth century B.C. or earlier a kingdom had flourished

---

[1] See Scott Keltie, *The Partition of Africa* (1893), 16, for the map of Africa according to Eratosthenes. The views of Eratosthenes have been preserved in Pliny.

[2] See map in Scott Keltie, *op. cit.*, 18. For a convenient summary of Ptolemy's ideas, see Warmington in *Cambridge History of the British Empire*, VIII, 65-70, 75.

with the city of Meroe as capital. Candace was not a name but a title, similar to Pharaoh, borne by the queen-mother who is said to have been the effective authority in the country.[1] The eunuch had possibly gone to Jerusalem to offer gifts on behalf of his queen, a practice not unusual among Gentiles. But more probably he was a pilgrim, a Jewish proselyte who had visited Jerusalem on his own account. He was literate, and read from the Septuagint, the Greek version of the Old Testament made for the Jews of Alexandria.[2] At his request Philip interpreted the passage he was reading, identifying Jesus with the Suffering Servant. He was baptized forthwith. Philip then left him, and he "went on his way rejoicing" into Africa. There the curtain falls. Nothing further is known of him. Irenaeus claims him as a missionary to his people, and Eusebius, who does the same, reports a later legend that his name was Judich. But we do not know. He flits across the stage and disappears.[3]

Passing from history in the New Testament to tradition in the Apostolic Age, we find no apostle reported as evangelizing on African soil. True, tradition sent Thomas to India, and as his route would lie, it is claimed, via the Nile and across to the Red Sea, a possible period in Alexandria would be feasible. Dr. J. N. Farquhar, who came to regard this tradition favourably, went so far as to say: "We may think it possible that Thomas was one of the men who proclaimed Christ in Egypt, Cyrene and further west."[4] But the luminous haze of legend is scarcely favourable to the recovery of historic fact.

A tradition resting on the solid authority of Eusebius records that John Mark, the evangelist, was an active missionary in Egypt, and first established churches in the city of Alexandria. Eusebius introduces the report with a cautious "they say". As Harnack remarks: "We have no means of checking this statement."[5]

[1] Jackson and Lake, *The Beginnings of Christianity*, IV (1933), 95–9, where bibliography is supplied.
[2] Jackson and Lake, *op. cit.*, II (1922), 89–90, where the quotation from Isaiah is classified as "showing substantial agreement" with the LXX. Also Henry J. Cadbury in V (1933), 66–7.
[3] Irenaeus, *Against Heresies*, III, XII, § 8; Eusebius, *Church History*, II, I, § 13. Jackson and Lake, *op. cit.* IV, 95–9.
[4] J. N. Farquhar, "The Apostle Thomas in North India", in *The Bulletin of the John Rylands Library*, X (1926), 89. But compare Streeter's critical comment, *The Primitive Church* (1929), 29–30.
[5] Eusebius, *Church History*, II, XVI; Harnack, *The Mission and Expansion of Christianity* (2nd. ed. 1908), II, 162. Mark's name crept into apocryphal Christian literature in connexion with Alexandria, cf. M. R. James, *The Apocryphal New Testament* (1924), 204.

So much for what we know of the introduction of Christianity into Africa in the Apostolic Age. In pursuing the story, developments in Egypt and ,in North Africa, with any missionary activity coming from them, will be considered in turn.

(3) *The Early Church in Egypt.*

Both the nearness of Egypt to Palestine and the large population of Jews settled there make it highly probable that Christian activity began quite early, for we know that the pioneer Christian missionaries went first to the synagogue. The Jews in Alexandria itself numbered 200,000, while throughout Egypt the Jewish population is reported by Philo as reaching a million. Indeed, Harnack goes so far as to say it is more than a conjecture that a larger number of Jews were converted to Christianity in the Nile valley than anywhere else.[1] Yet the whole story of Christian beginnings in Egypt is a blank in our annals. It is only with the episcopate of Demetrius of Alexandria (A.D. 189–232) that the Church in Egypt appears on the stage of history.[2] It is then sufficiently established to have an influential head in the bishop of Alexandria, who seems to have claimed jurisdiction over the whole country. It was Demetrius who was apparently the first to appoint three other bishops, a number increased to twenty-three by his successor.[3]

Christianity developed in Egypt in two different types of environment. On the one hand there was the Greek-speaking population of the towns of the Delta, and notably of Alexandria, which shared the religious and cultural influences common to the Hellenized provinces of the Empire. It was for the Greek-speaking Jews of Alexandria that the sacred Hebrew scriptures had first been translated into another tongue.[4] Here Greek philosophy was at home, and the influence of Platonic ideals notable on Jew and Christian alike. Contemporary with Demetrius were Pantaenus, Clement and Origen, the first the founder, and the others in turn the most distinguished heads of the world-

---

[1] Harnack, *op. cit.*, I, 6 and n. 2; II, 159, n. 2.

[2] Harnack (*op. cit.*, II, 160–2) summarizes under eight items only all that is known of the Church in Egypt prior to Demetrius.

[3] Westcott, in *D.C.B.* I, 803; Lightfoot, *Philippians*, 230; Harnack *op. cit.*, II, 164.

[4] Known as the Septuagint (LXX) from the tradition of there having been seventy translators (cf. H. G. Meecham, *The Oldest Version of the Bible* (1932), 3, n. 1). The Pentateuch had been translated before the middle of the third century B.C., the rest of the Old Testament by about 130 B.C. (cf. Prologue to *Ecclesiasticus* written *c.* 130 B.C.).

famous Catechetical School of Alexandria, a centre of Christian scholarship without rival in the then Christian world. Here the attempt was made to offer a reasoned and reasonable presentation of Christian truth, not only for the training of Christian believers, but also for the pagan nurtured in Greek philosophy. This was a genuine missionary activity, though it did not look towards the native population of Egypt or the undeveloped peoples beyond.

This native Egyptian population, later known as the Copts,[1] provided the other type of environment to which Christianity was exposed. The popular Egyptian religion was much concerned with magical mysteries, dominated by the famous cult of Osiris. This centred faith and practice in the hope of a future life and preparation for securing it through Osiris who, though slain by Evil, had triumphed in a resurrection. To carry out successfully the magical rites by which he had overcome the enemy was therefore the ambition of the Egyptian devotee, though a moral demand was not wanting, for there was weighing of good and evil before passing to the enjoyment of future felicity. That Christianity, with its proclamation of a Saviour who had conquered death, should therefore find a sympathetic hearing was to be expected. Clearly, also, the danger of syncretism would be especially acute.

While the progress of the Christian faith among the native Egyptian population cannot be traced as an unfolding story, it can nevertheless be measured at different times and by different means. Eusebius of Caesarea (c. 260–339), the learned historian of the early Church, has placed on record the story of martyrdoms during the persecutions of the third and early fourth centuries. Not only in Palestine, but also in Tyre and in Egypt he was an eyewitness of the sufferings of Christians, and in addition draws upon valuable contemporary sources for his narrative. The outbreak of persecution under the Emperor Septimius Severus occurred with the edict of A.D. 202 whereby fresh conversions to both Christianity and Judaism were forbidden. The evident intention was not to eradicate but to hold in check religious movements whose surprising expansion may have been held to be inimical to imperial stability. The edict gave opportunity, however, to the enemies of Christianity to assert themselves. The persecutions that broke out were

[1] From the modern Latin Coptus, an adaptation of the Arabic *quft* (also *qubt*), itself most probably an adaptation of the Coptic *gyytios* representing the Greek *aigyptios* (Egyptian).—*O.E.D., s.v.*

largely confined to Egypt and North Africa. Eusebius testifies to the faithful witness of Egyptian Christians: "This was especially the case in Alexandria, to which city, as to a most prominent theatre, athletes of God were brought from Egypt and all Thebais according to their merit, and won crowns from God through their great patience under many tortures and every mode of death."[1] The Thebais, or territory of Thebes, lay some 500 miles up the Nile, so that a considerable expansion of Christianity had taken place by this date. In the later persecution when Maximin ruled Syria and Egypt, Eusebius was himself an eyewitness of martyrdoms in the Thebais: "We also, being on the spot ourselves, have observed large crowds in one day; some suffering decapitation, others torture by fire. . . . As soon as sentence was pronounced against the first, one after another rushed to the judgment seat, and confessed themselves Christians."[2] Eusebius names bishops and other leaders of the Church in Egypt "who suffered deaths illustriously at Alexandria and throughout Egypt and Thebais".[3] Egyptian Christians also suffered outside their country; some were taken to labour in copper mines in Palestine; others suffered in Phœnicia; some who had been sent to minister to the confessors in Cilicia "received the same sentence as those whom they had gone to help being mutilated in their eyes and feet".[4] No section of the hard-pressed Christian fellowship held a prouder record than did the Egyptian Christians under their fiery trial. As in apostolic days, so now dispersion through persecution led to the further expansion of the Church. Eusebius quotes from a statement of Dionysius of Alexandria, who with others was exiled to Libya "to a village near the desert called Cephro", in which he says: "At first we were persecuted and stoned; but afterwards not a few of the heathen forsook the idols and turned to God. For until this time they had not heard the Word, since it was then first sown by us."[5] This vivid testimony as to the expansion of Christianity in Egypt by the third century is confirmed by evidence from the fourth supplied by the lists of episcopal attendances at Church synods. About A.D. 320 a synod was attended by almost 100 bishops. Athanasius also reported "close upon 100 bishops in Egypt, the Thebais, Libyae, and Pentapolis". At Sardica (343) there were

[1] Eusebius, *Church History*, VI, 1 (McGiffert's trans.).
[2] *Ibid.*, VIII, IX, §§ 4–5.　　　　[3] *Ibid.*, VIII, XIII, § 7.
[4] Eusebius, *Martyrs of Palestine*, XIII, §§ 1–3, 6; X, § 1. *Church History*, VIII, VII, §§ 1–6.
[5] Eusebius, *Church History*, VII, XI, § 13.

94 Egyptian bishops either actually present or who signed later.[1]

The use of the Egyptian language by the Church is decisive evidence of its expansion among the original Egyptian population of the Nile valley. The Greek language in the form of the *Koinē* or "Common Greek" that became current after the time of Alexander was for several centuries the general medium of intercourse in the Mediterranean world. The canonical Christian writings were all in Greek, as were, indeed, all the writings of the Apostolic Age. Greek even continued to be the language of the Church in Rome to the end of the second century. It was natural then that in Egypt, with its outstanding centre of Hellenic culture, Alexandria, Greek should at first be the general medium for Christian use.[2] But when the Christian message reached beyond the cultivated Greek-speaking population to the original Egyptian inhabitants, some translation of the New Testament books was required. Of the native Egyptian dialects in use, three became the media for new versions of the scriptures; the Sahidic of Upper Egypt, the Bohairic of the Nile Delta, and the Bashmuric intermediate to these. Dating is difficult, but the Sahidic version is regarded as the earliest, probably made in the third or early fourth century. We have the statement in the life of Anthony (born *c.* A.D. 250) that as a young man he heard the Gospels read in church; this suggests an Egyptian version, as he knew no Greek, but as the translation might have been oral, the evidence is not conclusive.[3] Pachomius, however, in the fourth century gives such place to the study of scripture in the rules for his Egyptian monks as to imply the existence of a vernacular version. The Bohairic dialect of the Delta, in a more cultured, Greek-speaking region, would

---

[1] Harnack, *op. cit.*, II, 170. The evidence from episcopal lists, however, is an imperfect measure of expansion. Its significance depends on the conditions required for the establishment of a new see.

[2] It has been suggested that the earliest Gospels in circulation in Egypt were not the canonical ones, but the apocryphal Gospel according to the Hebrews and Gospel according to the Egyptians, the former in Aramaic or a Greek translation for Jewish readers, and the latter in Greek for Hellenized Egyptians. See P. D. Scott-Moncrieff, *Paganism and Christianity in Egypt* (1913), 55–60, 65–8. Of particular interest was the discovery in 1935 of a fragment of the Fourth Gospel in the John Rylands Library. Though a tiny scrap, it was identified as written in a hand of the first half of the second century, and is the earliest known fragment of any part of the New Testament we possess. Sir Frederick Kenyon remarks: "It shows that a codex of the Fourth Gospel was circulating in mid-Egypt before the middle of the second century." — *Bulletin of the John Rylands Library*, XX (1936), 45–55; Sir Frederick Kenyon, *The Bible and Archaeology* (1940), 226.

[3] *D.C.B.*, I, 125a; *E.R.E.*, IV, 116b.

naturally be used later as a medium for the scriptures, probably only in the seventh or eighth century; this was the version, however, which became the official one for the Coptic Church.[1] Such translations are indisputable evidence of the need created by the expansion of the Church amongst the vernacular-speaking population, and the placing of the earliest version in the third or early fourth century shows that by that time the need had become insistent. Harnack makes so bold as to say for Egypt as a whole: "Certain it is that the Christians had long ago outstripped the Jews numerically, and by the opening of the fourth century they were over a million strong."[2]

Side by side with these canonical Books, however, there appeared an apocryphal Egyptian literature that witnessed to the appetite it sought to satisfy. There are various Lives and Panegyrics of the Virgin, and fragments of Narratives of the Ministry and Passion. Students of the literature remark on the highly emotional and uncritical quality of it, not to speak of the free handling of incident without concern for historical accuracy. Dr. M. R. James registers the warning that "the Copts were tireless in producing embroideries upon the Biblical stories, and perhaps in rewriting older documents to suit their own taste".[3]

This serves as a reminder that the expansion of Christianity in any region must always be measured in two dimensions—the area of population that becomes attached to the new faith, and the depth to which the new religion penetrates in reshaping faith and life. In this second respect growth was more gradual in Egypt. Perhaps the most striking exhibition of it, as well as the more secure (for the evidence is archaeological), is seen in the disposal of the dead. Excavations at Antinoë in Upper Egypt, for example, have brought to light a cemetery containing Christian dead indicating the slow transition from earlier Egyptian custom. Thus the embalming of the dead continued, a practice which had been connected with the belief in the passage of the soul to and fro between the realms of Osiris and the

---

[1] K. Lake, *The Text of the New Testament* (1908), 42–5; A. Souter, *The Text and Canon of the New Testament* (1913), 64–9.

[2] Harnack, *op. cit.*, II, 177.

[3] M. R. James, *The Apocryphal New Testament* (1924), 152. In relation to Infancy Gospels he says: "the reckless identification of the Virgin Mary with all the other Maries of the Gospels is characteristic of these Egyptian rhapsodies. . . . These documents on the whole show great negligence in the use of ancient sources and great licence on the part of the writers; and I think this is rather characteristic of the Christian literature of Egypt."—*Ibid.*, 88, 89.

tomb. Mummification, it appears, was continued by Egyptian Christians until the beginning of the fifth century. The Church opposed the practice and it eventually disappeared. It seems that the opposition of Anthony did most to end it. Apparently offerings of food were still made to the dead by Christians, a survival of the Egyptian idea of the necessity of magical food for the deceased. A Christian cemetery in the oasis of el-Khargeh has tombs of the pre-Christian pattern to which chambers with niches for offerings are attached. Moreover, the custom of burying with the dead wine jars and baskets for bread is revealed at Antinoë. It is suggested these may refer to a mystic Eucharist, for the custom of placing the holy elements in the coffin was at one time practised. Other objects, such as images of saints and evangelists, have been found replacing the figures of the gods of an earlier period. In a striking case of a supposed Christian priest, he is depicted on the outer wrapping holding a cup in one hand and corn-ears in the other (probably emblems of the Eucharist), with the swastika on his shoulder and the boat of Isis below.[1] The pull of the old religion, with its vivid conception of the future and hope of a life beyond, together with such means as were believed necessary to realize this hope, gave to Egyptian Christianity a distinctive character. In the words of Harnack's concise estimate: "Christianity in Egypt more than anywhere else perhaps, with the exception of Greece, adjusted itself to certain cardinal traits of the old national religion. . . . If the Egyptians were for the most part Christians by the middle of the fourth century, then they had created a sort of national religion for themselves out of the new religion by grafting on the latter to the cravings and remnants of the old."[2]

Another mark of the extent to which the Church was established in Egypt is the activity of the Copts in Christian art. As the late O. M. Dalton has pointed out, they made remarkable developments, more particularly in decorative design, after the fourth century. They seem to have derived methods and motives from Iran, probably by way of Syria, but they developed their own forms of expression. They were active producers and

[1] P. D. Scott-Moncrieff in *E.R.E.*, IV, 115b, 454–5. The early Christians seem to have continued pagan custom in keeping the mummified body in the house for a time, with occasional exposure to relatives and friends. It is suggested that this may be the origin of the later custom of preserving the remains of saints in reliquaria.—P. D. Scott-Moncrieff, *Paganism and Christianity in Egypt* (1913), 105–6. The placing of the Eucharistic elements with the dead witnesses to a belief in sacramental efficacy before that doctrine was developed by the Roman Church and may be due to Egyptian Gnostic sects.—*Ibid.*, 180–2. [2] Harnack, *op. cit.*, II, 176–7.

distribution was wide: bronze vessels of Coptic type have been recovered even in Anglo-Saxon cemeteries.[1]

An outstanding contribution was made by Egyptian Christianity to the whole of Christendom in the development of the monastic life. An ascetic element in the Christian ideal present from the Apostolic Age, and developed in the Christian reaction to the sensual pleasures of pagan cities, was encouraged from the philosophic side by the view of spirit as opposed to sense, so that, as liberation from the thraldom of sense was achieved, a growing spiritual experience could be realized. Such a development of an ascetic Christian ideal was found in Alexandria. It seems to have made a special appeal to many Egyptian converts.

Anthony is the father of the eremitic life. He was of Coptic descent. As a young man of twenty, on hearing the story of the rich young ruler (Matt. 19: 17 ff), he disposed of his goods and eventually retired into the desert. Many were fired by his example and colonies of hermits sprang up, notably in the deserts of Nitria and Scete in Lower Egypt. Ammonius, the father of monasticism in the Nitrian desert, exercised a strict discipline among the hundreds of hermits settled there. Apparently Negroes from lands to the south were occasionally found joining the native Egyptians as monks in the desert. One of them left his career on record. He had been a slave, but of so obstreperous a character that his masters refused to retain him. After a dark career as a brigand chief, he turned monk and inhabited a solitary cell in the Nitrian desert.[2] The real founder of the monastic life in community, however, as distinct from the solitary anchorite, was Pachomius, a Copt like Anthony. He founded a monastery on an island in the Nile in the Upper Thebaid. The life, while apparently less austere than that of the monks in the northern Libyan desert, was more systematized. Occupations were followed and sufficient food for an active life allowed. A common garb and the duty of obedience to a superior in control were also parts of his system. At his death towards the middle of the fourth century some eight monasteries existed modelled on his plan. The appeal of the monastic life to the untutored Egyptian Christian was so considerable that in this same fourth century the State took action to secure the discharge of civic duty. Whether the monastic life appealed as offering an escape from onerous social

---

[1] (O. M. Dalton), *Guide to the Early Christian and Byzantine Antiquities* (British Museum, 2nd ed. 1921), 31–2.
[2] Duchesne, *Early History of the Christian Church* (1912), II, 393.

and civic obligations, rationalized as the choice of the better way, or was a genuine choice of self-denial, the result was the same. A seriously depleted community was left behind to serve as citizens. Hence in 365 a law of Valens decreed that all who left the cities of Egypt for the monastic life of the desert should be compelled either to return to discharge their civic duties or to hand over their property to relatives who would.[1] Much resentment was caused among patriotic citizens at later periods that the land should be so largely denuded of able-bodied defenders in times of peril. Considerable power came to be wielded by these monasteries and their heads who rivalled the Egyptian episcopate in their influence. In the controversies of the time they were violently active, even invading Alexandria with fanatical riot and bloodshed and so staining the Christian name. There is little doubt that the extravagant extension of monasticism in Egypt beyond what was required to fulfil a genuine sense of vocation greatly weakened the life of the Church in that country.

The leading part played by the Church in Egypt in the great theological controversies of the fourth and fifth centuries can only be touched upon here in so far as it affected the relation of Egyptian Christians to ecumenical Christianity and to the imperial power. With the accession of Constantine as sole Emperor in A.D. 323 not only were Christians throughout the Empire relieved of oppressive statutes, but the material privileges of a state religion became theirs. The unity of the Church was, however, threatened by internal controversy. Arius and Athanasius had become protagonists in a dispute as to the relation of Christ the Son to the Father, and Alexandria had been the storm centre. Constantine decided to seek a solution for this and other matters in dispute by a common council of the bishops. Accordingly in 325 there met at Nicæa the first Ecumenical Council of the Church. With the acceptance of a creed,[2] for the first time proposed to the whole Church as a standard of doctrine (only two bishops at Nicæa, both Egyptians, refusing to subscribe to it),[3] the main purpose of the Council was temporarily achieved. Temporarily only, however, for the victory at Nicæa was the victory of a minority whose leaders, moved by deep conviction as to the significance of the issue at

---

[1] Moeller, *History of the Christian Church* (4th ed. 1912), I, 360.
[2] This original "Nicene Creed" is distinct from the Nicene Creed in current use. Cf. A. E. Burn, *An Introduction to the Creeds* (1899), 98.
[3] McGiffert in *Nicene and Post-Nicene Library*, I, 20.

stake, and clear-sighted as to their objective, were able to secure the support of the Council. Arianism still spread, and spread beyond the frontiers of the Empire. We shall meet it again in connexion with the Vandal invasion of North Africa. Harnack has stated concisely the reason for this success: "The Arians made the transition from heathenism to Christianity easier for the large numbers of the cultured and half-cultured whom the policy of Constantine brought into the Church. . . . The Arian monotheism was the best transition from polytheism to monotheism. It asserts the truth that there is *one* supreme God with whom nothing can be compared, and thus rooted out the crude worship of many gods."[1] Meanwhile Arianism was the cause of much sorry discord in the Church in Egypt.

In the course of the Arian controversy there emerged the question which was to dominate dogmatic discussion during the fifth and sixth centuries, namely, the nature of the union between the divine and the human in Christ. Many factors other than the simple search for truth entered into the ensuing controversies in which the bishops of Alexandria took a leading part. We are concerned with the limited issue of the effect of these controversies upon the development of Christianity in Egypt. Two of the factors other than theological must be noticed. There was first the ecclesiastical ambition of the bishops of Alexandria apparent from 325.[2] This involved a keen rivalry with the see of Constantinople and much high policy was primarily concerned with this ambition.[3] Rome would not have been Rome had she looked on unmoved; Alexandria was supported when Constantinople was to be checked, but the procedure could be and was reversed with disaster to Alexandrian ambitions. Then there was always the imperial concern that for the security and well-being of the Empire there should be unity within the Church as a State Church, a concern entirely.

[1] Harnack, *History of Dogma*, IV (1898), 43-4: cf. *ibid.*, 39-40: "These created beings which mediate between God and the creature are, however, according to Arius, to be adored, i.e. *it is only as a cosmologist that he is a strict monotheist, while as a theologian he is a polytheist.*" Italics in original.

[2] "The Council of Nicæa is the first step taken by the Bishop of Alexandria in aspiring to the primacy of the East."—*Ibid.*, IV, 59.

[3] "The Alexandrian bishops from Athanasius to Dioscurus have something in common. They strove to make themselves the masters of Egypt and the leaders of the Church of the East. Their resistance to the power of the State was not less strong than their hatred of the parvenu, the bishop of New Rome, whose aspirations after power they wished to put a stop to. We can only compare them with the great Popes, and the comparison is so far a just one inasmuch as they aimed at making Egypt a sort of independent ecclesiastical State."—*Ibid.*, 190-1.

reasonable. But this meant that the Emperor felt constrained to take a hand in settling bitter controversy that threatened disruption, and to support with the imperial power such decisions as might be reached by the majority of bishops, when, indeed, these decisions were not already determined by imperial policy. Here is a situation at the least stimulating, and at the most exasperating to any national feeling, and so it proved for Egypt.

The outstanding landmark in the lengthy Christological controversies was the Council of Chalcedon in 451. Convened by imperial edict, it was attended by some 600 members. On the critical doctrinal issue it determined that Christ was "perfect alike in His divinity and perfect in His humanity, alike truly God and truly man . . . the same Christ in two natures unconfusedly, unchangeably, indivisibly, inseparably".[1] Thus the "Orthodox" formula, asserting two natures in one person, was formally endorsed as the doctrine of the Church and the acts of the Council given imperial confirmation. Moreover, public disputation against the Council's decision was expressly forbidden. But in Egypt other teaching had long been current, namely, that the two natures in Christ were both resolved into one by the incarnation, whence the party name of Monophysites. So tenaciously was this view held (less on theological grounds than in opposition to irksome political control[2]) that the majority of Egyptian monks at Chalcedon begged to be excused from signing on the ground that if they did they would be killed forthwith on their return home.[3] A minority in Alexandria, it is true, accepted the Orthodox formula, and were forthwith dubbed Melkites or "Caesar-Christians".[4] But so violent was the feeling in opposition that troops had to be despatched from Constantinople to secure the peace, and the newly elected bishop could not move without a military escort.[5] Through a succession of rioting and tumult the spirit of faction became yet

---

[1] Harnack, op. cit., IV, 220. "The Emperor had now got what he wished. He had shown that he ruled the Church, and he had got a formula according to which he was able henceforth to decide what was orthodox and what was heretical."—Ibid., 221.

A careful narrative of the sequence of events at the Council is provided in B. J. Kidd, A History of the Christian Church to A.D. 461 (1922), III, xvi.

[2] "Monasticism which was hostile to the State, the aspirations after independence on the part of the Egyptians, and jealousy of the influence of the Byzantine patriarch, all played a part behind Monophysitism."—Harnack, op. cit., IV, 227, n.2.   [3] Ibid., IV, 224.

[4] As Schaff aptly terms them.—History of the Christian Church (5th ed., 1893), III, 776. Melkite is derived from the Hebrew melech, king.

[5] B. J. Kidd, op. cit., III, 407.

more bitter and deplorable deeds of violence, as earlier under Cyril, again stained the record of the Church in Egypt. The network of monastic settlements now enmeshed much of the country, and the cry "One Nature!" became indeed a battle-cry of these fierce ascetics. Thus with the exception of the small party of Melkites in Alexandria, the Egyptian Church had virtually separated from the Orthodox Communion as recognized by the Emperor and supported by imperial power. During the sixth century the struggle issued in the appearance of Monophysite sects in Egypt, Syria, and Armenia, whence derive the Coptic, Jacobite and Armenian Churches of to-day. The Emperor Justinian (527–565) attempted in vain the role of reconciler; the Empress Theodora favoured the Monophysite view, and actively assisted in promoting it. Persecution of Coptic Christians by the official Orthodox party, with the Emperor's power behind them, both in the reign of Justinian and of his successors, left a rankling resentment that persisted for many a generation.[1] Such was the unhappy state of the Church in Egypt at the time when a new national force and religious faith were coming to birth in Arabia—a rival power that Egyptians would soon hear hammering at the gate.

(4) *Missionary Expansion beyond Egypt.*

There were two directions, as permitted by geographical conditions, in which expansion from Egypt could take place— along the Mediterranean littoral to the bulge of Cyrenaica, and southwards along the Nile valley.

That there were Christians quite early in Cyrenaica seems clear. The existence of a Jewish community in contact with Jerusalem is attested in Acts (2:10; 6:9); these more enlightened Jews of the Dispersion, when converted, were not unnaturally among the first missionaries to the Gentiles (11: 20; 13: 1). That their own home settlements received the Gospel early is to be safely presumed. We know nothing, however, about Christian beginnings in Cyrenaica (alternatively known as Pentapolis). Catacombs are said to have been discovered in Cyrene belonging to the period before Constantine. By the middle of the third century there was a Church organized in a number of dioceses under a metropolitan resident in Ptolemais.

[1] T. W. Arnold says the rough handling of the Copts and the indignities suffered have not been forgotten by their children to the present day. He records that Justinian is said to have had 200,000 Copts put to death in the city of Alexandria alone, while the persecutions of his successors drove many to the desert.—*The Preaching of Islam* (2nd ed., 1913), 102 and n. 1.

Of the desert shores of the Syrtes farther west, lying between Cyrenaica and Africa Pronconsularis, Harnack says: "There were no churches there, but perhaps one or two Christian settlers at the end of the fourth century."[1] While the Church in Cyrenaica was most probably an independent planting, it eventually came under the ecclesiastical direction of the bishop of Alexandria.

The greater opportunity for missionary expansion lay to the south. Here along the Nile valley, beyond the southern boundary of Upper Egypt, was the region of Nubia, with Abyssinia lying beyond to the south-east and impinging on the Red Sea coast. Nubia, known also as Ethiopia to the ancients, was not a single political unit in Byzantine times; the southern boundary of Egypt varied with political and military fortunes, but may be taken as passing just below the First Cataract, and including the island of Philae, the most famous centre in all Egypt in Roman times for the worship of Isis, and one of the last pagan strongholds to yield to Christianity. The First Cataract was the ethnological as well as the geographical boundary. As early as 2000 B.C. the Pharaoh set this as the frontier no Negro should pass save in special circumstances.[2] There is good evidence, however, of active commercial intercourse, and of Egyptian influence on Nubian culture. The people were of mixed Hamitic and Negro descent.[3] The Blemmyes of the eastern desert, a Hamitic people represented by the Bisharin of to-day (a division of the Beja), were restive neighbours who from time to time invaded Upper Egypt. Soon after the middle of the third century A.D., having conquered the kingdom centred in Meroe which had inherited an ancient culture, they grew still more menacing. Thereupon Diocletian withdrew the imperial garrisons from the regions south of Philae, and brought Negro people from the western desert, the Nobadae, to settle there and so serve as a buffer state. In the course of the fourth century, however, the Blemmyes established themselves in the Nile valley just south of Philae, and in the middle of the fifth we find the Nobadae making common cause with them in attacks upon Egypt. In a treaty with the Emperor, by which the peace

[1] Harnack, *Mission and Expansion*, II, 178–9 and 179 n. 2.
[2] This decree, on the stele near the cataract, is quoted in Seligman, *Races of Africa*, 111.
[3] "There arose in Nubia a hybrid population, blending the characters of Egyptian, Negro, and Beja, and it is this type—which can clearly be defined in the graves of the Middle Empire—that has in the main persisted in Nubia to the present day . . ."—Seligman, *op. cit.*, 113.

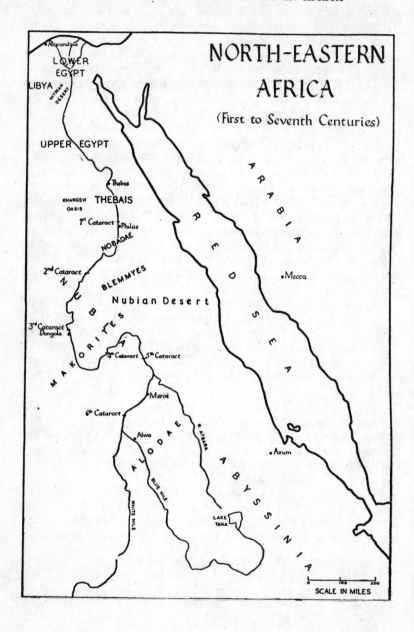

NORTH-EASTERN AFRICA

(First to Seventh Centuries)

was secured for a century, a special clause made provision for the Nobadae to visit the temple of Isis at Philae, evidence of the strength of the cult in Nubia at that time.[1] By the sixth century four peoples may be distinguished as in occupation of Nubia: the Nobadae between the First and Second Cataracts; the Blemmyes in the eastern desert; the Makorites south of the Nobadae, around Dongola, and the kingdom of Alwa with its capital near Khartoum.[2]

The first reference to any Christian contact with this interesting territory would appear to be the remark of Origen (185–253) who says in his commentary on Matthew when dealing with the apocalyptic passage in chap. 24 (and more particularly with reference to verse 14), that it is not claimed the Gospel has been preached to all the Ethiopians. This would seem to suggest that some contact at least had been made with the borders of the country in his time.[3] There is no evidence, however, of the effective establishment of Christianity there before the sixth century.

The first enterprises of which we have knowledge belong to the reign of Justinian (527–565), and are rival Orthodox and Monophysite missions. According to a contemporary account[4] the pioneer missionary to the Nobadae was one Julian, an old man of great worth, a presbyter in attendance on the patriarch of Alexandria, Theodosius, who was Monophysite. Julian had heard of these people beyond the frontier of Egypt, and was moved with a deep concern for their spiritual welfare. Being in Constantinople with the patriarch at the time, he laid his concern before the Empress Theodora. She, we are told, received the proposal with joy, and promised full support for the undertaking. She acquainted Justinian with her intention, who, though not opposed to the enterprise in itself, could not countenance a Monophysite as the agent of it. He took immediate action by despatching an embassy with rich gifts for the king and people of the Nobadae, and instructions to the governor

[1] *E.R.E.*, VI, 378b.
[2] F. Ll. Griffith in *Encyclopaedia Britannica*, 14th ed. (1929), XVI, 585b.
[3] " . . . *sic et nondum est praedicatum evangelium regni in toto orbe. Non enim fertur praedicatum esse evangelium apud omnes Aethiopas maxime apud eos, qui sunt ultra flumen* . . ."—*Origenis Opera Omnia*, ed. Lommatzsch (1834), IV, 271.
[4] *The Third Part of the Ecclesiastical History of John, Bishop of Ephesus*, translated by R. Payne Smith (1860), IV, 5–9; 49–53. John of Ephesus wrote in Syriac. Only Part III has survived, in a MS. discovered in an Egyptian convent. Not only was the author contemporary with the events here described, but he lived in Constantinople and claimed personal knowledge of the reports received there.

of the Thebais to speed the embassy on its way. Theodora, not to be outdone, sent an express letter to the governor informing him of the situation, and bidding him detain the imperial embassy until Julian had reached his destination, or his life would answer for it: "I will immediately send and take off your head." The governor, knowing the mettle of the Empress, acted as she desired; indeed, Julian and his party were allowed to seize the transport ostensibly prepared for their rivals who had come in first. The upshot was that Julian, who had received a generous welcome from the king and nobles of the Nobadae, was able to declare his mission unhindered. There was ready response, whereupon he warned the king of the rival embassy and succeeded in securing its rejection. Thus the Nobadae were gained to the Christian faith and came under the jurisdiction of the Monophysite patriarch of Alexandria. Julian remained two years in the country, though he found the heat extremely trying. To Theodore, bishop of Philae, who had been his helper, he handed over the care of the work, and returned to Constantinople to report to the Empress.

Meanwhile the Orthodox mission despatched by the Emperor, having failed to secure an entry among the Nobadae, seems to have turned to a neighbouring people of Nubia, the Makorites, and to have succeeded in winning converts to the faith. The success of an Orthodox mission is attested by gravestones inscribed with Greek Byzantine texts.[1]

It was some twenty years before further provision was made for the converts among the Nobadae. Then the patriarch Theodosius, as one of his last acts, commissioned Longinus, a priest who had long attended on him, to proceed there as bishop, an appointment Theodora had herself desired. For some three years he was frustrated in his attempt to set out, but finally in disguise slipped through the fingers of the imperial officials and reached his field, where he was accorded a great welcome. This was about 568. He is said to have "built them a church, and ordained clergy, and taught them the order of divine service and all the ordinances of Christianity". Indeed, John of Ephesus says he was present at court when a special ambassador from the Nobadae arrived and reported to the Emperor: "Though we were Christians in name, yet we did not really know what

[1] K. S. Latourette, *History of Expansion of Christianity*, II (1939), 233. Latourette conjectures that the Orthodox mission may eventually have fared better than the Monophysite, since Justinian survived Theodora for eighteen years, and "Justinian, with his usual attention to details, may be supposed to have given some thought to the spiritual care of these converts of his envoys."

Christianity was until Longinus came to us."[1] After some five years Longinus ventured to visit Alexandria, though he was still subject to imperial arrest, in response to a call to take a hand in securing a new patriarch, a step that involved him in a sorry business.

Meanwhile the success of the Christian mission among the Nobadae had stimulated the Alodæi, of the kingdom of Alwa to the south of the Makorites, and with whom the Nobadae were on friendly relations, to ask for a mission. Attempts of Longinus' opponents in Alexandria to enter this new field failed through the insistence of the king that he only knew Longinus who had baptized the Nobadae, and would receive him only. Longinus, who had now returned from Alexandria, set out on the difficult journey to the south. The natural obstacles of desert and climate were great enough—he is said to have lost seventeen camels on the way—but in addition the Makorites were unfriendly, so a circuitous route through the land of the Blemmyes had to be taken to reach the Blue Nile. If the Orthodox mission to the Makorites had succeeded as we assume, it is possible that the king of the Makorites was acting as the Emperor's friend in endeavouring to intercept Longinus.[2] But we cannot tell. Longinus was welcomed with great joy; "and immediately upon his arrival he spake unto the king and to all his nobles the word of God, and they opened their understandings, and listened with joy to what he said; and after a few days' instruction, both the king himself was baptized and all his nobles; and subsequently in process of time, his people also".[3] Of the further personal activities of Longinus, how long he stayed in Nubia and whether he ever left, we do not know. Christianity in Nubia, however, struck root and flourished. Christian kingdoms resisted the encroachments of Islam for eight centuries, and in places for nearly a thousand years. But that belongs to a later part of the story.

Beyond the Nubian kingdoms, in mountainous highlands to the south-east, lay Abyssinia. The kingdom of Axum, in the north of the country, had received Christianity in the time of

[1] John of Ephesus, op. cit. IV, 8; E. A. Wallis Budge, A History of Ethiopia (1928), I, 113–18. Budge supplies the text of an inscription of Silko, king of the Nobadae, and suggests that it was he who was primarily responsible for the kingdom with Dongola as its capital becoming Christian. In his inscription he celebrates victories over the Blemmyes and ascribes them to God, apparently the God of the Christians.

[2] Griffith speaks of the Makorites as still stoutly pagan at the time of the conversion of Alwa. Ency. Brit. (1929) XVI, 585b.

[3] John of Ephesus, op. cit., IV, 51.

Constantine. The story of its introduction as given by Rufinus is as follows:[1] a certain philosopher, Merope of Tyre, set out to visit India (a term then also covering Southern Arabia and lands bordering the Red Sea) in company with two lads, Frumentius and Aedesius. On their return journey the ship put into a harbour for necessaries where the people proved hostile. All save the two youths were put to death. These were spared and taken to the king. He was pleased with them, and appointed each to a position of trust, Aedesius the younger to be his cupbearer, and Frumentius to act as his private secretary. So faithful did they prove that the king at his decease granted them their freedom. The queen-mother, however, prevailed on them to remain and administer the affairs of the kingdom during her son's minority. Frumentius in due course made inquiry whether among the traders any Christians were to be found. Hearing that there were, he provided them with facilities for assembling together, and encouraged them in the faith. When they had both discharged the obligation they undertook, they were free to depart; Aedesius returned to Tyre, but Frumentius, with a deep concern for the little Christian community he had nurtured in the country, proceeded to Alexandria and laid the need before Athanasius who was then bishop. It was agreed that no more suitable appointment than that of Frumentius himself could be made; he was consecrated bishop, and returning to the kingdom saw many converted to the faith.

Rufinus claims to have this story from Aedesius himself, and such facts as are known confirm his narrative. The scene of the story is the kingdom centring in Axum, and embracing part of the modern Eritrea and of Abyssinia north of Lake Tana. That Frumentius was bishop in Axum in 356 we know on the authority of Athanasius himself.[2] What king on the Abyssinian side of the story can be linked up with these events? A king of Axum, 'Ezana[3] by name, probably of the second quarter of the fourth century, has left inscriptions recording his campaigns. In the earlier he is pagan; in the last, commemorating a victory over the Nubians, he acknowledges "the Lord of Heaven Who in heaven and upon the earth is mightier than

---

[1] Rufinus, *Hist. Eccles.* I, IX, in *Patrologia Latina*, ed. Migne Tom. XXI, (1878). Socrates translates it almost word for word in his *Ecclesiastical History*, I, XIX. Sozomen, *Hist. Eccl.*, II, 24, also gives the story, direct from Rufinus, cf. *Nicene and Post-Nicene Fathers*, II (1891), 23, n. 1, and 222.

[2] Athanasius, *Apologia ad Constantium*, §29, the date of which was A.D. 356. See A. Robertson in *Nicene and Post-Nicene Fathers*, IV, 236.

[3] In its Greek form, Aeizanas.

everything which exists".[1] The symbols on his coins also change, the later ones having the cross. His father, Ella Amida, may well be the king of Rufinus' story and 'Ezana the prince during whose minority Frumentius and Aedesius served the kingdom. If this identification be correct, then Frumentius did finally succeed in securing the conversion of the king, the "Constantine of Abyssinia", but only as his reign was drawing to a close. With the official establishment of Christianity in the country the work of Frumentius reached its climax, but the conversion of Abyssinia still remained a task for the future.[2]

Abyssinian legend speaks of the Nine Saints who helped to build up the Christian Church in the country. They probably came from Syria towards the end of the fifth century. At this date they may well have been Monophysite confessors expelled after Chalcedon; certainly from this time the Church in Abyssinia is Monophysite. Littmann even surmises that these Christian missionaries may have influenced the style of church architecture in the direction of a basilical plan: "The ancient shrines were now changed into Christian sanctuaries, the high places were dedicated to the saints, and the sacred sycamore trees to the Virgin Mary."[3] Friendly relations were maintained with the Christians of Southern Arabia during the sixth century. But Abyssinian Christianity is then shrouded from our view for six hundred years. One event of first-rate significance would seem to have occurred by this time—the translation of the scriptures into Ethiopic. Dating is difficult, but Dillmann regarded the translation as having been made from a Greek text between the fourth and the sixth century.[4] Other scholars favour the later date, and regard the translation as having been made from Syriac. A date in the sixth century would have much support.[5]

The missionary activity in lands to the south of Egypt thus

[1] The text of the inscriptions is given by Wallis Budge, *A History of Ethiopia* (1928), I, 247–9 (when a pagan); 252–8 (when a Christian).
[2] Budge, *op. cit.*, I, 147–53, 242–59; Jones and Monroe, *History of Abyssinia* (1935), 24–5, 28–9. K. S. Latourette also places the king of the inscriptions in the fourth century; *op. cit.*, I (1937), 236. R. Bell, however, prefers a date for 'Ezana in the later part of the fifth century, and finds in Frumentius' appointment to Axum a possible step to extend the influence of the Athanasian party against the Arians; *The Origin of Islam in its Christian Environment* (1926), 31. E. Littmann also accepts a fifth-century date for the king, *E.R.E.* I (1908), 57b.   [3] *Ibid.*, 58a.
[4] C. R. Gregory, *Canon and Text of the New Testament* (1907), 405–6; R. H. Charles in *H.D.B.*, I, 791–3; T. H. Robinson, "The Syriac Bible" in *The Bible in its Ancient and English Versions* (ed. H. Wheeler Robinson, 1940), 97.   [5] A. Souter, *The Text and Canon of the New Testament* (1913), 73.

appears as originally the concern of individuals moved by the need of their heathen neighbours, and prepared to devote themselves to meeting it. But they were themselves representatives of different Christian communities, and their converts became associated with their type of the faith. A Coptic patriarch of Alexandria exercised control in Nubia and in Abyssinia, though Orthodox activity in Nubia is also attested, and Syrian Christianity seems to have made its contribution to the Abyssinian Church.

CHAPTER 4

THE ENTERPRISE BEGUN
(B) NORTH AFRICA

As in the case of Egypt, so also in North Africa an impenetrable veil shrouds from view the beginnings of the Christian Church and its early growth until the end of the second century. Then the veil is withdrawn and we discover a well-established community in Carthage with a diocesan organization and some diffusion of the faith throughout the country. Before reviewing the extent and growth of the Church in this part of Africa, it will be well to notice some general features of the situation that are significant for its progress.

(1) *The Roman Provinces.*

The provinces of North Africa were only brought under imperial control by a steady process of expansion, as was characteristic of the growth of the Empire, in order the better to secure the *pax Romana* in existing territories. Geographical conditions set a limit to this process, the Sahara to extension southwards and the Atlas mountains to an effective control of the west. Thus to the original Africa Proconsularis were added the province of Numidia to the west, and the two provinces of Mauretania Caesariensis and Mauretania Tingitana between it and the Atlantic coast, the four covering the area occupied by the modern Tripoli, Tunis, Algeria and Morocco. Berber tribes were the earliest inhabitants in historical times. A Semitic element had been introduced with the Phoenician coastal settlements, and some Jewish communities had also appeared. Some would even argue for Jewish co-operation in the early Phoenician undertakings. The foreign element in the population that had been the last to arrive was due to Roman colonization. It consisted in the main of discharged soldiers— veterans sent specifically to colonize or soldiers who remained in Africa when their service there was completed. These were the standard-bearers of Roman civilization.[1] They became small resident landowners, by contrast to the Italian owners

[1] Professor E. Albertini notes that they included men from Italy, Gaul, Spain, Asia, and the Danubian countries, and that "since many of them married African wives, their descendants were quickly merged in the Berber population".—*Cambridge Ancient History*, XI (1936), 481.

ROMAN AFRICA and AFTER

(First to Seventh Centuries)

--- Roman Provinces in the Early Third Century --

-- -- Southern boundaries ill-defined.

Scale

of large estates who remained in Italy, but they were never more than a small fraction of the total population.

Agriculture was the almost universal occupation. Africa became the granary of Italy with wheat its principal export. Oil and wine, fruit and vegetables were also in regular supply for overseas markets.[1] The necessity to safeguard the agricultural community and to extend it, led to measures against the nomadic pastoral tribes upon the borders. A line of military posts along the desert fringe secured the southern frontier, while westwards in Numidia the pastoral peoples had either to turn agriculturist or move out. Mauretania was another proposition, and the western frontier was more difficult to determine.[2]

In both language and religion the three elements in the population made their contribution. The Berber dialects never disappeared; they are referred to collectively as Libyan. Punic, the language of the ruling race until the arrival of Rome, also continued in extensive use. Latin held its place by the side of these without displacing them.' "The truth of the matter probably was", says Albertini, "that in the upper and middle classes many people were bilingual or even trilingual, speaking Libyan or Punic in private and Latin in public; whereas many of the illiterate poor conversed freely in Libyan and Punic only and knew little Latin."[3] We shall find here a point of considerable significance for the Christian Church.

In religion there had been the development one might anticipate. The Berbers still venerated the spirits of natural objects on which life depended, such as springs and trees. But to these had been added the deities of Phoenicia which had migrated to Africa. The old Phoenician religion, indeed, remained more primitive in Carthage than in the homeland where it became modified by Greek influence.[4] Names were changed in course of time, but it was still the old Baal and Ashtoreth (Ashtart) of Hebrew history that later masqueraded as Saturn and Coelestis.[5] There was no gainsaying the continued popularity of these deities; the appeal of the old religion of Punic days remained as strong as ever. Gods of the Roman

---

[1] *Cambridge Ancient History*, XI (1936), 486.
[2] R. Syme in *Cambridge Ancient History*, XI, 147–8.
[3] *Op. cit.*, 487. It is said that when a sister of the Emperor Septimius Severus, a native of Leptis Magna, went to visit him in Rome, he was constrained to blush because of her defective knowledge of Latin—Paul Vinogradoff in *Cambridge Mediaeval History*, I (2nd ed. 1924), 545.
[4] *E.R.E.*, IX, 889a.   [5] *Cambridge Ancient History*, IX, 487.

pantheon came in beside them but were far from displacing them.

Recent archaeological work in North Africa has revealed the amazing development in material culture that took place in Roman times, from Leptis Magna in Tripolitania to Thamugadi (the modern Timgad) in Numidia and beyond. Indeed, these dead cities of Roman Africa have been claimed to be the most beautiful archaeological museum in the world. French and Italian experts, in the two decades between the wars, have recovered from the sand what are still most impressive memorials of that bygone day, such as the hippodrome at Leptis Magna with its seating capacity for 50,000, or at Timgad the thirteen public baths that may still be seen, lending vividness to the motto of a citizen of Timgad: "Hunting, bathing, gambling, laughing, that's life."[1] By the time of Septimius Severus at the end of the second century, who adorned Leptis Magna as worthy the birthplace of an Emperor, Africa seems to have become effectively romanized. Tertullian, contemporary of Severus, can write, primarily with respect to Africa: "Surely a glance at the wide world shows that it is daily being more cultivated and better peopled than before. All places are now accessible, well known, open to commerce. Delightful farms have now blotted out every trace of the dreadful wastes; cultivated fields have overcome woods; flocks and herds have driven out wild beasts; sandy spots are sown; rocks are planted; bogs are drained. Large cities now occupy land hardly tenanted before by cottages. Islands are no longer dreaded; houses, people, civil rule, civilization, are everywhere."[2] A caveat should be entered, however, against overlooking the great mass of the Berber population living outside the towns, little subject if at all to the romanizing process that functioned through town and city life, and always living near to subsistence level. The fact that these masses remain inarticulate while the cultured groups leave their record in monuments and literature, may, if we are not cautious, lead us to distort the picture.[3]

(2) The Church in the Roman Period.

Into these favoured provinces of the Roman world came Christianity, probably from Rome, and probably first to

[1] "In Roman Africa", *The Times*, March 27, and April 3, 1928.
[2] Tertullian, *de Anima*, xxx, quoted in Harnack, *Mission and Expansion* (2nd ed., 1908), II, 275, note 1. Some allowance must doubtless be made for Tertullian's rhetorical gift.
[3] Albertini underlines this warning concerning the unprivileged masses, *loc. cit.*, 491.

Carthage.[1] That it spread much farther afield is shown by the martyrdoms with which the African Church first appears on the stage of history. Twelve Christians, seven men and five women, were tried, condemned and executed in Carthage on July 17th, A.D. 180, for refusing to deny the faith. They came from Scillium in Numidia. They bore Latin names, which shows that at least they belonged to the romanized layer of the population. A certain Namphamo, claimed as the first martyr, also came from Numidia, the name in this case being Punic.[2] As from this point the story of the Church in Africa unfolds before us, we find a devotion under persecution not excelled elsewhere, and a fervent fidelity to the faith expressed in Puritan ideals that gave Montanism a second home in Africa. The names of Tertullian, Cyprian and Augustine add an imperishable lustre to the history of the African Church. Yet there are serious imperfections to record. Nowhere did party spirit run more rife than in the Donatist conflict of the fourth century that drained away energy sorely needed by the Church to fulfil her witness to a pagan world. As we shall see, social and racial antagonisms intensified the bitterness of the conflict, but on that very ground the failure was the greater, for the Church's task was to bring in the new order "where there cannot be Greek and Jew, circumcision and uncircumcision, barbarian, Scythian, bondman, freeman: but Christ is all, and in all".[3] Moreover, this very self-consuming strife involved the neglect of any real evangelistic mission both to the unreached within the imperial territories and still more to those upon and beyond the imperial frontier. The greatest failure to be laid at the door of the African Church is its failure to evangelize.

From the first appearance of the African Church in the light of history in A.D. 180 to the Vandal invasion in 429, marking the end of the Roman period, we have two and a half centuries of opportunity, divided into two by Constantine's Edict of Milan of 313, whereby the Christian religion received complete toleration within the Empire. It is at this mid-point that the Donatist controversy arises. The growth of the Church in the period before Constantine was considerable. It can be tested indirectly at different points by the extension of the episcopate

---

[1] Tertullian states that for Carthage Rome is vested with apostolic authority. —de Praescr., 36. Quoted by Lietzmann, *Cambridge Ancient History*, XII (1939), 536. On the tradition that Philip the Apostle visited Carthage, see *Anecdota Oxoniensa*, Semitic Series, Part VII 292–3; cf. P. W. Schmiedel in *Ency. Biblica*, III, 3701.

[2] B. J. Kidd, *A History of the Church to A.D. 461* (1932) I, 110–11. Duchesne, *Early History of the Christian Church* (1909), I, 188, 286. The site of Scillium remains unidentified. [3] Col. 3: 11.

in the African provinces. Harnack in discussing this evidence accepts the following stages of growth as reasonably correct: about A.D. 220 with the demise of Tertullian, some 70 to 90 bishoprics; about A.D. 250, in Cyprian's day, nearly 150; by the beginning of the fourth century, in the time of Constantine, not less than 250.[1] This trebling of the episcopate in less than a century is certainly evidence of striking progress, even when allowance is made for Gibbon's criticism that "the practice of appointing bishops to the most inconsiderable towns, and very frequently to the most obscure villages, contributed to multiply the splendour and importance of their religious societies".[2] Another measuring rod of extension is the enumeration of places where it is known Christian churches existed at a given date. It is surprising that Tertullian, our earliest authority, mentions four places only outside Carthage where Christian churches are to be found. Harnack is able to name only eight places, including Carthage, known to possess Christian churches previous to Cyprian; a further eighty-eight mentioned by Cyprian; with twenty-nine others mentioned after Cyprian but before A.D. 325, and adds the general comment: "With map in hand we can see the equable distribution of Christianity over the various provinces (with the exception of Mauretania), equable, i.e., when we take into account the nature of the soil and the presumed density of the population. The only parallel to this diffusion occurs in some of the provinces of Asia Minor."[3] Churches clustered most thickly about Carthage, the metropolis in both spiritual and secular affairs. In the opening years of the fourth century came the great persecution under Diocletian, comparatively short in duration (A.D. 303–305), but the sternest test the African Church had yet had to face. There were martyrs and there were apostates. The fidelity of the martyrs won fame for the Church as far afield as Caesarea where Eusebius records their faithful witness; the apostates were not a few, and on Augustine's testimony included seventy bishops.[4] These events also attest the numerical growth of the Church. Only spasmodic persecution continued after the abdication of Diocletian in 305, until Galerius issued an edict of toleration,

---

[1] Harnack, *Mission and Expansion*, II, 286.
[2] Gibbon, *Decline and Fall of the Roman Empire*, ed. Bury (9th ed., 1925), II, 62. Cf. Harnack, "One must never forget that the organization of the Church in Northern Africa evidently required a bishopric even where there were but a few Christians, i.e. in every township," *op. cit.*, II, 281.
[3] Harnack, *op. cit.*, II, 286–97.   [4] *Ibid.*, II, 285, n. 3.

shortly before his death in 311. And so we pass to the period of Constantine and after; persecution now belonged to the past, but the Church faced new perils in its alliance with the State. There was, nevertheless, greatly enlarged opportunity to pursue its mission in a pagan world, an opportunity that in Africa was wilfully thrown away in a controversy that rent the Church asunder. In 311, the year of the edict of Galerius, Mensurius, the bishop of Carthage, died. Caecilian, his arch-deacon, was elected his successor with popular approval, and was consecrated by Felix, a suffragan of Carthage. But there were disgruntled elements which formed themselves into an opposition party and disputed his succession.[1] They secured as allies certain Numidian bishops who showed petty vexation at being ignored in the consecration of Caecilian. The charge was then preferred that Caecilian was no true bishop since he had been consecrated by Felix who was a *traditor*. This charge, that Felix had surrendered the scriptures during persecution, remained to be proved, but meanwhile the opposition mustered some seventy bishops and in 312 consecrated Majorinus as bishop. There was schism in Carthage which brought the inter-vention of Constantine, for he sought a united Church as spiritual companion to a united Empire. When certain imperial benefactions were to be disbursed, under the terms of the Edict of Milan, Caecilian and his clergy alone were beneficiaries. The party of Majorinus lodged an appeal with the Emperor, and within the next seven years a succession of five investiga-tions took place. At the Council of Rome in 313 the prosecution failed, but complained that the alleged crime of Felix was not gone into; therefore an inquiry took place the following year at Carthage before the proconsul, when Felix was cleared of the charge against him. Later the same year, at the Council of Arles, the case of Caecilian was reviewed, the aim being to pacify the African Church, so that while Caecilian was again approved, the Council "seems to have sanctioned some division of the episcopal authority in any African diocese between Catholic and Donatist claimants to the see, for the sake of peace".[2] The Donatists refused the proffered olive branch and appealed direct to the Emperor. At length he responded and at Milan in 316 the case was argued before him.

[1] "His consecration was contested by the united forces of disappointed ambition, detected fraud, and personal pique."—B. J. Kidd, *op. cit.*, I, 534, whose admirable account of the course of the controversy is here followed.
[2] *Ibid.*, I, 539-40.

Again the verdict was for Caecilian. Meanwhile Majorinus had died, c. 315, and the Donatus whose name provided the party label succeeded him. A final investigation at Thamugadi in 320 proved a boomerang for the Donatists. The very charge they had made against Caecilian was proved beyond doubt against their own Majorinus. When in 322 Constantine inaugurated a period of tolerance, there followed a quarter of a century, not indeed of internal peace for the African Church, but of the suspension of a policy of imperial repression. With the failure, however, in Numidia (where the main strength of the Donatists was to be found) of an attempt at reunion through imperial commissioners, themselves Christians, there followed once again repression of the malcontents. It was effective in that it gave the Church in Africa a period of peace. This lasted from 348 until the accession of the pagan Julian in 361. In the following year he lifted the ban on the Donatist exiles and allowed them to re-occupy their churches. This they did with every gesture of provocation. "The running sore of the Church of Africa was opened again."[1] By the time of Augustine the Donatists themselves were split into parties and were excommunicating each other, but together they outnumbered the Catholic members of the Church.[2]

The rivalry of Donatist and Catholic led to the spectacular increase in the number of bishops we find at the beginning of the fifth century, the total given by Harnack being from 500 to 700.[3] The learned Father Mesnage, who has examined the evidence with care, points out that while the Catholics occasionally declined to compete in the race for bishoprics (as at the Council of Carthage in 390), yet it was too much to expect that such self-restraint should persist, with the opposing party growing so rapidly. Thus in 397 the Catholic primate of Carthage admitted having had an episcopal consecration almost weekly. There is also evidence (from a document of 411) of bishops being placed, not only in villages, but also on the estates of landed proprietors. Mesnage concludes there was nothing to choose between the two parties in this matter. Indeed, they would set up two, three, or even four bishops to oppose one, to such a length did the competition run.[4] Suitable episcopal candidates naturally ran short, so that the less worthy, to state it mildly, were appointed; best of all was to

---

[1] B. J. Kidd, op. cit., II, 114. [2] Ibid., 385.
[3] Harnack, op. cit., II, 286.
[4] Mesnage, Le Christianisme en Afrique, I, Origines (1914), 143–5.

secure your opponent's priest and ordain him bishop. One Donatist bishop stigmatized the priest he lost in this way as his Absalom.[1]

Augustine was now active with his pen, and in 401 stated the Catholic attitude as being to receive from the Donatists "all the good things they had of God—baptism, ordination, continence, virginity, faith in the Trinity and so forth. ... When therefore they return to the Catholic Church, they do not receive from her what they had before; but they receive from the Church what they had not, viz. charity, which makes what they had of benefit to them."[2] When further attempts at conference failed, the Catholic bishops appealed to the State. The Conference of Carthage held in 411 under an imperial commissioner sounded the death knell of Donatism. There were present 286 Catholic bishops and 279 Donatist, a grand total of 565.[3] Judgment went against the Donatists and an edict enforced it. Order was restored in ecclesiastical affairs, but the price was high.[4] And a new peril was approaching. Within twenty years the Vandals were in Africa.

The significance of the controversy has been variously assessed. Leaving on one side the personal ambitions and jealousies of unworthy leaders, some have stressed the African strain of rigorism that expressed itself in the Montanism of the third century, and gave persistence to the Donatists of the fourth. The idea of the Church is the matter ultimately in dispute, and the manner in which holiness is conceived as its mark. Harnack crystallizes the issue as the striving of Christendom "against the secularization that was imposed upon it by the removal of the attribute of holiness, and with it of the truth of the Church, from *persons* to institutions".[5] While the dogmatic theologian of necessity concentrates attention upon this element in the debate, the historian is aware of other

---

[1] Mesnage, *op. cit.*, 147

[2] Augustine, *Ep. lxi*, quoted in B. J. Kidd, *op. cit.*, III, 12. Cf. Harnack, *History of Dogma*, V, 146.

[3] Mesnage, *op. cit.*, 147–65. Some 137 dioceses were probably duplicated in representation, with both a Catholic and a Donatist bishop attending.

[4] B. J. Kidd comments on the resort to force: "Repression had been proved to be the only method so far successful in the cause of peace and good order; and we cannot wonder, though we must profoundly regret, that Augustine was at last won over to give it his countenance. It was a step not less disastrous in the after-history of the Church than the Conversion of Constantine. The Fathers, as a whole, were on the side of toleration."—*Op. cit.*, III, 17.

[5] Harnack, *History of Dogma*, V, 40 (italics in original). For Augustine's exposition on this point, cf. *ibid.*, 144–8. Also De Pressensé, *D.C.B.*, I, 218.

motives in a complex situation; in particular, of the social and national antagonisms that added heat to the controversy and made so intransigent much of the Donatist party. Harnack notes that the Donatists appear as the African national party.[1] Mesnage is still more explicit, and suggests that an important factor in their success in securing conversions among Berbers was their attitude of revolt against Roman authority.[2] He cites as parallel situations the support of Nestorius by Babylonia and Persia after the Council of Ephesus (431) less from a taste for his teaching than from the opportunity to express racial and national independence against the dominating Empire; and the case of Egypt after Chalcedon, which we have already noticed, where the refusal of the Council formula was determined less by dogmatic considerations than by those of nationality and race.[3] Further, it was in Numidia, where the main strength of the Donatists lay, that there arose under their aegis those bands of wandering mendicants known as Circumcellions. They exhibited a revolutionary frenzy that threatened the stability of society. There were indeed Donatists who disowned them, and some who invoked the civil power against them. Augustine says they only understood Punic, but it seems most probable that they were really Berbers who had learned Punic through prolonged contact with their Carthaginian neighbours.[4] They represented at bottom the social and racial revolt of a repressed peasantry.

The penetration of Christianity in North Africa at the conclusion of the Roman period may be measured in three ways, geographically, socially and linguistically. In geographical extent the limit to its influence was the Roman frontier. Christianity had reached it at several points, especially where there were military posts of importance. No bishopric is known beyond the Roman frontier.[5] Mesnage argues convincingly that, as the existence of ruins of churches and other Christian remains are adduced as evidence of the spread of Christianity,

[1] Harnack, *op. cit.*, V, 39.
[2] "Il parait bien certain que, si le donatisme prit tant d'extension parmi les indigènes, c'est qu'il représentait la résistance au gouvernement étranger. Ils se firent donatistes parce que leurs maîtres étaient catholiques, comme plus tard, après avoir embrassé l'Islam, ils se firent ouahbites parce que leurs maîtres étaient orthodoxes."—Mesnage, *op. cit.*, 140.
[3] *Ibid.*, 140–41, n. 2.
[4] H. Leclercq, *L'Afrique Chrétienne* (2nd ed. 1904), I, 346.
[5] Mesnage, *op. cit.*, 182.

so the absence of these in the interior is valid evidence of the failure to evangelize.[1]

Socially and racially there was a triple stratification in Africa. The solid base was Berber; next came the inhabitants of Punic stock and culture, and finally as the topmost and the thinnest layer, the Graeco-Roman population. Christianity won its largest successes with the Roman and romanized top layer, and penetrated much of the second Punic layer. It seems only to have touched the Berbers slightly, and that largely through fervent Donatist propaganda that was less interested in the soundness than the number of conversions. Certainly the indigenous tribes that kept the frontiers were almost untouched.[2]

The evidence of language is significant. Latin was the official language of the Church in Africa; services were in the Latin tongue, and Christian literature was in Latin. The earliest translation of the Bible into Latin, the Old Latin Version, may have been made in Africa. The Punic language was used in preaching, though Augustine did not find it easy to secure priests who were fluent in it. In one case he was obliged to ordain a simple reader as bishop. Moreover, Augustine himself had to use an interpreter when addressing a Punic congregation.[3] For the benefit of converts who knew Punic only, the Bible was translated into their tongue during worship, but so far as we know no written translation of the Bible into Punic was ever made.[4] The mother tongue of the Berbers fared even worse. Not only was no portion of the Scriptures translated, but apparently no attempt was made to have preaching or services in the Berber tongue. If the Berbers were to hear the word, it was in general through the Latin language they must do so. As a further point of linguistic interest it has been remarked that both Tertullian and Cyprian make liberal use of a military vocabulary. It is more than the occasional use of such language by Paul; and while Tertullian was a soldier's son, Cyprian's use demands another explanation. It is suggested that this may reflect the early contact of Christianity with the military camps, of which Lambaesa in Numidia was the most important, and also the fact that the Roman contribution to colonization in Africa consisted largely of discharged soldiers. Once again it is the romanized element in the population that is mainly in view.[5]

[1] Mesnage, *op. cit.*, 206–7. The argument from silence is less perilous with archaeological than with literary data.   [2] *Ibid.*, 198–9, 225–6. [3] *Ibid.*, 262, 263.   [4] Harnack, *op. cit.*, II, 279, n. 3.   [5] *Ibid.*, 280.

Note

Thus the evidence all converges upon the same point, namely, that the successes of Christianity in North Africa were among the Roman population and the Punic element mainly to the extent to which it was romanized, while only those Berbers were won who came within the circle of romanizing influence. The Berber converts who were gained during the competitive campaigns of Catholic and Donatist belonged to areas such as Numidia, already firmly held by the Roman power. Mesnage reviews the Christian situation at the end of the Roman period by reference to three different zones. First, the romanized towns which were for the most part Christian, but with the spirit of paganism still alive among many, both communicants and catechumens; next, the countryside which had been colonized and brought partly under Christian influence, but with pagan cults in active operation; and finally, the uncolonized areas and those where the Roman writ scarcely ran, still definitely pagan.[1]

(3) *The Vandals and After.*

And so we pass to the Vandal period. The sack of Rome by Alaric in 410 had sorely shaken that ancient world. Augustine was moved to write of the Christian security and hope amid world cataclysm. He was still in Hippo when the Vandals under Gaiseric (or Genseric) landed in Africa from Spain in 429, but died in the following year while Hippo was besieged. By a treaty of 435 the Empire recognized the settlement of the Vandals in Numidia. In 439 they captured Carthage and in 442 the Emperor recognized Gaiseric as an independent ruler. The Vandal kingdom in Africa survived for almost a century until Belisarius conquered it in 533 for the Byzantine Empire.

The Vandals were Arian Christians, and some of their kings ardent Arians. There was thus a double motive for the displacement of Catholic clergy, the religious and the political, for

---

[1] Mesnage, *op. cit.*, 326–8. He calls attention to the fact that Christian remains relating to the veneration of the Virgin Mary are extremely rare, and draws the conclusion that the Church deliberately refrained from encouraging it because of the risk due to survival of pagan ideas and in particular of the cult of the Punic Astarte. *Ibid.*, 285–6. Sherwin-White has pointed out that the Romans failed to master the mountain blocks in Roman Algeria (and the mountain peoples, i.e. Berbers, in them) for the same reason that they were checked in Germany, namely, the forests. He also argues that the development of towns was due primarily to the need for security, since these forested, mountain strongholds of the Berbers (the Aurès and Jurjura in particular) were never brought under effective Roman influence.—A. N. Sherwin-White, "Geographical Factors in Roman Algeria." *The Journal of Roman Studies*, XXXIV (1944), 1–10.

he who was friend to the Emperor was no friend to the Vandal king. Anti-Roman feeling meant anti-Catholic. While the treatment of the Catholics varied under the different rulers, there was from the time of Gaiseric an Arian Established Church. At first, however, the Catholics were only dispossessed and their clergy replaced by Arians in certain districts. It was under Huneric, Gaiseric's successor, that the oppression of the Catholics became severe. By an edict of 484 all Catholics within his dominion were to turn Arian on pain of having the imperial edicts against heresy set in motion against them. No Catholic clergy were any longer to function and all their churches were to be handed to Arian clergy. These latter were charged with carrying out the edict and are said to have done so ruthlessly. "Perhaps", says Dr. Ludwig Schmidt, "Catholicism might have been quite rooted out in Africa if the king had not died prematurely on December 23, 484."[1] This was the high water mark of persecution, though under later rulers there was ebb and flow until with Hilderic the Catholics were once more free. It had been a testing-time for the Catholic Church but did not permanently disable it. It is interesting to notice that while Latin was the diplomatic and legal language of Vandal Africa, the Vandal vernacular was used for the services of the Church. This meant that the Arian clergy were mostly German. Once again, through absorption in internal conflict and the limitation to a national language there was no Christian outreach to non-Christian neighbours. The mass of the Berbers remained pagan.[2]

Note

With the advent of Byzantine rule the Catholic Church recovered its place in Africa. The number of bishoprics had fallen considerably during the Vandal period. Mesnage takes 675 as the figure for the year 430. From the list of bishops convened to meet in Carthage in 484 at the time of Huneric's drastic edict, he calculates a total of 574 sees in Africa. In the next fifty years the number was apparently reduced to some 250 or even less; since in 534, after the expulsion of the Vandals, 220 bishops met in Carthage, such an estimate is quite reasonable.[3] But now a new era dawned. The "Hundred Years' Captivity", as Catholic clergy called it, was over.[4] In the year of the Council of Carthage, 534, Justinian decreed the

[1] In *Cambridge Mediaeval History*, I (2nd ed., 1924), 312.
[2] *Ibid.*, 320–1.
[3] Mesnage, *Le Christianisme en Afrique, II, Déclin et Extinction* (1915), 12, 53–4.   [4] Leclercq, *L'Afrique Chrétienne* (1904), II, 247.

restoration of all church buildings and appurtenances, recognized the bishop of Carthage as a metropolitan, and conferred special privileges on the churches of his diocese. Arians, Donatists, Jews and pagans were all made subject to certain disabilities.[1] But more than this, the Church was recognized as a pillar of the state, so that to propagate the Christian faith was at the same time to consolidate imperial power. Justinian pursued the policy in Africa of encouraging to become Christians all those chiefs and kings who sought his goodwill. He gave it as a definite instruction to his administrators that they should do all they could to incline the people to Christianity. In the case of native rulers, an investiture with robes of office and the bestowal of honorific titles went with the change. Religious propaganda for imperial expansion was the policy. As Mesnage drily remarks, it was found more economical to make use of the Gospel than military power for the security of distant territories! The policy was so far successful as to bring within the pale of the Church a number of Berber peoples not hitherto touched—to bring them in, that is to say, as far as the ruler's nominal assent was given. Such conversions, presumably not based on catechetical instruction, and undertaken from political motives, were just as permanent as the political interests of those concerned.[2] Given a new situation in which these interests changed, the robe of office of the Berber chief could be as easily doffed as it had been donned, together with the religion of the imperial court which it symbolized. Thus while the century or more of Byzantine rule appears to shine with fresh conquests for the faith in the winning of hitherto resistant Berber peoples, the actuality gives little ground for satisfaction. With the Arab invader came a challenge to all easy loyalties and an uncovering of the situation as it really was.

[1] Leclercq, *L'Afrique Chrétienne* (1904), II, 247–9. Cf. Procopius, *History of the Wars*, IV, xiv, 14: "For the Emperor Justinian did not allow any Christian who did not espouse the orthodox faith to receive baptism or any other sacrament." (Dewing's translation.)
[2] Mesnage, *op. cit.*, II, 70–2.

CHAPTER 5

THE ORDEAL WITH ISLAM
SEVENTH AND EIGHTH CENTURIES

THE only world religion to arise after Christianity was Islam. It has ever since been the most resistant of all to Christian missionary effort. The rapidity of its spread was spectacular. To take the westward expansion alone, within ten years of its founder's death it had invaded Egypt, and within a century it had swept across North Africa to the Atlantic, penetrated the Iberian peninsula and crossed the Pyrenees. In the process the Christian enterprise in Africa was overwhelmed.

(1) *The Rise of Islam.*

In its origin Islam is bound up with the career of one man, Muhammad, a citizen of Mecca. Though the actual year of his birth is not known the usually accepted date is about A.D. 570. Of his life before his call at forty years of age, tradition tells many things, but reliable facts are few. A recent biographer has summarized them thus: "Only this is certain, that he belonged to a respected but not wealthy family, that he lost his father early in life, and grew up in a poor home, but that he later gained economic independence through his marriage."[1] That he was sincere in his claim to be the chosen mouthpiece of Allah is now generally conceded. His own early misgivings, the fact that his first disciples belonged to his own family, and the steady adhesion of so upright a character as Omar all support it. For some ten years or more after his call he declared his message to the people of Mecca. Converts were gained, apparently more among the poor unfortunates than the influential citizens of the place. An African slave, Bilal, was among these converts, and displayed under cruel persecution the loyalty for which his race is distinguished. Muhammad called him "the first-fruits of Abyssinia". He is still famous throughout the Muslim world, says Arnold, as the first *mu'adhdhin*—the officer who chants the call to prayer.[2] Had Muhammad been concerned with a religious message pure and simple, he might have been content with such results. But

---

[1] Tor Andrae, *Mohammed the Man and his Faith* (1936), 54.

[2] T. W. Arnold, *The Preaching of Islam* (2nd ed., 1913), 14–15; Fr. Buhl in *Encyclopaedia of Islam*, I (1913), 718–19.

there is evidence that he already regarded temporal power as essential to his religious purpose. Any hope of securing political supremacy in Mecca steadily receded as opposition to him hardened. Then came the crisis in his fortunes when, in 622, he and his disciples left Mecca for Yathreb, called El Medina or "The City" in recognition of the event.[1] From this "Year of the Flight" Muslim chronology begins. In Medina Muhammad became politically powerful. He welded into one religious community the disciples from Mecca and those in Medina who had received them, thus making a landmark in the development of the new faith.[2] For ten years he ruled in Medina, until his death in 632. After fluctuating fortunes Mecca had capitulated to him, and treaties were made with Arab tribes that had submitted one after another, until in his last years he was master of Arabia.

The extent to which Muhammad was influenced by Christianity is difficult to determine. That he was indebted both to Judaism and to Christianity is admitted. There is no evidence of any Christian community in the neighbourhood of Mecca and Medina, and it seems clear that, with the exception of the south, Christianity obtained no footing within the Arabian peninsula. Around it, however, were Christian churches, in Syria on the north-west, in Mesopotamia on the north-east, and in Abyssinia to the south-west. There was thus no direct contact with Christian churches possible for Muhammad except on expeditions outside his native territory. Some would accept as historical the tradition that he had been to Syria as a caravan trader and made such contact with Christian churches there.[3] Muir, indeed, links with this the suggestion that if Muhammad had there seen a purer form of the faith, then "in the sincerity of his early search after truth, he might readily have embraced and faithfully adhered to the faith of Jesus".[4] There is, however, some scepticism about such visits.[5] On the other hand, the emphasis in the early Meccan period on the coming judgment has directed attention to this element in

[1] This is the usual explanation, but it has been called in question; cf. Fr. Buhl in *Ency. Islam*, III (1936), 83a.

[2] "The laws of the Medina congregation are the first draft of the theocratic constitution which gradually made Islam a world empire and a world religion. In the community of believers the old tribal constitution was abrogated in all essentials."—Tor Andrae, *op. cit.*, 190–1.

[3] Muir, *The Life of Mohammad* (ed. Weir, 1912), 20–2; R. Bell, *The Origin of Islam in its Christian Environment* (1926), 69.   [4] *Op. cit.*, 21.

[5] Tor Andrae, *op. cit.*, 49–51. ". . . we can hardly assume that Mohammed ever visited Christian Syria".—*Ibid.*, 50.

Syrian Christianity, and led to the suggestion that the initial impulse in Muhammad's religious awakening may well have been a missionary sermon by some wandering Syrian preacher.[1] That the use of scripture in public worship and private devotion in the Oriental churches was known to Muhammad and had impressed him is clear from his reference to Christians (as also to Jews) as the People of the Book. He was moved by a desire to supply religious texts for his own people in connexion with his message. It is agreed that the term *qur'an*[2] which Muhammad used of his prophecies is just the Syriac *qeryana*, the name for the Scripture lesson in Christian public worship.[3] He had no direct access to the Bible, for there was no Arabic version of it in his time.[4] One is tempted to wonder whether, if there had been, he might not have found there the satisfaction of his quest and even become a Christian preacher to the Arabs. As it was his knowledge of Christianity was gained in other ways, and was both fragmentary and distorted as the Koran reveals.

Note

Of contacts between Islam and Christian Churches during Muhammad's lifetime there are two accounts we may notice. During the Meccan period when persecution of his converts became severe, Muhammad consented to a number migrating across the water to find asylum in Christian Abyssinia. These were treated with every consideration by the king, and a second emigration took place.[5] Not only did this create a favourable impression of Christians at the time, but its influence has lasted down the centuries, and was active in securing the sympathy of both Egyptian and Indian Muslims for Christian Abyssinia at the time of the Italian aggression.[6] This experience of genuine goodwill in time of trouble when he and his people were still without power and prestige is evidently reflected in the Medina oracle which, after declaring the enmity of Jews and idolaters, says of the Christians: ". . . and thou wilt find the nearest in love to those who believe to be those who say, 'We are Christians'; that is because there are amongst them priests and monks, and because they are not proud".[7]

Note

[1] Tor Andrae offers a persuasive statement of the case, and even suggests that Nestorian monks from Arabian churches in Mesopotamia may have visited Hejaz. *Op. cit.*, 113–27, 132, 148. But cf. Bell *op. cit.*, 69–70.

[2] The form *Koran* is the customary one.

[3] Bell, *op. cit.*, 90–1; Tor Andrae, *op. cit.*, 132–3.

[4] Harnack, *Mission and Expansion*, II, 153, n. 2.

[5] Muir, *op. cit.*, 70, 86–7; Tor Andrae, *op. cit.*, 177–8; T. W. Arnold, *op. cit.*, 15–16.

[6] "Abyssinian Conflict seen from Egypt," *Manchester Guardian*, August 8, 1935; "Islamic Sympathy with Abyssinia", *The Times*, November 5, 1935.

[7] *Sura V*, 85–6 (Palmer's translation).

The second incident has reference to the Christian Church of the Najran in South-western Arabia, and the terms imposed upon them by Muhammad. At a time when many tribes of Arabia were sending their emissaries and submitting to Islam, these South Arabian Christians sent an embassy to Muhammad in Medina. They were prepared to submit to his rule but not to accept Islam. They consented to pay tribute, and in return were guaranteed protection for life, land and property, their churches and the practice of their religion.[1] Here was a practical expression of the tolerance for Christians enjoined in the Koranic text.

(2) *The Conquest of Egypt.*

Egypt was in an unhappy state at the time of Muhammad's death. We have already seen how persecution of Coptic Christians by the Orthodox party had made wider the breach between them and only served to intensify the national spirit. Heraclius (Eastern Emperor, 610–641) had appointed in 631 an ecclesiastic, Cyrus, as both patriarch and imperial representative. His policy towards the Coptic Church was sternly repressive in an endeavour to dragoon it into conformity with the Orthodox communion; at the same time as civil administrator he had to increase taxation, which scarcely added to his popularity. During his ten years of office he aggravated a situation already difficult enough, and left a reputation that led, in later Coptic tradition, to his identification with Antichrist.[2]

Meanwhile Arab conquests in Syria and Mesopotamia had displaced Byzantine rule in those rich provinces and secured for the Arabs the fertile crescent that overarched on the north their own desert peninsula. In 640 an Arab army invaded Egypt under 'Amr ibn al-'As. Within a couple of years, with the fall of Alexandria, the campaign was complete. The rapidity of the conquest with comparatively small forces was largely

---

[1] The text is quoted in Bell, *op. cit.*, 178–9. Cf. Tor Andrae *op. cit.*, 239–40. Muslim tradition speaks of an embassy of Muhammad to the king of Abyssinia and of the latter's conversion to Islam. Muir gives grounds for doubting the king's conversion, and points out that certain of Muhammad's declarations could be readily assented to by a Christian, more especially if of Arian or Nestorian leanings.—Muir, *The Life of Mohammad* (Revised ed., 1912), 92, n. 1; 372–73. Budge in reporting the story, while admitting that the difference between Islam and Christianity may not have appeared significant to the Abyssinians, suggests that the real reason for any acknowledgment made by the king was political in character.—Budge, *A History of Ethiopia*, I, 271–3.

[2] C. H. Becker in *Cambridge Mediaeval History*, II (1913), 349–50.

favoured by the disaffection prevailing among the Copts to whom the Arabs came as deliverers from an oppressive imperial rule.

This was the first introduction of Islam into Africa, if we except the temporary sojourn on Abyssinian soil of the refugees from Mecca. Yet the entry was not religiously aggressive. Tribute was to be paid, but this was no heavier than imperial demands had already been, while on the other hand all fear of persecution from imperial quarters was removed. Religious toleration was granted by the conquerors, the Coptic patriarch was restored to office, and Church property was left in Christian possession. This is the less surprising when it is remembered that there was an Arab national as well as a Muslim religious aspect of the conquest. "One of the most illuminating discoveries", says Sir T. W. Arnold, "made by modern historians in regard to Muslim history is the recognition of the fact that, the enormous expansion of Islam in the second half of the seventh century, was not the result of a great religious movement stimulated by a proselytizing zeal for the conversion of souls, but was an expansion of the Arab tribes, breaking through the frontiers which their powerful neighbours in the Roman and Persian Empires had grown too weak to defend."[1] The Arab pride of race rather than the Muslim sense of brotherhood was at first in the ascendant. There are words attributed to the first Caliph of the Umayyad dynasty (the fourth Caliph from the Prophet) indicating that the great distinction was to be an Arab: "I found that the people of Egypt were of three sorts, one-third men, one-third like men, and one-third not men, i.e. Arabs, converted foreigners, and those who pretend to be Muslims, the Copts."[2] The situation at first was that of a military occupation. The soldiery were Arab, but the existing administrative officials were still required at their posts. The governor was an Arab, and the revenues of the country were controlled by the new rulers. The Copts had but recently experienced a dozen years of Persian occupation, to be brought back to Byzantine rule by Heraclius, and it may be the Arab rule was also expected to be of limited duration.[3] There was no religious landslide to the conquerors at first, and no direct pressure exerted on their part to produce it.

There were, however, restrictions placed upon "the people

---

[1] T. W. Arnold, *The Caliphate* (1924), 23-4, reporting Caetani.
[2] A. S. Tritton, *The Caliphs and their Non-Muslim Subjects* (1930), 1-2.
[3] T. H. Weir, *E.R.E.*, VIII (1915), 900b. cf. R. H. Charles, *The Chronicle of John, Bishop of Nikiu* (1916) 200.

of protection" as the adherents of the tolerated faiths (Christians and Jews in particular) were called. The so-called "Covenant of Omar" the second Caliph, professed to state what these were for the Christians. They included the payment of tribute, hospitality to Muslims, prohibition of erection of new churches or monasteries, avoidance of all advertisement or display of Christian practice (no cross, for example, to be shown publicly), certain distinctions in dress and in saddles and the use of weapons, and even limitation in the height of their houses. Tritton has shown decisively that the covenant does not represent early practice but that its contents appeared gradually, and concludes: "In the first century it is ignored. In the second some of its provisions are sometimes observed. By 200 it existed in the traditional form, but with many minor variations."[1] Clearly social and religious restrictions such as these would, as they were applied, exert an indirect pressure to acceptance of Islam. To what extent did they appear in Egypt and with what effect on the Christian Church?

The payment of tribute was imposed from the outset, and indeed the incidence of taxation upon the Christians seems to have been the principal factor in their apostasy. There is direct evidence from papyri for the last quarter of the first Muslim century relating to taxation. There were then in operation a poll-tax, a land tax and various requisitions for the army and other purposes. There is no evidence of a Muslim paying taxes.[2] The rate of the poll-tax was three or four dinars per adult male (the traditions usually say two). Some idea of what this meant in terms of the current value of money is given by such evidence as this (also from the papyri): that a sheep cost half a dinar; that a ship-builder got two dinars a month for wages and expenses, a sawyer eleven dinars yearly and a labourer sixteen.[3] Priests were sometimes exempt, and monks apparently always. Monasteries, however, were assessed for requisitions and the returns indicate they were wealthy. The great desert monastery of St. Mary Deipara boasted eight estates, and that of Barbaros ten.[4] The land tax was paid in cash and kind; the papyri show it to have been larger than the poll-tax. The holdings were small for the most part, and the pressure of taxation such as to lead many Egyptian peasants to desert them. One papyrus

[1] Tritton, op. cit., 233.
[2] "This might be chance but, considering the testimony of Muslim historians, it is certain that they did not pay." Ibid., 198.
[3] Ibid., 199, where references to papyri are supplied. Budge gives the value of the dinar as ten shillings.—Op. cit., I, 270, 273.   [4] Tritton, op. cit., 200.

contains a list of 180 fugitives from one district alone, for the government took stern steps to prevent the exodus, so fatal to the revenue. It led eventually to the introduction of a pass system.[1] There must be added to the picture the unauthorized exactions of subordinate officials among people who all too often regarded official appointment as the heaven-sent opportunity for personal profit. Increases in the tribute were made from time to time, though accurate information is hard to come by.[2] With these increases, however, Muslims themselves became in due course subject to the land tax and certain other demands. Conversions to Islam meant a fall in the revenue, for every convert was automatically exempt from the poll-tax. If all the data were available, the approximate number of conversions could therefore be calculated from revenue returns. As it is, we have to be content with such sidelights on the situation as the proposal of the governor of Egypt in the caliphate of Omar II (717–720) that in future converts should not be exempt from the poll-tax. The Caliph, however, piously replied that "God had sent Muhammad to call men to a knowledge of the truth and not to be a collector of taxes". But such was the number becoming Muslims that this policy of making the converts pay had to be introduced to support the revenue, though there was no consistent pursuit of it. The governor of Egypt in 744, just a century after the conquest, promised exemption again to all converts, and 24,000 Christians are said to have come over in response. The Abbasid Caliphs (750–1258) were Muslims first and foremost, in contrast to the Arab dynasty of the Umayyads, and it was therefore natural that the first of the line should repeat the offer with like results, for "many both rich and poor, denied the faith of Christ by reason of the magnitude of the taxation and the burdens imposed upon them" (Severus).[3]

Distinction in dress seems only to have been legally required after the Arabs settled down to the civilized life of the conquered provinces, and there arose some temptation to imitate them. The *zunnar* or girdle became distinctive of both Jew and Christian. Colour was also a distinguishing mark. Mutawakkil, the Abbasid Caliph, was the first, apparently, to give precise orders about dress; Christians were to wear yellow cloaks and

[1] Tritton, *op. cit.*, 134–35, 202–3.
[2] "The phrase 'doubled the tribute' is so common that clearly it is not to be taken literally."—*Ibid.*, 211.
[3] T. W. Arnold, *The Preaching of Islam* (2nd ed. 1913), 103–4.

turbans, and even their slaves a yellow patch in front and behind. Christian women were to wear a yellow wrapper out of doors. A century and a half later Al Hakim, the mad Caliph of Egypt, ordered non-Muslims to wear black. Three centuries on we find blue prescribed for the Christians and yellow for the Jews. To issue an edict and to have it steadily observed were not the same thing, and doubtless the strictness of the enforcement varied according to the whim of the authorities. Nevertheless there is evidence that some Christians denied their faith and some went into banishment on such occasions.[1]

The most serious restrictions for any religious group are those bearing on the practice of their faith. The covenant of Omar forbade the building or repair of churches and monasteries and the obtrusion of Christian worship in any way upon the Muslims. The facts show that this is far from reflecting the actual situation at the outset. Under the Umayyads (661–750) new churches, convents and monasteries were built and others restored. For a century and a half, with one doubtful exception, there was no suggestion of a ban on new churches. Then under the Abbasids a change of policy began to appear. Mutawakkil, at the end of the first century of Abbasid rule, ordered all new churches to be destroyed. He also prohibited the carrying of the cross in procession, and the reading of services in the street, implying that this had previously been done.[2] Nevertheless the fact that much Christian activity could proceed unhindered, as well as contact be maintained with Christians elsewhere, is illustrated by the case of the monastery of St. Mary Deipara and its famous library, situated in the Nitrian desert west of the Nile. In 927 its abbot journeyed to Baghdad to secure remission of the poll-tax that had been demanded of the monks. His appeal was successful. He then journeyed through Iraq and Syria, visiting Christian centres and securing manuscripts for the monastery library. When he returned home in 932 he brought with him no fewer than 250 volumes with which to enrich the collection.[3] The success of the abbot's appeal, the range of his journeyings and the extent of the treasures he brought safely to his monastery all bear their own testimony.

The disabilities of the Christians were, nevertheless, sufficiently severe to encourage the appeal to force, and from time

[1] Tritton, *op. cit.*, 115-26; *Ency. Islam*, IV, 1241–2.
[2] *Ibid.*, 42–3, 46, 50, 107.
[3] W. Wright, *Catalogue of the Syriac Manuscripts in the British Museum*, Part III (1872), iv.

to time Coptic discontent expressed itself in revolt. Within the second century (A.H.) there were half a dozen risings, ranging from the Delta to Upper Egypt, and more occurred in the following decades. The Copts were severely handled and lost their power to stage further trouble.[1] Periods of persecution with consequent apostasy are recorded, the climax being reached in the eighth century of Muslim rule. A first attempt by the mob to destroy all the churches in Egypt was foiled by the authorities, but a general attack on Egyptian churches afterwards broke out, the Christian monks, it is alleged, causing disastrous incendiary outbursts in Cairo by way of reprisal. Fifty-nine churches and many monasteries are said to have been destroyed. A generation later, churches were again wrecked by the mob amidst a general persecution of the Christians. A popular Christian festival in which Muslims had long shared, associated with the annual inundation of the Nile, was at this time definitely abolished.[2] The Coptic Christian community became sadly reduced. But the remnant has survived.

In the absence of an overwhelming religious crusade by the Arab conquerors, how should we account for the apostasy of so large a proportion of Coptic Christians? There were several reasons. Self-interest appears to have been the earliest motive to operate. The pressure of taxation we have already noticed. Among Christians becoming government officials, there was often secession to Islam. Romance too played its part, for no Christian could marry a Muslim woman, and conversions to secure the bride were by no means unknown.[3] Persecution at intervals undoubtedly encouraged apostasy, but there were also considerable periods of peace when the Church might have recruited her strength, but failed to do so.

If these were external causes springing from the new environment, there were also internal factors. We have already seen that for all its rapid extension and fervid enthusiasms, the Church in Egypt was beset with internal weaknesses. It was thus without the power to resist successfully the attractions that came with the rival faith. Coptic-Melkite squabbles still continued, and apart from the shame of Christians bribing Muslim Arabs to take their side in a quarrel, the continuing rivalry sapped the strength sorely needed for other ends.[4] These other ends were, in particular, the strengthening of the Christian community by the education of its members, and

---

[1] Tritton, *op. cit.*, 144.   [2] *Ibid.*, 58–9, 110–11.   [3] *Ibid.*, 35–6.
[4] *Ibid.*, 20–1, 47–8, 79; T. W. Arnold, *op. cit.*, 108.

Note 1

the training of a succession of pastoral workers to care for the moral and spiritual welfare of Christians in town and village. Pastoral neglect is alleged as a definite cause of apostasy.[1] Those who might have helped to secure the Church in the evil days that came upon her had all too often retired to the monastic life. The warnings this total situation conveys are plain to read.

5

(3) *North Africa subdued.*

The Arab advance from Egypt to the west was dictated by military necessity. The occupation of Alexandria demanded protection on the flank, and hence there followed the occupation of Barca. This brought the Arabs to the confines of the ancient Proconsular Africa in its eastern section known to them as Tripolis. An expedition to the west was organized and Gregory of Carthage, who had recently revolted from his Byzantine masters, was defeated in 647. The Arabs then withdrew with their booty. It was thirty years before the next move westwards, which brought a stage nearer the permanent occupation of North Africa. 'Ukba ibn Nafi, a nephew of 'Amr the conqueror of Egypt, invaded Proconsular Africa and founded the famous Kairawan as a military camp. A change of Egyptian governor brought the supersession of 'Ukba by Dinar whose conciliatory policy was in sharp contrast to that of the haughty leader of Arab horse. Among Dinar's achievements was the winning of Kusaila, a powerful Berber chief, to co-operation with the Arabs. But 'Ukba regained the command and swept westward to Tangier, and beyond to the Atlantic coast. He had, however, by his attitude forfeited Kusaila's support. A rising of the Berbers caught the expedition on its return, and 'Ukba met his death in 683. Once again there was no Arab control west of Barca. 'Ukba was venerated as a martyr and became Sidi 'Ukba to the faithful. C. H. Becker draws an interesting contrast between 'Ukba and Dinar that is significant for understanding the situation in North Africa. 'Ukba represented the proud Arab spirit of military conquest, with no concern for the finer issues of diplomacy. The effects of his successes were shortlived; they disappeared with the power that had produced them. "Many Berbers," says Becker, "had indeed accepted Islam as long as a contingent of Arabian troops was in their neighbourhood, only to secede as soon as the latter had withdrawn." Dinar, by contrast, distinguished the Byzantines as the real enemy

[1] T. W. Arnold, *op. cit.*, 107–8.

to Arab ambitions and saw in the Berbers potential allies. In his period of control he successfully pursued a conciliatory policy that was reversed on 'Ukba's return. Dinar appears, tested by the judgment of history, as much the greater man. He foreshadowed the policy which was to be so successful in winning the Berbers not only to Arab collaboration but also to Islam to a degree to which they had never been won to Christianity.[1] After an intermittent attempt to recover the lost ground, a new commander, Hassan, appeared who carried the campaign to success. He was an astute leader and pursued the wise policy of Dinar. He too saw the Byzantines as the enemy and the Berbers as potential friends and allies. He succeeded in taking Carthage in 697, though it was only finally secured by power at sea. At first the Berber tribes were hostile. A woman of the Zenata, Kahina by name, appeared as a prophetess and for a time had successes, but was finally vanquished by Hassan in 703. The Berber tribes were now won over more and more to alliance and friendship and Islam. The consolidation of Arab power in North Africa was the work of Hassan's successor, Musa ibn Nusair, who took over control in 708. His subjugation of the western Berbers gave him control of the territory of Morocco and command of the western route to the Sudan. In 711 his Berber general Tarik, governor of Mauretania, was commissioned to cross to Spain, apparently less with the idea of immediate conquest than of raiding a rich and fertile kingdom. Tarik crossed with 7,000 Berber troops, and landed near a rock which has since borne his name, Gibraltar.[2] He met with amazing success and half of Spain was in his hands before the year was out. This was a Berber conquest; they were Muslim Berbers, it is true, but it was Berbers and not Arabs who laid low the Gothic kingdom. Musa, apparently taken by surprise at the speed of events, hastened across with an army the following year and completed the conquest, thus associating Arab arms with the final victory.

Concurrently with these conquests came the conversion to Islam of the peoples of the Maghreb, as the Arabs termed North Africa. As in the time of the Byzantine rulers who seized from the Vandals control of northern 'Africa, so now with the Arab conquerors, the Berber chiefs along with their political submission adopted the religion of the new masters. The cases of two outstanding leaders are illuminating. Kusaila,

[1] C. H. Becker in *Cambridge Mediaeval History*, II (1913), 368-9.
[2] Gebel Tarik—Hill of Tarik.

Ibn Khaldun tells us, together with his lieutenant Sekerdid, both Christian chiefs, turned Muslim with the Arab invasion. But later, restive under the new rule, they renounced both it and Islam. Kusaila, however, was taken prisoner and only escaped death by embracing Islam once again. As he died fighting the Arabs, he had probably turned Christian at the end.[1] The other case is that of Kahina, the heroic woman who at first defeated Hassan but was finally vanquished by him. A Jewess by religion, she did not, it is true, renounce her faith, but strangely enough advised her two sons to do so. They became loyal Muslims, and the elder was granted the chieftainship of his people. The amnesty wisely offered by Hassan after Kahina's defeat and death led her people to recognize Arab rule, become Muslim, and furnish Hassan with a contingent of 12,000 fighting men. Ibn Khaldun claims that their subsequent conduct attested the sincerity of their conversion.[2] Small wonder, with such facts as these, that Mesnage asserts it is plain as day that apostasy became general, acceptance of Islam going step by step with the Arab conquest. It was self-interest that dominated. If to become Muslim meant survival, then Muslims they would be. By the time of Musa the greater number of Christian and Jewish chiefs had professed the new religion and the pagan tribes had almost all been won, in the sense that Islam was accepted by the chiefs in the name of their people.[3] The Arab policy of assimilation fostered the movement to Islam. Intermarriage of Arabs with Berber women led to racial intermixture. The Semitic and Hamitic stocks after all had much in common. Musa's sons married Berber wives whose sons rose to distinction. Musa himself is said to have selected the finest of the slaves taken in war, offered them Islam, military service (after due probation) and their liberty.[4] "The commixture of Arabs and Berbers, which gave the impress to the whole of the Islam of the West, was a slow process. Centuries passed, but in the end Islam has attained what Phoenicians and Romans strove for in vain. . . . As Mommsen says, the Phoenicians and Romans have been swept away, but the Berbers have remained, like the palm trees and the desert sand."[5]

[1] Ibn Khaldun, *Histoire des Berbères*. I, 208, quoted in Mesnage, *Le Christianisme en Afrique*, II, 134-5.
[2] Ibn Khaldun, *op. cit.*, I, 214-15, quoted in Mesnage, *op. cit.*, II, 136.
[3] Mesnage, *op. cit.*, II, 137, 140.   [4] T. W. Arnold, *op. cit.*, 313-14.
[5] C. H. Becker, in *Cambridge Mediaeval History*, II, 365.

In the immediate sequence of events, it was the conquest of Spain by joint Berber and Arab arms that set the seal on the Berber conversion to Islam, particularly in Mauretania. The victorious campaigns that carried them through Spain, across the Pyrenees and into the heart of France exactly suited the eager temperament and martial ardour of the Berber tribes; moreover, there was rich booty to be shared, but only among the converted. That proved no obstacle. Thus by the early decades of the eighth century there were few tribes remaining that had not turned Muslim. A further stage was reached in the ninth century with the setting up of the Idrisside dynasty whose founder initiated a persecution against Jews and Christians, ignoring all right to survival of the People of the Book. The climax came with the rise to power of the Almohades whose founder, 'Abd-ul Mu'min, well called "the flail of God", carried fire and sword from the Atlantic to the Libyan desert, purging the faithful of the dross of heresy and almost, it would seem, extinguishing the last remnants of Christianity in the Maghreb.[1]

There was also a peaceful penetration by the new religion with methods that seem to copy the Christian monastic system. Missionaries concerned for the conversion of the people went into the more remote pagan areas, sometimes as preachers, sometimes as hermits, establishing themselves in a lonely spot and scrupulously practising all the religious routine of the devout Muslim. The Berbers around would reverence such self-abnegation, and seek their faith. Among these converts were devoted disciples who themselves accepted the same vocation with the inestimable advantage that they belonged to the people in language and outlook. Following such lonely witnesses came establishments of a monastic type in which novices were trained who then moved out among peoples recently converted or whose conversion was little more than nominal, and sought to establish them in the faith. In particular the Kabyles, so difficult of access in their mountain fastnesses, are said to have been reached by such methods as late as the turn of the fifteenth century.[2] Islam had now struck its roots into the soil.

(4) *The Disappearance of the Church in North Africa.*

There is nothing in the story of North Africa comparable to the survival of the Coptic Church in Egypt. After the early

[1] Mesnage, *op. cit.*, II, 153, 157, 222.
[2] *Ibid.*, 171–5 (where authorities are given); T. W. Arnold, *op. cit.*, 127–9.

Arab conquests, there is only a trickling stream that finally disappears.

In estimating the growth of the Church in earlier centuries we have taken the evidence of the bishoprics as one standard of measurement. By that same test the tragic situation stands stark before us. By contrast with the seven hundred of Augustine's time there were not above thirty or forty left to survive the Arab conquest at the turn of the seventh century. From the mid-eleventh century to the early twelfth a bare half-score at the outside may be counted. Then came the flare of persecution under the Almohades, the fiery "Unitarians", leaving few vestiges of Christianity behind. A solitary bishopric survived.[1] Ibn Khaldun at the close of the fourteenth century still knows of a few villages with a Christian population, and at the end of the fifteenth century a small Christian community, distinct from the foreign merchants, was to be found in the city of Tunis. And after this, unbroken silence.[2]

We have already seen that it was not the Arab practice in the early period of expansion to offer the alternative "Embrace Islam or die" for the People of the Book. There is no evidence that any such dilemma was presented to Christians in North Africa until the later persecutions. It is of course true that apostates were given this choice, but to the Muslim an apostate is one who has forsaken Islam and reverted to his earlier faith. Thus Kusaila was an apostate to Islam when he became Christian a second time, and was then offered the drastic alternative. If a Christian refused in the first instance to accept Islam, he could claim protection, as we have seen in the case of Egypt, on payment of tribute, and there is nothing to show that the same opportunity was not granted to Christians in North Africa. Indeed, the very practice of this procedure by the Muslims who occupied Spain indicates it was known to them at home in Africa.

In seeking an answer to the question why the Church vanished from the North African scene it is to be remembered that, as compared with the prosperity of Roman times, the Church was probably much reduced by the devastation of the Vandal wars and the bitter Arian persecution of the Catholic population. Procopius surveys the scene from the vantage-ground of the contemporary historian who as a colleague of Belisarius had first hand knowledge of the field in the drawn-out conflict

[1] Mesnage, op. cit., II, 189, 219, 220–2, 243.
[2] T. W. Arnold, op. cit., 129–30.

between Byzantine and Moor (as the Berber tribes were called). He refers again and again to the devastation and depopulation that accompanied the protracted struggle.[1]

The Christian element in the population was still further reduced during the early Arab raids and the more serious campaigns that followed. It seems that those among the romanized section of the population who could do so fled to Italy and Spain, and some apparently as far as Germany.[2] Others, unable to escape by sea, probably moved south into the interior, as we shall see. Such a contributory cause as the lack of pastoral oversight for hard-pressed Christian communities almost certainly aggravated a difficult situation. We know this was true of Egypt, and yet after the Arab conquest the Christian churches of the Maghreb became an additional care of the patriarchate of Alexandria. By such historical causes the glory of the North African Church was already greatly diminished.

There is one feature in the situation, however, inherited from the days of prosperity, already noticed as disquieting, which now leaps to the forefront in its significance. It is the comparatively small proportion of Berber Christians in the African Church, and the apparently poor quality of those that did exist. Yet the Berbers were the large majority of the people and the only indigenous population. With the arrival of the Arabs little was left of the Romans and Byzantines, but the Berbers remained in strength. Yet in the west they were still largely pagan and in the central Maghreb, while some tribes in the old province of Africa had a Christian veneer, they were still a small minority. Mesnage is not too severe in his judgment when he says that the death-blow the African Church received in the eighth century had as its two principal causes the slight advance she had made among the Berbers,

[1] Procopius, *History of the Wars*, Book IV. "But men were being killed indiscriminately and women with their children were being made slaves, and the wealth was being plundered from every part of the frontier and the whole country was being filled with fugitives."—IV, viii, 22. "While the Roman army was occupied in Byzacium, he [a Berber chief] had plundered many of the places in Numidia."—IV, xiii, 18. "Even the populous city of Tamougadis . . . was emptied of its population by the Moors and razed to the ground . . . "—IV, xiii, 26. "They made raids everywhere and wrought unholy deeds upon the Libyans, sparing no one whatever his age, and the land became at that time for the most part depopulated. For of the Libyans who had been left some fled into the cities and some to Sicily and the other islands. But almost all the notables came to Byzantium . . . "—IV, xxiii, 27–9. (Dewing's translation.) Cf. also IV, xix, 20, xxi, 17; xxii, 5–6.　　　　　　　　　　　　　[2] T. W. Arnold, *op. cit.*, 125.

and the almost general apostasy of those there were in the hour of trial.[1]

This judgment is supported by the absence of any church liturgy or portion of scripture in the language of the Berbers. Elsewhere, as in Syria and Egypt, these were provided and provided because they were needed. If in North Africa they were not provided, it is more likely that this was because there was no need for them than that here alone a different policy was adopted.

One element in the situation, both interesting in itself and bearing on this question, remains to be considered. It is the matter of apparent Christian survivals among tribes now definitely Muslim. Are these not evidence that the tribes in question were Christian before conversion to Islam, and that therefore the Christian Berbers were at least numerous enough to include them? First it will be well to review some of the evidence.

The Kabyles, a people of the highlands behind the Algerian coast, retain features that betray a Christian origin. The cross is a constant emblem; it is tattooed on the person, and is used in design on pottery and on doors; not the Greek cross only, which might simply reflect primitive art, or early belief,[2] but the Latin also. In social life monogamy is the regular form of marriage. Poverty does not account for it. Further, there are expressions in use that are reminiscent of Christian liturgical forms such as the *Dominus tecum, vobiscum*. Moreover, missionary testimony is unanimous that the Kabyles themselves have the tradition of a Christian ancestry. If the Kabyles were not already Christian when the Arabs came, what then? The probable alternative is that Christians from the coastal districts who could not get away to Europe to escape the Arab flood, sought refuge in the highlands to the south, where amidst the mountain fastnesses they were secure from the invader. They were too few to absorb those among whom they came to live; rather matters fell out the other way. The romanized exiles, escaping among a crowd of their own retainers and peasant farmers, became in time "berberized". That there were Christian priests and even bishops among them is also to be supposed, but cut off from all intercourse with the outside world, and from the opportunity of living a civilized life (the Kabyles, for example, had no written language), they gradually degenerated until only the marks we have mentioned survive

[1] Mesnage, *op. cit.*, II, 286. [2] Wysner, *The Kabyle People* (1945), 165-8.

as evidence of their coming. Such is the reconstruction proposed by Mesnage as probable. It has much to commend it. As he concisely puts it, Kabylia became Christian not by evangelization but by emigration.[1] This reconstruction at least demonstrates that the Christian survivals in Kabylia cannot be used without further ado as evidence that the Kabyles had been converted before the Arabs came.

There are peoples of the Sahara that provide similar evidence of practices traceable to a Christian origin. The Mzabites occupy the oasis of Mzab in the southern territory of Algeria. The present population is given as about eleven thousand.[2] Their form of government before the coming of the French was virtually a republican federation. Its officers could be distinguished as clerical and lay, the former being in three grades according to age and training—disciples, graduates (lettrés), and members of the ecclesiastical council each charged with a particular duty. A striking feature is that women are organized in what is virtually, to use Christian terminology, an order of deaconesses. These are recruited from among the widows. They have duties at funerals and marriages and the oversight of women whose husbands are away. A leader among them in each community is responsible for the religious instruction of the women. This leadership of women is an amazing feature in a Muslim society. Further, there is the practice of public confession, and graded penance, the extreme penalty in practice being excommunication. There is even a kind of baptismal ceremony. In the matter of confession the deaconesses officiate for the women. Lavigerie, when apostolic delegate for the Sahara and the Sudan, reported the visit of a professor from his Seminary at Algiers to the Mzabites, who inquired whether they had any religious books besides the Koran. When they said they had, he asked if these books spoke of Muhammad. "No, they do not speak of him." "What do they say then?" "They say we should pay honour to Jesus, son of Mary." Lavigerie also quotes a letter sent by one of the clergy in the Sahara describing vividly the spiritual discipline exercised on Mzabite traders who, amidst the seductions of city life, have relaxed their standards. They are brought to book with a public confession in which the final formula of absolution is

---

[1] Mesnage, op. cit., II, 198–204. G. Yver in Encyclopaedia of Islam, II (1927) 599b. Dr. Robert Brown had earlier drawn attention to the same possibility: Leo Africanus, The History and Description of Africa, edited by Dr. Robert Brown (1896), III, 770, n. 91. [2] Fitzgerald, Africa, 400.

pronounced: "I pardon you, as God pardons you."[1] That there is a Christian history behind these survivals seems clear. But of what nature? Again the oasis, like the rock-begirt highland, is an asylum in time of upheaval. That Christian exiles retreated south across the sands to Mzab is certainly feasible. Mesnage suggests the period of the Almohad crusade. This, at least, seems historically more probable than that the Church in North Africa reached across unconverted tribes on her immediate borders to evangelize an oasis of the Sahara. If this interpretation is accepted, once again the Christian survivals are but evidence of the exodus of Christians from the romanized territories to the north, Christians who were unable to maintain themselves with their faith in the new environment.

The Tuareg are another people for whom an earlier Christian allegiance has been claimed. They are sometimes termed the "Berbers of the Sahara". The characteristic veil worn by the men only, for which custom there is no satisfactory explanation, has led to their being called "the veiled people of the desert". The Tuareg country occupies much of the west Central Sahara, with notable settlements in the highlands of Ahaggar and Air. Henry Barth on his famous travels through North and Central Africa in 1849–55 had much to do with them. He says: "It seems clear that a great part of the Berbers of the desert were once Christians (they are still called by some Arabs 'the Christians of the desert'), and that they afterwards changed their religion and adopted Islam; notwithstanding which they still call God 'Mesi' and an angel 'anyelus', and have preserved many curious customs which bear testimony to their ancient creed."[2] Francis Rennell Rodd, who has made a recent study of these people, has also been impressed with what he is inclined to regard as Christian survivals. He found among the Tuareg tribes inhabiting the mountains of Air in the Central Sahara the characteristic "Agades cross", the upper arm of which ends in a loop. The principal occurrence of the Latin cross (ignoring cross-hilted weapons) he found on the large shield of sun-dried hide, though it is here only part of a larger design, of which he says: "It resembles nothing so much as the Christian cross standing on a radiating mass representing light or glory."[3] In respect of language, certain

[1] Mesnage, op. cit., II, 227–37. Lavigerie in Annales de la Propagation de la Foi, Tome 41 (1869), 29–34.
[2] Barth, Travels and Discoveries in Central Africa (1857), I, 227–8.
[3] F. R. Rodd, The People of the Veil (1926), 235, 284–5.

words in the vocabulary are alleged to point to a Christian origin. Such are (with suggested derivations) *Mesi* for God (Messiah), *Amanai* for God (Adonai), *amerkid* for religious merit (Latin *merces*), *abekkad* for sin (Latin *peccatum*), *tafaski* for feast day (Latin *Pasca*), and *angelous* for angel (Latin *angelus*).[1] The status of woman is also remarkable for a people professing Islam. Monogamy appears to be an old tradition associated with the status of Tuareg women and not a consequence of economic pressure. They may own property, and they have a share in public life. They never veil the face.[2]

The occurrence of the cross among a Muslim people is at first sight startling, but does not of necessity demand a Christian origin. The so-called "Agades cross" with a loop as the upper arm is almost identical with the ancient Egyptian *ankh*, the handled cross or key of life.[3] Again, to regard the cross on the shield with a background of radiation as a relic of an earlier Christianity is not a necessary supposition. The cross on a shield has been found on a prehistoric rock carving in Tibesti, a mountain group of the Central Sahara south of the Fezzan.[4] The cross seems to have been a very general symbol to represent radiation.[5] Libyans depicted on the Egyptian monuments are shown with cruciform devices among their tattoo-marks, which still survive among the Berbers. That these are in origin sun-symbols is as probable as any other explanation.[6] In the matter of vocabulary thought to point to Latin sources, words are borrowed under varying sets of circumstances. That the Tuareg now in Air were at one time in the Fezzan to the south of Tripolis seems probable, as also that they migrated south (first to Bornu) during the period of Arab pressure in the eighth century.[7] That the Church of North Africa, however, reached in effective missionary activity to this distance from its own citadel needs stronger evidence than the apparent borrowing of a few terms current in Christian circles. Where so much is highly hypothetical, as

[1] F. R. Rodd, *The People of the Veil* (1926), 277–8.   [2] *Ibid.*, 167–71.
[3] *E.R.E.*, IV, 326.   [4] O. Bates *The Eastern Libyans* (1914), 148, 208–9.
[5] *E.R.E.*, IV, 324. The radiated cross was known in ancient Assyria.
[6] O. Bates, *op. cit.*, 140 (Fig. 52), 187.
[7] So Rodd, *op. cit.*, 376. H. R. Palmer goes farther and suggests that they were only moving into the Fezzan in the time of the Vandal invasion of North Africa, having come from the valley of the Upper Nile, and even speculates on their links with the Blemmyes. Rather remarkable evidence is afforded by a series of human faces found on pottery from Blemmyes' territory, where the mouth in several cases seems to be covered by a veil, the *litham* (as the Arabs called it) of the Tuareg.—*J.A.R.*, XXXI (1932), 153–61; XXXIII (1934), 288–90. Cf. Rodd, *op. cit.*, 376.

in the case of Tuareg origins and migrations, statements can be tentative only, but it seems entirely reasonable to assert that, apart from certain alleged survivals for the most part otherwise explicable, there is no convincing evidence of any Christian activity among the Tuareg by the North African Church.

Such, then, is the situation in respect of three cases where Christian survivals have been reported among Berber tribes. While at first sight these features would seem to indicate an earlier Christian profession before they turned Muslim, yet in view of alternative explanations with some historical foundation, such early Berber conversions can scarcely be claimed as the historical probability of the case. The charge that the great failure of the African Church was the failure to evangelize therefore stands. Two features of its organization bear this out. One is the fact that the diocese was centred in the urban community. The Romans had inherited the municipal organization of Phoenician times, and the Church modelled her ecclesiastical structure upon it. Harnack points out that the Berbers lacked this municipal organization, and so were left out of the work of a Church so organized.[1] The other feature to notice is the part played by monasticism in Africa. The first monastery was established by Augustine in Hippo. It was a community of clerics, and bishops who came from it established similar monasteries in their own dioceses. This union of the cleric and the monk was typical of Africa. In the fifth century so considerable was the expansion that we can cite about fifty localities that had these institutions. But unlike the monasteries of Ireland that sent out evangelists into the countryside, or St. Martin's monastery of Marmoutier in Gaul which was a great centre for evangelization, those of Africa were established in towns already Christian and only served within the existing dioceses. They made no attempt to conquer pagan territory.[2] Yet it was this very use of a monastic system, as we have already seen, that was adopted by Muslim missionaries with such success among the Berbers.

Was the African Church becoming conscious of its responsibility to the surrounding pagan tribes at the end of the Roman period? This has been thought possible. But if so, it began too late. The opportunity that lay before it in the surrounding

[1] Harnack, *Mission and Expansion*, II, 281, n. 1.
[2] E. C. Butler, "Monasticism", in *Cambridge Mediaeval History*, I (2nd ed. 1924), 532. Mesnage, *op. cit.*, I, 289–97.

Berber tribes was the immediate missionary challenge, as we now review the situation. The failure to win these peoples rooted in the soil was the judgment passed in advance on the Church itself. As has already been pointed out, there were three layers to the population in North Africa. The topmost layer, Roman and romanized, was very largely Christian; the second, Punic, stratum was more or less effectively penetrated; but both layers were too thin. When, after the wounds inflicted by the Vandals, the Arabs came, the topmost layer was finally ripped off and the second was partly destroyed with it, but the hard substratum of Berber population still stood firm. True, Berber tribes were also displaced by the Arab advent, but the bulk of them remained. The African Church, once the home of Tertullian, of Cyprian, and of Augustine, came to an end, because the only peoples it had really won were swept away.

And so the sad fact confronts us that North Africa is the land of the vanished Church. If the interpretation we have set forth of the historic situation be correct, then there is no more vivid warning that to fail to share the faith with all around is to let it die.

Note

CHAPTER 6

THE CRESCENT ACROSS AFRICA
EIGHTH TO FIFTEENTH CENTURIES

WHAT the Christian Church of the early centuries failed to do in Africa, Islam now did. It swept across the barrier of the Sahara to the Western Sudan, converting great Negro kingdoms to the faith; it moved from the Upper Nile into the Eastern Sudan; and through prosperous settlements on the eastern shores of Africa it established its influence as far south as Mozambique. The very map thus shows, in this sweeping arc of progress, the crescent across Africa. As this great movement that changed the religious face of much of the continent represents a major factor in the missionary situation up to the present time, it is advisable briefly to review its expansion.

(1) *Islam in the Sahara and the Western Sudan.*

The conversion of the Berbers of the Maghreb to Islam was a slow process. Indeed, it would seem that only when Berber independence under their own dynasties was secured did Islam really strike root, and even then it was modified by the national character. This is in harmony with the earlier Berber attitude to Roman and Byzantine. The result of this independent spirit was continual turbulence boiling over at times into open revolt of Berber against Arab. As always, this was reflected in some displacement of peoples. Some Berber tribes were pressed down into the desert fringe and even beyond. Among these may have been the Sanhadja, Berbers of the desert. Their early history is unknown. One group of tribes under this name were desert nomads in the western Sahara, bordering on the Senegal, to which river, indeed, they gave their name.[1] In the eleventh century a Sanhadja chief, returning from the pilgrimage to Mecca, came by way of Kairawan where, in conference with a professor of law, he realized the necessity of a teacher of Muslim doctrine for his people. Not without difficulty one was found who was prepared to face life in the Sahara, Ibn Yasin. His efforts to impart the true faith to the tribesmen, who were little more than nominal adherents of Islam, proving a failure, he withdrew to solitude on

[1] According to Ibn Khaldun, Sanhadja was pronounced *Zanāga*. Under this name were a number of Berber tribes, some nomad in the Sahara, some settled in the Maghreb.—G. Marçais in *Ency. Islam*, IV (1934), 152a.

90

an island in the Senegal. A few disciples he had made were with him and they constituted a *ribat* or monastery. Among them were two brothers, chiefs of the Sanhadja, Yahya and Abu Bekr. This new thing among the Sanhadja excited interest, and the monastic group grew to a thousand. From their *ribat* they were named by Ibn Yasin, Al Murabitin, whence Almoravides, by which name they are known to history. A preaching mission on which Ibn Yasin now sent them having failed, with the fierce zeal of a reformer he determined to compel the people to the faith. In 1042 he left his monastic retreat and led his followers in a holy war against the stiff-necked tribesmen. His monks achieved as warriors the success denied them as preachers, and their ranks soon swelled with new-won Almoravides. Ibn Yasin was a stern disciplinarian and restrained the normal excesses of the Berber warrior. Their numbers grew until, with a well-equipped army thirty thousand strong, Ibn Yasin, with Yahya as his general, was master of the tribes of the western Sahara. When Yahya died, c. 1056, his brother, Abu Bekr, succeeded to the command. Ibn Yasin died three years later on campaign in southern Morocco, but the movement he had initiated swept on to new victories. Abu Bekr was soon called south to deal with disaffection in the Sahara, and handed over the army command to Yusuf, a transfer of authority that proved permanent. Yusuf won fresh laurels for Almoravid arms, not only securing North Africa as far east as Algiers, but being invited to Spain by the Muslim princes to safeguard them from Christian attack, he established Almoravid rule there also. Thus appeared the Empire of the Two Shores under a Berber dynasty, extending from the Senegal in West Africa to the Ebro in Spain.[1] But the hardy desert tribesmen became effete with the luxuries of civilized life and forgot the stern standards of their founder. So the Almoravides made way in their turn for the Almohades or Unitarians. Their founder, Ibn Tumart, not only wrote in the Berber language, but allowed the call to prayer to be made in that tongue, an interesting contrast to the Christian practice we have already noticed.[2] These uncompromising reformers pledged themselves to put an end to error, and claimed the right to use violent means to do it. The Almohad Empire was likewise of the Two Shores, but included the whole of North Africa, from the Gulf of

---

[1] T. W. Arnold, *op. cit.*, 314–16; E. Doutté in *Ency. Islam*, I (1913), 32–3; A. Bell, *ibid.*, 318–20; E. W. Bovill, *op. cit.*, 47–55.

[2] T. W. Arnold, *op. cit.*, 316.

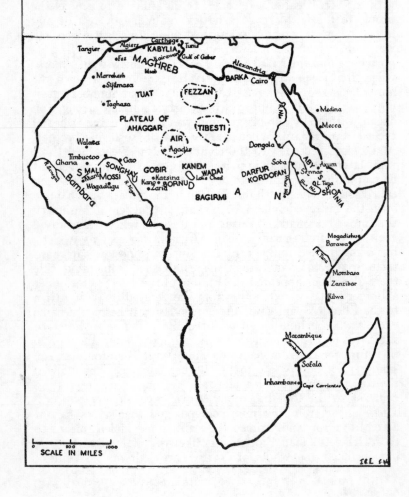

ISLAM IN AFRICA
Seventh to Sixteenth Centuries

Gabes to the Atlantic. Within a century and a half it had disintegrated.[1] But meanwhile, under both Almoravides and Almohades, a Berber dynasty had united North Africa and Spain at a time when trans-Saharan traffic was flourishing with Negro kingdoms of the Sudan, kingdoms that about this time received the Muslim faith.

When Abu Bekr had surrendered his command to Yusuf he remained in the south and for some fifteen years waged war in the Sahara and the Sudan, taking the city of Ghana, renowned in that day, about 1076. Ghana lay in the Western Sudan, not far from Walata (with which, indeed, some have sought to identify it), and west of the Niger Bend. It seems to have been founded about A.D. 300 and, according to tradition, had "white" rulers at first. These were in time succeeded by a Negro dynasty of the Mandingo race. The kingdom grew until it extended from the Niger westwards to the Atlantic and north to the Sahara, and was the leading state of the Sudan. It reached its zenith in the half-century before the rise of the Almoravides to power. Ghana's commercial relations were important. It lay at the southern end of the western caravan route that ran from Sijilmasa in Morocco on through Taghaza in the desert, famous for its salt mines. Cloths and brocades, copper and salt were among the principal imports, while the export of outstanding value was Ghana's gold dust. This was obtained by the method of silent trading from a people on the Senegal.[2] The volume of the trade with the Sudan is indicated by the geographer Ibn Hauqal (c. 975), who reported seeing in Awdaghost (fifteen days' journey west of Ghana) a "cheque" for forty-two thousand dinars made out to a merchant of Sijilmasa.[3] This traffic carried with it cultural

[1] A. Bell in *Ency. Islam*, I, 314–18.
[2] Silent trading refers to the practice of commercial interchange without the parties meeting face to face. In this case the foreign merchants placed their goods on the river bank and withdrew. The local people then emerged, placed what they regarded as the equivalent of gold dust beside each pile of merchandize, and likewise withdrew. If the merchants on returning were content, they took the gold dust and retired; if not, they left the piles untouched until agreement was reached. The author found among Ibibios and Ibos in Nigeria the same custom ascribed to Europeans; manufactured articles, so perfect and uniform, were obviously the product of spirit agents with whom Europeans conducted silent trade! Cf. Bovill, *op. cit.*, 59–61. John Campbell found in South Africa a Koranna tradition to the same effect concerning silent trade on the east coast with merchants from the Great Water, i.e. the Indian Ocean.—John Campbell, *Travels in South Africa*: *A Second Journey* (1822), II, 351.
[3] J. H. Kramers in *The Legacy of Islam* (1931), 101–2, who points out that the word used is the Arabic *Sakk* from which our "cheque" has been derived.

contacts for Negroland with North Africa and Muslim Spain. We owe to El Bekri, a member of an Arab family of Muslim Spain, our earliest account of Ghana. He wrote about 1067 a geography, the African section of which has fortunately survived. He evidently depended upon the reports of merchants trading in the Sudan for what he knew of it. Ghana, he tells us, consisted of two towns in a plain, six miles apart, one of which was Muslim and the other pagan. The Muslim town boasted twelve mosques and men of learning, jurists and others, were to be found there. The king, however, was a pagan, and the court was therefore in the pagan town. Near the court of justice there was a mosque for the convenience of Muslims in attendance on the king. The majority of his ministers are also said to have been Muslim, as were the court interpreter and the treasurer. The name of the pagan town, El Ghaba (the wood), was due to the thickets with which it was surrounded and which were sacred to the spiritual affairs of the nation. Here, he says, were the priests, and here were the royal tombs. The prisons also were situated here, from which there was no reprieve. This sounds very much like the widespread regard in pagan Africa for the departed ancestors of the chief as communal divinities upon whose favour the continued welfare of the community depends.[1] El Bekri reports an available army of 200,000 men, 40,000 of whom were equipped as archers. Most of the houses were of clay with thatched roofs, but there were also fine houses built of stone. This development had taken place and Islam filtered into the country at a period contemporary with the Norman invasion of England.[2]

The conversion of Ghana to Islam was hastened by the campaign of Abu Bekr and his Almoravides, Berber troops from the Sahara, for whom the prospect of booty was doubtless an attraction, though the religious motive was powerful. There were several results of this Berber conquest. First and foremost, it was now in the latter part of the eleventh century that the conversion of tribes in the northern belt of the Sudan became

[1] For an account of such an ancestor cult, with the sacred thicket as a burial-place and the "priest" in attendance (though among Bantu), see Smith and Dale, *Ila-Speaking Peoples of Northern Rhodesia* (1920), II, 180–86.

[2] The question has been raised whether any other non-pagan religion had penetrated to this region previous to Islam. M. Delafosse held the view that Jewish-Syrian tribes from Cyrenaica may have been the founders of Ghana—*Ency. Islam*, II (1927), 139b; Mesnage, *op. cit.*, II, 160, n. 4 (quoting from a letter of Delafosse). On the other hand C. K. Meek says: "The early religion of Ghana appears to have been a mixture of Christianity and animism."—*Northern Nigeria* (1925), I, 63.

more general. Then again, Ghana was taken by Abu Bekr in 1076 and the Negro dynasty overthrown. Berber rule took its place until the death of the victor. The kings of Ghana later regained their independence but with a much reduced territory. The chief of one of the small states that had resulted took Ghana in 1203. Thereupon the Muslims of Ghana withdrew, not willing to live once more under pagan rule, and established Walata, which replaced Ghana as the terminus of the caravan route. And thirdly, a cordon of Berber tribes settled along the desert fringe of the Sudan. Timbuktu was founded about this time by Tuareg who moved north and south with the seasons and finally established a settlement on this north-western point of the Niger Bend. Timbuktu was Muslim from the first and grew to be a commercial metropolis and a centre of learning of recognized standing in the Muslim world. Ghana itself slowly decayed until it was taken by the Mandingo king Sundiata and razed to the ground. It had enjoyed a history of nearly a thousand years.[1]

As Ghana fell a yet more powerful kingdom rose that spread to truly imperial dimensions, the renowned empire of Mali.[2] There was a considerable extension of Islam in the Western Sudan during the time of its ascendancy. The early history of the kingdom is unknown, save that about the year 1050 the the reigning sovereign, Baramendana, was converted to Islam. The motive is reported to have been his desire to terminate a drought. He later made the pilgrimage to Mecca, a practice followed faithfully by his successors, which did much to promote the spread of Islam. It was Sundiata, the conqueror of Ghana, who laid the foundations of Mali's imperial greatness in the thirteenth century. He not only pursued a vigorous policy of military conquest that raised his little kingdom to a powerful state, but developed a wise administration of his territories, and is said, for example, to have encouraged

[1] E. W. Bovill, *op. cit.*, 57–66; G. Yver in *Ency. Islam*, II (1927), 139–40; H. A. R. Gibb, *Ibn Battuta* (1929), 380, n. 21. It has been suggested that the Akan stock, to which the Ashanti and Fanti of the Gold Coast belong, may be historically connected with the ancient Ghana. For evidence bearing on this, see W. T. Balmer, *History of the Akan Peoples* (n.d.), 27; F. C. Fuller, *A Vanished Dynasty* (1921), 1; H. H. Johnston, *The Colonization of Africa* (2nd ed., 1913), 14; W. W. Claridge, *A History of the Gold Coast and Ashanti* (1915), I, 4–5, 6–7. On the origin of Timbuktu cf. De Vaux in *Ency. Islam*, IV, 776a.
[2] The name Mali is said to be the Fulani pronunciation of Mande or Manding, and so is strictly the name of the ruling tribe rather than a town. It was the name used by Arab authors for the chief town, though it is now known the two successive capitals of the empire were Djeriba and Niani,— H. Labouret in *Ency. Islam*, III, 203; H. A. R. Gibb, *op. cit.*, 379, n. 19.

agriculture and the more extensive cultivation of cotton. Soon after his defeat of the Soninke dynasty of Ghana in 1235, he transferred the capital from Djeriba to Niani, south of Segu on the Upper Niger; it was this capital, lying some three hundred miles north-east of the modern Sierra Leone, that became known as Mali. After a reign of twenty-five years he died in 1255.

His most distinguished successor was his grandson Mansa Musa (1307–22), whose fame reached from Arabia to Spain. Under him the empire reached its zenith. A famous pilgrimage to Mecca made his name familiar throughout the Muslim world. Mansa Musa took the occasion to make the journey a tour of his empire, going out by way of Walata and Tuat to Cairo and returning from Egypt by the eastern route. The magnificence of his caravan was long remembered. In a stately cavalcade five hundred negro slaves, each bearing a staff of gold, preceded him. Part of the burden of his baggage train of camels was a large supply of gold which was distributed with lavish hand, particularly in Cairo, Mecca and Medina. He was a pious Muslim and was clearly quite sincere in his purpose of pilgrimage. He took back with him to the Sudan the Arab poet, Es Saheli of Granada, whom he had met in Mecca. News reached him, while crossing the Sahara on the return journey, that Gao and Timbuktu had been taken and added to his empire, and with them the kingdom of Songhay which stretched from the Mali frontier eastwards beyond the Niger Bend. He determined to call at Gao, the Songhay capital, where he received the conquered king as his vassal, and took two of his sons with him to Mali. Two splendid mosques were built in Gao and Timbuktu; Es Saheli superintended the work, which meant the introduction of an Arab style of architecture. The empire of Mali now extended some twelve hundred miles from the Atlantic to the Niger boundary of Hausaland between the two natural barriers of the equatorial forest on the south and the Sahara on the north. Development of foreign relations and commercial prosperity proceeded side by side. One result of the Negro sovereign's renown was literally to place Mali on the map. Fourteenth-century maps of Africa and after produced in Europe bear across the desert such inscriptions as "King of Mali" and "Musa Mali".[1]

Twenty years after Mansa Musa's death in 1332, the famous traveller Ibn Battuta visited the Negro empire. It was now

[1] E. W. Bovill, *op. cit.*, 74.

past the zenith, for Songhay had asserted its independence. Ibn Battuta spent some eight months in the country visiting, among other places, Mali, Timbuktu and Gao. His is the first account we have by an eye-witness of any kingdom of the Sudan. He was impressed by the faithful observance of Muslim rites: "They are careful to observe the hours of prayer, and assiduous in attending them in congregations, and in bringing up their children to them. On Fridays, if a man does not go, early to the mosque, he cannot find a corner to pray in, on account of the crowd. It is a custom of theirs to send each boy [to the mosque] with his prayer-mat; the boy spreads it out for his master in a place befitting him [and remains on it] until he comes to the mosque.... Another of their good qualities is their habit of wearing clean white garments on Fridays. Even if a man has nothing but an old shirt, he washes it and cleans it, and wears it to the Friday service. Yet another is their zeal for learning the Koran by heart. They put their children in chains if they show any backwardness in memorizing it, and they are not set free until they have it by heart. I visited the qadi in his house on the day of the festival. His children were chained up, so I said to him, 'Will you not let them loose?' He replied, 'I shall not do so until they learn the Koran by heart'."[1] Not all that Ibn Battuta saw was pleasing to him, but he has high praise for the effectiveness of the judicial system. He testifies to the complete security he found in the country so that no inhabitant or traveller need fear molestation. Indeed, if a foreign merchant were to die there, his possessions would be secure until the claim of the rightful heir was established.[2]

The hegemony of the Sudan exercised by Mali for two and a half centuries (c. 1238–1488) passed in due course to Songhay. Its rulers had been Muslim from the start, and the relations with Egypt and the Sultanates of North Africa, in particular with Fez, had led to stimulating contacts for the teachers of the faith. The early *imams* of the Great Mosque at Timbuktu are said to have studied at the University of Fez. This connexion of learning with the mosques strengthened the hold of Islam upon the people. If in the time of Ghana Islam was planted in the Sudan it was in the time of Mali that it struck deeper roots.[3]

[1] Translation by H. A. R. Gibb, *op. cit.*, 330.   [2] *Ibid.*, 229–30.
[3] H. Labouret in *Ency. Islam*, III (1936), 203–4, 240–1; E. W. Bovill, *op. cit.*, 67–80.

The kingdom of Songhay is said to have been founded in the seventh century. There were thirty kings of the first dynasty, the sixteenth of whom was converted to Islam early in the eleventh century, after which all the rulers were Muslim. In 1335 one of the two young princes taken by Mansa Musa to Mali after the conquest of Gao, the Songhay capital, managed to escape and was proclaimed king with the title of Sonni (Liberator) which was borne by his successors. Under him Songhay regained its independence. The most distinguished of his successors was Sonni Ali (1464–92), who conferred on Songhay by military conquests the hegemony of the Sudan. The enemies of Mali were now besetting her. Sonni Ali was not content to be one among many sharing the spoil; he rather designed to succeed to Mali's imperial rule. The career of conquest began in 1468 with the capture of Timbuktu and continued for twenty years. At his death after a few months' rule by his son, with whom the dynasty came to an end, power was seized by his general and minister, Muhammad Ture, who took the name Askia, by which his dynasty is known. It lasted a century. With his accession in 1493, Askia appeared truly devout in his practice of Islam. This has been attributed to political astuteness, for he needed the support of the leaders of religion to secure his position. Sonni Ali, though nominally Muslim, left a reputation for neglect of religion; careless in his prayers, ignorant of the Koran, turning to soothsayers and magicians for consultation, he was condemned in later times as an unbeliever. He shows how little the claim to be converted to Islam might mean at times in the Sudan. Lady Lugard speaks of Sonni Ali as the last of the great pagans, and points out how he and the Muslim Askia met at a dramatic moment in the history of the Sudan: "Standing as they do side by side on the field of history, Sonni Ali and his great minister must be taken as representing in the Soudan the genius of paganism and the genius of Islam clasping hands in a salute before their respective roads cross and part."[1] Pious Muslim biographers rejoiced over Askia, says Dubois, as "a brilliant light shining after a great darkness; a saviour who drew the servants of God from idolatry and the country from ruin. The Defender of the Faithful, who scattered joy, gifts, and alms around him".[2] There is no doubt that during his outstanding reign of thirty-five years a great impetus was given

[1] Lady Lugard, *A Tropical Dependency* (1905), 173.
[2] Felix Dubois, *Timbuctoo the Mysterious* (1897), 109.

to the spread of Islam. Within three years of his accession he made the pilgrimage to Mecca, and established an institution there to assist future pilgrims from the Sudan. He is also said to have received investiture, on the proposal of the Caliph of Egypt, as Caliph for the lands of the Sudan.[1] Before his return he consulted with learned men in Cairo on questions of administration and government, and on his return instituted many reforms. He gave full support to learning, and the University of Sankore flourished at Timbuktu; her scholars studied abroad in Fez, Tunis and Cairo, and even became teachers in Morocco and Egypt. Dubois speaks of the libraries they had possessed in Timbuktu, of which he only discovered scattered fragments.[2] Askia lifted his kingdom to the place Mali had occupied. His expeditions ranged as far west as the Senegal, and east to the boundary of Bornu. He sought to compel the pagan state of Mossi to embrace Islam, says the *Tarikh es-Sudan*, but without success save in the case of prisoners of war: "The Emir sent an ambassador to the king of Mossi demanding his conversion to Islam. The monarch replied, saying he must take counsel with his ancestors who were in the other world." The reply being unfavourable, war was declared, when "the arms of Askia were victorious, and he destroyed their fields and villages, making men, women and children his prisoners, and compelling them to be converted".[3] Askia's internal reforms bore the marks of a great organizer. His measures to assist commerce included unification of weights and measures and inspection of markets.

Lady Lugard has appraised him, though a distinguished general, as "more remarkable for the qualities which usually characterize great civilians. He appears to have been a man of liberal principles and large views, naturally humane, and disposed to temper justice with mercy, more than usually cultivated, active, wise and firm. . . . His mother was a woman of remarkable piety who brought up her children with care."[4] His end was pitiable. His successors were corrupt and in-

[1] M. Delafosse in *Ency. Islam*, IV (1934), 489a. In the judgment of Delafosse Askia was "superficially a convert to Islam but tolerant to those who were still pagans".

[2] F. Dubois, *op. cit.*, 285–88, 307. Dubois had a complete copy made of the famous *Tarikh es-Sudan* (History of the Sudan), of which Barth, who had seen a complete copy in Gando, was only able to make extracts.—Barth, *Travels*, lxvi. It is especially valuable as the work of a local historian, Es-Sadi of Timbuktu (born 1596). Cf. F. Dubois, *op, cit.*, 312–15. For an interesting account, see Lady Lugard, *op. cit.*, 154–7.

[3] F. Dubois, *op. cit.*, 111–12.   [4] Lady Lugard, *op. cit.*, 171.

competent, and within a couple of generations the kingdom was overthrown.[1] The Moorish conquest began in 1591; the climax came three years later with the setting out of a caravan of deported citizens from Timbuktu to Morocco. It proved a long drawn out and sorry story. The Moroccan Sultan's greed of gold remained unsatisfied, but the territories of Songhay were devastated and the contacts of the Sudan with the outside world greatly reduced.[2]

To the south-east of Songhay, between the Niger and Bornu by Lake Chad, lay the seven Hausa states, of which Kano on the desert border has become the best known with its great walled city, terminus for caravans from Tripoli and Egypt. According to the Kano chronicle it was Mandingos who brought Islam to Hausaland in the fourteenth century, for an entry under Yaji's reign (1349–85) reads: "In his time the Wanga-rawa came from Melle, bringing the Muhammadan religion. There were about forty of them, led by Abduraman. They commanded the king to observe the times of prayer and he complied." A mosque was built and the Muslim judicial system introduced.[3] Ibn Battuta, who paid his visit to the Sudan at this time, speaks of Gobir, another of the Hausa states, as still pagan.[4] A celebrated teacher of Tuat, al-Maghili, toured in the Sudan about 1500, preaching the faith, and was evidently active in Kano and Katsina at this time, strengthening the work of earlier Muslim missionaries.[5] In the fifteenth century Kano became tributary to Bornu, the powerful state of the Central Sudan which had accepted Islam in the eleventh century.[6] Muslim influence would therefore also come from the east. Askia's conquest of Kano, Katsina and Zaria extended the frontier of the Songhay empire to Bornu, but with the invasion of the Moors the Hausa states, which had regained independence, increased in prosperity, Katsina replacing Gao in commercial importance, and Kano inheriting the glory that had belonged to Timbuktu as the greatest port for the trade across the desert. Both cities had been centres of Muslim learning from the fifteenth century, teachers of law and of theology returning from the pilgrimage to Mecca being accus-

[1] M. Delafosse in *Ency. Islam*, IV (1934), 488–9; E. W. Bovill, *op. cit.*, 82–101; F. Dubois, *op. cit.*, 89–121; C. K. Meek, *Northern Nigeria*, I, 66–8.
[2] E. W. Bovill, "The Moorish Invasion of the Sudan", in *J.A.S.*, XXVI, 245–62, 380–7; XXVII, 47–56.
[3] C. K. Meek, *op. cit.*, I, 89.   [4] H. A. R Gibb, *op. cit.*, 336.
[5] T. W. Arnold, *op. cit.*, 320; G. Yver in *Ency. Islam*, II, 292a.
[6] G. Yver in *Ency. Islam*, I, 751b.

tomed to spend some time there in the instruction of native students.[1] Thus it would seem that on the whole Islam was introduced into the Hausa states by peaceful methods. It is well to remember, however, that the growth of Islam among the Hausas was no smooth upward progress. As Westermann has reminded us: "It is characteristic of the Hausa peoples, whose interest is centred on outward things, and who are but little susceptible to deep religious impressions, that after the partial success of Mohammedanism there should have been repeated lapses into heathenism. A struggle between the two religions was constantly going on in the majority of the Hausa states. Heathen and Mohammedan rulers appear to alternate until the occupation by the Fula. There are repeated complaints by the Hausa chroniclers that only the lower classes followed Islam, and that the religion was despised by the wealthy. It sometimes even happened that inconvenient preachers were put out of the way at the instigation of the worldly disposed kings."[2] The situation was transformed in the early nineteenth century through a religious revolution when Islam greatly strengthened its hold.

It will be convenient, before surveying the expansion of Islam farther east, to look back upon this historical review of early Islam in the Western Sudan and inquire what were the factors facilitating its spread, and what was the actual measure of its expansion and hold upon the people. To some extent these two questions are intertwined. First among the factors that led to Islam becoming established south of the Sahara was the activity of the Almoravides, desert Berbers who devoted their fierce energy to the propagation of the faith. It is one of the ironies of history that the very people whom the Church of North Africa failed to win to the Christian faith should have provided the agency by which the religion most resistant to Christianity was propagated. The fact that Islam carried with it the prestige of learning facilitated its spread. A religion with a book, and with teachers who have been trained systematically in its doctrines, makes a great appeal to a preliterate people. Delafosse states one of the two great causes of the expansion of Islam among Negroes to be their ardent desire for knowledge. He goes so far as to say: "If there were in Africa no other establishments of learning than the Quranic schools, it may be presumed that the whole of Africa would become

---

[1] G. Yver, in *Ency. Islam*, II, 292a.   [2] *I.R.M.*, I (1912), 629.

Mussulman in a more or less short space of time, so imperious is the desire for knowledge, and above all for the power to read and write, among these people who realize their ignorance and suffer from it."[1] Again, there was for the Negro of the Sudan the influence of the prestige of Muslim lands in the Middle Ages. Spain, North Africa and Egypt not only represented for him the highest development of human culture, but did in fact enjoy a civilization that outdistanced that of the rest of Europe at the time.[2] To take medicine as an illustration, there was the Egyptian Jew, Isaac Judaeus (c. 900), court physician in Kairawan, whose medical works were translated into Latin and had much influence on Western medicine during the Middle Ages. His disciple, Ibn al-Jazzar, was a Muslim whose principal writing, *Provision for the Traveller*, translated into Latin under the title *Viaticum*, was much valued because of its account of internal diseases. Or take for Spain the name of Abulcasis (c. 1000), court physician in Cordoba, whose surgical treatise, early translated into Latin, is said to have laid the foundations of surgery in Europe. It was still being printed in Western Europe in the fourteenth century. There were treatises on drugs whose Latin translations survived fifty or more printings.[3] Or to take an example from the industrial arts, the lustre pottery produced in Muslim Spain was so exquisite a treasure that it is said to-day to rank only below Chinese porcelain in the eyes of collectors. Indeed, orders for it were placed by cardinals and popes, and in reference to it Cardinal Ximenes is said to have been responsible for the witticism: "They lack our faith but we lack their works."[4] It was on the pilgrimage to Mecca that Negroes of the Sudan made direct contact in North Africa and Egypt with such things and saw them associated with the Muslim name. On their return, as to-day with African travellers, many would gather round to hear of the wonders of lands across the desert, wonders that lost nothing in the telling. The pilgrimage served yet another purpose in bringing the pilgrim into touch with teachers at mosques and academies on his route, thus deepening his understanding of his religion.

The question of the probable extent of Islam in the Western Sudan at the dawn of the modern period is difficult to answer.

[1] *I.R.M.*, XV (1926), 543.
[2] Lady Lugard in *A Tropical Dependency* gives a brilliant sketch of the culture of Muslim Spain at the time when the Sudan was in contact with it.
[3] Max Meyerhof, "Science and Medicine" in *The Legacy of Islam* (1931), 325–6, 330–2. [4] J. B. Trend, "Spain and Portugal", *op. cit.*, 14–15.

Doubtless allowance must be made for the pardonable exaggerations of Muslim historians recounting the conquests of the faith. Yet there is enough reliable evidence that the expansion of Islam was considerable, though there was clearly ebb and flow. But conversion to Islam was by no means universal. The Bambara, for example, a branch of the Mandingo stock, living in the French Sudan, have proved resistant to Islam through the centuries, though surrounded by Muslim peoples. The Mossi are agriculturists, centring upon Wagadugu south of the Niger Bend, who have sturdily remained pagans, despite Muhammad Askia's reported attempt to convert them.[1] There were physical obstacles that compelled the Muslims to stop where they did. The thick forest proved an effective barrier to an army of horsemen, and the tsetse fly was also an enemy of repute that all invaders had to face, for neither horses nor cattle (save a dwarf variety that has acquired a tolerance to the trypanosome) could long survive in the fly's forest domain.[2] Delafosse has directed attention to two respects in which expansion was restricted. First, one cannot argue from the conversion of a ruler to that of his people. Speaking from a wide experience of this very part of Africa, he says: "These chiefs, when they have become Mussulman, do not at·all like to be imitated by the lower orders, since they wish to maintain the distance which separates them from the latter. Most frequently, far from favouring the conversion of their subjects, they try to oppose it, and if it is accomplished in spite of them they regard it with disfavour. This is why it has been repeatedly observed that in small Native states Islam is only practised by the sovereign, his children and some of the highest dignitaries, while the king does nothing at all to propagate the new religion among the mass of the population."[3] A second observation of significance is that agriculturists are slower to embrace Islam than town dwellers and traders: "It has been justly said that Islam is chiefly a religion of nomads or of city dwellers and not at all a religion of peasants. Now in Negro Africa the nomads are rare, the cities are not numerous, the community is absorbed in agricultural work, indeed its whole character is more distinctively rural than one could find elsewhere. . . . We see

---

[1] G. Yver, in *Ency. Islam*, I (1913), 642a; T. W. Arnold, *op. cit.*, 321; C. G. Seligman, *Races of Africa* (1930), 63–4.
[2] Cf. *Report of the Commission on Higher Education in West Africa* (Cmd. 6655, 1945), 5.
[3] *I.R.M.*, XV (1926), 542. Cf. H. Labouret in *Ency. Islam*, III (1936), 240a.

the agricultural tribes resisting for centuries the onslaughts of Islam and setting themselves, fierce, desperate and stubborn, like a barricade against the propaganda from the towns. One is often a witness of a return to paganism on the part of people whom circumstances have forced to pass from city to rural life."[1] Through movements in the eighteenth and nineteenth centuries, Islam made its greatest progress in the Western Sudan. The result has been to produce what is in the nature of a vast reservoir of Muslim peoples from the Mandingo to the Hausa, only needing the protection of friendly colonial governments and the development of means of communication for traders and others to filter through in increasing volume to the peoples of the Guinea coast. But this situation belongs to a later period.

(2) *Islam in the Central and Eastern Sudan.*

We are less well informed about the spread of Islam in the Central and Eastern Sudan. The Central Sudan includes the region around Lake Chad. There are three states in this region, Kanem to the north and north-east of the Lake, and Bagirmi to the south-east, both within the French Equatorial Africa of to-day; while the third, Bornu, to the west of Lake Chad, falls within Nigeria. Islam first appeared in the eleventh century in Kanem, introduced by one al-Hadi al-Othmani. In the middle of the century El Bekri reported the country as pagan. In 1086, however, a new dynasty, according to tradition, was founded by one Hami who is said to have been the first Muslim king: he was making the pilgrimage to Mecca when he died. In the thirteenth century the kingdom of Kanem, which now included Bornu on the west of Lake Chad, held the hegemony of the Central Sudan. Under Dunama (1221–1257) the kingdom extended from the Niger to the Nile. Islam spread considerably in Kanem at this time. It was in this reign that Muslims from Kanem are said to have established a centre in Cairo. A series of wars disturbed the next two centuries. At the beginning of the fifteenth century the centre of gravity had moved to the west of Lake Chad, and the dynasty set up its capital in Bornu, under which name the history is then told. Vigorous rulers in the sixteenth century lifted the kingdom

---

[1] Delafosse in *I.R.M.*, XV, 544, 545. As an illustration of this from two sections of the Mandingo, the Bambara (noticed above) are agriculturists, while the Diula, who are merchants and traders, are fervent Muslims.—H. Labouret in *Ency. Islam*, III, 239b.

to a new level of prosperity. It continued so powerful that it served as a bastion to hold back the surging Fulani in the nineteenth.[1]

Bagirmi, to the south of Lake Chad, was only founded in the sixteenth century by rulers who came from the east. Abdullah (1561–1602) was the first to embrace Islam. The rulers, however, were more intent on increasing their own power and wealth than on spreading their religion.[2]

In the Eastern Sudan we are concerned with the states of Wadai, Darfur and Kordofan, between the Central Sudan states and Nubia, and with Nubia itself. While Arabs had been settled in both Darfur and Wadai since about 1400, there is no evidence of conversion to Islam at that time. In Darfur a new dynasty appeared two centuries later founded by Suleman Solon (1596–1637), son of an Arab woman, a Muslim succeeding pagan kings, who made Islam the state religion.[3] It was his grandson, however, Ahmad Bokhor (1682–1722) who really established the new religion in the country. Mosques were built, government reorganized, and a general advance in civilization experienced. Much that was pagan in practice still survived in the Muslim era. C. H. Becker calls attention to the principal annual festival in the spring when sacrifices were made to the ancestral rulers at their tombs. With the coming of Islam these sacrifices continued to be offered, the only difference being that in the case of Muslim kings, as time passed, passages from the Koran were read along with the sacrifices.[4]

The effective entrance of Islam into the neighbouring region of Kordofan was late. Merchants of the country claim descent from Arabs who, they assert, came from Egypt in the twelfth century. Such Arab immigration seems to have taken place in much of the Eastern Sudan, though without producing any marked religious result among the pagans. A king of the Muslim dynasty of Darfur, Muhammad Tirab (1752–85), conquered the country and the conversion of the tribes began.[5]

Wadai, the westernmost of this group of states, received Arab settlements from about 1400, but not till the seventeenth century did the process of conversion begin. It is said to have been due to a preacher named Salih who came about 1615,

[1] C. K. Meek, *op. cit.*, I, 78–85; G. Yver in *Ency. Islam*, I, 751–2; II, 714.
[2] G. Yver in *Ency. Islam*, I, 571; Westermann in *I.R.M.*, I, 627–8.
[3] H. A. MacMichael, *A History of the Arabs in the Sudan* (1922), I, 91–2.
[4] C. H. Becker in *Ency. Islam*, I, 915–17; T. W. Arnold, *op. cit.*, 322.
[5] Delafosse in *Ency. Islam*, IV, 497a; T. W. Arnold, *op. cit.*, 320; H. A. MacMichael, *op. cit.*, I, 93–4.

though of his origin or career little seems to be known. Some twenty years later Salih's son (or nephew), gathering his father's converts and the resident Arabs together, proclaimed a holy war against the pagan princes, and established a new dynasty which survived for three centuries.[1]

(3) *Islam in Nubia and Abyssinia.*

In both Nubia and Abyssinia Christianity had preceded Islam. In the one, after many troubled centuries, Christianity disappeared. In the other it has survived. In the region south of Egypt, from Aswan by the First Cataract, conventionally described as Nubia, were two Christian kingdoms when the Arabs conquered Egypt. The northern kingdom was that of Makurra, with its capital at Dongola in the neighbourhood of the Third Cataract, from which the modern district of Dongola takes its name. The southern was the kingdom of Alwa, with its capital at Soba near Khartoum at the junction of the Blue and White Niles. Ten years after the conquest of Egypt the Arabs invaded Nubia as far as Dongola; the capital was besieged and its church destroyed. A treaty, however, was entered into whereby, in return for an annual delivery of slaves, the Nubians received corn, oil and clothing. It was a treaty between people and people rather than between Muslim and Christian, however, for one of the contracting parties is described as "the Muslims, non-Muslims and the protected peoples".[2] The mutual tolerance implied by the treaty seems to have been the rule for a considerable time, though a century later the king of Dongola, Kyriakos, is said to have invaded Egypt to secure the release of a Coptic patriarch who had been imprisoned, and is reported as having achieved his object. Muslim traders steadily moved in from the north and even reached the southern kingdom of Alwa by the tenth century. For this century we possess the record of a contemporary, Ibn Selim, whose account of "Nubia, Mukurra, 'Aloa, the Bega, and the Nile" was written between A.D. 975 and 996. Muslim settlers from Egypt had secured land in the extreme north of Nubia and were to all intents and purposes independent. These immigrant Arabs apparently found in Nubia a more congenial physical environment than in Egypt. At the same time a number of Nubians between the First and Second Cataracts

---

[1] Delafosse in *Ency. Islam*, IV, 1075–6; H. A. MacMichael, *op. cit.* I, 68. Westermann claims that Islam had a footing in Wadai in the eleventh century. —*I.R.M.*, I (1912), 628, n. [2] Tritton, *op. cit.*, 142.

had become converts to Islam. The kingdom of Makurra included the whole territory between Egypt and Alwa. Soba in the latter kingdom is described by Ibn Selim as a beautiful city, with great monasteries, churches rich with gold, and fine gardens to embellish the whole. One of the suburbs was inhabited by Muslims. The people of the country were Christians, with bishops appointed by the patriarch of Alexandria. They used Greek writings which they translated into the vernacular.[1]

In the early years of the thirteenth century Abu Salih, an Armenian, wrote of the Nubia of his day.[2] The northern kingdom of Makurra probably then included seven dioceses, and there were certainly many monasteries and churches. Abu Salih also describes the southern kingdom of Alwa, and speaks of 400 churches there. The Christians were of the Monophysite persuasion. Slaves were the principal export item of Nubia in interchange with Muslim merchants.[3] The geographer Yakut, a contemporary of Abu Salih, reports that Suakin[4] was inhabited by Begas who were Christians.[5]

In the thirteenth century the Egyptian rulers actively intervened. In 1275 Dongola the capital was taken and an Egyptian nominee placed on the throne, thus making Nubia a virtual dependency for the time being. It was not, however, till 1316 that we hear of the first king to be a Muslim,[6] and even then the population remained Christian. Ibn Battuta, in the middle of the fourteenth century, refers to the Nubians as Christians, but speaks of the king as a Muslim. From this time historical records are scarce, but the conversion to Islam had begun and was gradually accomplished. Rivalries in the Nubian royal family were weakening to the kingdom; these rivalries had been the occasion of Egyptian intervention in the thirteenth century.[7] The immigrant Arab chiefs steadily acquired greater influence, and through intermarriage an absorption of the native inhabitants into the Arab tribes went on. In Alwa doubtless similar influences were at work. A crisis in Alwa's fortunes occurred when the Fung, a people related to the Shilluk of the Nile valley,[8] joined forces with

---

[1] H. A. MacMichael, *op. cit.*, I, 169–71.
[2] His work was composed *c.* A.D. 1208. MacMichael warns that his account must be read critically. [3] H. A. MacMichael, *op. cit.*, I, 177–78.
[4] On the Red Sea coast, south of the present Port Sudan.
[5] Another, however (Ibn Sa'id, 1214–87), says they were part Christian and part Muslim, *ibid.*, I, 179. [6] *Ibid.*, I, 186. [7] *Ibid.*, I, 181–5.
[8] *Ibid.*, I, 49–50.

the Arabs and captured Soba, the capital. Soon after, in 1504, 'Omara Dunkas, the first king of the Fung, founded the Sudanese kingdom of Sennar which lay astride the Blue Nile south of Soba. From here the Fung advanced north and west and so extended their rule over neighbouring territories.[1]

The transition from Christianity to Islam was a slow one, for in the sixteenth century there is a Portuguese report of the surviving Nubian Christians seeking help from the Christian king of Abyssinia.[2] But in the following century the Christian witness had disappeared.

From its first introduction Christianity had lasted close on a thousand years. That it should have survived so long in a kingdom ringed round by Muslim peoples and deeply penetrated by Muslim influences is a tribute to the root it had taken in the land. This is also reflected in the Nubian language, of which Dr. Griffith says: "Perhaps the chief interest of the language is its use in the writings of the Nubian Church. Probably to fortify their independence against Muslim encroachment, the Nubians adapted the Greek alphabet, with necessary additions from the Coptic and perhaps the Meroitic alphabets, to the purpose of writing their own language. The rare examples of Nubian writing that have been discovered, besides graffiti and two legal documents, comprise portions of a lectionary, homilies and edifying narratives, obviously translated from Greek and not from Coptic. The earliest dates from the end of the eighth century, the latest from the beginning of the fourteenth."[3] The isolation of the Nubian Church from stimulating contact with fellow Christians, and the failure to produce the Christian leaders required for its own nourishment, seem to have completed what external factors had begun.[4]

That Christian Nubians carried their religion farther afield in the course of so many centuries would be reasonable to expect. There are some indications that this was the case, but the evidence is tantalisingly meagre. Such fragments of evidence as exist appear to warrant the view that the Central and Western

---

[1] H. A. MacMichael, op. cti., I, 34, 75, 189; II, 355. MacMichael gives a local history (Manuscript D7; translation in II, 358–405) which "represents the only known attempt by a native historian to give a detailed chronological account of the Fung and Turkish days".

[2] Alvarez, Narrative of the Portuguese Embassy to Abyssinia (Stanley's translation, 1881), 352.

[3] F. Ll. Griffith in Ency. Brit. (14th ed., 1929), XVI, 286a.

[4] E. Graefe in Ency. Islam, I, 1072–3; S. Hillelson, ibid., III, 943–6; T. W. Arnold, op. cit., 109–13.

Sudan, in their pre-Muslim period, not only received influences from the Nile valley but that Coptic Christian influences were among them. It is even said that Christianity, probably in some diluted form, may have reached Ghana in its early days,[1] and that the princes who founded the kingdom of Songhay in the seventh century were Christian.[2] In several Hausa states Christian influences are also said to be observable.[3] That these all come from Coptic Christians in the Nile valley seems to be the reasonable conclusion.[4] MacMichael has suggested that the Tungur, an ancient pre-Arab tribe from Nubia who migrated to the west, were Christian before they left. They seem to have retained the observance of certain rites of the Coptic Church.[5] But such streams of influence all ran into the sand long before the central reservoir that supplied them had dried up.

In Abyssinia matters fell out the other way. Islam made a bold bid to win the kingdom, but the Christian Church survived. Two external factors that influenced the situation were, first, the physical barrier of the highlands making penetration more difficult, and second, the presence of others of the same faith, the Portuguese, at a critical moment. The period following the rise of Islam is shrouded in mystery as far as Abyssinia is concerned. The early struggles between the rival faiths are inferred in the light of later events. "The history of Abyssinia", says Littmann, "from about 650 to 1270 is shrouded in darkness. During this time many wars must have been fought between Christians and pagans, and also between Christians and Mohammedans. The outcome was that political conquest and missionary activity spread far to the south, and that the centre of the empire was transferred to the southern provinces."[6] Abyssinian legendary history recounts the exploits of Christian missionaries in this period. The Abyssinian Church continued to recognize its dependence on Alexandria, and the king applied when necessary for a metropolitan or *abuna* to be chosen by the patriarch of Alexandria, a request customarily allowed by the Egyptian Sultan of the day.[7]

---

[1] C. K. Meek, *op. cit.*, I, 63.
[2] Delafosse in *Ency. Islam*, IV, 495b.   [3] C. K. Meek, *op. cit.*, I, 72–3.
[4] Meek suggests that the eighth and ninth centuries are a possible period of special exodus when troubles in Egypt led to the expulsion of certain disaffected tribes into the Libyan desert, but this would not be Nubian influence. *Ibid.*, II, 163-64.   [5] H. A. MacMichael, *op. cit.*, I, 66, 128.
[6] E. Littmann in *E.R.E.* I (1908), 58a.
[7] Tritton, *op. cit.*, 86.

When the light of history again shines upon the scene we find Muslims have already penetrated into Abyssinia. About 1270 the existing dynasty was overthrown by Yekuno Amlak (1270–85) who claimed to represent the ancient Solomonic line. This king made furious onslaughts on the Muslims who ravaged much of the kingdom, an indication of their serious increase.[1] With the restored Solomonic dynasty came a literary revival that lasted to the eighteenth century, and by producing literature, largely religious, in Ge'ez or Ethiopic, undoubtedly contributed to the consolidation of the Abyssinian Church. Translations from Coptic and Arabic were supplemented by original compositions. Soon chronicles of contemporary history were prepared which from the fifteenth century preserved a valuable record of the kingdom.[2] Once again the use of the language of the people is found linked with Christian survival under stress of stormy times.

It was early in the fourteenth century that the Arab wars against Abyssinia began; they lasted for over two hundred years and wellnigh brought the Christian kingdom to destruction. To the middle of this period belongs one of the great kings of Abyssinia, Zara Ya'kob (1434–68). He seems to have realized how ominous for his kingdom and its religion was the growing Arab power, and he came to the conclusion that he must find support outside his country. He therefore entered into communication with the Pope, and is said to have been the first king of Abyssinia to do so. He doubtless hoped for more than spiritual help in his conflict with the enemies of the Church.[3] The crisis came in the reign of Lebna Dengel (1508–40). The conjunction of an outstandingly able leader with the use (if limited) of firearms on the Muslim side nearly proved fatal for Christian Abyssinia. The leader was a Somali chief, Ahmad ibn Muhammad Gran, Muslim ruler of a border state, who with great energy and resource pressed home the invasion of Abyssinia. From Shoa he penetrated to Axum in the north; the land was ravaged, churches were destroyed, and in Axum itself the cathedral church was burned. While many chiefs with their people then turned Muslim, some Christians elected to retain their faith and to pay tribute. Yet so great was the success of the invader that the Abyssinian chronicles claim nine men out of ten turned Muslim at this time. It must be

---

[1] Budge, *History of Ethiopia*, I, 285.
[2] Jones and Monroe, *A History of Abyssinia* (1935), 53–5.
[3] Budge, *op. cit.*, I, 310–11.

remembered, not only that a chief taking the initiative might carry his followers with him, but that there were chiefs, once Muslim, who for one reason or another had entered the service of the Christian king and taken the Christian name, but who now re-affirmed their loyalty to Islam.[1] The struggle went on for fifteen years. The heel of the Muslim was on the neck of the Christian kingdom. Then the king, with his faithful Abyssinians, was reinforced by help from Christian Portugal. Lebna Dengel had sent more than once for help. After long delays at last it was on the way. But Lebna Dengel was now dead, and his successor Galawdewos (Claudius, 1540–59) sat on the uneasy throne of the battered kingdom. In 1541 there arrived some 400 armed Portuguese commanded by Christopher da Gama (son of Vasco). Now firearms were matched with firearms; the tide of battle swayed, then turned. After a severe initial setback, in which the Portuguese lost their brave commander, the allies were victorious. Ahmad Gran was slain in 1543.[2] The kingdom rose again. Islam did not secure the great advances it had made, but neither did the tide recede to its starting-point. There was a permanent accession to Islam remaining after the Christian victory. A traveller of the following century estimated that one in three of the Abyssinians was Muslim.[3] Thus at the dawn of the modern period the Church of Abyssinia remained, with the Coptic Church of Egypt, the only surviving Christian witness in the continent of Africa. These alone were the fruit of Christian effort when fifteen centuries had passed.

(4) *Arab Colonies in East Africa.*

The coast of East Africa to Zanzibar, as we have already seen, was well known to the ancients. Arab, Persian and Indian traded there in pre-Islamic days, with the Arab in the van. Arab traders settled on the coast at least as early as the first century and married women of the coast tribes. From such intermarriage came the Swahili, the mixed race of African and Arab.[4] Tradition speaks of specific settlements made in Islamic times as far south as the Zambezi, the earliest permanent Arab settlements of which we have knowledge. From Oman in the south-east corner of Arabia came the pioneering party. A

[1] Jones and Monroe, *op. cit.*, 82–3; T. W. Arnold, *op. cit.*, 117–18.
[2] Budge, *op. cit.*, I, 330–35; II, 338–41. An account of the Portuguese expedition by Castanhoso, a member of it, is available in *The Portuguese Expedition to Abyssinia in 1541–1543* (Whiteway's translation, 1902).
[3] Guidi in *Ency. Islam*, I, 119–20; T. W. Arnold, *op. cit.*, 113–17.
[4] W. H. Schoff, *Periplus of the Erythraean Sea*, 28; A. Werner in *Ency. Islam*, IV, 1215b.

rebellion had failed and they had to flee. Their point of settlement on the coast is not known. This was about A.D. 695. Half a century later a number of Arabs (known as Zaidiyah or Emozaidi), banished for schismatic views, crossed to East Africa and settled on the coast north of the Tana River. Early in the tenth century some families from Central Arabia, driven out by oppressive sheikhs, also crossed to Africa. These founded Mogadishu and Barawa just north of the Equator. Later in the same century Persians from Shiraz sought a home across the water. The story goes that the Sultan's son by an Abyssinian slave, finding no future for himself at home, came to East Africa. He is said to have founded the colony of Kilwa (c. 975) on an island off the coast. Daughter settlements in due time appeared until by 1500 there were fifteen or more such colonies, from Mogadishu to Inhambane. Mombasa, Zanzibar, Kilwa, Mozambique and Sofala were names of importance among them. Cape Corrientes marked the southern terminus, partly because the vessels the Arabs used were adapted to the regular monsoons of the Indian Ocean but not equal to the stormy waters farther south, and partly because of perils associated with such strange waters in the mariner's imagination. Many of these colonies were on islands off the coast, there being trade relations only with the mainland. They grew wealthy with a commerce that extended to the shores of India and enjoyed a high civilization on the material side. Here were towns with well-built houses, generously provided with terraces, courts, and gardens, and made beautiful with carved woodwork and embossed metal decoration, with silks and carpets and tapestries of the eastern trade. This trade, which extended as far as China (fragments of Ming ware have been found on the ruined sites of the coast towns), also brought rich dress materials and personal ornaments, glassware, choice furniture, and jewelled weapons of tempered steel. The sheikhs were dressed in silk and velvet and cloth of gold. The women were decked in all the finery the commercial prosperity of the settlements could provide. The cultural side of life, however, lagged behind. There is nothing to indicate interests beyond the material level. "It is difficult, indeed, to understand how the great age of the Arabs in East Africa could have been so rich in wealth and comfort and yet so poor in culture."[1]

Relations among the various colonies were anything but harmonious. They constituted a series of city states that were

[1] R. Coupland, *East Africa and its invaders* (1938), 39.

often at war with one another. One and another would hold the hegemony of a section of the coast. They were all Muslim in religion and mosques adorned with minarets graced all their towns, but they made no effort to propagate their faith among the peoples of the mainland. Indeed, it was a major interest to secure from them instead a steady flow of slaves for export. Africans were active in their service and in trade with them, and there was intermarriage with African women, the children all counting as "Arab" in the next generation; but otherwise the settlements were self-contained Arab colonies, a fringe of Islam along the littoral of eastern Africa.[1]

Our survey of the expansion of Islam in Africa has taken us north and west and east. Throughout North Africa west of Egypt Christianity disappeared and Islam became and has remained the religion of the people. In the west the Berber tribes became Muslim, while the peoples of the Sudan were partly converted, but have held the faith more lightly than the Berber capable of fierce fanaticism. Christian Nubia in the east eventually succumbed, while the long conflict of Islam for Abyssinia won only partial success. Farther south a string of island and coastal settlements remained little more than a series of isolated colonies—there was never the unity of an Arab empire among them—until the nineteenth century.

Truly a giant crescent across Africa.

[1] R. Coupland, *op. cit.*, 21–40; G. M. Theal, *History and Ethnography of South Africa before 1795*, I (1907), 182–99.

CHAPTER 7

THE ENTERPRISE RENEWED
FIFTEENTH AND SIXTEENTH CENTURIES

THROUGHOUT the Middle Ages Christian access to Africa for the propagation of the faith was denied by the Muslim occupation from Egypt to the Atlantic. Christian soldiers might serve the Sultans of Morocco and Tunis, Christian merchants might have quarters for residence assigned them, and even slender Christian communities survive for a time under tolerant rulers, but a Christian missionary who sought to exercise his vocation would have short shrift. Yet valiant attempts were made from time to time by devoted men to win once more for the Church of Christ the lands that had been lost. These efforts demand brief attention before we turn to the effective renewal of the enterprise under the aegis of the Portuguese.

(1) *Christian faces Muslim.*

Until the persecuting fury of the Almohades swept through the land, Christians were a tolerated sect, and small communities survived the Arab invasion on payment of the tribute. They were isolated, often in highlands to which they had escaped for refuge, but relations with the outside world were not completely severed. Under a beneficent ruler a temporary prosperity might be enjoyed. Such was the case in Mauretania under the Hammadite dynasty in the eleventh and twelfth centuries. In the two principal cities, Draa and Bugia, were Christian communities. That of Bugia was without a bishop in 1075; with the consent of the Muslim king the chosen candidate set out for Rome, and with him were despatched all the Christian slaves, together with letters and gifts for the Pope. Gregory VII consecrated as bishop the priest sent to him, and replied in most cordial terms to the message of the king. A papal offer of service was apparently accepted at a later date when several hundreds of expert workmen were sent from Italy to beautify the capital city of Bugia. The terms of the letter suggest that Gregory may have even entertained the hope of winning a Hammadite prince to the Christian faith.[1]

In addition to these rare communities were other groups of Christians for whom the papal See had continuing concern,

---

[1] The full text of the papal letter is given in Mesnage, *op. cit.*, II, 209-10.

apparently hoping through them to win some of the Muslim rulers. There were settlements of Christian merchants, mainly from Italy, in some fifteen of the ports of North Africa from Tangier to Tripoli. They were granted quarters in which as Christians they might worship in their own churches and have their own priests. Naturally all proselytizing was strictly forbidden. Even the Almohades, fanatical as they were, had the common sense to realize the value of this external trade, and 'Abd-ul Mu'min himself renewed in 1160 the existing trade agreement with Genoa.

A second group consisted of Christian troops in the service of the Sultans. They first appear in the eleventh century. They were not fugitives and renegades but were recruited in Europe with the consent of the Christian powers concerned, and with the approval of the Papacy. They were established in the state capitals, Marrakesh, Tlemcen, Bugia and Tunis. The Sultans felt more secure with such a bodyguard of professional soldiers who were above local rivalries and outside the intrigues of the court. It was understood they would remain Christian in religion, and chaplains were regularly allowed them.

A third group were Christian immigrants from Spain, found in Morocco, for the most part transferred under compulsion—a group known as Mozarabic Christians, a term applied by Muslims in Spain to the Christian communities among them.[1] There were several bishoprics apportioned them and their number led Innocent IV to speak of the Moroccan Church. That they were not the relics of African Christianity is shown by the fact that their language was Arabic, not Berber. Although removed by force they were tolerated as a protected people, and constituted from the thirteenth century another Christian group. These Christian groups all afforded points of contact for the Church in Europe, and their interests were not forgotten.[2]

The Christian mission to Muslim lands in Africa was undertaken in particular by Franciscans and Dominicans. Francis of Assisi himself visited Egypt in 1219 during the Fourth Crusade, when the Christian army was engaged in the siege of Damietta. With him was a group of the Brothers Minor. From the Christian army he crossed to that of the Muslims and preached before the Sultan; the story of his challenge to ordeal by fire to

[1] Spanish *Mozarabe*, a corruption of the Arabic *Musta'rib*, denoting persons not Arab by race but assimilated to them.
[2] Mesnage, *op. cit.*, III, 3–15, 40–4; E. W. Bovill, *op. cit.*, 115–22; Schmidlin, *Catholic Mission History* (1933), 225–6.

I

decide which of their two religions was the true one is not as well authenticated as the fact of the visit. The courteous reception he and his companions received at such a time of military tension reflects great credit on the Muslim Sultan.[1] It was shortly after this, in November 1219, that Damietta fell to the crusaders, a heavy blow for the Muslims at that time. A Franciscan mission to Tunis, possibly in the same year, had short shrift from their own co-religionists in the place. The friars had no sooner landed than they began to preach, but their denunciation of Islam aroused such violent hostility that it was all the Christian merchants could do to save their lives and pack them back to Europe. In 1219 also there went a band of five Franciscans to Morocco, but their deliberate invectives hurled at their Muslim listeners were such that Sabatier is led to say that here "the thirst for martyrdom becomes the madness of suicide". The five devoted if misguided men—the friars Bernard, Pietro, Adjutus, Accurso, and Otho—were all martyred in 1220; their story became famous in Franciscan annals.[2] Other missionaries followed with the same fervid devotion and carelessness of martyrdom characteristic of the Order. In Egypt, where they cared for the spiritual needs of European merchants and prisoners, some seven missionaries of the Order sealed their service with martyrdom.[3]

The preaching friars also found a field of service among Muslims. The precise date of the arrival of Dominicans in Africa is not known; either just before or after the death of the founder in 1222 has been suggested. At any rate, by 1234 they are found working with considerable success. Their methods were a contrast to those of the Franciscans, for "the more spontaneous Franciscans braved dangers and sought martyrdom, while the more logical and prudential Dominicans avoided difficulties."[4] In Africa they are found working among Christian soldiers and Christian slaves, seeking contact with apostates and those hovering on the brink of apostasy, offering instruction to interested Muslims on the Christian use of images in worship, and generally so comporting themselves as to remain in favour with the Muslim authorities.[5] Their early devotion to the study of theology and their selected vocation of preaching, and

[1] Sabatier, *Life of St. Francis of Assisi* (1895), 228–30; E. L. Butcher, *The Story of the Church of Egypt* (1897), II, 128–9; *Cambridge Mediaeval History*, V, 314; VI, 731.

[2] Sabatier, *op. cit.*, 224–6; *Cambridge Mediaeval History*, II, 753.

[3] Mesnage, *op. cit.*, III, 62–3; *The Catholic Encyclopaedia*, VI, 293.

[4] Schmidlin, *op. cit.*, 230, n. 21.   [5] Mesnage, *op. cit.*, III, 66–9.

teaching naturally led them to emphasize special missionary training for those working in the non-Christian world. This consisted in the two practical subjects of language and method of presentation of Christian truth to non-Christians. Already, in the thirteenth century Raymond of Penafort founded colleges for the study of languages in Murcia and Tunis, the latter being specially established for the study of Arabic. On the question of method Raymond sought the assistance of Thomas Aquinas; it was given in his *Summa Catholicae Fidei contra Gentiles* which marked the beginning of a theological approach to Islam.[1]

Among those who laboured for North Africa Raymond Lull stands as the most commanding figure. The time was unfavourable. The Crusades of the late thirteenth century had aroused the Muslims of Africa to renewed hostility. His was a spiritual crusade. The *Art of loving the good* (1290) was to be turned into Arabic for the conversion of Muslims; with that purpose in view all direct argument on the Trinity or the Incarnation was avoided. In 1292 at the age of sixty he made his first voyage to Tunis. At the first attempt, however, he shrank back; he let the boat sail without him. The mental conflict that followed induced an illness that only vanished when he finally set sail. After a brief opportunity of discussion with Muslims in the city opposition was aroused, he was imprisoned, tried and deported. It was fifteen years before he returned. In the interval he became a Franciscan tertiary (the Third Order, for laymen), the Franciscans having found his *Art* more acceptable a treatise than the Dominicans had done. He made his second missionary attempt in 1307 when seventy-five, this time landing at Bugia. The time was extremely unpropitious, and Lull was anything but tactful, opening with the public challenge: "The law of the Christians is holy and true, and the sect of the Moors is false and wrong, and this am I prepared to prove." The natural upshot was imprisonment (though the mob was ready to martyr him). Thanks to the intervention of influential Christian merchants in the place, restrictions were relaxed and he was even allowed to receive Muslim visitors with whom he continued his discussion. In six months he was repatriated. His third and last journey was made in 1314 when he was eighty-two years of age. He visited both Bugia and Tunis, and in the latter city is said to have had his most successful mission, gaining several influential converts.

[1] Mesnage, *op. cit.*, III, 71-4; Schmidlin, *op. cit.*, 229.

The end came in Bugia to which he had returned. Like Stephen he was stoned to death and received the martyr's crown.[1]

And so three centuries passed during which Franciscans, Dominicans and others toiled on the hard soil of Islam with little to show. Then came the grand era of maritime discovery; the New World in the West burst on the astonished eyes of Europe, and the sea-route to the East opened up the rich lands of Asia. The Christian merchants in North Africa slipped away to more profitable fields. The Franciscan and Dominican missionaries heard the call of the new lands and transferred their work to more responsive peoples. Soon only Christian slaves were left in Muslim Africa, and the devoted "Pères Rédempteurs" who sought to alleviate their lot. The once cherished hope of recovering the lost lands of the Church in Africa had faded.

(2) *Portuguese Prowess.*

Just as the hope of recovery in the north was finally fading, there appeared an undreamt-of opportunity in new lands south of the desert. The veil was lifted from the whole of the unknown African coastline by the prowess of the Portuguese until, as the climax of three-quarters of a century of enterprise, Vasco da Gama completed the task five years after the discovery of the New World, the first to sail by the Cape route to India. One name stands without peer in the whole story—the name of Prince Henry of Portugal, known to history as Henry the Navigator. He was born in 1394, and was the third surviving son of King John I and his queen, Philippa, daughter of John of Gaunt. In 1415 when his cousin, Henry V, was victor at Agincourt, Prince Henry won distinction in the capture of Ceuta from the Moors, the first Portuguese acquisition of territory in Africa. Three years later he settled on the promontory of Sagres in the extreme south-west of Portugal overlooking the Atlantic. Here he built an observatory and studied such maps as were available and worked out plans for journeys of exploration. For the next forty years this was his home, together with his port, the nearby Lagos. He sent out his captains in expedition after expedition down the African coast, and they crept along, fearfully at first, each one registering some new advance, until the truth was learned of regions long dreaded because unknown. When in North Africa he had secured important information about the lands to the south and the trade with

[1] E. A. Peers, *Ramon Lull* (1929), 227–8, 235–45, 325–33, 268–72.

them, especially in gold, a commodity of which Europe was in great need at that time. The possibility of making direct contact with these southern lands by sea suggested itself to him and was a mainspring of his undertakings. He would outflank the Muslim lands of Africa. Fortunately we have the record of a contemporary, the faithful chronicler Azurara, as to the motives that moved the Prince. Azurara specifies five reasons that inspired him to carry on the work in the earliest and darkest days. First was a scientific reason; he wanted to know what lay beyond the Canary Islands and Cape Bojador, the existing limit of navigation to the south: "he sent out his own ships against those parts to have manifest certainty of them all". We know that this scientific interest was not limited to exploration of the West African coast, but that the discovery of a route to India by sea was a master ambition. The second reason was commercial; should a Christian population perchance be found, trade profitable to both parties might be carried on and "many kinds of merchandise might be brought to this realm". The third reason was political: to discover the real strength of the national and religious enemy, the Muslim Moors, and what territory they occupied, "because every wise man is obliged by natural prudence to wish for a knowledge of the power of his enemy". Fourthly, he had never found in Africa a Christian ally; "therefore he sought to know if there were in those parts any Christian princes in whom the charity and the love of Christ was so ingrained that they would aid him against those enemies of the faith". And finally, a direct missionary reason: "The fifth reason was his great desire to make increase in the faith of our Lord Jesus Christ and to bring to him all the souls that should be saved", to the Prince's carrying out of which purpose Azurara adds his personal testimony.[1]

A chronological summary records the stages but gives no conception of the hopes and fears of that great adventure into the unknown. Within a year or two of his settlement at Sagres, Madeira was re-discovered by Prince Henry's captains, and they sailed down the African coast to Cape Bojador, but for twelve years he could get none to pass beyond it. To the actual perils of the unknown ocean—for they believed that currents

[1] G. de Azurara, *The Chronicle of the Discovery and Conquest of Guinea.* Translated from the Portuguese by C. R. Beazley and E. Prestage (1899), I, 27–30. Azurara finished his *Chronica de Guiné* in 1453, during Prince Henry's lifetime. He held a post in the Royal Library and was eventually in charge of it. An abridged version of Azurara is provided in *Conquests and Discoveries of Henry the Navigator* (1936), ed. Almeida.

THE PORTUGUESE IN AFRICA

Fifteenth to Seventeenth Centuries

beyond the Cape were so terrible that no ship could ever return—were added mythical dangers that lost nothing in their transmission through mediaeval legend. It was current knowledge among seamen that any Christian passing Bojador would be changed into a Negro as payment for his pains. There were maps that showed in this ocean "the horrible giant hand of Satan raised above the waves to seize the first of his human prey that would venture into his den". And Muslim writers, who ought to know, declared the tropic sun poured down liquid flame so that mariners venturing so far would soon be cooked in the boiling waters.[1] Small wonder that year after year Cape Bojador was reached but never rounded. At last in 1434 Prince Henry specially commissioned one of his captains, Gil Eannes, to this undertaking, who resolved not to return till it was accomplished, "and as he purposed, so he performed—for in that voyage he doubled the Cape, despising all danger, and found the lands beyond quite contrary to what he, like others, had expected".[2] This was the great advance, the breaking of the lock that threw open the door to further discovery. Inhabited stretches of coast were in due course reached. In 1441 Moorish captives were brought back, as on most later expeditions; in 1442 the first Negro slaves—and gold dust, a sign at last of the realizing of a main objective of the expeditions. More slaves were brought the following year, and in 1444 a group of merchant adventurers set out with one Lançarote, who had received the Prince's licence, to prosecute the enterprise. In 1445 the River Senegal, frontier of the Sahara and Sudan, was passed and Cape Verde, the most westerly point of Africa, discovered. The next year an expedition reached the River Gambia. But now the commercial exploitation of the new discoveries claimed the interest of the Portuguese, so that our chronicler says of 1448: "After this year the affairs of these parts were henceforth treated more by trafficking and bargaining than by bravery and toil of arms."[3] Before the next great advance Prince Henry died in 1460.

The religious aspect of the expeditions was prominent. A papal Letter of Indulgence was granted, covering all engaged, in which the work was commended as being undertaken "for the destruction and confusion of the Moors and the enemies of Christ, and for the exaltation of the Catholic faith".[4] That these feelings were shared by those engaged is suggested by

[1] C. R. Beazley, *Prince Henry the Navigator* (1895), 171–2.
[2] Azurara, *op. cit.*, I, 33. [3] *Ibid.*, II, 289. [4] *Ibid.*, I, 53.

Azurara in speaking of the capturing of Moorish prisoners, of which one occasion will be typical: "And for this good booty, and all the grace that God had shown them in those days, they rendered Him much praise for His guidance and the great victory He had given them over the enemies of the faith. And with the will and purpose to toil still more in His service, they embarked again in their boats and returned to their ships."[1] Of the sincerity of Prince Henry's interest in the conversion of the captives brought back to Portugal we are left in no doubt, and Azurara claims that the greater part became Christian.[2] He even suggests that one Negro lad of unusual capacity, who made progress in Christian truth ("and many Christians there be who have not this knowledge as perfectly as he had"), was being prepared by Prince Henry as a missionary to his own countrymen, but the lad died before the purpose could be effected.[3]

Before we leave the period in which Prince Henry personally directed the task of exploration, we salute him. Without his courageous pursuit of purpose the course of history that is to unroll before us in an Africa unknown before his time must have been long delayed. The tribute of the biographer who was one of the first to direct attention to his achievement does not make too large a claim: "The coasts of Africa visited, the Cape of Good Hope rounded: the New World disclosed: the sea-way to India, the Moluccas, and China, laid open; the globe circumnavigated, and Australia and New Zealand discovered: such were the stupendous results of a great thought and of indomitable perseverance in spite of twelve years of costly failure and disheartening ridicule. . . . True it is, that the great majority of these vast results were effected after his death; and it was not granted to him to affix his quaint signature to charters and grants of territory in those Eastern and Western Empires which at length were won by means of the explorations he had fostered." Yet tracing these to their source they "all lead us back to that same inhospitable point of Sagres, and to the motive which gave to it a royal inhabitant".[4]

In a generation from Prince Henry's death the outline of

---

[1] Azurara, *op. cit.*, I, 73–4.
[2] *Ibid.*, I, 83; II, 277–8, 288.   [3] *Ibid.*, II, 179.
[4] R. H. Major, *The Discoveries of Prince Henry the Navigator and their Results* (2nd ed. 1877), 299-300. See, too, the tributes to Prince Henry's work by C. R. Beazley in *Prince Henry the Navigator* (1895), 310–12; and by C. P. Lucas in *Historical Geography of the British Colonies*, III, West Africa (2nd ed., 1900), 28–9.

Africa had been completed. The Rio Grande in West Africa was the limit reached in his lifetime. In the following two years (1461-62) a further 600 miles of coast were explored. A lofty mountain range abutting on the coast they named Sierra Leone from the roaring of the thunder round its summit. They journeyed on as far as a Cape they named Cabo Mesurado where Monrovia stands to-day. Then came a lull until, in 1469, Fernando Gomez entered into a five years' contract whereby the trade of the coast was allowed him, and as one condition he undertook to explore 300 miles of coast each year, beginning from Sierra Leone. By 1470 the explorers had reached the coast later called La Mina, important for the trade in gold, and may have reached the kingdom of Benin. At any rate, the island of San Thomé was sighted on the Saint's day in that year, and probably Fernando Po as well, named after its discoverer. Annobon (discovered on New Year's Day) and Principe completed the islands of the Gulf of Guinea. In 1471 the Equator was crossed, the first crossing from north to south ever recorded on the western coast of Africa. Ten years later the building of a fort on the Gold Coast (La Mina) was determined on. It became the first European settlement on the Guinea Coast. To expedite the work the king had the stones cut and dressed in Portugal. These and other necessary materials, together with supplies for 600 men, were despatched by special fleet to La Mina. This first European settlement was founded with Christian rites: "They reached La Mina on the 19th of January, 1482. On the following morning they suspended the banner of Portugal from the bough of a lofty tree, at the foot of which they erected an altar, and the whole company assisted at the first mass that was celebrated in Guinea, and prayed for the conversion of the natives from idolatry, and the perpetual prosperity of the Church which they intended to erect upon the spot."[1] Diogo d'Azambuja, the Portuguese commander, in state conference with the African chief told him of the Christian faith, and said that if he would accept it the king of Portugal would make an alliance with him and trade relations would be profitable to them both. To make this possible the Portuguese wished for land on which to build their settlement. In due course the site was granted and a fort and church completed and dedicated to St. George.[2]

Two years later, in 1484, an expedition under Diogo Cam

[1] R. H. Major, *op. cit.*, 201.
[2] *Ibid.*, 201–3; W. W. Claridge, *History of the Gold Coast* (1915), I, 44–7.

reached a mighty estuary and ascended it a little.[1] People on the southern bank were friendly; they belonged to the kingdom of Congo. It was this mightiest of the rivers of Africa whose estuary had been discovered. On the south of it Diogo Cam erected one of the stone pillars surmounted by a cross, by which the Portuguese claimed on these voyages of discovery their right of possession.[2]

At this time the King of Portugal, John II, added to his titles that of Lord of Guinea. This name was used by the Portuguese of the lands they discovered from the Senegal onwards to Elmina and beyond. It was the coast from which came gold—gold first traded through the Sudan kingdom of Ghana—and this fact is claimed to favour this derivation of the name.[3]

The discoveries now came in quick succession leading to the Cape. On his second voyage in 1485 Diogo Cam passed 600 miles beyond the Congo to the south. In 1486 Bartholomew Diaz commanded an expedition that reached the Cape in 1487 and pressed on eastward as far as the Great Fish River. Here Diaz was compelled to turn by his long-suffering crews. Their tempestuous experience in passing the Cape led Diaz to christen it Cabo Tormentoso, but on his return with such thrilling news of discovery, John II thought otherwise and christened it Cabo de Bona Esperança, and Cape of Good Hope it has since remained. For a decade there was delay, and then King Manuel commissioned an expedition under Vasco da Gama.[4]

---

[1] The date, 1484, is accepted by R. H. Major, *op. cit.*, 204; J. Scott Keltie, *The Partition of Africa* (1893), 39; W. H. Bentley, *Pioneering on the Congo* (1900), I, 19; and C. P. Lucas, *The Partition and Colonization of Africa* (1922), 33. Schmidlin prefers 1483, *op. cit.*, 276; and H. H. Johnston 1482, *George Grenfell and the Congo* (1908), I, 70. Also for 1482 see J. Cuvelier, *L'Ancien Royaume du Congo* (1946), 255–6; cf. E. Prestage in Camb. Med. Hist. VIII, 524.

[2] R. H. Major, *op. cit.*, 203–4. Pictures of two of Diogo Cam's crosses, with full Portuguese inscription, are reproduced in Wilmot, *Monomotapa* (1896), Appendix D. On a second expedition of Diogo Cam to the Congo in 1485 they reached the dangerous rocks above Matadi and inscribed a record of the achievement. This was first discovered in 1900. Photographs and decipherment of the inscriptions, in which crosses figure, are given in H. H. Johnston, *op. cit.*, I, ix, 71–2. cf. *The Times* July 16, 1953.

[3] The name first appeared as the Portuguese *Guiné*, derivation uncertain. The connexion with Ghana is tempting, but some prefer to link the name with the city of Jenné, southwest of Timbuktu, also famous in the gold trade. See H. H. Johnston, *A History and Description of the British Empire in Africa*, n.d., 48, n.; W. T. Balmer, *History of the Akan Peoples*, n.d., 27; *Ency. Brit.* (14th ed., 1929), *s.v.* For the Portuguese use of the name, see R. H. Major, *op. cit.*, 96–7: 204–5.

[4] It is said that Pedro de Covilham, previous to his entry of Abyssinia in 1490–91, had collected much information about the eastern seas, and had even sent the King of Portugal a map indicating the possibility of a sea-route to India by the Cape.—Budge, *History of Ethiopia*, I, 180; Alvarez, *op. cit.*, 269.

They set sail in July 1497. On Christmas Day Da Gama caught sight of land and therefore christened it Natal. In January 1498 they reached a river on the eastern coast of Africa where two Muslim merchants engaged in the African trade were found. It was the River Quilimane, one of the mouths of the Zambezi. They had reached the southern end of the string of Arab settlements. Mozambique, Mombasa and Malindi were reached in succession with the help of local pilots. A skilful Arab pilot took the fleet from Malindi on the last stage across the Indian Ocean, and on May 17, 1498, the first men from the west to come all the way by sea sighted the shores of India. Within two generations of the passing of Cape Bojador Prince Henry's master ambition had been realized.[1]

(3) Missions in Western Africa.

The completing of the sea route to the East opened up new vistas of prosperity for Portugal and led to the establishment of her Eastern Empire. The rewards were greater than in Africa, where climate soon began to take its toll. To the Church, however, the opportunity was presented to establish herself a second time in Africa. On the Guinea coast experiences were disappointing. In the kingdom of Congo there seemed prospect of continuing success.

The earliest missionary activity was on the islands off the Atlantic coast. The Canaries, in which the papacy was interested from the fourteenth century, were first colonized by a Norman baron in 1402. Spanish Franciscans (for he recognized Castilian suzerainty) worked among the native Guanches. By 1476 four of the larger islands are said to have been converted. The missionaries were the protectors of native rights in the early days. Intermarriage between Spaniards and Guanches produced eventually a common stock. Franciscans were with the discoverers of Madeira in 1420. A century later Funchal, the capital, was made an episcopal see (1514), and was before long raised to archiepiscopal rank (1539) with the dioceses of Angra (in Azores), Cabo Verde, San Thomé and even Goa (in Western India) as suffragans. But such an unwieldy province

---

[1] R. H. Major, *op. cit.*, 242–50; G. M. Theal, *op. cit.*, I, 212–28; J. H. Kramers in *The Legacy of Islam* (1931), 96. The chroniclers of Da Gama's voyages do not agree in their dates. Correa, for example, places the arrival in India in August, 1498. See Mendelssohn, *South African Bibliography* (1910), I, 384, for the reference to *The Three Voyages of Vasco da Gama, and his Viceroyalty from the Lendas da India of Gaspar Correa.* Translated by H. E. T. Stanley (1869).

was soon reduced; Funchal was a simple bishopric again in 1551, and twenty years later itself a suffragan of Lisbon. Franciscans were also the first to work in the Azores (from 1431) and the Cape Verde Islands (1456). The Madeiras and Azores were without inhabitants, and the Cape Verde Islands may have been, before European colonization.[1]

As early as 1462 a missionary Prefect for Guinea was appointed by Pius II. He was a Portuguese Franciscan who had been active in the conversion of the Canaries, Alphonso of Bolano.[2] There was little progress, however, to report upon the Guinea coast. The Negro chiefs, it is true, were dazzled by the power and magnificence of their Portuguese visitors and inclined to view their religion favourably in this reflected light, but the motive of conversion in such cases was unequal to producing in the convert any change of life. There was occasional rivalry with Islam, for the Portuguese made contact with vassals of Mali in Senegambia. Indeed they visited Mali itself. In 1483 an embassy set out from Elmina for the interior and visited the Mandingo capital.[3] It was in Senegambia that Diogo Gomez, one of Prince Henry's captains, about 1457 met the Negro chief Nomimansa before whom Gomez and a Muslim sheikh discussed Christianity and Islam. The chief declared himself for Christianity, took the name of Henry and asked for baptism, which Gomez as a layman declined to give. A missionary is said to have been sent later to instruct the chief.[4] In Senegambia also, a generation later, a chief of the Negro Wolof, Behemoi, sought alliance with the Portuguese, but was told that conversion was an indispensable condition. Feeling he could not comply during the civil war and so alienate his supporters, he delayed and was defeated. He escaped to safety and reached Lisbon where a great welcome awaited him. After instruction he and his twenty-five companions received baptism in 1489. He was knighted by the king the following day. On his return Dominicans accompanied him to work for the conversion of his people, but he is said to have expelled them later. One account speaks of the fiery-tempered Portuguese commander stabbing him to death on charge of treason. This would seal the fate of any mission.[5] In Sierra Leone Portuguese Jesuits were active from the latter part of the sixteenth[6] century. At the beginning of the

---

[1] Schmidlin, op. cit., 241; Cath. Ency. III, 243-4; VI, 318, 603; K. S. Latourette, op. cit., III, 242. [2] Schmidlin, op. cit., 242.
[3] H. Labouret in Ency. Islam, III, 203b, where the record of the journey is quoted. [4] R. H. Major, op. cit., 174-7.
[5] R. H. Major, op. cit., 215-17; Schmidlin, op. cit., 242.
[6] (Correcting H. C. Luke); cf. F. W. Butt-Thompson, Sierra Leone (1926), 26-7.

seventeenth century the Jesuit Father Barrerius won over the king of Sierra Leone who was "wonderful desirous of Baptisme". He agreed to surrender all wives but one, though the one he chose as wife declined to be baptized. He was named Philip, after Philip III of Spain. His sons and many people were also converted. He is reported to have made good progress as a Christian. In the latter part of the seventeenth century Andalusian friars worked in Sierra Leone with some success but later left the field.[1] At the other end of the Guinea Coast lay the kingdom of Benin. About 1485 a request from the king for missionaries reached Portugal; his real desire seems to have been for Portuguese armed help rather than for Christianity. The mission was naturally unsuccessful. Nevertheless, a king of Benin is said to have been baptized in 1491. A century later Father Barrerius the Jesuit baptized a king of Benin who, when at first refused, had threatened to turn Muslim. About 1655 Spanish friars visited Benin, baptized the king, and were having encouraging success, when the Portuguese compelled them to withdraw. The vicar general of San Thomé is even said to have imprisoned the Spanish prefect apostolic, so bitter was the feeling between Portuguese and Spanish at the time.[2] It is perhaps not without significance that out of more than fifty of the famous Benin bronzes and ivory carvings that have survived, dating for the most part from the sixteenth century, the great majority are representations of Portuguese warriors. This is tangible evidence of the aspect of the newcomers that most impressed the Negro mind.[3]

Of the kingdom of Congo a different story has to be told. There was a response more encouraging than any met elsewhere in Western Africa; yet the Christian mission had a chequered career, and its work finally faded out. Here the Portuguese first met a Bantu people. When Diogo Cam had reached the estuary of the Congo in 1484 he took back to Portugal some of the natives of the country, leaving Portuguese as surety for their safe return. They were soon sufficiently proficient in Portuguese to be instructed in Christianity in Portugal. In 1485 they were sent back with Diogo Cam[4] by John II with presents for the king of Congo. The king made a request for

[1] H. C. Luke, *A Bibliography of Sierra Leone* (1925), 52, 54; Schmidlin *op. cit.*, 281, 469.

[2] R. H. Major, *op. cit.*, 211; Schmidlin, *op. cit.*, 242, 282, 470.

[3] J. E. Lips, *The Savage Hits Back* (1937), 93.

[4] On 1485 as the date of his return, deduced from a Portuguese inscription at Matadi, see H. H. Johnston, *The Colonization of Africa* (1913), 80, n. 3.

missionaries from Portugal, and a priest was left behind to instruct king and people. Diogo Cam by his fair dealing won the esteem of the Negroes, quickly sensitive to character, and his name was remembered to the nineteenth century.[1] The answer to the king's request was the arrival of the first missionary party in 1491. The composition of this first party is not certain. It seems to have consisted of both Franciscans and Canons of St. John the Evangelist.[2] The missionaries baptized the chief of Sonyo, the village where Diogo Cam had first landed, and then proceeded to the king's town, Mbanza Kongo, where they were graciously received. The king and his wife were duly baptized and took the names of John and Eleonora after the King and Queen of Portugal. The king's eldest son was also baptized with the name of Alphonso, that of the Portuguese Infante. The capital was re-named San Salvador and a church erected. Alphonso gave every evidence of the sincerity of his conversion; the king was not so stable. His second son, Mpanzu, remained pagan and headed the party of reaction. The Christian opposition to polygamy was much resented (the women whom the king had dismissed were not silent), and devoted adherents of the old religion were much displeased. The king relapsed, Alphonso was banished, and the mission left without countenance or support. Mpanzu had triumphed. But his triumph was limited. On the king's death there was a trial of strength between Alphonso and Mpanzu.[3] Pigafetta, reporting the account of the Portuguese Lopez, supplied a vivid narrative of the conflict in which a sign like that of Constantine, a solar halo with five flaming swords, appeared and greatly enheartened the Christian side.[4] But whatever the embroidery with which legend has adorned the story, the fact remains that Alphonso

[1] "The natives still preserve the memory of his name; one of the king's counsellors told us, a year or two ago, that the first white man to reach their country was Ndo Dioko Kam (i.e. Dom Diogo Cam)."—W. H. Bentley, *Pioneering on the Congo* (1900), I, 19, n.

[2] So Van Wing, *Études Bakongo* (1921), 36 and n. 2, who reports ten Franciscans. Cf. Hildebrand, *Le Martyr Georges de Geel et les débuts de la Mission du Congo, 1645–1652* (1940), 70. The claim that Dominicans were the pioneers cannot stand; they arrived with the second party in 1511—Van Wing, *op. cit.*, 36–7; Schmidlin, *op. cit.*, 277, and n. 2. Cf. K. S. Latourette, *op. cit.*, III, 242; Du Plessis, *Evangelisation of Pagan Africa* (n.d.), 16, n.; J. Cuvelier *op. cit.* 272.

[3] The length of the period between the King's baptism in 1491 and his death is uncertain. Bentley places his death "shortly after" in 1492, *op. cit.*, I, 26; Van Wing in 1500, *op. cit.*, 36; Schmidlin puts it as late as 1507, *op. cit.*, 277.

[4] F. Pigafetta, *History of the Kingdom of Congo*, Rome, 1591 (trans. Hutchinson, 1881), 82. Lopez' reports are stamped as unreliable; cf. Schmidlin, *op. cit.*, 275.

succeeded to the chieftainship and did so as a Christian. His reign was long and throughout he remained a loyal disciple. He gave active support to the mission and asked for more missionaries; fresh parties arrived from time to time.[1] He himself was reputed to be an effective preacher. He is said to have learned Portuguese and to have studied Portuguese law, which he did with an independent mind. He sent his son and other youths of rank to be educated in Lisbon, a number for the priesthood. In 1513 he sent a legation to wait upon the Pope at Rome. His son Henry, who had been educated in Lisbon and ordained to the priesthood, was in 1518 given episcopal rank as titular bishop of Utica, the first Negro to receive the high dignity. He was appointed by Leo X Vicar Apostolic of Congo, with residence at San Salvador. How he fared is uncertain.[2] Despite the energetic support given by Alphonso to the Christian cause, there is little evidence of radical change among the population. In externals, however, a veritable Portuguese mantle had been thrown over dusky society. Portuguese names were liberally bestowed; the chief became king with his secretary of state producing public documents in current European style, and an imitation of the feudal system even seems to have appeared with dukes and lords. In the reign of Alvaro II (1574–1614), a sable "marquis" was sent as special ambassador to the papal court.[3] That there were Negro clergy is implied by the sending of candidates to Lisbon to be trained for the priesthood, but that they and others failed to live up to their high responsibilities is clear. With the establishment in 1534 of a bishopric at San Thomé and the subordination of Congo to it, the bishop attempted reform but was refused obedience. By the middle of the sixteenth century the Jesuits had arrived, the first party consisting of three priests and a brother. They are said to have had 5,000 baptisms in three months. A generation later a Jesuit who came to Congo at the king's request baptized 1,500, and a second four years later, 1,000. This last is said to have found many Christian villages.[4] There is some reason, however, to suspect the continuance of much Congo custom under a fair exterior of outward compliance. Emil Torday, who has examined

Note

---

[1] Van Wing reports three such occasions, in 1505, 1511 and 1521, respectively.—_Op. cit._, 36–7.

[2] He is said to have died before quitting Europe (_Cath. Ency._ IV, 234); to have died after reaching Congo on the way from the coast to San Salvador (Pigafetta, _op. cit._, 91); and to have reached San Salvador and been kept there virtually as a prisoner by his father for safety's sake (Schmidlin, _op. cit._, 278, n. 5). Cf. Van Wing, _op. cit._, 37–8.

[3] _Cath. Ency._, IV, 235.   [4] Schmidlin, _op. cit._, 278.

the influence of the kingdom of Congo on the Bushongo of Central Africa, is critical of contemporary reports. There was opposition to Portuguese domination and hostility to "the friends of the slavers".[1] In the sixteenth century Franciscans and Carmelites sent missionaries to the Congo. In the seventeenth, the Capuchins appeared; they were mostly Italian by nationality, and were sent at the request of Paul V. They were reinforced on at least five occasions during the century by parties from five to forty-five in strength. One of the missionaries, Father G. Antonio Cavazzi, wrote an account of his observations and experiences that is one of our authorities.[2]

South of the kingdom of Congo lay the territory of Angola (a fraction of the Portuguese colony of to-day), the chief of which was a vassal of the king of Congo. It seems certain that some Christian influence had percolated into the country from the north, but no progress was made until Portuguese settlement in the sixteenth century. Jesuits are said to have accompanied an expedition of 1560, but accomplished nothing. The effective entry was made in 1574; ten years later the chief was a convert and many of his subjects had been baptized. There were restive elements, however, in the country and these attacked the Portuguese whose commander, Paulo Diaz (grandson of Bartholomew who reached the Cape), took up the challenge. By the end of the century Portuguese authority was secure. Diaz founded San Paulo de Loanda where a cathedral was built. Angola was made an episcopal see in 1596. In the course of the seventeenth century the centre of gravity moved from San Salvador to Loanda. In this century the Jesuits were active in Angola; they established a monastery, as did three other orders.[3]

The mission in Congo was the first considerable Christian mission in Africa since the days of the early Church, and the first at any time south of the Sahara with any continuity of history. Yet it has disappeared. It was not overwhelmed by Islam. It seems just to have faded out. Holman Bentley describes what he and others found on his arrival on the Congo:

[1] Emil Torday in *Africa*, I (1928), 163. "Under the ever vigilant eyes of the Portuguese, Alvaro II was forced to cloak with pseudo-European appearances the true Kongo custom which must have prevailed at his court, and consequently it was hidden to the travellers and missionaries whose records we possess."

[2] Schmidlin, *op. cit.*, 279–80, K. S. Latourette, *op. cit.*, III, 243; *Cath. Ency.*, III, 324, 468.

[3] Schmidlin, *op. cit.*, 280–1; H. H. Johnston, *Colonization of Africa* (1913), 89–90. For Capuchins on the Congo see *Aequatoria*, 1948 (No. 4), 128–31.

"When we reached San Salvador in 1879, it was to all intents and purposes a heathen land. King and people were wholly given to fetishism and all the superstitions and cruelties of the Dark Continent. Some of the ruined walls of the cathedral remained, the chancel arch and part of a Lady Chapel. The sad relics of a failure." A large crucifix and some images of saints were in possession of the chief, and were paraded round the town in time of drought. Some old people were called *minkwikizi* (believers), but only functioned at great funerals with relics of Christian rites. The common charm for hunting was a *santu* (from *santa cruz*), a flat wooden cross, which lost its power if the owner were guilty of any immorality. Old crucifixes were found among the insignia of some chiefs and also an occasional Portuguese missal. Once or twice came evidence of a trickling tradition of Christian teaching: "When we were holding our services at San Salvador on two occasions after the sermon, have people, visitors to the town, risen to urge the people to listen to the teaching, and to receive it; for old relatives had told them long before of a Saviour who died for us and now the same story was brought to them again by us."[1] David Livingstone had evidence of the decay in Angola when on his famous journey to Loanda in 1854. Speaking of the capital itself, he wrote: "There are various evidences of its former magnificence, especially two cathedrals, one of which, once a Jesuit college, is now converted into a workshop, and in passing the other we saw with sorrow a number of oxen feeding within its stately walls." At Massangano he found two churches and a hospital in ruins, and the remains of two convents, one reputed a Benedictine establishment. He pays tribute to the service of the Jesuits to the country in introducing coffee plantations and many varieties of foreign fruit trees, and for their faithful teaching. "All speak well", he says, "of the Jesuits and other missionaries, as the Capuchins, etc., for having attended diligently to the instruction of the children. They were supposed to have a tendency to take the part of the people against the Government, and were supplanted by priests, concerning whom no regret is expressed that they were allowed to die out."[2]

[1] W. H. Bentley, *op. cit.*, I, 35–6. Illustrations of ruins and crucifixes are given in Bentley, *loc. cit.*, and in H. H. Johnston, *George Grenfell and the Congo*, I, 71–3.
[2] Livingstone, *Missionary Travels and Researches in South Africa* (1857), 394, 401–2, 405, 410–11.

(4) Missions in Eastern Africa.

The Portuguese made no settlement at the Cape. In South-East Africa, however, there was commercial attraction, for here was gold. But first the sea route to India' was to be made secure. The Arabs on the coast did not relish the coming of European rivals to win the wealth of oriental trade. In 1500 a fleet commanded by Cabral left Portugal for India. The king's instructions were that peace and friendship were to be offered to those prepared to become Christian and engage in commerce. Eight Franciscans went as missionaries; and there were also chaplains for the fleet.[1] Before Cabral's return to Lisbon the following year another expedition sailed; at Mossel Bay in South Africa, a watering-place for the ships, this commander had erected a small stone chapel dedicated to Saint Bras. This was the first Christian place of worship in South Africa.[2] In 1502 Vasco da Gama, now Admiral of the Eastern Seas, led an expedition on which tribute from the Arab colony of Kilwa was obtained, the first from any eastern state. The king devoted it to the service of religion.[3] Year by year expedition followed expedition. In 1505 it was decided to establish forts to secure the trade route—on the African coast, at Kilwa and Sofala. Kilwa was easily taken and then "the Franciscan friars in the fleet landed and set up a cross, before which the canticle *Te Deum Laudamus* was chanted, and when this was completed the place was given up to plunder".[4] For these were Muslims. The background of the Muslim occupation of Portugal must be remembered. At Kilwa was built the first Portuguese fort beyond Angola. In a month the fleet was at Mombasa which was taken with difficulty. The commander, Francisco d'Almeida, showed a clemency in the hour of victory unusual in that day. Of the thousand or so captives taken he set four-fifths at liberty—strange magnanimity when dealing with a Muslim foe! At Malindi the Portuguese were welcomed; Mombasa had been Malindi's rival. In the same year Sofala to the south was occupied without a fight. The fate of Kilwa and Mombasa induced the Muslims there to show the better part of valour. This was not a colony like the others, for they themselves were only tenants of a Bantu chief. They may have regarded the climate as their most powerful ally, for so it proved.[5] In 1509 a decisive naval engagement was fought in the Indian Ocean

[1] G. M. Theal, *History and Ethnography of South Africa before 1795*, I, 229–33. [2] *Ibid.*, 236. [3] *Ibid.*, 239. [4] *Ibid.*, 246. [5] *Ibid.*, 250–1, 265.

with a fleet under the flag of the Egyptian Sultan; the Portuguese were victors and for a century held unchallenged command of the eastern seas. India was now far more important than eastern Africa, and when in 1510 Goa was made the head of a viceroyalty, of the four great governments which it comprised the eastern coast of Africa was one.

Behind Sofala, on the coast south of the Zambezi, lay the tribe of the Makalanga, the Bantu people with whom the Portuguese were brought into contact in East Africa. The Mashona of Southern Rhodesia to-day are descended from them.[1] Their paramount chief was known by the title *monomotapa*.[2] Legend had enlarged his kingdom beyond all reasonable bounds. An Italian map of Africa of 1623 shows the great bulk of Africa south of the Zambezi as *Monomotapae Imperium*.[3] This kingdom was a magnet to the Portuguese; its trade in gold passed through Sofala. It was at this point in East Africa that the pioneer missionary effort was made.

The Society of Jesus was the Order that first came. The year was 1560, twenty years after its foundation and eight after Francis Xavier's death. Xavier had traversed the east coast in 1541 on his journey to the East, but had made no contact with pagan African or Muslim Arab, preaching only to Christian Portuguese. A discussion with Muslims in Malindi was the one exception.[4] The pioneer was Father Gonçalo da Silveira. He belonged to a noble family of Portugal and had been sent to Goa in 1556. Three years later a request came from South-East Africa asking for missionaries.[5] In 1560 Father Silveira and two priests landed at Sofala. The letters they sent back to Goa are extant.[6] Moving inland, they made contact with a chief in the neighbourhood of Inhambane. He seems to have been flattered by the attention of the powerful Portuguese, and readily consented to conversion. Many of his tribe were con-

[1] C. Bullock, *The Mashona* (1927), 17–19. The ruins of stone buildings at Zimbabwe, and numerous others less famous and imposing, lie within their territory. The most recent research supports the claim of Bantu origin and medieval date for these buildings.—Caton-Thompson, *Zimbabwe Culture* (1931), 194–9. When the Portuguese arrived the kingdom of Monomotapa was in a decline, and its invasion by other Bantu tribes added to the confusion of the period.

[2] The meaning of the title is disputed, but is probably "chief of the mountain" —Prestage in *Cambridge History of the British Empire*, VIII (1936), 90. The name is also used for the kingdom, and is then capitalized in the text.

[3] The map, which is in the archives of the Vatican, is reproduced in facsimile in A. Wilmot, *Monomotapa* (1896), 2.

[4] Schmidlin, *op. cit.*, 283.

[5] G. M. Theal, *op. cit.*, I, 306.   [6] Wilmot, *op. cit.*, 162, n.

verted with him. Father Silveira wrote jubilantly to Goa:
"Thanks be to God and to the Holy Virgin, the Queen of Tongue
as well as the king's sons and daughters, his household court and
relations—in a word, all the subjects of that kingdom are now
Christians. . . . On my way from Tongue to the spot where I
was to sail for Mozambique I have baptized many chiefs or
little kings. Those of Tongue are Mocarangas."[1] Some 400
persons are said to have received baptism in this brief period.
The king received the name Constantino and his principal wife
Isabel.[2] But the country of Monomotapa was the objective. In
September 1560 Silveira left Mozambique with his companions
and after a perilous journey reached Sena, a Portuguese post on
the Zambezi. Here he found some "ten or fifteen Portuguese
and some Indians already Christians". The Portuguese had
deteriorated sadly. Silveira spent his interval of waiting in
seeking to restore a moral tone; he also baptized some 500 Bantu,
mostly dependants of the Portuguese.[3] At length permission to
proceed to the *monomotapa* was received. Silveira reached the
capital on Christmas Day. The king sent the customary gifts to
a distinguished stranger—money, servants and cattle—and
inquired what gold and land and women he wanted. Silveira's
declining them provoked the remark: "This man is not as others
who come with much toil by sea and land to seek for treasures."
Silveira presented the king with a statue of the Virgin, whom
the king then saw in his dreams enthroned in light. He and his
mother desired baptism, and after instructing them and a
number at the court, Silveira baptized them. The king took the
name Sebastian and his mother Mary. The Muslims at the
capital were dismayed at the turn of events. They told the king
Silveira was an arch-enchanter and that the ceremony of
baptism was part of his enchantment. He was in reality a spy
of the Viceroy of India. The plot succeeded. It was decided that
Silveira's life must be taken. He became aware of his impending
fate. Antonio Caiado, a Portuguese adventurer at the royal
kraal ranking as a king's counsellor, warned him, but Silveira
answered: "I know well that the king has determined to put
me to death, but I am ready when it shall please God to give my
life and my blood for His service." He refused to leave, and
waited with calmness for the end. "I am more ready to receive
death than my enemies are to give it to me", he said later to
Caiado; "I pardon willingly the king and his mother, for they

[1] Wilmot, *op. cit.*, 164.　　　　[2] G. M. Theal, *op. cit.*, I, 308–9.
[3] Wilmot, *op. cit.*, 168–9; G. M. Theal, *op. cit.*, I, 309.

are seduced by the Muslims". Later he was strangled while
lying tranquilly asleep. It was March 16, 1561, when the proto-
martyr of South Africa sealed his witness with his blood.[1] So
ended the Jesuit mission of the sixteenth century to South-
East Africa, leaving no trace of Christian influence.

The murder of Silveira was a challenging affront to Portuguese prestige. An expedition to retrieve it arrived in 1570
under Francisco Barreto. After many vicissitudes they reached
the *monomotapa* and secured a treaty.[2] But the force was decimated in malaria-ridden country and the horses sickened with
tsetse poison. Barreto met and conquered human obstacles,
but was beaten by disease.[3] Samuel Purchas puts it quaintly:
"The Benomotapa fearing the Portugals forces, offered reasonable conditions, which Barretto refusing, was discomfited, not
by the Negro, but by the Ayre, the malignity whereof (the
sowre sauce of all these Golden Countryes in Africa) consumed
his people."[4] The Jesuits did not at once return to the field.

A second mission was attempted, this time by the Order of
Preachers. In 1577 two Dominicans were settled at Mozambique.
The work extended and soon reached to Sofala, Sena and Tete.
The missionaries both cared for the spiritual welfare of the
Portuguese and worked for the conversion of the Bantu. Their
African converts, however, were among those already in the
service of the Portuguese. In 1586 Dos Santos was sent by the
Order to Sofala. He resided there for three and a half years and
during that period baptized some 1,700 persons, mostly Bantu.
He wrote a valuable eyewitness account of the country and the
mission. The Dominican hero of South-East Africa is Friar
Nicolau do Rosario. He was shipwrecked on the African coast,
and posted by Dos Santos to Tete on the Zambezi. He was

[1] G. M. Theal, *op. cit.*, I, 310–12; A. Wilmot, *op. cit.*, 170–4. A translation
of the account of the martyrdom of Father Silveira, from the folio edition in
the Vatican of the History of the Society of Jesus, is given in Wilmot,
Appendix C. Dr. Ricards has identified the place of the martyrdom as Zumbi,
some 600 miles from the Zambezi mouth.—Mendelssohn, *South African
Bibliography* (1910), I, xxxi, n.

[2] Barreto stated three conditions: the expulsion of the Muslims, the admission of Christian missionaries, and a cession of gold mines. While the *monomotapa* nominally accepted these, he probably had no intention, as Theal
remarks, of carrying out the first and last.—G. M. Theal, *op. cit.* I, 331.

[3] Livingstone pointed out that Barreto passed through a district abounding
in tsetse, and what he thought was poison administered to his horses by the
natives was in reality the tsetse fly.—*The Zambesi and its Tributaries* (1865),
3–4.

[4] *Purchas his Pilgrimage, or Relations of the World*, by Samuel Purchas
(folio ed., 1626), 761.

serving as chaplain with a Portuguese force that was helping a friendly tribe when they were ambushed by the enemy. Only Rosario survived, and he as a prisoner. He was bound to a tree and killed with arrows.[1] With the seventeenth century the Dominicans secured many able recruits to the Order. The year 1578 was a tragic one for Portugal, when King Sebastian met his end fighting the Moors in Morocco. In a disputed succession Portugal then fell to the Spanish crown and in 1580 Philip II became her king. For sixty years she lost her independence. Portuguese of rank and ability now sought service increasingly with the Church, and South-East Africa received its share of these capable missionaries. In 1612 ecclesiastical control was removed from the care of the Archbishop of Goa, and a "Prelature Nullius" extending from Cape Guardafui to the Cape of Good Hope was established, with the administrator's headquarters in Mozambique.[2]

The kingdom of Monomotapa now came under the care of the Dominicans. A new ruler, Kapranzine, who was anti-Portuguese, had succeeded to the chieftainship, and the country was soon involved in the turmoil of civil war (1628–31). A near relative of the *monomotapa*, Manuza, had been under Dominican instruction, and with Portuguese help was himself established as *monomotapa*. In the course of the war he was baptized and took the name of Philippe. In one of the critical battles he and his companions believed they saw a cross in the sky which greatly enheartened them. Kapranzine's son and heir was taken prisoner and sent to Goa where he was entrusted to the Dominican fathers.[3] Manuza was succeeded in 1652 by a pagan, which caused the Dominicans deep concern. But he soon sought baptism, and received it in August 1652 as Domingos with his wife Luiza. So great was the satisfaction in Portugal that a special service of thanksgiving was held in Lisbon, and the same was done in Rome by the Father-General of the Order. A painting of the event was made for the Dominican House in Rome.[4] Meanwhile Kapranzine's son, who had been sent to Goa as prisoner of war, had been baptized, entered the Dominican order, and became one of the ablest preachers in the country: "In 1670 the general of the order sent him the diploma of Master in Theology, equivalent to Doctor of Divinity, and this

---

[1] G. M. Theal, *op. cit.*, I, 342–3; Du Plessis, *A History of Christian Missions in South Africa* (1911), 13–14.
[2] The term survives to-day, though it is now limited to Portuguese territory.—*Cath. Ency.*, X, 611.   [3] G. M. Theal, *op. cit.*, I, 457–62.
[4] *Ibid.*, 478, where a reproduction of the picture of the baptism is given.

man, born a barbarian, heir to the most important chieftainship in Southern Africa, died as vicar of the convent of Santa Barbara in Goa. Fiction surely has no stranger story than this."[1] But the fond hopes of consolidation in South-East Africa proved illusory. As the century closed the Dominican work was in a decline; so too was the revived work of the Jesuits in the Zambezi valley.[2]

An instructive report by the Portuguese Jesuit Manuel Barreto, submitted to the viceroy in 1667, enables us to gauge a little the position of Christianity on the lower Zambezi at that time. There were in the country sixteen places of worship, six of which were Jesuit, nine Dominican, and one under a secular priest. Nine of these were in Portuguese territory, five in the kingdom of Monomotapa, and two in Manika. Barreto admits that simony was prevalent, and laments the evil living of the Portuguese. He has, however, ambitions for Christian development that appear inordinate against the existing background—an archbishop at Mozambique, with two or three episcopal coadjutors, and priests in proportion.[3] But no such arrest of the decline was possible. The heyday of both Jesuit and Dominican lay in the past. Few relics of their teaching now remain. Dr. Donald Fraser thought that one trace might be found in the lovely canoe songs of the Zambezi with the theme: "We have no mother but Mary."[4] There are folk-tales still current, so strongly reminiscent of Old Testament narratives that they appear as echoes of them.[5]

The year 1652 in which the *monomotapa* was baptized, an event which caused such joy in Catholic Europe, was the very year in which Jan van Riebeeck with the first Dutch settlers landed at Table Bay. Thus we arrive at the watershed of Roman Catholic effort and Protestant settlement in Southern Africa. But before proceeding to the story of that settlement we must notice the position of the Muslims in the Arab colonies, and the Jesuit attempts to win Abyssinia to the Church of Rome.

In Mombasa and Malindi lying north of Zanzibar, Augustinian missionaries worked from the end of the sixteenth century and reported conversions. Urban VIII sent an interesting letter to one of the converted rulers described as King of Mombasa and Malindi, and greeted as "Son much beloved in Christ", in the

---

[1] G. M. Theal, *op. cit.*, I, 478. Schmidlin, *op. cit.*, 472.
[3] G. M. Theal, *op. cit.*, I, 484–6, cf. 494–6.
[4] E. W. Smith, *The Christian Mission in Africa* (1926), 9, n. I.
[5] J. Torrend, *Bantu Folk-Lore from Northern Rhodesia* (1921), 145.

course of which he says: "The blessed Augustine himself—the bright light of your Africa and the whole Church—makes his voice thrill through your ears by means of the Augustinian missionaries." These conversions, however, proved very unreliable. Converts relapsed to Islam and Christians were massacred. There was no real progress to report in these Muslim settlements.[1]

(5) *The Jesuit Mission in Abyssinia.*

Since in Abyssinia there was already a Christian Church surviving from the early centuries, the Jesuit mission of Portuguese times was not here concerned with the conversion of non-Christians but with securing the adhesion to Rome of the existing Church.

The identification of the fabled Prester John[2] with the King of Abyssinia had led John II of Portugal, when Bartholomew Diaz sailed south in 1487, to attempt contact by the overland route. His envoy was Pedro de Covilham who reached Abyssinia and was well received but not permitted to return to Portugal.[3] In 1520 an embassy from Portugal, travelling via India, reached the country and found de Covilham settled there. The chaplain to the embassy, Francisco·Alvarez, wrote an account of the country and their visit, the first account by a European eyewitness.[4] He gives a valuable account of Christian practice as he found it observed and writes with a spirit of tolerance of those elements the European visitors scarcely found congenial. Thus the shouting and leaping in connexion with worship he admits may be accepted as done to the glory of God, for God may be served in many ways.[5] He gives accounts of services of baptism[6] and ordination[7] he attended. He frankly expressed

---

[1] Schmidlin, *op. cit.*, 285; Wilmot, *op. cit.*, 158–61.

[2] The legend of Prester John, which arose in Europe in the twelfth century, was by the fourteenth connected with Abyssinia. Portuguese explorers along the West African coast returned with stories of a great Christian king in interior Africa that linked up with the Prester John tradition; so that when John II despatched Bartholomew Diaz on the expedition that took him beyond the Cape, the discovery of the kingdom of Prester John was a principal motive.—Jones and Monroe, *op. cit.*, 59–62; R. H. Major, *op. cit.*, 211–12. A sixteenth-century map, assigning vast territory to the kingdom of Prester John, is reproduced in Jones and Monroe, 78.

[3] R. H. Major, *op. cit.*, 212–14.

[4] *Narrative of the Portuguese Embassy to Abyssinia during the years 1520–1527.* By Father Francisco Alvarez. Translated from the Portuguese by Lord Stanley of Alderley (1881). On the various translations of this work, see Budge, *History of Ethiopia*, I, 180, cf. 331.   [5] Alvarez, *op. cit.*, 23–4, 257.

[6] *Ibid.*, 240–44.   [7] *Ibid.*, 246–52.

to the *abuna* (the head of the Abyssinian Church) his amazement at the ordaining of children and even infants in arms as deacons, to which the old man replied that they would learn, and that he was very old and it might be long before his successor could be appointed from Cairo.[1] The Portuguese celebration of the Mass, the Prester thought impressive. The embassy was six years in the country, and finally left in 1526 with letters from Lebna Dengel for the authorities in India and Portugal.[2] An Abyssinian envoy went with them to Portugal, and a Portuguese, Bermudez, remained as hostage. It was Bermudez who took to Portugal the king's pleas for help when hard pressed in the crisis of the Muslim invasion. Bermudez later attempted to get himself installed as *abuna* of Abyssinia but was foiled.[3]

It is said that Ignatius Loyola had himself desired to serve in Abyssinia, but the Pope would not agree. Of three who were appointed later only Andrew de Oviedo with several priests reached the country in 1557, but Galawdewos (Claudius) the king, as a Monophysite, had no intention of surrendering to the control of Rome. Moreover, he had unpleasant memories of Bermudez' claims. Oviedo and his companions could do little more than care for the Catholics they found in the territory. Fremona near Axum was the centre of the mission. For twenty years Oviedo continued and then died at his post.

Pedro Paez, who was sent to Abyssinia in 1589, was captured by pirates on the way from Goa, and served as a galley slave for seven years. In 1596 he was redeemed by the Society, and eventually reached Abyssinia in 1603. He settled at first in the monastery of Fremona near Axum. His linguistic ability was remarkable: he is said to have learned to read, write and speak the ancient Ge'ez within twelve months of arrival and was soon recognized as an eloquent preacher in that language. The linguistic task accomplished, he turned to the educational and started a school at Fremona for both Portuguese and Abyssinian pupils. The opinion Bruce the traveller formed of him was that "he was the most capable and most successful missionary that ever entered Abyssinia".[4] One appraisal of him says: "He was a brilliant linguist and rapidly acquired a thorough knowledge not only of Amharic

---

[1] Alvarez, *op. cit.*, 250–2.   [2] *Ibid.*, 368–74, 389–400.
[3] For material relating to Bermudez, see *The Portuguese Expedition to Abyssinia in 1541–1543, as narrated by Castanhoso* (1902), to which are added some letters that passed between the kings of Portugal and Abyssinia, and Bermudez' own account of events.   [4] Budge, *op. cit.*, II, 377.

but of Ge'ez. He was an able schoolmaster, and he later trained himself to be an expert architect, mason and carpenter. But above all he was a man of great patience and discretion; he never tried to move too fast."[1] When, after a period of civil war, Za Dengel was established on the throne, he received Paez, was convinced by his instruction, and declared himself for Rome and the reform of the Abyssinian Church. Paez was for steady reform, but the king was impetuous and provoked rebellion. The *abuna* took a step said to have had but a single precedent in Abyssinian history, and released the people from their oath of allegiance. In the course of the rebellion Za Dengel lost his life.[2] The next king, Susenyos (Sisinnius, 1607–32), also became a Catholic, as did his brother, Se'ala Krestos.[3] In 1622 the king publicly proclaimed his Roman Catholic faith. The future was full of hope for the Jesuit mission when Paez died. "The king and his subjects", says Wallis Budge, "had to mourn the loss of a true friend, and the wisest counsellor that Europe had sent into the country."[4]

In response to the king's request for a patriarch, the Pope nominated Alphonso Mendez, a Spanish Jesuit. It proved a most unhappy choice. In all ways that Paez had been wise, Mendez was foolish. He is described as overbearing and bigoted. It is enough to list the changes he attempted as soon as he was given power: all priests to be re-ordained, the people to be re-baptized, churches to be re-consecrated and the liturgy to be changed; the king was to swear fealty to him as the papal representative; images were to be introduced into the churches. Hostility to the changes, too deep-seated to be dealt with by royal authority, compelled the king to a drastic step. He withdrew all the reforms of Mendez and then abdicated in favour of his son, Fasiladas (Basilides).[5] He issued a proclamation (as Wallis Budge renders it) to the following effect: "Hearken, Hearken, Hearken. Originally we gave you the Roman Faith believing it to be a good one. But Yolyos, Gabriel, Takla Giyorgis, Sarsa Krestos, and even the ignorant peasants of Lasta have died fighting against it. Now therefore we restore to you the Faith of your ancestors. Let your own people say their mass in their own churches; let the people have their own altars for the Sacrament, and their own Liturgy, and let them

---

[1] Jones and Monroe, *op. cit.*, 93.
[2] Budge, *op. cit.*, II, 378–9.
[3] Ras Se'ala Krestos—The Rasselas of Samuel Johnson's story.
[4] *Op. cit.*, II, 389. [5] *Ibid.*, II, 390–3.

be happy. As for me I am old and worn out with war and sickness, and am no longer capable of governing; I nominate my son Fasiladas to succeed me as king."[1] There followed, from the Roman standpoint, the apostasy of Abyssinia. Fasiladas, always loyal to his father when king, now determined to clear out the Jesuits root and branch, and he acted on his resolution. Mendez and others succeeded in escaping after a series of adventures.[2]

Jerome Lobo, a Jesuit who accompanied Mendez and remained until the expulsion of the Order, has left a narrative that is a valuable contemporary record.[3] In respect of the Church as he found it, he admits that the Abyssinian Christians "notwithstanding their separation from the Roman Church, and the corruptions which have crept into their faith, yet retain in a great measure the devout fervour of the primitive Christians". There are naturally features in their form of the faith of which he is critical, but he finds observances of which to approve: "They have however preserved the belief of our principal mysteries, they celebrate with a great deal of piety, the Passion of our Lord, they reverence the Cross, they pay a great devotion to the Blessed Virgin, the angels, and the Saints. They observe the festivals, and pay a strict regard to the Sunday. Every month they commemorate the Assumption of the Virgin Mary, and are of opinion, that no Christians beside themselves, have a true sense of the greatness of the Mother of God, or pay her the honours that are due to her. . . . Every week they keep a feast to the honour of the Apostles and angels; they come to Mass with great devotion, and love to hear the word of God. They receive the sacrament often, but do not always prepare themselves by confession. . . . The severity of their fasts is equal to that of the Primitive Church: in Lent they never eat till after sunset." Lobo found less acceptable the energetic and tumultuous expression of the congregation in public worship: "No country in the world is so full of churches, monasteries and ecclesiastics as Abyssinia; it is not possible to sing in one church or monastery without being heard by another, and perhaps by several. They sing the Psalms of David of which as well as the other parts of the Holy Scriptures, they have a very exact translation in their own language.

[1] Budge, op. cit., II, 393. [2] Ibid., II, 399–401.
[3] Lobo wrote his narrative in Portuguese, but apparently only a French translation was published (Paris, 1728). Dr. Johnson produced an abridgment of this in English under the title A Voyage to Abyssinia, by Father Jerome Lobo (1735).

. . . The instruments of musick made use of in their rites of worship, are little drums, which they hang about their necks, and beat with both hands. . . . They begin their consort by stamping their feet on the ground, and playing gently on their instruments, but when they have heated themselves by degrees, they leave off drumming and fall to leaping, dancing, and clapping their hands, at the same time straining their voices to their utmost pitch, till at length they have no regard either to the tune, or the pauses, and seem rather a riotous, than a religious assembly. For this manner of worship they cite the Psalm of David, 'O clap your hands all ye nations'. Thus they misapply the sacred Writings, to defend practices, yet more corrupt than those I have been speaking of.''[1]

Rome made one further attempt with a mission of six Capuchin friars; two entering by Mogadishu and two by Massawa were all killed; the remaining two gave up the attempt. Three other Capuchins tried to enter by Massawa, but all were taken and put to death. The Muslim Turks who controlled the Red Sea coast willingly acceded to the request of Fasiladas to let no priest pass alive. The net result of the Jesuit mission was to render the Abyssinians bitterly hostile to the Roman Catholic Church, and this attitude lasted long.[2]

We have reviewed the attempt to renew the Christian enterprise at the dawn of the modern period. It had no permanent success. On the Guinea coast results were too spasmodic. In the Congo and Angola an early prosperity proved deceptive. In East Africa the one bright hope of Monomotapa faded out. Among the missionaries engaged upon the task were many of the highest personal devotion. Moreover, the Church of Rome had the field to herself; there was little rivalry in the missionary enterprise, save as the various monastic orders and the secular clergy might show it to one another. The African attitude to the newcomers was friendly when the initial Portuguese contact had been made by a tactful and wise commander. All the advantage of prestige attaching to Europeans on their first arrival by sea was theirs; the Portuguese represented a stage of culture and civilization new to the Guinea Coast and Central Africa at least, and Africans were alert enough to appreciate it. True, the very fact of the influence of prestige suggestion

[1] Lobo, op. cit., 45–6, 59–60, 61–2.
[2] Budge, op. cit., II, 401–2; Schmidlin, op. cit., 287; Jones and Monroe, op. cit., 88–101.

might lead to conversion from mixed motives, but that is often the beginning, from which the Church has had to develop a purer and a stronger faith. In this case she did not. The failure has occasioned deep concern, as well it might.

An adequate analysis of the situation displaying all the influences at work cannot be attempted here, but the following major factors are worthy of attention. The first contact was made with the rulers of the people, chiefs and petty kings. This was entirely natural in the circumstances, for these were independent chiefdoms. But the motive of self-interest was bound to play a leading part, and we have evidence it did. The offer by the king of Portugal of his alliance on condition of conversion tied up the Christian mission from the start with questions of political advantage. But the missionaries on their side demanded monogamy which was difficult to concede, for the chief as a polygamist was deeply involved in the prevailing social system. Further, his approach to his ancestors was regarded by his people as necessary for communal security. When therefore the motive for conversion was political, there would be little likelihood of a change in the way of life. Sons of chiefs in particular received the advantages of education; some were sent to Portugal, others were the special care of missionaries on the spot. Here again there were deep-seated, political implications, for the missionaries were prepared to go to great lengths to secure the chieftainship for an heir whom they had trained. The friar Manuel Sardinha, for example, is said to have raised an army of 20,000 men from tribes hostile to the Makalanga and so opposed to the ruling *monomotapa*, with which the cause of the Dominican-trained Manuza was carried to success.[1] Any expansion of Christianity due to its identification with a particular political regime is likely to be temporary only and to wane with the regime. It was so in these Portuguese territories; when Portuguese power faded, Christianity faded too. While many circumstances in both cases are in sharp contrast, one is reminded nevertheless of the superficial Christian expansion among the Berbers in Byzantine times, with as rapid a withering before the Arab blast. In neither case were the roots of the Christian Church set deep in native soil.

A second factor of major importance was the practice of mass baptisms. These were inevitably carried through with no adequate instruction. The ease with which consent was given

[1] G. M. Theal, *op. cit.*, I, 461.

aroused no misgiving in the missionary's mind.[1] Those who had lightly taken the Christian name would as lightly discard it when danger threatened or discipline was strict. In 1581, for example, a Jesuit who came to the Congo baptized 1,500 persons, but the converts thus secured could tell nothing more about their baptism than that they had eaten salt.[2] The Jesuits who had resumed work on the Zambezi reported there was no difficulty in getting people to call themselves Christians, but to abandon polygamy or observe the ordinances of the Church was quite another matter,[3] Mesnage refers to these same territories in West and East Africa when passing strictures on the baptism of large numbers without adequate instruction, a practice that fills the church with "demi-Christians" who disappear as soon as trouble assails.[4] The Jesuits, it is true, with their customary efficiency gave attention to education, but this was not broadly based in the local language and in practice was therefore restricted to the intelligent minority who could profit by it. Thus the teaching members of the second Jesuit mission to the Congo and Angola (1623–69) offered Latin for the sons of Portuguese and the more intelligent African youth, and also some instruction in the Portuguese language. There was indeed singing in the Congo vernacular, and children were organized into choirs for the purpose. But an educational programme in the language of the people far more comprehensive than this was demanded for the securing of an instructed Christian community with reasonable chance of survival in days of testing.[5]

The necessity of an instructed membership for stability of faith raises the question of Christian literature in the language of the people. Latin was in use for the liturgy, and the Scriptures remained entirely untranslated. Not that there were no gifted language students among the missionaries. The Jesuit Father Cardozo produced in Lisbon in 1624 the first manual of religious instruction to appear in a Congo vernacular. He also prepared a little book of prayers in Kimbundu, a language of Angola.[6] Father Giacinto Brusciotto published at Rome in 1650 and later works on the Congo language.[7] The Jesuits

---

[1] G. M. Theal points out how Bantu courtesy might prompt an expression of agreement without in the least implying a change of creed. *Op. cit.*, I, 308–9.
[2] Van Wing, *op. cit.*, 40; Schmidlin, *op. cit.*, 279 and n. 8.
[3] G. M. Theal, *op. cit.*, I, 494.
[4] Mesnage, *Le Christianisme en Afrique*, II (*Déclin*), 283.
[5] Van Wing, *op. cit.*, 50.   [6] *Ibid.*, 48 and n. 1, 2.
[7] H. H. Johnston, *George Grenfell and the Congo*, I, 74; J. R. Hildebrand, *op. cit.*, 261–3.

Father Pacconio and Father Dias, who both studied Kimbundu produced, the former a catechism in 1642, and the latter in 1697 a small grammar of the language.[1] These were meagre contributions, however, to appear in the second century of effort. Without the regular use of the vernacular in worship and the translation of the Scriptures, the ritual of the Church became liable all too easily to misinterpretation against a pagan background. A piece of evidence on this point, as decisive as one could hope to get, is supplied by David Livingstone. When in Loanda in 1854 he had wanted to show his faithful Makololo from the Zambezi a place of Christian worship: "But here the frequent genuflexions, changing of positions, burning of incense, with the priests' backs turned to the people, the laughing, talking and manifest irreverence of the singers, with firing of guns, etc., did not convey to the minds of my men the idea of adoration. I overheard them, in talking to each other, remark that 'they had seen the white men charming their demons'; a phrase identical with one they had used when seeing the Balonda beating drums before their idols."[2]

Inadequate pastoral oversight was a further weakness. It is true that the admission of Africans to the priesthood was not delayed; but it was a heavy burden that was placed upon them. A number of both Africans and Asiatics were admitted to the Dominican Order, apparently under the impression that their influence would be more effective than that of Europeans over their own people. Asiatics, Eurasians and Africans were thus found in the ranks of the Dominicans in South-East Africa, but they proved unequal to the spiritual demands of the missionary situation. Such co-workers may render excellent service even at the earliest stage under the direction of those whose long Christian nurture has equipped them for such a task, whereas the African convert is at first too near his own past to have the full responsibility of spiritual direction handed over to him. There are, of course, always brilliant exceptions.[3] In con- nexion with the inadequacy of the staff for Christian instruc- tion and pastoral care, the absence of women missionaries was notable. Women missionaries can best serve women, who are the mothers and as such the most effective teachers of the next generation. Father Barroso of San Salvador, later Bishop of Mozambique, has called attention to this and cites it as

---

[1] H. C. Withey, "The Kimbundu Language of Angola" in *M.R.W.*, XIV (1901), 282–3.   [2] Livingstone, *Missionary Travels in South Africa*, 392.
[3] K. S. Latourette, *op. cit.*, III, 243; G. M. Theal, *op. cit.*, I, 464, 496.

a principal cause of what he terms the disaster in the Congo.[1]

The trader follows the missionary pioneer. Portuguese who followed the Christian teachers to the Congo did not commend the faith that had been preached. The Abbé Proyart, who was on the Congo in 1776, speaks of the duty of a Christian prince who favours missionaries, not to send on their track "a set of men who have nothing of the Christian but the name, which they dishonour and whose worse than heathenish conduct makes the idolaters doubt whether the gods whom they worship be not preferable to that of the Christian religion."[2] In the lands of the lower Zambezi prazos or great estates were developed by many Portuguese, almost on feudal lines; their owners, practising cruelty and oppression and indulging selfish passions, were so little an example to an African Christian community that the Jesuit, Father Manuel Barreto, feared the wrath of the Almighty would be poured out on them for their sins.[3]

The active pursuit of the slave-trade accompanied the Christian mission and was not thought amiss. Indeed, the very mission possessed slaves of its own; a Jesuit monastery at Loanda was endowed with 12,000.[4] When the slave-trade was developed between Angola and Brazil, the bishop of Loanda, on a chair of stone by the quayside, bestowed his episcopal blessing on the departing cargoes, promising them future felicity when the stormy trials of life were over.[5] Father Barroso was a spokesman for those who later acutely felt the shame of it, and saw in the condonation of the traffic a major cause of ultimate missionary failure.[6] It was destined, however, to grow to yet more alarming proportions and to cast its deadly blight on Africa far from the white man's actual settlements before the Christian conscience was aroused.

This leads us to the next scene in the African missionary drama.

[1] In a paper read before the Lisbon Geographical Society, 1889, and reported by W. H. Bentley, op. cit., I, 39-40.
[2] Quoted by W. H. Bentley, op. cit., I, 37, from Pinkerton's Voyages, xvi, 563.
[3] G. M. Theal, op. cit., I, 485.
[4] J. Richter, Geschichte der evangelischen Mission in Afrika (1922), 8.
[5] Ibid., 8-9.
[6] W. H. Bentley, op. cit., I, 37-9.

CHAPTER 8

A PERIOD OF PAUSE
SEVENTEENTH AND EIGHTEENTH CENTURIES

BEGINNING with the great age of maritime discovery and the arrival of the Portuguese in Africa, the fortunes of that continent have been increasingly bound up with the fortunes of Europe. The clue to happenings in the one continent is to be found in developments in the other. There were events in Europe in the sixteenth century that produced marked repercussions on Africa in the seventeenth. The Reformation with the rise of Protestant powers in Northern Europe in opposition to the Roman Catholic empires of Spain and Portugal not only revolutionized political relations in Europe itself, but transformed the situation overseas. Africa did not escape.

Pope Alexander VI had generously apportioned all newly discovered lands between Spain and Portugal. He had indeed been called in to arbitrate to avoid any unworthy rivalry between two loyal Roman Catholic powers who had been the pioneers in geographical discovery. According to the final decision accepted in the Treaty of Tordesillas (1494), a meridian 370 leagues west of the Cape Verde Islands was to be the boundary. This line reserved the whole of the African territories to Portugal and gave her Brazil in South America, while Spain retained the rest of the Americas, but secured the Philippines as a foothold in the East opened up by Portugal.[1] It was scarcely to be expected that Protestant powers would respect the papal ruling when they were able to contest it. But to do so they must be seafaring peoples. The English and the Dutch were Protestant powers of growing repute with sturdy, seafaring stock, and they became the chief contestants. This produced a change of scene in Africa that for the next two centuries became the setting for missionary activity. Overshadowing all there loomed the grim spectre of the slave-trade, with ever-increasing menace to the African people. Missionary effort became so weak as almost to disappear. By the merest margin of activity the tenuous thread of its existence was preserved.

[1] Prestage in *Cambridge Medieval History*, VIII (1936), 524–5; cf. 493. The fact that the Pope had issued several bulls at different times on this matter seems to be responsible for the varying definitions of the line quoted by historians. Cf. R. H. Major, *op. cit.*, 273; H. A. L. Fisher, *History of Europe* (1935), II, 483–4; *Cath. Ency.*, XI, 455; XII, 302.

(1) *Developments in Guinea*

English adventurers became active on the Guinea Coast by the middle of the sixteenth century, entering the Portuguese domain for trade, but not at first attempting to secure any foothold on the coast. The first English voyager to Guinea appears to have been William Hawkins of Plymouth, father of Sir John, who traded there in the course of voyages to Brazil, in the years 1530–32.[1] He was engaged in honest trade. After 1550 others followed him, but the unenviable reputation of being the first Englishman to engage in the slave-trade belongs to Sir John himself. In 1562 he secured 300 Negroes in Sierra Leone and sold them to the Spaniards in the West Indies.[2] For his next slave-trading voyage Elizabeth lent him one of her ships, the *Jesus*.[3] As individual voyagers increased, a number of English merchants combined to secure a royal patent for trade monopoly in Guinea. Two such were granted by Elizabeth.[4] But there was no attempt to displace the Portuguese on land. With the seventeenth century activity increased; the year 1618 saw the Company of Adventurers of London trading into Africa receive a royal charter. By this Company two forts were built, one on the Gambia, and one at Coromantine on the Gold Coast, the first English footholds in Guinea of the Portuguese. These forts were as much for defence against European rivals on the coast as against any African attack. This was not a slave-trading Company, but in 1631 appeared a second African company that was—also with a royal charter. The demand for labour in the West Indies was increasing.[5]

The Dutch now came upon the West African scene and played a leading part. This was the manner of their coming. Both Charles V and Philip II had failed to stamp out the sturdy Protestantism of the northern provinces of the Netherlands. With the rise of the Dutch Republic and the renouncing of allegiance to the King of Spain in 1581, the Dutch at war with Spain were at war with Portugal as well.[6] Dutch sea power had been steadily growing and overseas enterprise soon

---

[1] Richard Hakluyt, *The Principal Navigations, Voyages, Traffiques, and Discoveries of the English Nation* (1903–5 edition), XI, 23–4.
[2] *Ibid.*, X, 8. [3] *Ibid.*, X, 9, 17, 25.
[4] In 1588, the very year of the Armada, and 1592.
[5] Lucas, *Historical Geography of the British Colonies*, III, West Africa (2nd ed. 1900), 57–9.
[6] Through the death of King Sebastian without issue, Portugal had fallen to the Spanish Crown in 1580.

began. In 1621 the Dutch West India Company was incorporated, and in 1623 embarked on a lengthy war with the Portuguese in Brazil. In the course of this, the Dutch struck at the Portuguese in Guinea. In 1637 a Dutch fleet besieged Elmina, in four days the fortress fell, and their first famous fort upon the Guinea Coast, the proud castle of St. George d'Elmina, was lost by Portugal for ever. The fort of St. Anthony at Axim, second in importance, was taken by the Dutch in 1642, and others followed.[1]

The English and the Dutch were the peoples with leading interests on the Guinea Coast in the seventeenth and eighteenth centuries, but they were not the only Europeans to arrive. In addition to the French, who established themselves in the neighbourhood of the Senegal, came Danes and Swedes and Brandenburghers. The principal Danish fort was Christiansborg at Accra, dating from the mid-seventeenth century. About the same time came the Swedes and the Brandenburghers, but their tenure was brief. Danes and Dutch succeeded to their forts.[2] While the clash of political rivalry had often introduced the newcomers, they were induced to stay by the great profit of West African trade, but it was the trade in men. In the seventeenth century this began to dominate.

There were no colonies yet on the Guinea Coast, but just trading settlements each provided with a fort for its defence. A chart of the Gold Coast of the year 1760 shows the number to be thirteen English, eleven Dutch, one Danish and one of Brandenburg.[3] Some features of these English fort-settlements in the eighteenth century are worthy of notice. There was no seizure of land from Africans; rent was paid. In the case of Cape Coast Castle it amounted to £72 per annum. It was stated for the Company of Merchants trading to Africa, which controlled the forts: "We recognize the sovereignty of the natives as lords of the soil and entitled to rent."[4] There was no oppression of local chiefs; indeed, matters sometimes fell out the other way. Profit from private trading and the rapid promotion due to heavy mortality from the deadly climate seem to have been the attraction for those who served the Company. The liquor traffic was a growing evil; one officer said of Africans around the forts: "The whole race will perjure themselves for brandy."[5]

---

[1] Lucas, *op. cit.*, 64-5.   [2] *Ibid.*, 66-9.
[3] E. C. Martin, *The British West African Settlements, 1750-1821* (1927), viii.   [4] *Ibid.*, 49.   [5] *Ibid.*, 46.

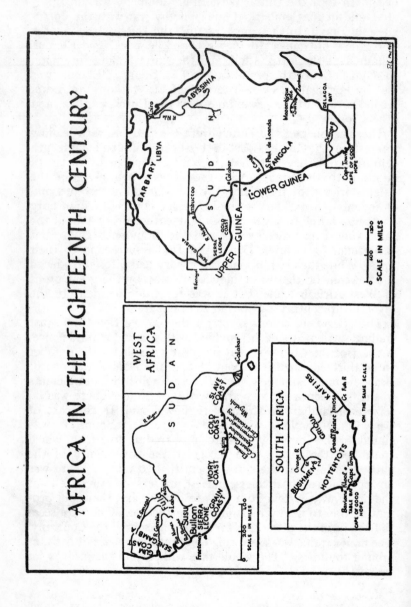

AFRICA IN THE EIGHTEENTH CENTURY

The Dutch West India Company recognized the obligation to Christianize the overseas regions it controlled, though this was not explicit in its charter as was the case with the Dutch East India Company. As far as the Guinea Coast was concerned, chaplains were part of the regular establishment of the Company's stations. William Bosman, who was on the coast in the seventeenth century, tells us something of them. In a list of officers at each fort, the "Preacher" always stands second, next to the Director-General. There is also a "Clerk of the Church" though he is last but one. The Preacher enjoyed a place at the Governor's table. Bosman proceeds: " . . . we are very Religious; we are obliged to go to Church every day, on forfeiture of twenty-five Styvers, except on Sundays and Thursdays, when the forfeiture for omission is doubled: But I know you will reply, this is a forced service of God, and consequently not always accompanied with the most sincere Intentions: And to confess the Truth, it is not much better; for were not the restraint laid upon us, some would rather pay a visit elsewhere than to the Church."[1]

The story of an African chaplain who served the Company in the eighteenth century deserves recording. A Negro boy, native of the Gold Coast, was sold to the captain of a trading vessel who presented him to a Dutch merchant. The latter named him Capitein (after his first master), which was later expanded to Jacobus Elisa Johannes Capitein. After three or four years, at the age of eleven, his master took him to Holland for education. In 1737, when he was about twenty years of age, he entered the University of Leyden, and as the climax of his five years' study delivered a Latin oration on the theme that slavery is not contrary to religious liberty. This was published and went through four editions. He was then ordained to the ministry of the Dutch Reformed Church, being the first African to receive Protestant ordination. He proceeded to the Gold Coast as chaplain to the Company at St. George d'Elmina. He made a beginning with vernacular Christian literature, for he translated into Fanti the Twelve Articles of the Apostles' Creed, published in 1744. His marriage was unfortunate. He wished to marry an African, but the Amsterdam authorities (in whose Presbytery he had been ordained) objected because she was unbaptized. He then married a European—interesting evidence of the benevolent

[1] William Bosman, *A New and Accurate Description of the Coast of Guinea* (1705), 98–9.

151

attitude to inter-racial marriage at the time. His was a hard
lot; the Europeans seem to have disregarded his office because
of his colour, and his own people virtually ostracized him. His
career was short and troubled, for he died at the age of thirty,
leaving an embarrassed estate.[1] His sheer loneliness, though
living in society, may well have quenched his spirit. The
Negro is peculiarly sensitive to his social environment; warm,
personal relationships will secure his utmost devotion, where
the imposition of an abstract duty will leave him callous.[2]
This is a characteristic admirably expressed in his loyalty to
his chief, which the African does not lose with education. A
brilliant contemporary of Capitein also illustrates this characteristic. Anthony William Amo, of Axim on the Gold Coast, was
taken to Europe when very young and became a protégé of
the Princess of Brunswick. He pursued his studies at Halle, in
Saxony, and at Wittenberg where in 1734 the University conferred on him the Doctor's degree. In recognition of his personal
merit the Court of Berlin conferred on him the title of Counsellor
of State. Yet when his friend and benefactress, the Princess,
died he fell into a deep melancholy; and although he had then
been thirty years in Europe, resolved to leave for his native
land. He returned to Axim where he is said to have lived as a
recluse.[3] Such cases enforce the necessity, not so much of
administrative supervision as of fellowship in Christian work
for the African leader to render of his best. It is probable that
cases of disappointment in early mission work are due in the
main to this support of personal fellowship not having been
available. Another case is that of Philip Quaque who served as
chaplain under the English Company. As his appointment was
in conjunction with the Society for the Propagation of the
Gospel, we introduce him in a later section when reviewing
missionary endeavour in the period.

While there were no true colonies on the Guinea Coast, a
British Crown colony did appear in Senegambia for a brief
period in the eighteenth century—the first in West Africa. In
the constitution of the new colony the interests of religion were
not overlooked. "Two ministers and a schoolmaster" appeared
on the establishment. But there was difficulty in inducing
appointees to face an insalubrious climate. Non-resident

---

[1] J. Du Plessis, *Evangelisation of Pagan Africa*; 122, n.; Abbé Grégoire in
West African Celebrities (1905), 19–23, where Capitein's first work, an elegy
in Latin on the death of Manger, minister at the Hague, is printed in full.

[2] Cf. Joyce Cary, *The Case for African Freedom* (1941), 39–40.

[3] Abbé Grégoire in *West African Celebrities*, 15–17.

ministers are complained of to the Colonial Secretary. As French rivalry was a feature of the situation on the Senegal, it is scarcely surprising to find an emphasis on Protestantism, with some regard to it as a political instrument. Thus the Governor's Council of thirteen was to include nine Protestant inhabitants chosen by him. The two ministers were to be sent out "to the end that the Church of England may be established both in principle and practice". The Governor was to see that places of worship were set apart where the English service was to be used and "God Almighty be devoutly and duly served". The hope followed that "the inhabitants may by degrees be induced to embrace the Protestant religion". Liberty of conscience was to be allowed, but no ecclesiastical jurisdiction of the See of Rome could be permitted. The anti-papal bias and the political complexion of these recommendations are clear. One Governor frankly suggests as a remedy for French control of Senegambia through the priests, "our religion, a very excellent political engine in such a case".[1] Remembering the state of religion in England during the earlier part of the eighteenth century, such a view of it as useful to the administration is easy to understand, though any hope of success in winning the inhabitants of the province was as remote as the missionary motive itself. There is no evidence that the proposals were ever put into effective operation.

(2) *Settlement at the Cape.*

It was not only on the Guinea Coast that the Portuguese were losing their possessions to the Dutch. From the end of the sixteenth century, companies formed in towns of the Netherlands sent their fleets to the East. In 1602 the Dutch East India Company was formed and from that time the share of the Dutch in the eastern trade increased by leaps and bounds. The Cape formed a convenient port of call, and from 1616 all outward bound fleets touched at Table Bay. Ships of the English East India Company also called here for refreshment, where like the Dutch they would barter with the Hottentots for sheep and oxen. Moreover, the sorrel of the Cape was an excellent remedy for the scurvy that was a major trial on these voyages. It was good policy to keep on friendly terms with the inhabitants or food would be withheld. An English traveller, John Jourdain of the English East India Company, was there in 1608 and recorded that the Hottentots, after bartering their

[1] E. C. Martin, *op. cit.*, 69, 71-2, 95.

animals, whistled some away and offered them again, a fraud the English overlooked for the sake of good relations. Jourdain also thought the place suitable for a settlement, and expressed the opinion that the Hottentots might be brought first to "civility" and then to a knowledge of God.[1] In 1620 a group of Englishmen did attempt to stake a claim, in ignorance of the fact that prior possession had been taken for the Dutch East India Company. These Englishmen, whose impetuous action received no countenance in England, when placing on record the reasons for their step also expressed the pious hope that the Hottentots would in due time become servants of God.[2] The only direct action the English ever took was to land occasional groups of convicts there.[3] Meanwhile both the Dutch and English Companies used Table Bay and their ships were sometimes there together.

The first settlement was due indirectly to a shipwreck. The *Haarlem*, engaged in the East Indies trade, was stranded in Table Bay in 1648. The shipwrecked crew spent five months on shore. The experience was so favourable that two of the crew presented a memorial to the Company on their return to Holland that a permanent station should be established at so suitable a spot. They denounced current ideas that no good could be expected of the Hottentots, for their own experience had been far otherwise; they also testified to their capacity to learn Dutch, and they expressed hope of their future progress in contact with a Dutch settlement: "By maintaining a good correspondence with them, we shall be able in time to employ some of their children as boys and servants, and to educate them in the Christian Religion, by which means, if it pleases God Almighty to bless this good cause, as at Tayouan and Formosa, many souls will be brought to God, and to the Christian Reformed Religion, so that the formation of the said fort and garden will not only tend to the gain and profit of the Honourable Company, but to the preservation and saving of many men's lives, and what is more, to the magnifying of God's Holy Name, and to the propagation of His Gospel, whereby, beyond all doubt, your Honours' trade over all India will be more and more blessed."[4] The suggestion that the Company should introduce Christianity in the shape of the Reformed

---

[1] G. M. Theal, *op. cit.*, I, 423-4. [2] *Ibid.*, 426.
[3] Leipoldt, *Jan van Riebeeck* (1936), 74-80.
[4] J. Du Plessis, *History of Christian Missions in South Africa* (1911), 20-1. For a fuller report on the Hottentots from this memorial, see Leipoldt, *op. cit.*, 87-9.

faith was no new policy; the obligation of the state to Christianize was the view held in Holland.

The Company decided to attempt the settlement, and an expedition was prepared. It was under the command of Jan van Riebeeck who had seen service in the East as a factor of the Company, though his training had been that of a surgeon. He had been with the homeward bound fleet that rescued the men of the *Haarlem*. The three ships he now commanded sighted on the voyage a Moorish pirate—a reminder that Northern Africa was firmly in non-Christian hands. They anchored in Table Bay on April 6, 1652. Van Riebeeck was destined to guide the little community for the next ten years. The 126 persons of 1652 had become 381 permanent residents at the time of his departure.[1] During this important formative period of the settlement, not originally intended by the Company as a colony but as a useful port of call for fleets engaged in the eastern trade, there appeared intimations of those problems that were to mark the chequered course of South African history.

First and foremost was the relation of the newcomers to the native population, the Dutch to the Hottentots. Within three days of their arrival, van Riebeeck issued his first proclamation in the course of which he dealt with this question. The responsibility for good relations was to rest upon the Dutch. All were to be answerable for their own arms and weapons, and in case of theft were themselves to receive the punishment: "All arms and tools shall be debited to those who have received them, and anyone who loses his weapons or tools shall receive fifty lashes and forfeit his grog for eight days or undergo such heavier punishment as the importance of the case shall demand. If anyone ill-treat a native, or beat or push him—no matter whether he be in the right or not—he shall receive in the presence of the aggrieved native, fifty lashes, so that the natives may be made to understand that the deed has been done against our will, and that we desire to associate with them in all kindness and amity, according to the objects and orders of our Lords Principal. . . . Everyone is earnestly ordered and admonished to show all friendliness and amiability to the natives, so that in course of time they may be made accustomed to us by our friendly intercourse and help and realize the object of our Lords Principal."[2] No one was to stray beyond the

[1] Leipoldt, *op. cit.*, 118, 219.
[2] *Ibid.*, 110–11, where the full text is given. Du Plessis quotes the relevant paragraphs, *op. cit.*, 22.

settlement or barter with the natives without the Commander's consent. The Hottentots in the immediate neighbourhood of the settlement seem to have been less dependable than the larger groups in the interior. Despite various provocations, peace was maintained for seven years, but in 1659 the cattle thefts had become so serious that the Council decided to resort to force. This was the first armed conflict to occur. Within a year peace was restored by negotiation. In the course of discussion the Hottentots' grievances were stated, when they complained of the loss of more and more of their grazing land taken by the Dutch, and pertinently asked, "if they came to Holland, would we allow them to do so".[1]

Within two months of his arrival van Riebeeck requested slaves for the heavy and dirty work of the settlement. This request was several times repeated; he also suggested more than once how useful Chinese would be. These never came in his day, but the slaves did, and thereby another strand was woven into South Africa's fateful destiny. Five years later slaves were demanded in connexion with the agricultural policy the Directors wished to be pursued; until 1657 all residents had been the Company's servants, but in that year the first free farmers were granted land. Van Riebeeck had favoured a farming community of small peasant proprietors who would themselves till the soil. This was not realized, and the sinister alternative of slave labour was pursued. In 1658 the first slave cargo arrived; a ship from Amsterdam had met a Portuguese slaver from Angola, and seized half of her cargo of 500 slaves, but of these only 170 survived to reach the Cape. Van Riebeeck logged the event with the comment: "They were mostly girls and small boys, from whom in the next four or five years little service is to be expected."[2] A school, however, was soon set up for them, with the *Ziekentrooster* (Comforter of the Sick) in charge. He was to hold morning and afternoon classes and van Riebeeck noted in his log the encouragement to be offered: "In order to animate the said slaves diligently to attend to be instructed in learning Christian prayers, he has been ordered at the end of the lesson to give each slave a quid of tobacco and a nip of brandy."[3] A few weeks later a consignment of 228 slaves from the Guinea Coast came to Table Bay.[4] The new order was now in operation.

Those who recommended the settlement had envisaged in

[1] The record of the discussion was logged by van Riebeeck. It is quoted in Leipoldt, *op. cit.*, 206–8.　　[2] *Ibid.*, 182.　　[3] *Ibid.*, 189.　　[4] *Ibid.*, 190.

connexion with it an extension of the Reformed religion. The East India Company had this obligation written into its charter, Article XIII of which provided "that ministers and school-masters shall be settled at the most suitable places, for the admonition of the persons abiding there, and for the advancement of non-Christians and the instruction of their children, in order that the Name of Christ may be extended and the interests of the Company promoted."[1] There was a regulation prayer with which every Council of the Company was formally opened; this, with the interpolation of special references to the local situation, was employed by van Riebeeck at each meeting of the Council. There was a petition that the interests of the Company might be advanced and "in time possibly tend to the propagation and spread of Thy true Reformed Christian Faith among these wild and brutal folk, to the glorification and honour of Thy holy Name and to the benefit of our Lords Principal." This cautious reference to missionary expansion is no more lacking in disinterestedness than the proposals of the British in Senegambia a century later, which we have already noticed. The Directors, who strictly prohibited any private trading on the part of their agents (van Riebeeck had slipped here in the East), took occasion to remind their servants while at their devotions of this obligation. In the prayer assigned for their use they were to request that they might "resolve only that which may conduce to the magnification and glory of Thy Most holy Name and the greatest service to our Lords and Masters, without in any way whatsoever considering our own advantage or individual profit". It is understandable that Dr. Godee Molsbergen should call the prayer a mixture of commercialism and piety; Dr. Leipoldt's terms are somewhat scathing: "No other trading company so sanctimoniously protested its utter dependence upon the Almighty, and yet so consistently acted as if all the Deity's functions had been specially entrusted to it."[2] We are sharply reminded, as with the Portuguese of the fifteenth and sixteenth centuries, so now in a measure with the Dutch of the seventeenth, that their conception of the Christian religion prescribed different attitudes from our own.

The one official concerned with religious duties at the Cape was the "Comforter of the Sick" or catechist. Ordained

---

[1] Du Plessis, op. cit., 21, n. 2. See also G. Warneck, Outline of a History of Protestant Missions (3rd English ed., 1906), 43-4.
[2] Leipoldt, op. cit., 100-2.

ministers, when they passed as chaplains with the fleets, would preach and administer the sacraments. Some thirty ministers gave help in this way during the first thirteen years.[1] The catechist was not to transgress the bounds of his vocation; van Riebeeck was instructed from Batavia to see to this, for the Consistory there had heard that he "conducts service in a manner only permitted to a properly ordained minister, and he ought to know that he may not reap another man's harvest, as is the commandment of our Lord Jesus".[2] This stricture anticipates the acute problem that was to arise with the coming of the first Moravian missionary. The duties of the catechist, in addition to visiting the sick, were to conduct evening prayers, on Sundays to read a sermon, and to teach the Heidelberg catechism. The catechist Wylant, who accompanied the expedition, made a fruitless attempt to teach some Hottentot youths reading and writing and to learn their language, "in order by that means to bring them to the light of the truth".[3] Of two Hottentots who were sent to Batavia for education, one died and the other, on his return, slipped back to his own people, probably another case of sheer loneliness of spirit in the new environment. A promising Hottentot convert was the girl Eva who acquired an excellent knowledge of Dutch, and was a useful interpreter in dealings with the tribes. Wylant's successor, Pieter van der Stael, reported to Amsterdam Eva's baptism on May 3, 1662, a few days before van Riebeeck's departure: "Dominie Sybelius again delivered a sermon, and baptized a grown-up woman, the first-fruits of these aborigines called Hottentoos."[4] It was not till 1665 that the first ordained minister was appointed to the Cape, Johan van Arckel. Unhappily he survived less than six months, but had in that time won his place with the resident Dutch community.[5]

A practical question of some importance was that of the baptism of slaves. For twenty-five years or so baptism automatically carried with it emancipation. There was even a plan to assist these freedmen to develop a settlement of their own. But not all the freed slaves used their freedom worthily. It must be remembered that they had in the first instance been torn from that order of society which was their native inheritance, and as slaves they had been dependent upon the will of another. Suddenly to thrust them out from this protective environment and expect them to show initiative in developing

[1] Du Plessis, op. cit., 24.   [2] Leipoldt, op. cit., 138.
[3] Du Plessis, op. cit., 24–5.   Ibid., 27.   [5] Ibid., 32.

their own resources was asking too much: it was likely to render them idle and a burden to society. Such many became. Stricter laws were therefore enacted, only allowing emancipation after a time limit of age or service, provided there was profession of Christianity and ability to speak Dutch.[1] The practice prevailing at the Cape with regard to the baptism of the children of slaves was to accept them, with an admonition to the owners to have them instructed in the Christian faith.[2] Van Arckel, during his brief tenure of office, had baptized several slave children with this condition.

Profession of Christianity in the early days also made inter-racial marriage acceptable. Religion, not colour, was the barrier. The first of such marriages at the Cape was that between Jan Wouters and Catherine, the baptized daughter of a Bengal slave, in 1656. Van Riebeeck allowed marriages with coloured women, but these were only placed on a legal footing on profession of Christianity. This happened in the case of Eva, the Hottentot interpreter, whose marriage to a Dane, the assistant surgeon, was recognized with an official wedding after her baptism. By enactment of 1682, however, marriage between Europeans and freed slaves of full colour was prohibited.[3]

With the passing of the seventeenth century there was a waning of interest in the spiritual welfare of Hottentots and slaves. In 1709 a Danish missionary, J. G. Böving, called at the Cape on the way home from India. He speaks of the "lovelessness and grievous sin" of the colonists in opposing the evangelization of their slaves, because then they could no longer buy and sell them. His attempt to address the Hottentots through an interpreter was received by them with ridicule. The eighteenth century opened with the first fair promise blighted.[4]

One accession to the spiritual resources of the colony must be chronicled. This was the arrival of Huguenot refugees in 1688 and following years. In 1685 the Edict of Nantes, which gave recognition to the Huguenot community in France, was revoked, and Huguenots left her soil for that of her Protestant neighbours, Holland and England. Men and women of such sterling character, who had left their homeland rather than surrender the faith they had embraced, and who had suffered the loss of possessions, were of the quality to bring strength and prosperity

---

[1] Du Plessis, *op. cit.*, 42, where the full conditions are stated.
[2] *Ibid.*, 34-5. [3] *Ibid.*, 28, 32, 42; Leipoldt, *op. cit.*, 152, 168, 180.
[4] Du Plessis, *op. cit.*, 48.

to any new settlement where their religious faith would be welcomed. As their accession benefited the other lands to which they went, so it was in South Africa. Du Plessis calls their advent an unmixed blessing. They were settled in an area which the Hottentots had been ordered to leave, and so constituted a kind of "buffer state" between the Dutch colonists and the African population. It is a tribute to the French colonists that relations between the races were never more friendly than in the generation after their arrival.

In the latter part of the seventeenth century Islam made its first appearance at the Cape. It was introduced as the professed religion of Malays who were brought to the colony by the Dutch from their eastern possessions.[1]

(3) *The Growth of the Slave-trade.*

The European slave-trade which began in the days of Prince Henry as a cloud no bigger than a man's hand, by degrees so enveloped the African scene that in the eighteenth century "the African trade" had one predominant meaning—the trade in men. The sinister effect of this development on missionary hopes is plain to see.

During the fifteenth and sixteenth centuries the trade in slaves from Africa was almost entirely Portuguese. We have already observed from the pages of Azurara how, on the earliest voyages down the West African coast, Negro slaves were taken back to Portugal, and how Prince Henry was interested in their conversion to Christianity. Before his death, some 700 to 800 Negro slaves were being imported into Portugal annually.

With the discovery of the New World and the development of its vast resources a new demand appeared; first, for labour in the mines, and later, and on a far greater scale, labour for the plantations. The native population was not equal in numbers or physique to this new demand, so Africans were caught and carried overseas. In the sixteenth century the Portuguese did a brisk trade from their African possessions at first via Portugal,

[1] T. W. Arnold, *Preaching of Islam*, 350. A strange episode occurred a century later at Delagoa Bay. An Englishman, William Bolts, having been granted a charter by Maria Theresa of Austria in 1775, proceeded the next year to Delagoa Bay where he entered into agreement with the chiefs, ran up the Austrian flag, and began to build up a considerable commercial settlement. He seems to have thought Islam better suited than Christianity to African needs, for he brought over a Muslim teacher from India to win local Africans to that faith. The settlement was short-lived; tropical disease and Portuguese protests combined effectively to end it.—Scott Keltie, *The Partition of Africa* (1893), 83.

but in due course there was direct traffic between Africa and America. The development of the sugar plantations in the West Indies and Brazil greatly increased the demand. A document in the archives of the Lisbon Geographical Society, purporting to be a return of the year 1548 from San Salvador, states that there were ten or more European exporters of slaves, and that from the port of Pinda twelve to fifteen ships, each with a cargo of 400 to 700 slaves, sailed annually.[1] While the Portuguese went on steadily supplying their own colony of Brazil, after 1600 they begin to slip out of the larger picture.

The Dutch and the English superseded the Portuguese as carriers of slaves to the New World. The Dutch were carriers only, for their main colonial empire lay in the eastern seas. Their possessions in the West were few. England, however, with the development of the American colonies in the seventeenth century, and the growth of the West Indies, came to have an interest in the traffic that was bound up with the prosperity of her overseas possessions. Nevertheless during the seventeenth century the Dutch held an easy lead. Even in 1672, when the Royal African Company of England took over the West African trade, the Dutch are said to have exported ten times as many slaves as the English.[2] Under the Royal African Company, however, the trade began to grow. Between 1680 and 1688, for example, they shipped slaves at a rate that varied from 5,000 to 9,000 annually; in the same period 15,872 slaves were sold in Jamaica alone at an average price of £13 1s. 9d. This Company and other English traders were landing in the plantations some 25,000 Negroes every year.[3]

With the eighteenth century the English took the lead. The growth of British sea power provided the great opportunity. By an article of the Peace of Utrecht of 1713 the French contract to supply slaves to the Spanish colonies in America passed to the English. From this time the development of the slave-trade became a definite object of British policy. Chatham, for example, gave it special attention.[4] The American Colonies resented the large numbers of Negro slaves being introduced, not indeed on humanitarian so much as on economic and political grounds, but they were powerless to resist.[5] It is estimated that by 1770 about half the total trade was in British

[1] W. H. Bentley, *Pioneering on the Congo*, I, 38–9.
[2] C. P. Lucas, *op. cit.*, III, 83.   [3] *Ibid.*, 84.
[4] W. E. H. Lecky, *History of England in the Eighteenth Century* (Cabinet ed. 1904), II, 134.   [5] *Ibid.*, 246–7.

hands, with a fleet of 192 slave-ships with capacity for 50,000 slaves.[1] French, Portuguese, Dutch and Danes were the other principal carriers. It was valued not merely as an activity profitable in itself, but as the keystone in the arch of British commercial prosperity, more especially in relation to the West Indies, the wealth of whose sugar plantations was greatly prized. A writer of the period expressed the contemporary view: "How vast is the importance of our trade to Africa, which is the first principle and foundation of all the rest; the main spring of the machine, which sets every wheel in motion: a trade which arises almost entirely of ourselves, our exports being chiefly our own manufactures, or such as are purchased with them, and the returns gold, ivory, wax, dyeing woods and negroes the first four articles of home consumption, or manufactured for exporting the last affording a most prodigious employment to our people, both by sea and land without whom our plantations could not be improved or carried on, nor should we have any shipping passing between the colonies, and mother country; whereas by their labour our sugars, tobacco, and numberless other articles are raised, which employ an incredible number of ships, and these ships in their turn must employ a much greater number of handicraft trades at home; and the merchandises they bring home and carry out, pay such considerable sums to government, that of them consist the most flourishing branches of the revenue; so that both for exports and imports, the improvement of our national revenue, the encouragement of industry at home, the supply of our colonies abroad, and the increase of our navigation, the African trade is so very beneficial to Great Britain, so essentially necessary to the very being of her colonies, that without it neither could we flourish nor they long subsist."[2] This is a measure of the task awaiting the abolitionists, but for the moment we are rather concerned with the easy acceptance of the traffic in eighteenth-century England as indispensable to prosperity.

Nor was the slave-trade repugnant, for the most part at least, to the Christian conscience. It is to the credit of the Papacy that with the opening of the New World to European exploitation, one voice a century was raised in protest (the Indians were at first in mind)—that of Pius II in the fifteenth, Paul III in the sixteenth, Urban VIII in the seventeenth and Benedict XIV in the eighteenth.[3] But any results were negligible. We

[1] R. Coupland, *The British Anti-Slavery Movement* (1933), 22.
[2] *A Treatise upon the Trade of Great Britain to Africa* (1772), 4, 5, quoted in E. C. Martin, *op. cit.*, 1–2.   [3] Paul Allard in *Cath. Ency.*, XIV, 39.

have seen Portuguese and Dutch in Africa sincerely make their Christian profession while sharing in the trade. It was not otherwise with the English. Lord Dartmouth, a recognized leader in the Church, when Colonial Secretary replied in 1775 to a colonial protest: "We cannot allow the colonies to check or discourage in any degree a traffic so beneficial to the nation."[1] When the article in the charter of the colony of Georgia which forbade slavery was repealed in 1749, George Whitefield was one who advocated the change.[2] John Newton first made his contact with the slave-trade in his youth when scorning all religion, but after his conversion still visited West Africa in its interest. After his marriage in 1750 he made three voyages to Guinea as commander of a slave-ship. That he had no qualms of conscience on this business is shown by what he wrote of this period: "I never knew sweeter or more frequent hours of divine communion than in my two last voyages to Guinea."[3] His earliest biographer who knew him, says: "It seems, from the account he gives, that he had not the least scruple as to the lawfulness of the Slave Trade; he considered it as the appointment of Providence: he viewed this employment as respectable and profitable: yet he could not help regarding himself as a sort of jailor; and was sometimes shocked with an employment so conversant with chains, bolts and shackles."[4] The Society for the Propagation of the Gospel received in trust three estates with their Negroes under the will of General Codrington, for the purpose of endowing theological and medical studies. On the abolition of slavery the Society received £8,823 8s. 9d. in respect of compensation for the slaves on its estates.[5] It was the Quaker community in the American colonies that made the first effective protest, and a handful of Christian men in England who, realizing the iniquity of the traffic, devoted themselves to its uprooting.

The effect on Africa was disastrous. The propensity to inter-tribal warfare was intensified. The original arrangement whereby prisoners of war were enslaved when a conflict occurred, and condemned criminals were sold as slaves no longer met the large demands of traders. Wars of aggression specifically to secure slaves were therefore promoted; a whole class of African middlemen existed who secured slaves in the interior and

---

[1] W. E. H. Lecky, *op. cit.*, II, 247.   [2] *Ibid.*, 248.
[3] R. Cecil, *Memoirs of the late Hon. and Rev. W. B. Cadogan, John Bacon, Esq., and the Rev. John Newton* (New ed., 1812), 305.   [4] *Ibid*, 314.
[5] C. F. Pascoe, *Two Hundred Years of the S.P.G.* (1901), I, 197, 199. The Society, it should be said, made efforts for the conversion of the Negroes on these and other plantations.

brought them down by land or water to the coast. Private kidnapping became a source of gain. European traders violated on their ships the sacred laws of hospitality, and seized those who were their unsuspecting guests.[1] The effect on the depopulation of Africa, though it cannot be accurately measured in statistics, must have been drastic. Taking into account the loss of life in Africa and on the Middle Passage, and including the Arab trade of the nineteenth century, as high a figure as 100,000,000 lives has been suggested as the cost to Africa.[2] Trade should open up a country. This trade closed it. From the Gambia to Angola, the slave-trade dominated: "Its effect, and it could hardly be otherwise, was to lock up Africa. Game preserves cannot be anything but locked-up lands, uncultivated and unopened areas. The West Coast of Africa was a great preserve for human game."[3]

(4) *The Thin Thread of Continuity in Missionary Enterprise.*

Roman missions in both West and East Africa entered on a period of decline in the seventeenth century, and in the eighteenth almost disappeared. Political changes made their work less easy, and the diminished power and prestige of Portugal reduced their opportunities.

The seventeenth century, it is true, saw the setting up of a central authority to control all missionary enterprises, the Congregation of Propaganda, or simply the Propaganda, as it is shortly named. This was established in 1622 by Gregory XV. The missionary activities of the various Orders continued, but were now subject directly to a supreme ecclesiastical authority. In the nature of the case, however, it took a little time for the Congregation of Propaganda to exercise in fact the considerable powers with which it was invested. Its effectiveness in directing Roman Catholic developments in Africa belongs to a later stage.[4]

Augustinians from San Thomé visited the Guinea Coast at the end of the seventeenth century. Bosman reports meeting

---

[1] Thomas Clarkson, *Essay on the Slavery and Commerce of the Human Species* (1788), 33–5, records a particularly flagrant episode at Old Calabar in 1767. The late Dr. R. R. Moton, the distinguished successor of Booker T. Washington at Tuskegee Institute, stated that his own African ancestor on the mother's side was seized in this way and carried into slavery; R. R. Moton, *Finding a Way Out* (1920), 3–4.

[2] E. W. Smith, *The Golden Stool* (1926), 100, quoting Du Bois.

[3] C. P. Lucas, *The Partition and Colonization of Africa* (1922), 53.

[4] *Cath. Enc.*, XIII, 142–3; G. Warneck, *op. cit.*, 161–3. The official title is *Sacra Congregatio de propaganda fide.*

one at Whydah, who came "in order, if possible, to convert the Blacks to Christianity, but in vain. Polygamy is an Obstacle which they cannot get over. As for all the other Points they might have got Footing here, but the confinement to one wife is an insuperable Difficulty. This Priest invited the King to be present at Mass, which he also did And when I saw him next, asking him how he liked it, he said very well, and that it was very fine; but that he chose rather to keep to his Fetiche." The strength of the bond with the ancestors was illustrated in their reply to the priest when he threatened hell fire to those who would not repent: "Our fathers, grandfathers, to an endless number, liv'd as we do, and worship'd the same gods as we do: and if they must burn therefore, patience, we are not better than our ancestors, and shall comfort ourselves with them."[1] Whydah was a slave depot of importance. In the same region on the Slave Coast lay the kingdom of Arda, in the Dahomey of to-day. Philip IV of Spain promoted a Capuchin mission to the king of Arda which arrived in 1660. Five of the eleven members soon succumbed; the survivors, after vain attempts to win the king (polygamy was one obstacle), retired from the field in 1661.[2]

Various parties of Capuchin monks arrived in the Congo and Angola during the seventeenth century. Franciscan Recollects also came but their work was interrupted. The close of the century saw Jesuits, Franciscans and Carmelites in Loanda. In the eighteenth century French secular priests came to Congo, but the climate seems to have deterred them. Their stay was brief. By the end of the eighteenth century the French, Italian and Portuguese missionaries had evidently abandoned the Congo region. The slender continuity of effort on the west coast was centred in the see of Loanda in Angola.[3] On the eastern side a spectacular success had been achieved, as we have seen, in 1652, but after that the downhill course was all too clear. In 1697 the Jesuits began a seminary at Sena for the children of Portuguese and the sons of chiefs. They had several river stations but confessed that work among the Bantu was not successful. The Dominican convent at Mozambique was the principal centre of the Order. Reports in 1751 from both

[1] Bosman, op. cit., 385; Schmidlin, op. cit., 470.
[2] H. Labouret et P. Rivet, Le Royaume d'Arda et son Evangélisation au XVII⁰ Siècle (1929).
[3] Van Wing, Etudes Bakongo, 55-70; Schmidlin, op. cit., 471-2; J. R. Hildebrand, Le Martyr Georges de Geel et les débuts de la Mission du Congo, 1645-52 (1940); A. B. Keith, The Belgian Congo and the Berlin Act (1919), 21-2.

the Orders were anything but encouraging. Eight years later came the expulsion of the Jesuits. Dr. Theal has suggested that some may have turned inland and reached Dhlodhlo and Khami in Southern Rhodesia, where Christian relics have been found.[1] If so, their work died out.

The Protestant Churches were not yet ready to shoulder the missionary task. They were quite naturally concerned with establishing themselves as Christian communions and preparing their apologia. This struggle at first absorbed all their thought and energy. Moreover, political conditions in both Germany and England helped to delay any missionary endeavour. Only slowly did the Protestant Churches come to recognize the missionary obligation. Gustav Warneck has attributed this failure in Germany, the home of the Reformation, to two main causes: the needs of the world overseas had not yet come within the purview of German Protestantism, and the orthodox theology definitely discouraged all missionary ideas. When, however, in the course of the seventeenth century missionary ideas did begin to emerge in Germany, they took varying shape. Some recognized the duty of Christian rulers to Christianize heathen peoples subject to them, but did not admit any obligation of the Church to do so. Others did indeed admit the duty of the Church in this respect but urged that this was not the time. Others, again, asserted without qualification the duty devolving on the Church, "but such voices were very feeble".[2] In Holland, as we have seen, the duty of Christianizing heathen peoples was assumed to fall upon the colonial government. In England the seventeenth century was a time of unhappy strife, with a reaction against religion at the Restoration that compelled sincere Christians once again to a real concern for the faith in their own land.

Ignorance about the world across the seas was particularly the case in respect of Africa. *The History and Description of Africa* of Leo Africanus was, from the end of the sixteenth century, long accepted as the authority on that continent. The author was a Moor, born probably in Granada, who journeyed through North Africa, Egypt, and the Sudan in the first quarter of the sixteenth century. On one of his Mediterranean voyages he was captured by pirates who presented him to Pope Leo X. He was granted his freedom, professed con-

[1] Schmidlin, *op. cit.*, 472; G. M. Theal, *op. cit.*, I, 494–5, 497–8; G. W. H. Knight-Bruce, *Memories of Mashonaland* (1895), 7.
[2] G. Warneck, *op. cit.*, 25–6.

version from Islam, and was baptized, the Pope giving him
his own name.[1] He was encouraged to pursue in Rome the
life of a scholar, and there penned the memorable record of his
travels. Editions in Italian, French and Latin appeared on the
Continent during the sixteenth century, and in 1600 John Pory
presented it in an English version. It exercised, therefore, a
wide influence in Europe. Leo wrote from first-hand knowledge
practically throughout, and his freedom from credulity and
prejudice together with his unusual accuracy have impressed
later students of his pages. He recognizes four divisions of
Africa: "Barbaria, Numidia, Libya and the land of Negros."
In the last named he claims to have visited fifteen kingdoms,
though he admits many were vassal states, for he paid his
visit during the ascendancy of Songhay under Askia the Great.
It will be observed that the whole of the Africa he describes is
Muslim or under Muslim rule. Moreover, his Negroland was
only accessible by caravan across the desert, through the
impenetrable barrier of Islam in the north. There was little,
therefore, in this standard account to arouse among Protestants
a sense of missionary opportunity.

Travellers who skirted the coasts of Africa did little by their
reports to excite interest in her inhabitants. The author of
Some Yeares Travels into Divers Parts of Asia and Afrique
(London, 1634) wrote ungallantly of the West coast tribes:
"Let one character serve them all; they look like chimney
sweepers; are of no profession except rapine and villainy makes
one." With some three weeks' experience of the Cape he
stigmatized the Hottentots as "an accursed progeny of Cham,
who differ in nothing from 'bruit' beasts save forms . . . desper-
ately crafty and injurious".[2] While the original journals of Sir
James Lancaster, who commanded the first fleet of the English

---

[1] The sincerity of his conversion is questioned. Dr. Robert Brown, in his
edition of Pory's version, writes: "There is little doubt that Leo's change of
faith was dictated by self-interest. . . . Under Cardinal Ximenes' policy of
learned argument and costly presents, so many insisted on abjuring the creed
of the 'false Mahound', that the good Archbishop had to baptize the perverts
by means of a wet mop trundled over their heads. In this way 4,000 were
sometimes admitted into the Church in one day. During Leo's residence in
Morocco he must have frequently heard of similar occurrences."—*The
History and Description of Africa*, by Leo Africanus (ed. R. Brown, 1896), I,
xlii–iii.

[2] Quoted in Mendelssohn, *South African Bibliography* (1910), I, 705–6. Not
all readers had the perspicacity of Dean Swift, who wrote in his copy of the
book: "If this work were strypt of its Impertinencies, conceitedness, and
tedious Digressions, it would be almost worth reading, and it would then be
two-thirds smaller than it is" (quoted by Mendelssohn).

East India Company, do not survive, material from them has been preserved by Purchas, who says of Lancaster on his voyage in 1601, that in seeking food supplies from the Hottentots he "made signes to them to bring him down sheepe and oxen. For he spake to them in the cattels language, which was never changed at the confusion of Babell, which was 'moath' for oxen and kine, and 'baa' for sheepe, which language the people understood very well without any interpreter. . . . Their speech is wholly uttered through the throate, and they clocke with their tongues in such sort, that in seven weekes which we remained heere in this place, the sharpest wit among us could not learne one word of their language; and yet the people would soon understand any signe we made to them".[1] Edward Terry, travelling as chaplain to a British ambassador, touched at the Cape in 1615, and in his *A Voyage to East India* (1655) observes of the Hottentots: "These brutes devote themselves to idleness, for they neither dig nor spin . . . the sun shines not upon a people in the whole world more barbarous . . . beasts in the skins of men."[2] Small wonder that so cultivated a patron of letters as Lord Chesterfield should write a century later: "The Africans are the most ignorant and unpolished people in the world, little better than the lions, tygers, leopards, and other wild beasts, which that country produces in great numbers. The most southern part of Africa is the Cape of Good Hope. . . . This is the country of the Hottentots, the most savage people in the world."[3] Alexander Ross in his *Pansebeia or View of all Religions in the World* (1653), out of a total of 454 pages devotes six only to religions of Africa. Of these six, two relate to Islam and one to Christian Abyssinia, the remainder containing notices of Guinea, the Congo and South-Eastern Africa. This is a more comprehensive and well-informed account than most, but the proportion of the whole which it receives is eloquent of the ignorance prevailing.[4]

Despite the general apathy of the Protestant Churches in respect of the missionary obligation, and the widespread ignorance of Africa as a possible field of endeavour, there were

---

[1] *The Voyages of Sir James Lancaster, Kt., to the East Indies* (ed. Clements R. Markham, 1877), 63, 64.
[2] Quoted in Mendelssohn, *op. cit.*, II, 471.
[3] *Lord Chesterfield's Letters to his Son* (1821 ed.), I, 212–13 (Letter 90).
[4] *Op. cit.* (sixth ed., 1696), 68–74. Ross is a careful compiler and refers to his authorities for each section. He reports the Roman missions in Congo and Monomotapa.

made in the eighteenth century the first Protestant attempts to reach the Negro in his home. The Church of the United Brethren in Moravia holds pride of place. The Society for the Propagation of the Gospel claims the only English effort before the last decade of the century.

The spirit of Pietism which stood for a personal Christianity was bringing during the seventeenth century some life to a Protestantism long dominated by a dead orthodoxy. Not only was Pietism characterized by an emphasis on conversion but it stood for Christianity in action, the Christian message expressed in life. Holland and England shared with Germany in the movement. The Moravian Church of the Brethren was in this stream. Spener the founder of German Pietism and Francke his colleague, the missionary leader of the day, both came into personal contact with Count Zinzendorf, Francke exercising a deep influence upon him.[1] Ten years after the first persecuted brethren from Moravia had settled on the Count's estate, the first four missionaries were sent out, two to Negroes in St. Thomas (Danish West Indies) and two to Greenland. This was in 1732. Five years later the first Protestant missionary sailed to Africa. He was the Moravian George Schmidt, and his destination was the Cape.

Two pastors of the Dutch Reformed Church at Amsterdam had a concern for Christian work among Africans at the Cape. The Halle missionary, Ziegenbalg, on his way home from Malabar had been impressed by the spiritual destitution of the Hottentots, and had communicated to these pastors his sense of their dire need.[2] They turned to Count Zinzendorf. The man selected was George Schmidt. He had been six years in prison for his Protestant faith. The Directors in Amsterdam found him satisfactory and commended him to the Governor at the Cape: "Since the inclination of the aforesaid Schmidt is directed towards the pious object of, and may possibly be a blessed means for, leading the ignorant and uncivilized heathens to conversion, or at least to a more moral and better life, we have allowed him to proceed to you by this vessel, with recommendation that you grant him every help and assistance in this good purpose."[3] Schmidt arrived at the Cape on July 9, 1737, after a voyage of 120 days. The Council placed on record his arrival, with expressed approval of his mission but no great faith in it: "There has come to land here a certain person named George

[1] G. Warneck, *op. cit.*, 58–63; J. E. Hutton, *A History of Moravian Missions* (1923), 6–13.   [2] J. E. Hutton, *op. cit.*, 126.   [3] Du Plessis, *op. cit.*, 51.

Schmidt, with the purpose—if that be possible—of converting the Hottentots from heathendom to Christianity, we trust that his efforts may have the desired result."[1] Local comment on his proposed enterprise was hardly encouraging. This was the third generation from van Riebeeck's day, and the colony had grown. There were farmers settled far from Cape Town who held no flattering opinion of their Hottentot neighbours. On his first evening Schmidt heard some conversation at the inn: "I hear", said a farmer, "that a parson has come here to convert the Hottentots." "A parson?" retorted another. "The young man is no parson at all. What good can he ever do to the Hottentots? They are stupid; they have no money; and this man actually proposes to bear his own expenses. The poor fool must have lost his head." "And what, sir, do you think?" said the waiter to Schmidt. "I", answered Schmidt, "am the very man."[2] Schmidt established himself near a Hottentot settlement some 100 miles east of Cape Town in a valley called Bavianskloof (Vale of the Baboons). An entry in his journal shows how he made contact with the people: "Every evening I visited the Hottentots, sat down among them, distributed tobacco and began to smoke with them. I told them that, moved by sincere love, I had come to make them acquainted with their Saviour, and to assist them to work." He found their language, however, more than he could manage: "I attempted to master the Hottentot language, seeing that very few of the Hottentots understand Dutch. They have three kinds of clicks which I could not imitate; and I soon perceived that their language was too difficult for me to acquire. I therefore commenced to teach them to speak Dutch."[3] He certainly offered them no child's prattle in his evening gatherings; he read to them Zinzendorf's Berlin Discourses, and offered systematic theological lectures on the Epistle to the Romans. He did, indeed, on one occasion, record in his diary with surprise the fact that not much attention had been paid by the assembly to St. Paul's theology![4] Without attempting to justify a method of presentation that no modern missionary standard would approve, yet let one vital fact be borne in mind. It is recognized that the emotional factor is by no means negligible in teaching others. Even the dullest mind will respond to the lesson of the well-loved teacher. And the Hottentots knew that Schmidt cared for them and cared deeply. He was

---

[1] Du Plessis, *op. cit.*, 52.   [2] J. E. Hutton, *op. cit.*, 127.
[3] Du Plessis, *op. cit.*, 53–4.   [4] J. E. Hutton, *op. cit.*, 129.

not left without some harvest for his sowing, slender though
it was. As time went on one or two Hottentots seemed sufficiently responsive to lead Schmidt to consider them ready for
baptism. But he was not ordained and could not baptize. He
therefore applied to Count Zinzendorf for ordination, and in
1742 he received his Act of Ordination from Herrnhut. When
returning from Cape Town he acted on the new authority: "In
the course of our return journey I asked Willem, one of my
Hottentots, whether he desired to be baptized, upon which
he answered: 'If it be the will of the Lord.' I thereupon
explained to him what baptism signified. Shortly after we
reached a stream of water where I kneeled down and prayed
with Willem. I then asked him: 'Believest thou that the Son
of God died upon the cross; that thou art by nature deserving
of all condemnation, etc?' When he had joyfully replied in the
affirmative, I asked again: 'Desirest thou to be baptized?'
On his answering: 'If it be the will of the Lord', I caused him
to enter the water, and baptized him with the name of Joshua,
in the name of Father, Son and Holy Ghost. On the 2nd April
I baptized Afrika in similar manner, in a rivulet not far from
my hut, with the name of Christian; and the following week I
baptized four others."[1] This action precipitated controversy.
The Dutch clergy held the right to administer the sacraments
as their exclusive prerogative in a Dutch colony. Schmidt
declined to compromise by passing over all his converts to them
for baptism. Thereupon three formal charges were laid against
him, and submitted to Amsterdam: that his ordination was by
certificate and not by laying on of hands; that as a Moravian
he was a heretic (later withdrawn as untrue); that he had not
baptized in the presence of witnesses. His action was regarded
as a breach of church order that could not be tolerated and
Amsterdam condemned it.[2] He struggled on at Bavianskloof
until 1744, and then came back broken-hearted, it is said, to
Europe. All efforts to return with due authority proved un-
availing. He had given seven years of faithful service to a
people almost universally despised. He had secured converts.
He had taught Hottentots to pray; "they actually retire from
time to time to pray in solitude" Cape residents had remarked.[3]

[1] Du Plessis, op. cit., 58. [2] Ibid., 57–8; J. E. Hutton, op. cit., 130.
[3] Du Plessis, op. cit., 56. The rigidity in Christian practice that cut short
Schmidt's missionary career has naturally attracted much attention and the
narrative of his pioneer attempt commonly includes scathing reference to the
Dutch. Du Plessis has gathered a number of these references (Appendix II,
Note B, 418–19) and contends that the facts do not justify such extremity of
statement.

It was half a century before the mission was resumed. Schmidt lived on in quiet service, and when he died in 1785 his friends said there was a prayer for South Africa upon his lips.

The Moravian Brethren were interested in the Church in Abyssinia, thinking to find surviving in it the simplicity of apostolic times, and desiring to be of some service to it. Frederic William Hokker, a physician of experience in the East, offered to make the attempt to reach the country, and his proposal was approved. He reached Cairo in 1752. There he set himself to learn Arabic, and established friendly contact with the Coptic patriarch who rejoiced to hear of the work of the Brethren. A visit to Constantinople procured him the various passports and documents he required, for he proposed to attempt the journey to Abyssinia by way of the Red Sea where the Turks were in control. Political disturbances in Egypt, however, and other difficulties led to his temporary return to Europe in 1755. The following year he returned to Cairo with a helper. Much friendly intercourse with the patriarch and clergy of the Coptic Church took place; on one occasion two Abyssinian priests were present. In 1758 Hokker and his companion started on the journey to Abyssinia. They were shipwrecked in the Red Sea and marooned for several weeks. They at last reached the frontier port to Abyssinia, but without equipment, the loss of the physician's chest of medicines being the most serious. Indeed, the regent of Abyssinia had just requested a physician urgently, but the Brethren "would not venture to prepare medicines in a strange country, from, probably, unknown herbs". They sent, however, a letter to the *abuna* and then returned to Cairo on an adventurous journey by way of the Nile. In 1768 Hokker pluckily made a third attempt, but could go no farther than Cairo. Though the effort to reach Abyssinia was frustrated, the contact made in Egypt with the Coptic Church was, within the limits of the occasion, spiritually refreshing to that ancient communion. We are told that Moravian discourses delivered at Herrnhut and translated into Arabic for the patriarch and his clergy pleased them exceedingly.[1]

The Church of the Brethren, so indefatigable in its missionary labours, also attempted a mission in Guinea, though without success. It began with a mulatto, Christian Protten, who had been taken by the Danes to Copenhagen. There he was educated.

[1] David Cranz, *The Ancient and Modern History of the Brethren* (1780), 433-7, 489-92, 615.

He had already become a Christian when Zinzendorf met him in 1735 and invited him to Herrnhut. He volunteered to go as a missionary to Elmina, the Dutch fort and settlement. His offer was accepted, and a Moravian, Henry Huckoff, accompanied him. They sailed in 1737, the year of George Schmidt's arrival at the Cape. Within two months Huckoff was in his grave. Protten had no success as a missionary. He seems to have been unsuited to the work and is said to have been in danger of apprehension as a runaway slave. He was back in Europe in 1741. Fifteen years later he made a second attempt, this time at Christiansborg the Danish station. In five years he was once more in Europe. Then from 1763 until his death in 1769 he seems to have continued spasmodically in service at Christiansborg. He produced in 1764 a grammar of Fanti, which included selections from the Bible translated into that language.[1] The year before his death, in 1768, the Brethren attempted a renewal of the enterprise. Jacob Meder and four companions reached the coast in July of that year, during the rainy season. Within two months Meder and two helpers were in their graves. When the news reached Europe, volunteers came forward to fill the gap, and in 1770 a reinforcement of four missionaries, led by J. E. Westmann, joined the two survivors of Meder's party. They selected a site with the help of the Danish Governor of Christiansborg, but before the end of the year the four recruits had died, and Meder's surviving companions soon followed. A mortality of one hundred per cent in a staff of nine missionaries in so short a time was truly devastating. The Brethren decided to desist from their enterprise: "The Lord had so clearly closed up the road to the country with thorns, that they dared not try to brave it out there any longer."[2]

In England the earliest continuing organizations with a missionary purpose were the Society for Promoting Christian Knowledge (1699), and the Society for the Propagation of the Gospel (1701). The latter had as its sphere of work the West Indies and the American colonies, to which it appointed chaplains. The pastoral care of Europeans was, however, their main concern. John Wesley, who was a missionary of the Society in Georgia in 1736–37, found that the claims of the

[1] E. M. North, *The Book of a Thousand Tongues* (1938), 43.
[2] Holmes, *Historical Sketches of the Missions of the United Brethren for propagating the Gospel among the Heathen* (1818), 454–5; Hamilton, *A History of the Missions of the Moravian Church* (1901), 16–17; J. E. Hutton, *op. cit.*, 156; Du Plessis, *The Evangelisation of Pagan Africa*, 111–12.

settlers at Savannah left him no time for the plan he had cherished of preaching to the Indians.[1] In 1745 there was appointed as missionary to New Jersey Thomas Thompson; he had held a Fellowship at Christ's College, Cambridge, and in 1744 had resigned his curacy "out of pure zeal to become a Missionary in the cause of Christ". During his five years' service in New Jersey he interested himself in the instruction of the Negro slaves on the plantations, receiving some into the Church. But this aroused in him a desire to help the Negro in his home, and towards the end of 1750 he requested the Society to grant him an appointment to Guinea "to make a trial with the Natives, and see what Hopes there would be of introducing among them the Christian Religion".[2] His humble conception of his own contribution to the enterprise is expressed in his letter to the Society: "In an ordinary way one Labourer can do but little, yet . . . no Doubt it must be of divine Grace that the Conversion of that people is wrought, whether it be by many or by few; but if ever a Church is founded among them, some Body must lay the first Stone . . . and should I be prevented in my Intention, God only knows how long it may be before any other Person will take the same Resolution."[3] In 1751 the Society appointed him its missionary to the Gold Coast on a salary of £70 per annum. He sailed from New York to West Africa direct, calling at Fort James on the Gambia and at Sierra Leone before reaching his destination at Cape Coast Castle. Islam had already reached Sierra Leone and Ashanti.[4] Going inland at Sierra Leone he made his first contact with it; he found an old Mandingo teaching some children their lesson in Arabic on a board, and also heard the call to prayer in the local mosques five times a day. At Cape Coast he set himself to learn Fanti, but began to preach at once with the aid of an interpreter. He says of his first service in the chief's house: "I preached to them on the Nature and Attributes of God; his Providence; and of a Future State, having one to interpret to them. After coming to speak upon the Christian Religion, some of them made a Motion to go away, but I desired their patience a little longer, and they sat till I had done."[5] Finding the Castle without a chaplain, he added to his duties the pastoral care of the Europeans there. It was indeed part of his missionary

[1] C. F. Pascoe, *op. cit.*, I, 27.
[2] T. Thompson, *An Account of Two Missionary Voyages* (1758, reprinted 1937), 23.
[3] *Ibid.*, x–xi (quoted from *S.P.G. Journal*, II, 309).
[4] T. W. Arnold, *op. cit.*, 338–9.   [5] T. Thompson, *op. cit.*, 35–6.

duty, for the chief had remarked to him on the immoral lives of many that professed Christianity. He found the ground hard. He could not get the Africans to assemble more often than once a week; some even wanted liquor as the price of attending. Some of the mulattoes who had been christened in infancy were better disposed. Some adult Negroes were baptized. Within four years the climate broke his health; he returned to England in 1756. He reported just before his removal that all things considered, such "as the Prejudice of the people against him and his frequent interruptions by sickness, he could not well have had better success".[1] Despite his own discouragements, he gives "Grounds and Reasons" why he thought it probable that the people might be brought to the Christian faith.[2] It is an interesting sidelight on the outlook of the eighteenth century that so devoted a missionary should write, after he left the field, a defence of the slave-trade under the title *The African Trade for Negro Slaves shown to be consistent with the Principles of Humanity and with the Laws of Revealed Religion* (1772).[3]

Thomas Thompson was not only the first missionary of the Church of England to Africa: he was instrumental in winning the first African to receive Anglican ordination. In 1754 he sent three Negro lads to England for education. All were Cape Coast boys. They were put to school at Islington. After seven weeks "one of them could say the Lord's Prayer and the Apostles' Creed, and the other two answered well". They asked for baptism; two were baptized in 1759 (the third had died of consumption the previous year). One lost his reason and died in hospital. The sole survivor was Philip Quaque.[4]

Philip Quaque completed his training and took Anglican orders, the first non-European since the Reformation to do so. In 1765 he was appointed by the S.P.G. as their "Missionary, School Master and Catechist to the Negroes on the Gold Coast". He also received the appointment of chaplain to the Company of Merchants. He arrived on the coast in 1766, and gave half a century's service until his death in 1816. During his time in

---

[1] C. F. Pascoe, *op. cit.*, I, 255–6.   [2] T. Thompson, *op. cit.*, 81–7.
[3] *D.N.B.*, XIX, 703a, where E. I. Carlyle says of the book, that Thompson "without considering the subject very deeply, draws his arguments from Aristotle and his illustration from the Pentateuch". Granville Sharp published a reply in 1776 entitled *The Just Limitation of Slavery in the Laws of God. To which is added a Plan for the Gradual Abolition of Slavery in the Colonies.*—E. C. P. Lascelles, *Granville Sharp* (1928), 139.
[4] T. Thompson, *op. cit.*, 66–7; C. F. Pascoe, *op. cit.*, I, 256.

England he had forgotten his mother tongue, so that on his return he had to use an interpreter. In 1769 the Society felt impelled to urge him "to endeavour to recover his own language". The task of winning individuals to a Christian confession was a hard one. After nine years' work, there were only fifty-two baptisms, and these included Europeans and mulatto children. A principal obstacle to his work was the unworthy example of Europeans, even of the highest rank. One Governor openly ridiculed religion, public worship was sometimes suspended for nearly a year, and in general the effect was to offer the Negro the white man's vices rather than his religion.[1] Under the pressure of these discouragements, and with no missionary colleague who could share the burden, it is not surprising if Philip Quaque's devotion was found flagging. It is admitted that after 1774 he was tired of being settled in one place at Cape Coast, and began visiting other centres for months at a time. The Society even considered his removal to some other part of Africa where he might be more useful than at Cape Coast. In 1791, for refusing a peremptory order of the Governor "to attend him to Anamabu to take up arms in defence of the fort" as being inconsistent with his profession, he was suspended as chaplain, but on appeal to the African Company was reinstated with an increase of salary.[2] The one charge against him that appears substantiated is that he mingled the interests of trade with the pursuit of his profession. The home authorities admitted that he had "quite deviated from the Intentions of the Society, and his proper Line of Duty by paying more Attention to the Purposes of Trade than of Religion".[3] In harmony with this is the fact that at his death in 1816 five years' arrears of salary remained undrawn. It was the temptation to engage in trade to which he succumbed, a strong temptation to the African with his keen instinct for trading, and stimulated by the example of Europeans all around him, for officials regarded appointment to the Coast as offering this opportunity for private gain. The African Company erected a memorial to Philip Quaque at Cape Coast Castle testifying to his employment as missionary of the Society and chaplain to the factory for upwards of half a century. It was the mid-

[1] C. F. Pascoe, *op. cit.*, I, 256–7.

[2] E. C. Martin, *op. cit.*, 42, claims that his suspension was due to "his disreputable living", but that the cause was his refusal to go on military service seems clear.

[3] *Ibid.*, 42, quoting letter from S.P.G. in *Report of the Board of Trade on the Trade of Africa* (1789).

nineteenth century before another full-time appointment as missionary was made by the Society to the Gold Coast.[1]

Thus the seventeenth and eighteenth centuries slipped by with the Christian enterprise in Africa all but dormant, and the evil tentacles of the slave-trade so enveloping the continent that only the doughtiest champion could hope to set her free. But in this same eighteenth century deliverance was being prepared. The Christian faith became alive again, and inspired the leadership that dealt a death-blow to the slave-trade, and eventually to slavery itself. This same revival produced a missionary zeal that found in Africa a sphere that taxed its best endeavours.

[1] C. F. Pascoe, *op. cit.*, I, 258–9.

CHAPTER 9

ASSAULT ON SLAVERY

THE effective renewal of Christian enterprise in Africa came as the result of an extensive revival of religion that swept through Great Britain and America in the course of the eighteenth century. It not only changed profoundly the religious complexion of the British Isles and North America; it was the motive power behind far-reaching social reforms at home and produced an amazing record of self-denying service overseas. The evils and the evil of the slave-trade were exposed to the British public, and after a hard contested struggle lasting little less than a generation, the nation prohibited the traffic. Another quarter of a century's campaigning brought about within the British Dominions the abolition of the institution of slavery itself. While this epic struggle was proceeding missionary societies were springing up in Great Britain, North America and on the continent of Europe. The renewal of the Christian enterprise through these agencies produced an amazing expansion of Christianity throughout the world during the nineteenth century and after. The peoples of Africa through many vicissitudes shared in the general progress, so that little of non-Muslim Africa remained untouched after a century and a half of effort. Moreover, Roman missions were stimulated into new life in the process. The total achievement stands unparalleled for so short a time.

(1) *The Background of Religious Revival.*

Like all great movements that appear to spring suddenly into life, the evangelical revival had its antecedents. There were in later seventeenth-century England and surviving into the eighteenth fertile oases that were evidence of springs of spiritual refreshment in a dry and seemingly barren land. Among these were the Religious Societies that sought to nurture the spiritual life of the more devout in a difficult age. Through these circles like-minded Christians discovered one another; their spiritual witness reached to the continent of Europe where Spener and Francke, and through them Zinzendorf and the Moravians, were influenced by them. Their common concern in seeking to recover a vital spiritual purpose for life, not from a rational illumination merely but through the quickening influence of the Christian revelation, was inherited by the leaders of the evangelical revival.

That Christianity seemed in decay in England was no unfounded lament. Natural had displaced revealed religion through the ascendancy of Deism. This, the accepted attitude of the educated, admitted a belief in one God, but not a God who was in active providential control of His universe. Bishop Butler, who wrote the classical refutation of the Deists' position in his *Analogy of Religion*, stated in the Preface to that work in May 1736: "It is come, I know not how, to be taken for granted, by many persons, that Christianity is not so much as a subject of inquiry; but that it is, now at length, discovered to be fictitious. And accordingly they treat it, as if, in the present age, this were an agreed point, among all people of discernment, and nothing remained but to set it up as a principal object of mirth and ridicule, as it were by way of reprisals, for its having so long interrupted the pleasures of the world."[1]

Into this dark and depressing situation burst the fire of spiritual revival, bringing new hope to multitudes of men and women in the living of their own lives and in facing the problems of their age. Most though not all of the eminent leaders were ordained clergymen of the Church of England. The name of John Wesley stands at the head of the distinguished company. His own indebtedness to the Moravians shows one stream of influence that flows from the continent of Europe.[2] George Whitefield, also in Anglican orders, was the outstanding orator of the revival. Not only was he evangelist to England, Wales and Scotland, but five times he visited the American colonies, from Georgia to Massachusetts. With Wesley's death in 1791 Methodism outside the Establishment more and more developed its own life as a separate Communion. The generous support accorded to Whitfield by the Countess of Huntingdon led to the appearance in due course of the Countess of Huntingdon's Connexion.

While on the one hand the revival of religion deepened the gulf between the more spiritual and the more worldly-minded within the Church, on the other it brought together in a close fellowship those who shared in the spiritual awakening of the time. This is not to overlook differences, by no means negligible both in doctrinal outlook and in ecclesiastical sympathy, that existed among worthy men, but many of diverse views on such

[1] *The Works of Joseph Butler, Bishop of Durham* (1804 ed.), I, lxxi–ii.
[2] A. W. Harrison, *The Evangelical Revival and Christian Reunion* (1942), 41.

matters were brought together through the discovery of a common purpose—the vocation committed to them by God of devoting their lives to Him in the unfailing service of wayfaring mankind. Within the nation many among Dissenting congregations and in those of the Establishment began to find each other. An Arian tendency in theology had invaded many Dissenting churches; the Christocentric message of the revival changed the current of their thinking, and they too, the Independents more particularly, shared in the rising tide of spiritual experience. Thus the evangelical clergy began to find, through the revival, much in common with fellow-Christians in the Dissenting churches. The editorial board of the *Evangelical Magazine*, begun in 1793, was a case in point, for it was composed of both Churchmen and Dissenters. This discovery of one another worked to powerful effect in the anti-slavery movement which was soon to challenge the mightiest vested interest of the day.

The spiritual awakening was shared by Churches in North America and on the continent of Europe, and in due course many among them came into active partnership in the launching of a new missionary movement. The discovery of a common purpose among Christians called evangelical was now more than national: it brought together in mutual helpfulness if not in actual organization British and Americans, Dutch and Germans and French and Swiss in the new activities overseas.

(2) *The Clapham Sect.*

Of particular note among the Evangelicals of the second generation was the group of distinguished men known to history as the Clapham Sect.[1] John Venn, son of Henry Venn of Huddersfield who, in Lecky's words, inoculated with the evangelical doctrines the great manufacturing population of Yorkshire, came to Clapham as rector in 1792 and during his tenure of twenty-one years was accounted the leader of the group of outstanding men of evangelical persuasion within his parish. While these had received the evangelical inheritance from the generation that had preceded them, they were Evangelicals with a difference. "Absolute as was the faith of Mr. Wilberforce and his associates," writes Sir James Stephen, "it was not possible that the system called 'Evangelical'

[1] See Sir James Stephen's brilliant essay, "The Clapham Sect", in *Essays in Ecclesiastical Biography* (3rd ed. 1853), II, 289–385, which is drawn upon here. A recent study is J. A. Patten's *These Remarkable Men* (1945).

should be asserted by them in the blunt and uncompromising tone of their immediate predecessors. A more elaborate education, greater familiarity with the world and with human affairs, a deeper insight into science and history, with a far nicer discernment of mere conventional proprieties, had opened to them a range of thought, and had brought them into relations with society, of which their fathers were comparatively destitute."[1] But even if they were in this respect Evangelicals with a difference, they were not a tithe less true to their inheritance in the effort to spread in the world around them that experience of Christian brotherhood which they enjoyed among themselves. Among the topics they discussed at Clapham were the abolition of the slave-trade and the expansion of Christianity as well as many needed reforms nearer home. They not only discussed but they acted with resounding effect upon the world, as we shall see. They were comprehensive in the use of methods to attain their ends: parliamentary campaigns, the education of public opinion through the Press, the dissemination of evangelical literature and above all of the Scriptures, the encouragement and support of evangelical pulpits. The personnel of the group may be briefly introduced, as to the principal figures, for their activities were closely intertwined with the fortunes of Africa in their time.

Henry Thornton (1760–1815) was frequently the host to these friends in his house at Clapham Common, which he had purchased in 1792, when John Venn came to the parish, a house that had belonged to William Pitt. Henry Thornton was a wealthy banker. For more than thirty years he sat as Member of Parliament for Southwark. The generous son of a generous father (John Thornton of the first generation of Evangelicals is described in Cowper's "Charity"), he gave away six-sevenths of his annual income to the needy, revising this to one-third after his marriage when the responsibilities of a family came upon him. The most brilliant among the friends he entertained was William Wilberforce (1759–1833), "the very sun of the Claphamic system" Sir James Stephen calls him. Elected M.P. for Hull when only twenty-one, he was before long joined in the House by his friend William Pitt. With wealth and social station, natural endowment and popular admiration, he let the years go by in easy pleasure until his crisis came. As a boy of ten he had spent a couple of years in an uncle's home in London; his aunt, a sister of John Thornton, was of the evange-

[1] *Essays in Ecclesiastical Biography* (3rd ed, 1853) II, 311.

lical persuasion and an ardent admirer of George Whitefield's preaching. Familiarity with Scripture and habits of devotion were acquired by him at this time. But wind of these religious influences and their effect reached his mother. She took alarm. He was called home to Hull and was submitted to a course of treatment designed to obliterate all "methodist" impressions. The treatment appeared at the time to be entirely successful.[1] But some fifteen years later, when travelling on the Continent, these early impressions revived. In particular they seem to have been stimulated by the chance discovery and the reading of Doddridge's *Rise and Progress of Religion in the Soul*. Isaac Milner, the Cambridge don, was a travelling companion at the time. Later John Newton, then rector of St. Mary Woolnoth in Lombard Street, was sought out as a spiritual adviser. Wilberforce emerged from the crisis a sincere and humble Christian disciple. There was no gainsaying the transformation. Said a friend of the family: "If this is madness, I hope that he will bite us all." William Pitt wrote of "a new aera in your life".[2] Within two years the new disciple had discovered his vocation as apostle in Parliament of the British anti-slavery movement. His dedication to the task was an event of outstanding importance in the history of Africa.[3]

Another member of the Clapham fellowship was Granville Sharp (1735–1813). Through his interest in suffering Negro slaves brought to England by visiting West Indian planters, he devoted himself to studying the law on the subject, and eventually succeeded in securing from the Chief Justice, Lord Mansfield, the famous judgment of 1772 regarding the forcible detention of a slave: "I cannot say this case is allowed or approved by the law of England; and therefore the black must be discharged." As Professor Coupland comments: "Its

---

[1] R. I. and S. Wilberforce, *The Life of William Wilberforce* (1838), I, 4–9.
[2] R. Coupland, *Wilberforce* (1923), 39, 44.
[3] As a boy of fourteen he had written a letter to the Press "in condemnation of the odious traffic in human flesh". In 1780 he had requested a friend, bound for Antigua, to gather information for him on the subject. The Diary has an entry for Nov. 13, 1783, "Ramsay—negroes", recording thus a conversation with the Rev. James Ramsay, late of St. Kitts, whose *Essay on the Treatment and Conversion of Slaves in the British Sugar Colonies* (1784), a brave pioneer publication, was to arouse a furore of abuse. Thus out of his interest in and study of the subject came his call, so that the Journal for Sunday, Oct. 28, 1787, contains the entry: "God Almighty has set before me two great objects, the suppression of the slave trade and the reformation of manners."—R. I. and S. Wilberforce, *op. cit.*, I, 9, 46, 147, 149. Cf. R. Coupland, *op. cit.*, 91–3.

implicit extension to all a slave-owner's rights was obvious, and from that time all slaves in England . . . were recognized as free men. . . . Thus, mainly as the outcome of one man's work, slavery was deleted from the British Isles."[1] This might well be considered a sufficient life achievement, but in the course of African affairs we meet the doughty Granville Sharp again.

Zachary Macaulay (1768–1838), less well known to a later age than his distinguished eldest son, Thomas Babington, Lord Macaulay, had gone to Jamaica at the age of sixteen. Returning in 1792 through his disgust at what he had seen of slavery, he served in Sierra Leone, and gave nearly forty years of unstinted service to great causes on his return. The abolition of the slave-trade was his central concern, but he was active in missionary and educational movements.[2] Sir James Stephen speaks of the devotion with which he pursued the fight against slavery as a task divinely committed to him. He, too, was in the evangelical succession.[3]

James Stephen (1758–1832) was the lawyer of the group. He had practised in the West Indies, and while there had provided Wilberforce with information about slavery and the slave-trade. In 1794 he returned to England and in 1808 became a Member of Parliament.[4]

Charles Grant (1746–1823) was a member of the group with interests in the East. He returned from India in 1790, became a Director of the East India Company, and was three times its Chairman. Both in this capacity and as Member of Parliament his influence was used for many a religious and philanthropic cause. John Shore, Lord Teignmouth (1751–1834), an ex-Viceroy of India, also became one of the Clapham circle and among his Christian undertakings became the first President of the British and Foreign Bible Society, a position he adorned with honour for thirty years.

A tablet in Clapham Parish Church commemorates the "servants of Christ sometime called 'The Clapham Sect' who in the latter part of the XVIIIth Century and early part of the XIXth Century laboured so abundantly for the increase of National Righteousness and the Conversion of the Heathen and rested not until the curse of slavery was swept away from

[1] R. Coupland, *The British Anti-Slavery Movement* (1933), 55
[2] See Leslie Stephen in *D.N.B.*, XXXIV, 420.
[3] See especially Stephen, *op. cit.*, II, 330—1.
[4] His son is the author of the Essay on the Clapham Sect.

all parts of the British Dominions".[1] They had, indeed, many coadjutors, others likeminded who marched with them; but there was no other group so distinguished as this in the evangelical succession, with such decisive achievement to its credit. The tasks they pursued with courageous and unflagging devotion were regarded as obligations solemnly laid upon them by their Lord. With all the heroic self-denial and steadfast zeal of men on pilgrimage, they surmounted difficulties, challenged threatening opposition, and dealt many a mortal blow to evils of the time. Through service to the Negro in which they and others were devotedly engaged, the face of slave-ravaged Africa slowly began to change.

(3) *The Establishment of a Settlement in Sierra Leone.*

The judgment of Lord Mansfield in 1772 had created a new social problem. Homeless Negroes appeared, cast adrift by their former masters, and in London particularly the destitute black poor challenged humanitarian sympathies. With the recognition of the independence of the American colonies their numbers were increased, for of the Negroes who had fought on the British side both on land and sea some were brought to London. Granville Sharp had thought of a settlement in West Africa as a solution of the problem as early as 1783, but it was four years later before the first attempt was made. There was set up in 1786 a Committee for Relieving the Black Poor, and a certain Dr. Henry Smeathman produced a memorandum strongly advocating Sierra Leone as a suitable and salubrious locality for a settlement.[2] His commendation proved tragically misleading. Granville Sharp, however, supported the proposal, and the Government accepted the responsibility of transporting the Negroes to their new home. Smeathman's untimely death threw the whole burden of the enterprise on the shoulders of Granville Sharp. Captain Thompson, R.N., sailed in command of a party of 411 settlers on February 22, 1787. Among the company were some sixty women of ill repute, included without Granville Sharp's knowledge. The Government was active in ridding the country of undesirables; this was the year

[1] The tablet was erected in 1919. The names commemorated include those we have mentioned together with the fathers, John Thornton and Henry Venn, sometime Curate of Clapham. The full text is given in E. C. P. Lascelles, *Granville Sharp* (1928), 134.

[2] H. C. Luke, *A Bibliography of Sierra Leone* (1925), 85–6. Smeathman was a naturalist who had been in Sierra Leone but had grievously failed to recognize the climatic difficulties that would confront any new settlement.

in which the convict fleet sailed for Botany Bay. The voyage to
Sierra Leone was unhappily prolonged until May 9th, when
the rainy season was just beginning—the worst time of the
year at which to arrive. It was too late to build houses or plant
food crops, and the worst season for disease was upon them.
There were 130 survivors in March 1788. Granville Sharp
despatched a relief ship with supplies largely at his personal
expense, and the settlement was saved from immediate disaster.
Meanwhile Captain Thompson had secured by treaty twenty
square miles of land from a local chief, but when he left there
was no leader; Granville Sharp had placed his faith in a system
of frankpledge, but this ideal arrangement of a system of
mutual service by all members of the community assumed a
self-discipline which did not exist. Granville Sharp was acutely
distressed when he learned that some had even deserted from
the settlement to engage in the slave-trade, and he wrote
sternly to the settlers on the matter. It was clear that some
new arrangement must be made if the settlement were not to
disappear. And so arose the Sierra Leone Company.[1]

The inspiring idea behind the formation of the Company
was due to Granville Sharp. It was that the organization and
control of the settlement should be combined with the enterprise of legitimate trade, that is, the commercial development
of the natural resources of Africa as against the trade in men.
To foster such commerce as a means of displacing the slave-
trade was indeed a new idea. Two generations later David
Livingstone was to sound it as a trumpet call in initiating a
new campaign for African freedom: "I go back to Africa to
try to make an open path for commerce and Christianity."[2]
But to Granville Sharp belongs the honour both of a new conception and a new and daring project based upon it—daring,
because the slave-trade was still legal, and the new enterprise
would start from zero in the effort to compete with the most
lucrative traffic in the world. The idea was taken up and a
charter sought from Parliament. The aims were specified as
follows: "To colonize a small part of the coast of Africa, to
introduce civilization among the natives, and to cultivate the
soil by means of free labour, at the same time abjuring all
concerns whatever in the odious traffic of human bodies, and

---

[1] E. C. P. Lascelles, *op. cit.*, 81–4. Lascelles had access to the original
letters and papers of Granville Sharp, and is here followed when authorities
conflict. E. C. Martin, *op. cit.*, 103–8.
[2] *Dr. Livingstone's Cambridge Lectures*, ed. Monk (1858), 24.

binding itself neither to deal in slaves, nor to allow of any slave-trade in the territory; to maintain peace unless attacked; to punish crimes; to govern all equally according to the laws of England; to open schools for reading, writing and accounts, and to receive and instruct the children of the natives, if sent to the schools."[1] Despite the opposition of the Company of Merchants that already controlled the various British forts and trading settlements along the coast, the petition of the St. George's Bay Company, as it was at first called, was received by the Commons in February 1791, and by the end of May was carried to the Lords by one of its leading supporters, Henry Thornton. On June 6th the Royal Assent was given. The name had now become: The Sierra Leone Company. The able and experienced Henry Thornton presided over the Board of Directors which included Granville Sharp, William Wilberforce and Thomas Clarkson. That the philanthropic motive was in the foreground such names would guarantee, but this was made explicit in the first Report: "The Directors are endeavouring in the outset rather to lay the foundation of happiness to Africa, and of future prosperity to the Company, than to grasp at any premature advantages."[2]

No sooner had the Company assumed control than an event occurred of outstanding significance for the future welfare of the settlement. This was the arrival of a fresh troop of settlers. While the Company had been in process of formation, a new calamity had befallen the little outpost of civilization; a neighbouring chief had attacked and burned out the settlement in retaliation for wrongs he had suffered at the hands of other white men. Sharp and others had despatched a relief ship and sixty odd of the old settlers were found and brought back to a new centre named Granville Town. The settlement was saved, but new blood would strengthen the weakened community. A number of free Negroes who had fought on the British side in the American War of Independence and had been subsequently settled in Nova Scotia, disliked the climate and general situation in which they found themselves. They applied for admission to the Sierra Leone settlement. These Nova Scotians, as they are called, were welcomed by the Company. The Government agreed to collect and deliver them and sent for this purpose Lieutenant John Clarkson, R.N., the brother of Thomas Clarkson. In February 1792 Lieut. Clarkson arrived

[1] Quoted in Luke, *op. cit.*, 8.
[2] *Report of the Court of Directors of the Sierra Leone Company* (1791), 54.

with over twelve hundred Negroes from Nova Scotia. Until December of that year Clarkson officiated as Governor under the new regime of the Company. His manuscript diary throws a flood of light on the trials he had to endure through the ravages of disease on the one hand, and the discontent of the disappointed Nova Scotians on the other, and also bears witness to the Christian concern for his people by which he was animated.[1] He discharged the clerical duties until a chaplain arrived and says: "The sermons I in general read to the congregation are principally Bishop Watson's, given me by the Bishop of Nova Scotia, and occasionally as circumstances require a select one, from Blair. It is truly gratifying to me to see the orderly and decent conduct of my Sunday flock."[2] A letter from Henry Thornton received in August informed him that a suitable chaplain had been appointed, the Rev. Melville Horne, an Anglican clergyman who "has been in Wesley's connexion"; the letter added: "We have a very capable manager of an estate who has left Jamaica for Sierra Leone . . . His name is Macauley."[3] We shall meet these two again. Clarkson was a great gift to the settlement in these early months of rehabilitation. He had won the confidence of the Nova Scotians, and treated with wisdom and courtesy the neighbouring peoples and the officials of the Company. The purpose of the whole enterprise was larger than that of providing a settlement for Negroes in distress from England and Nova Scotia. It was viewed as the beginning of the attempt to bring Christianity and civilization to Africa, and an honourable commerce in place of the detested slave-trade. Twice in his Journal Clarkson speaks of it: "I have no other end in view than the happiness of those committed to my care as well as the general civilization of this benighted continent"; and again: ". . . this Colony established in hopes of spreading a general blessing throughout Africa".[4] John Clarkson was succeeded by William Dawes who in turn handed over the reigns of government to Zachary Macaulay, his second in command. From March 1794 until April 1799, Macaulay governed the colony, paying only one visit to England. Six months after his taking over the office, a heavy calamity befell the struggling settlement. England and France were now at war, and on September 28, 1794, a French

---

[1] The manuscript is in the possession of the Clarkson family. The diary for the period August 5 to November 5, 1792, has been printed in *Sierra Leone Studies*, No. VIII (March, 1927), 1–114. Cf. also Ingham, *Sierra Leone after a Hundred Years* (1894).   [2] *Sierra Leone Studies*, No. VIII, 23. [3] *Ibid.*, 28–9.   [4] *Ibid.*, 30, 55.

squadron, piloted by two Americans whose runaway slaves had taken refuge in the colony, sailed up to Freetown. Macaulay interviewed the commodore in hope of saving the place from destruction by stating its philanthropic purpose, but only had for his answer: "Citoyen, cela peut bien être, mais encore vous êtes Anglais." For a fortnight the French sailors worked their will upon the settlement; livestock were killed, stores were looted, instruments smashed and records ruined. "I had the mortification", says Macaulay, "to see a great part of my own labour, and of the labour of others for several years, totally destroyed." The Directors estimated the financial loss at £52,000. They had need be philanthropists. Macaulay set himself with dauntless courage to rebuild what had been cast down. The settlers had fled, provisions were exhausted, and disease was rife. His earlier cordial relations with neighbouring slave-dealers, despite his detestation of their trade, now bore fruit in the essential provisions and stores which they supplied. The settlers were drawn back into an ordered community. A desperate situation had been retrieved by outstanding personal courage and a religious faith that was incapable of extinction by disaster. But the strain had told, and exhausting attacks of malaria demanded a respite. Although a sick man he determined to make his return to England by the West Indies in order to experience life on a slave-ship. This he did by way of Barbados. On his return after eight months in England, he governed an increasingly prosperous colony. It is not to be wondered at that his devotion to the welfare of those he governed led to many settlers adopting Macaulay as their family name.[1]

The enterprise had been maintained to secure a base for Christian activity in Africa, but the cost had been heavy. The failure in 1799 to carry the Abolition Bill in Parliament was a setback in the general plan. The Company was strained to the limit of its resources and had, indeed, received occasional small grants from Parliament to enable the work to continue. In 1804 the Directors proposed a transfer to the Crown, and in 1807 the Act was passed by which the transfer was made. On January 1, 1808, Sierra Leone became a Crown Colony. Henry Thornton had worked devotedly for the enterprise, and in the end lost some two to three thousand pounds by it, but held that it was "on the whole well given".[2] The members of the

---

[1] Knutsford, *Life and Letters of Zachary Macaulay* (1900), 64–84; C. Booth, *Zachary Macaulay* (1934), 38–58. Charles Booth, a descendant of Zachary Macaulay, had access to his papers and private diaries. Lascelles, *op. cit.*, 84–7; Martin, *op. cit.*, 123–31.   [2] Martin, *op. cit.*, 133–43.

Company who were committed to the philanthropic side of its activities now constituted along with others the African Institution to further them. Zachary Macaulay became the first secretary; Henry Thornton was treasurer.[1]

The year 1807 in which the Act of transfer was passed was the year of the abolition of the slave-trade, the first resounding victory in the parliamentary campaign of the anti-slavery movement. British ships of war were now authorized, within the limits of international conventions, to seize slavers and liberate their cargoes. They could not be restored to their homelands; they were landed at Sierra Leone. Here was a new demand upon the sympathies of evangelical Christendom. Sierra Leone thus became the natural centre upon the West Coast for the work of the new Missionary Societies when they first arose.

(4) The Anti-Slavery Movement.

While the establishment of a settlement for free Negroes at Sierra Leone was a courageous and disinterested effort to deal with the immediate problem of liberated Negroes in need and at the same time was calculated to become the starting-point for honourable relations with Africans in their own home, yet little could be achieved while the slave-trade continued. To get rid of the nefarious traffic, and of slavery itself, was the major task upon which energy had to be concentrated.

In this Abolition Movement members of the Clapham Sect were again to the fore, but many streams of influence contributed to its strength. To the Quakers belongs the place of honour as being the first Christian community to experience an awakened conscience on the matter, and in due course to discipline their members when obdurate on the slavery issue. In the American colonies the Quakers were pioneers for abolition, not only of the trade, but of slavery itself. The first recorded protest is that of the group of Friends, probably from Holland, issued in 1688 at Germantown, Pennsylvania. Other appeals followed within a decade.[2] Effective action, however,

[1] The First Report stated that it was "the Society's fixed determination not to undertake any religious missions, and not to engage in commercial speculations". It was rather concerned to see that the laws abolishing the slave-trade became effectual, and to promote the development of the resources of Africa and the education of her peoples.—*Report of the Committee of the African Institution* (1807), 65–71.

[2] H. J. Cadbury, "An Early Quaker Anti-Slavery Statement", in *The Journal of Negro History* (1937), 488–93. This original protest is said to have been made by German Mennonites who identified themselves with the Quakers and were known as "German Quakers".

was delayed for another two or three generations. Then John Woolman had arrived. His conscience was awakened when, in 1742, he was preparing as an apprentice a bill of sale for a Negress. Study of the facts deepened his conviction of the evil of slavery. In 1758, in a memorable Friends' Yearly Meeting in Philadelphia, he voiced his protest against yet another shelving of the issue. His word had effect: "This appeal moved the hearts of the large assembly to a sense of their neglected duty. Sympathetic discussion followed, and finally the Truth triumphed over all opposition, and the first committee then appointed began its actual aggressive work. More than any other one man, Woolman aided the English-speaking nations to throw off the disgrace of slavery."[1] As with Wilberforce in England, so with this pioneer in America, it was a deep religious motive and not a rational humanitarianism that first prompted action and maintained the steadfast purpose. Among outstanding champions of the cause was Anthony Benezet (1713–84), a Quaker schoolmaster of Philadelphia, who was indefatigable in securing facts about the slave-trade and publishing pamphlets on the subject, as well as writing to persons of influence on both sides of the Atlantic in the endeavour to arouse their interest.[2]

In Great Britain also the Quakers were the first to organize support for Abolition and to seek to educate public opinion on the subject. In 1783 they appointed a committee for the purpose, and among other activities they circulated a tract of Anthony Benezet's. It was a Quaker who helped Thomas Clarkson to publish in 1786 the English edition of his Latin Prize Essay on slavery.[3] A year later Clarkson was instrumental in bringing together the Quaker supporters with other friends of the movement into a Society for the Abolition of the Slave Trade, of whose standing committee Thomas Clarkson and Granville Sharp were fellow-members. Its object was to procure and publish all relevant facts that would educate public opinion

[1] Rufus M. Jones, *The Quakers in the American Colonies* (1911), 396–7.

[2] W. Armistead, *Anthony Benezet* (1859), *passim*.

[3] In 1785 Thomas Clarkson competed for, and won with high commendation, the University Latin Essay prize at Cambridge on the subject *Anne liceat invitos in servitutem dare?* He found Anthony Benezet's *Historical Account of Guinea* a mine of information for his purpose. It was the work for this essay that led to his self-dedication to the anti-slavery movement. The English edition was published in 1786 under the title *An Essay on the Slavery and Commerce of the Human Species, particularly the African, Translated from a Latin Dissertation, which was honoured with the first prize in the University of Cambridge for the year 1785.*—E. L. Griggs, *Thomas Clarkson* (1936), 24–6, 30.

to demand the abolition of the traffic.[1] Clarkson was already in
touch with Wilberforce who, in this same year 1787, took up
the parliamentary leadership of the campaign for abolition.
The joint activity thus represented by Clarkson and Wilberforce was necessary for success—a public opinion that would
support such action and a leadership in Parliament that would
wisely yet insistently press for the reform. Thomas Clarkson
was at once busy with his pen and produced four new treatises
in the next four years.[2] Wilberforce prepared to launch the
attack in the House of Commons in the course of 1788. Those
of the Clapham fellowship who sat in Parliament were his
closest coadjutors, nicknamed the "Saints", of whom Professor
Coupland writes: "It was their selfless devotion to high causes,
their lack of all personal ambition, their scrupulous honesty
and candour, their frank appeal to conscience and Christianity,
that gave that little group a power in the House of Commons
out of all proportion to its numbers or its parliamentary gifts."
They were not bound to party, but for the most part remained
independent on principle: "It was, indeed, because of this
independence and because it was known to be grounded on a
refusal to obey the lesser loyalties of life, that the 'Saints'
were so great a force in Parliament and outside it. 'A brotherhood of Christian politicians'—there has never been anything
like it since."[3] Wilberforce had in his crusade a warm friend
and staunch supporter in William Pitt, though as Prime
Minister Pitt's possibility of action was limited by the views
of his colleagues. He did, however, direct the Trade Committee
of the Privy Council to inquire into the conditions of the African
trade. In the absence of Wilberforce through desperate illness,
Pitt moved the resolution that on the Committee's report the
House should consider the slave-trade. The issue with the trade
was now joined. The Abolition Committee, with Clarkson its
indefatigable courier, presented irrefutable records; Granville
Sharp met the Prime Minister in personal conference. Fox and
Burke declared themselves for Abolition. In April 1789 the
Privy Council Committee reported, and a month later the
subject was debated, Wilberforce, now restored, giving a

[1] R. Coupland, *Wilberforce*, 86, 88.
[2] *A Summary View of the Slave-Trade, and of the probable Consequences of
its Abolition* (1787); *An Essay on the Impolicy of the African Slave Trade* (1788);
a second edition, enlarged, of the *Essay on Slavery, etc.* (1788); *An Essay on
the Comparative Efficiency of Regulation or Abolition, as applied to the Slave
Trade* (1789); and *Letters on the Slave Trade, and the State of the Natives in
Africa* (1791).
[3] R. Coupland, *The British Anti-Slavery Movement* (1933), 80–1.

brilliant lead in a demand for immediate abolition of the trade. But the House was not prepared for action, and with a resolution "that this House will early in the next session of Parliament, proceed to consider further the circumstances of the Slave Trade" he had to be for the time content. But he was possessed of a great patience—the patience of one who can bide his time, yet ever maintain inflexibility of purpose.[1]

Two years passed, and Wilberforce prepared again to raise the issue. There was no underrating by him or his friends of the powerful interests marshalled to oppose them. On February 24, 1791, just six days before his death, the veteran John Wesley wrote him: "Unless the divine power has raised you up to be as *Athanasius contra mundum*, I see not how you can go through your glorious enterprise in opposing that execrable villany, which is the scandal of religion, of England, and of human nature. Unless God has raised you up for this very thing, you will be worn out by the opposition of men and devils. But, if God be for you, who can be against you? Are all of them together stronger than God? O be not weary of well doing! Go on, in the name of God and in the power of His might, till even American slavery (the vilest that ever saw the sun) shall vanish away before it."[2] In April Wilberforce opened the debate with a request "to bring in a Bill to prevent the further importation of slaves into the British islands in the West Indies". He spoke with eloquence, he was supported by Burke and Fox and Pitt. And again he lost. His motion was rejected by 163 votes to 88.[3]

This second failure meant a long delay, for France, already aflame with revolution, was growing aggressive and now threatening such equilibrium as existed on the continent of Europe. Not least harmful to the cause of the Abolitionists were the lurid accounts reaching England of Negro outrages where the slaves had gained the upper hand in the French West Indies. Every conservative instinct was strengthened; this was plainly no time for so drastic an interference with the existing system as the abolition of the slave-trade. If such was the reaction of the House of Commons, public opinion in the country at large, now educated in many ways to the grim realities of the slave-trade, was more sensitive to the cry from Africa and was more directly expressed at Westminster than

[1] R. Coupland, *Wilberforce* (1923), 103–34.
[2] *The Letters of the Rev. John Wesley, A.M.* (Standard ed., 1931), VIII, 265.
[3] R. Coupland, *op. cit.*, 140–4.

it had ever been before. Following the notice of an Abolition motion given by Wilberforce in 1792, some 500 petitions poured in to the Commons in support of immediate abolition. The opposition to Wilberforce's motion took the form of an amendment proposing the addition of the word "gradually". Pitt rose to close the night-long debate as dawn was almost breaking and reached, it is said, a height of parliamentary oratory he never excelled. "And now, Sir, I come to Africa", he said, after replying to arguments for gradual abolition. "If on the ground of injustice it ought to be abolished at last, why ought it not now? Why is injustice suffered to remain for a single hour?" But remembrance of the Terror in Paris and the horror of St. Domingo carried the amendment, and the substantive motion "That the Slave Trade ought to be *gradually*-abolished" was carried by 230 votes to 85. It seemed at least a vote for the principle of abolition, and the Commons did indeed fix a date, but the Lords still stood in the way. They saw to it that the session ended without a vote. In Professor Coupland's vivid words: "Sentence had been pronounced. A hundred thousand natives of West Africa had been condemned to death or penal servitude. Before another witness could attest their sufferings in the House of Lords, war had broken out between Great Britain and France. And year after year now, it was less and less possible for English ears to hear the far faint cry of Africa beyond the guns in Europe."[1]

It was a decade before the question of abolition again reached the point of parliamentary debate. Year after year until the end of the century Wilberforce moved for leave to introduce it, and year after year he was refused. In 1794 Clarkson's health gave way under the unceasing strain to which he had been subjected, and for wellnigh a decade he was unable to participate actively in the fray. The Abolition Committee itself lay dormant from 1796 to 1804. But in the latter year a revival of interest in the slave-trade took place. The Abolition Committee resumed its activity with two new members both Claphamites, James Stephen the lawyer from the West Indies and Zachary Macaulay now returned from Sierra Leone. For the first time since 1799 Wilberforce in 1804 moved his usual resolution which this time was successful; he then introduced and carried through the House his Abolition Bill, but once again the Lords, to whom the Bill had gone, let the session close without a vote. In 1805 the Bill was reintroduced (Pitt, now carrying a heavier burden than ever in the war against Napoleon, had wished it postponed), but it was lost on the second reading. Yet victory was not now long delayed. The Bill introduced on January 2, 1807, this time in the Lords, passed through all its stages and received the Royal Assent on March 25. It became operative on January 1, 1808. Enforcement of the law was the task of the British Navy, whose patrol of the West African coast introduced a new era in West African affairs—one which saw captured African cargoes restored to Africa.[1]

To have secured the abolition of the British slave-trade was a resounding victory. Only Denmark had already taken similar action. But with this the work of the Abolitionist crusaders was only partly accomplished. To have prohibited the trade was a safeguard, as far as British action was concerned, against further ravishment of Africa to provide slave labour for the colonies. But the slaves already in the colonies still continued slaves. The institution of slavery was still in existence; the crusaders could not be content till this, also, had gone. Parliament was not prepared to consider further measures at the moment, but inclined to attempt improvement in the lot of the slave by securing slave codes. Meanwhile the struggle against Napoleon had another seven years to run, and following his defeat came the depressing post-war years with their economic, social and political problems. In 1822 Wilberforce found himself compelled to hand over the parliamentary leadership of the anti-slavery crusade, which he had held for thirty-five years, to Thomas Fowell Buxton. The campaign for the abolition of slavery itself went on with renewed vigour. Members of the Clapham Sect were again to the fore; Wilberforce issued in 1823 *An Appeal to the Religion, Justice and Humanity of the Inhabitants of the British Empire in behalf of the Negro Slaves in the West Indies;* James Stephen's *The Slavery of the British West India Colonies Delineated* appeared in two volumes in 1824 and 1830; while from 1825 *The Anti-Slavery Reporter* (begun two years before) was edited by Zachary Macaulay. Buxton led the attack in the Commons in 1823, but the policy of ameliorative measures was again preferred to abolition. The policy was tried—and failed. The slave-owners would have none of it. Ameliorative measures were not for them. Ten years of waiting, of fruitless waiting, for promised improvements found public opinion stern and unrelenting in its sharp demand for abolition. In 1833 petitions began pouring in to

[1] R. Coupland, 213–28, 270–4, 302–21, 328–43.

Parliament; by early May it was calculated the number of signatures amounted to a million and a half. Then came the climax of the popular demand with a delegate assembly in London, attended by 330 men from all parts of the country. After the first day's session in Exeter Hall they met again and proceeded in a body to Downing Street: "Drawn as they had been from almost every place of note in the United Kingdom, they included in their ranks men of every calling and denomination; among them were to be seen, we are told, 'merchants, squires, bankers, magistrates, clergymen, and dissenting ministers.' Lord Althorp and Mr. Stanley received them; and after Mr. Samuel Gurney had read the address and commented on it, Mr. Buxton stepped forward and pointed out the extent of the movement which had sent the delegates thither. 'This, my lord,' said he, 'is the deputy from Cork—this is the one from Belfast; these are from Edinburgh, those from Dundee; this gentleman is from Aberdeen, that from Carmarthen; these are the delegates from Bristol, those from Liverpool, Birmingham, Manchester, Sheffield; these from York and Leeds', etc. . . . it was the first occasion on which public feeling so emphatically expressed itself, and it was felt to be called forth by no ordinary earnestness of purpose."[1] A Bill was introduced on July 5, and on August 29 it became law. Wilberforce lived until July 29, when the success of the measure and the final victory of the cause to which his life had been dedicated were already assured. The Act became effective at midnight on July 31, 1834, when slavery ceased to exist throughout the British Dominions. Twenty millions sterling were voted as compensation to the slave-owners. The Act of 1807 prohibiting the traffic had most closely affected the West Coast of Africa; the Act of 1834 had repercussions in the South; the Boers resented British interference with their slave labour, and this was a major factor stimulating the Great Trek of 1836–40 that later proved so fateful in British-Boer relations.

Thus for full fifty years the great anti-slavery campaign was carried on; it was maintained through thick and thin by a group of men to whom this was a crusade committed to them by Divine vocation. When the passing of the measure of 1807 was secured and Wilberforce found solitude "his thoughts turned wholly to humility and gratitude before 'the Giver of all good'. 'God will bless this country', he said".[2] So Buxton

---

[1] C. Buxton (ed.), *Memoirs of Sir Thomas Fowell Buxton, Bart.* (4th ed., 1850), 267. [2] R. Coupland, *Wilberforce*, 343.

and his colleagues accepted their victory twenty-six years later. It was this sense of an Unseen leadership and of being sustained by more than human power that, according to their own testimony, enabled the campaigners to plod on year after year, despite constant disappointment and rebuff, and finally to acclaim the triumph of right over injustice and self-interest. "The unweary, unostentatious, and inglorious crusade of England against slavery", says Lecky, "may probably be regarded as among the three or four perfectly virtuous pages comprised in the history of nations."[1]

The success of the anti-slavery movement was not only an achievement of Christian men; it was an indispensable prerequisite for the successful planting of Christianity in Africa. The self-criticism of Roman Catholic writers concerning their own earlier missions in this regard has already been noted. The first sustained Protestant efforts were to be without this incubus at least. But such a preparation, valuable as it was, remained negative nevertheless; it was but the removal of an obstacle to progress. There were still necessary those positive missionary activities that alone could communicate to Africa the Christian life and message. For this purpose suitable organizations were required. During the very years of the anti-slavery campaigns new missionary societies were appearing—a score or more sprang up, between 1792 and 1835, in England and Scotland, in North America, and on the continent of Europe. There had been nothing like it before. The Protestant Churches were at last awake.

[1] W. E. H. Lecky, *History of European Morals* (New Impression, 1902), I, 153.

CHAPTER 10

THE MISSIONARY AWAKENING
1792-1815

WHILE the series of dramatic military and political events was in progress, which culminated in the Congress of Vienna and in Waterloo, another series of a not less momentous character was taking place. A group of new Societies began to appear, that were destined to carry the Christian message, revitalized by the evangelical awakening, around the world. First in Great Britain, then on the continent of Europe and in North America they arose. Despite the unpropitious character of the times they set to work with enlightened enthusiasm, and long before political tranquillity was restored, had established pioneer missions in Asia and Africa. These beginnings, humble though they were, grew into enterprises without parallel in the expansion of the Christian Church. We stand on the threshold of an amazing century.

(1) *The Rise of New Missionary Societies.*

One of the earliest attempts to found a missionary society with evangelical support was made by Dr. Coke, personal friend of John Wesley and entrusted by him with the direction of overseas Methodist activities. There appeared in 1784 "A Plan of the Society for the Establishment of Missions among the Heathens", over the names of Thomas Coke and Thomas Parker, the latter a Methodist barrister. One of the Society's objects was stated to be: "To procure the best Instruction which can be obtained for such Persons, in the Language of the Country for which they are intended, before they go abroad," and another: "To print the Scriptures . . . for the use of any Heathen Country." It seems that the Society was intended to be undenominational, but the proposal met with little support. Dr. Coke was soon engaged to the limit of his powers with Methodist missionary developments in North America and the West Indies. The Plan proved abortive and we hear no more of it.[1]

It was William Carey who had the distinction of leading the way in 1792 when the Baptist Missionary Society was founded.

---

[1] The Plan is reproduced in full in Findlay and Holdsworth, *The History of the Wesleyan Methodist Missionary Society*, II (1921), 14–16. See also I, 64–5.

One contributory stream of influence sprang from the American colonies where Jonathan Edwards of Northampton, Massachusetts, published in 1747 a book entitled *An humble attempt to promote explicit agreement and visible union of God's people in extraordinary prayer for the revival of religion, and the advancement of Christ's Kingdom on earth.* The reading of this by English Baptist ministers of the Northamptonshire Association led to the appointment of a day in each month for such united prayer, and from 1784 this was done.[1] William Carey was himself a child of the Evangelical Revival. His chief helper in his early religious life was an Anglican clergyman, Thomas Scott, who had himself found escape from the arid desert of Deism into the joy of a vital religious experience. "If there be anything of the work of God in my soul," wrote William Carey, "I owe much of it to Mr. Scott's preaching, when I first set out in the ways of the Lord."[2] Between 1787 and 1789 Carey wrote his famous *Enquiry*, first published in 1792.[3] It was in May of that year, after a challenging sermon of Carey's at Baptist Association meetings and his personal appeal to take immediate action, that it was agreed: "That a plan be prepared against the next Ministers' Meeting at Kettering, for forming a Baptist Society for propagating the Gospel among the Heathens." On October 2, 1792, the Baptist Missionary Society was constituted. The first of the new missionary societies had been born.[4]

When Dr. Ryland of Bristol received, in 1794, William Carey's first letter from India, among the friends called in to hear it was a Congregational minister, David Bogue, who as a consequence published an appeal that Evangelicals other than Baptists might undertake their own mission overseas. At the same time there had appeared a book by Melville Horne, the chaplain of Sierra Leone, in which he made a very direct and

---

[1] *The Centenary Volume of the Baptist Missionary Society* (1892), 4; E. A. Payne, *The Church Awakes* (1942), 31; E. A. Payne, *Before the Start* (L.M.S. Triple Jubilee Papers, No. 2, 1942), 8.

[2] S. Pearce Carey, *William Carey* (8th ed., 1934), 35–6. It is striking to find so different a figure as John Henry Newman also confessing his debt to Thomas Scott to whom, he says, "humanly speaking, I almost owe my soul".—S. C. Carpenter, *Church and People, 1789-1889* (1933), 120.

[3] *An Enquiry into the Obligations of Christians to use means for the Conversion of the Heathens* (1792). It was reprinted in 1818, and facsimile editions of the first were issued in 1892 and 1942 by the Baptist Missionary Society. In his survey of the existing religious state of the world, Carey lists nineteen "Countries" of Africa, apart from Islands, five of which are classed as mainly Muslim and twelve as pagan. Significantly, Roman Catholics are only reported for the various African Islands.   [4] S. Pearce Carey, *op. cit.*, 81–7, 91–4.

searching appeal for missionary service.[1] Various meetings and appeals that followed culminated in the establishment in London, in September 1795, of "The Missionary Society". Similar influences north of the Tweed resulted in the founding of the Edinburgh and the Glasgow Missionary Societies in 1796. The London Missionary Society,[2] which was thus the second to arrive, began as an interdenominational organization as did also the Edinburgh and Glasgow Societies. David Bogue hailed this aspect of it on its formation: "We have now before us a pleasing spectacle, Christians of different denominations although differing in points of church government, united in forming a society for propagating the gospel among the heathen. This is a new thing in the Christian church. . . . Here are Episcopalians, Methodists, Presbyterians, and Independents, all united in one society, all joining to form its laws, to regulate its institutions, and manage its various concerns."[3] But in due course Episcopalians, Methodists and Presbyterians constituted their own Societies, the support of the London Missionary Society then falling in the main upon Congregationalists. Before the end of the century the Society had entered upon its historic work in South Africa, where lustre was added to its missionary annals by names of such distinction as Robert Moffat, John Philip, David Livingstone, and John Mackenzie.

One direct result of its establishment was the appearance of the first of the new Societies on the continent of Europe, the Netherlands Missionary Society, in 1797. This was due to the personal initiative of Dr. Vanderkemp, accepted for service by the London Missionary Society and their pioneer at the Cape.[4]

These events stimulated evangelical leaders within the Established Church. In 1796 Charles Simeon introduced at a meeting of the Eclectic Society[5] the question: "With what propriety, and in what mode, can a Mission be attempted to the heathen from the Established Church?" One who was present wrote across his notes of the discussion: "This conversation proved the foundation of the Church Missionary Society."[6] Three years went by before action was taken. In April 1799 the new Society

[1] *Letters on Missions addressed to the Protestant Ministers of the British Churches* (1794).
[2] In the original Plan the name was simply "The Missionary Society". "London" first appears in the official publications in 1818.
[3] *Sermons preached in London at the Formation of the Missionary Society* (1795), 130.
[4] *Report of the Directors* at the Fourth General Meeting (1789), 10–12.
[5] Founded in 1783 by a group of clergy and laymen.
[6] C. Hole, *The Early History of the Church Missionary Society* (1896), 25–6.

was constituted, with Claphamites active in its counsels—
William Wilberforce, Charles Grant, Henry Thornton, Zachary
Macaulay, Charles Simeon and John Venn were all officially
connected with it. Melville Horne and John Newton were additional members with West African experience. The first secretary was Thomas Scott, spiritual father of William Carey.[1]
The name became in due course Church Missionary Society.[2]
To secure the interest of the episcopate was a delicate business,
entrusted to the capable hands of Wilberforce. It was nearly
a year before he could report that the Archbishop of Canterbury
"acquiesced in the hope I expressed that the Society might go
forward, being assured he would look on the proceedings with
candour, and that it would give him pleasure to find them such
as he could approve".[3] During this year of waiting an important
decision was taken: on November 4, 1799, it was resolved to
attempt as soon as convenient a mission to Sierra Leone. This
was a natural beginning. A number of leading shareholders in
the Sierra Leone Company were also members of the C.M.S.
Committee. Moreover, Zachary Macaulay, returning from his
governorship of Sierra Leone that very year, had brought with
him twenty-five Negro children for further education in England. The twenty-one boys were placed under a master at
Clapham; the four girls under a lady at Battersea. Members
of the C.M.S. Committee became interested. John Newton paid
a visit in October: "Last week I was at Clapham, and saw the
twenty African blackbirds. . . . I am told the boys come forward
apace, behave well, and seem very happy, especially when they
see Mr. Macaulay." A visitor who saw the boys with several
Clapham friends reported: "They stood in a semicircle round
Mr. Macaulay while he questioned them in Scripture history.
Mr. Henry Thornton stood by Mr. Macaulay's side, evidently
much interested in the group before him, while Mr. Wilberforce,
on the outside of the group, went from boy to boy, patting them
on the shoulder as they gave good answers to the questions,
and giving them a few words of encouragement and an admoni-

---

[1] C. Hole, op. cit., 36–8.

[2] The name originally adopted was "Society for Missions to Africa and the
East", thus marking off its intended sphere from that of the Society for the
Propagation of the Gospel which at the time was active in America and
the West Indies. By degrees "Church Missionary Society" came into use,
the regular official style becoming "Church Missionary Society to Africa and
the East".—Ibid., 41, 42.

[3] Ibid., 58. It was not until 1815 that the first two bishops consented to
become Vice-Presidents.—Eugene Stock, The History of the Church Missionary
Society (1899), I, 110.

tion to teach the same truths to their countrymen."[1] In due course several were baptized by John Venn at Clapham.[2] Indeed when Sierra Leone was determined upon as the first field of activity, the question of training African children for the purpose was discussed. Thus the question of a native agency was early under consideration.[3] The Church Missionary Society, directed at the outset to work in Africa, was destined to play a large part in the evangelization of the continent.

During these years the background of international war had been growing steadily more sombre. In 1795, when the London Missionary Society appeared, the name of Napoleon was inspiring awe; 1799, when the Church Missionary Society was born, was the year of his campaign in Egypt. By 1805 he had an army more than 200,000 strong waiting to cross the narrow sea for the invasion of England. They waited until Trafalgar sealed the fate of any sea-borne expedition. But in the period when the threat was real, action was taken to establish a Society devoted to the circulation of the Scriptures. "If the present period", wrote the sponsors of the enterprise, "is not the most auspicious to such undertakings, neither is there any danger of its being fatal to them. 'The wall of Jerusalem', it is written, 'shall be built in troublous times.' In fact, how many successful efforts for the promotion of human happiness have been made amidst the clouds and tempests of national calamity! It also should be remembered that the present is the only period of which we are sure. Our days of service are both few and un- certain: whatsoever, therefore, our hands find to do, let us do it with our might."[4] A meeting was accordingly held on March 7, 1804, attended by some three hundred persons of various denominations, at which the British and Foreign Bible Society came into being. This was an enterprise in which Churchmen and Dissenters co-operated. The purpose was simply stated: "The sole object shall be to encourage a wider circulation of the Holy Scriptures without note or comment."[5] William Wilberforce, who could not be present in person at the meeting, wrote expressing his approbation of the project.[6] Other Claphamites were active in support: Granville Sharp

[1] C. Hole, op. cit., 49–50.
[2] On May 12, 1805, when eight were baptized, there were present Macaulay, Wilberforce, Thornton and Grant.—Ibid., 654.   [3] Ibid., 48.
[4] W. Canton, History of the British and Foreign Bible Society, I (1910), 11.
[5] Ibid., I, 18.
[6] The letter was discovered in the archives of the Society during 1943, and was printed in The Times, May 5, 1943.

presided at the meeting; Lord Teignmouth became first President and remained so for thirty years; Henry Thornton was appointed Treasurer, while Charles Grant, Zachary Macaulay and James Stephen were all officially associated with the Society, Wilberforce himself becoming a Vice-President. The founding of the Bible Society was one of the most significant steps taken at this time. We have already seen how, in earlier periods in Africa, for the bare survival of the Christian Church through the vicissitudes of the centuries, not to speak of its healthy growth, the possession of the Bible in the language of the people had proved indispensable. The modern Protestant missionary movement was now to march forward with special provision made to meet this fundamental need. In no continent has the demand for this service been greater than in Africa, with its more than five hundred languages and major dialects.

The next event in this remarkable series takes us to the United States. Some local societies had earlier been concerned with missionary advocacy and the raising of funds, but it was in 1810 that the first of the American sending societies appeared —the American Board of Commissioners for Foreign Missions. It traced its origin ultimately to the Evangelical Revival, though specific influences favoured its origin at that particular time.[1] Among these were William Carey's sermon and the founding of the Baptist Missionary Society, with Carey's own beginning in India. Then came news of the London Missionary Society whose activities "produced an indescribable effect upon large numbers of influential clergymen and laymen in this country, particularly, so far as is known, in the Northern and Middle States".[2] Another factor was the circulation of missionary literature, and in particular Melville Horne's *Letters on Missions*.[3] The rise of the British and Foreign Bible Society added a powerful impulse to the movement. This rising missionary enthusiasm was further stimulated by the passing through the States, in 1807, of Dr. Morrison of the London Missionary Society, the first Protestant missionary to reside in China. This fluid situation was finally crystallized by the

---

[1] "The American Board of Commissioners for Foreign Missions . . . had its origin neither in Bradford, nor Andover, nor Williamstown, nor any other single locality, but in the revivals at the end of the eighteenth and the beginning of the nineteenth century."—S. M. Worcester, *Discourse* (1860), 13. Dr. Samuel M. Worcester was the official spokesman at the Board's Jubilee in 1860. From his statement is derived the information here given about the early influences leading to its origin. [2] Worcester, *Discourse*, 12.
[3] "They keenly felt the expostulations of the Chaplain of Sierra Leone."— *Ibid.*, 12.

action of four Congregational divinity students. They presented a memorial to the General Association of Massachusetts in session at Bradford, stating their missionary concern, and asking whether a missionary society in their own country would enable them to fulfil their vocation. The memorial was received on June 28, 1810; on June 29th it was resolved: "That there be instituted by this General Association, a Board of Commissioners for Foreign Missions, for the purpose of devising ways and means, and adopting and prosecuting measures for promoting the spread of the gospel in heathen lands."[1] The four candidates were forthwith accepted, and an appeal issued to "the Christian public". A suggestion that the Board might co-operate with the London Missionary Society not proving practicable, it set out on its own independent career, the first of many American Societies that were to follow. Africa was entered in 1835.

Other Christian Churches in the States were subject to the same general influences, though particular events led to individual action being taken. Of the first five missionaries sent out by the American Board, two became convinced on the voyage to India of the necessity of believer's baptism, and resigned on arrival. One of these, Adoniram Judson, wrote in a letter received in January 1813: "Should there be formed a Baptist Society for the support of missions in these parts, I should be ready to consider myself their missionary." American Baptists were already concerned for overseas missions and were actually giving financial support to the Baptist Missionary Society in England. Judson's challenge led to the establishment in May 1814 of the General Missionary Convention of the Baptist Denomination in the United States of America for Foreign Missions. This has become, for the northern states, the American Baptist Foreign Mission Society of to-day with deep commitments in the Belgian Congo.[2]

Meanwhile the beginnings of the Wesleyan Methodist Missionary Society had appeared in England in 1813. Methodists had already pioneered in work overseas, but as the work had been at the instance and under the personal direction of Dr. Coke, in the name of the Conference, no separate organization had been felt necessary. Dr. Coke's departure for the East and his death at sea in May 1813, hastened this development,

---

[1] *First Ten Reports of A.B.C.F.M.*, 9–10, where the memorial is given in full.
[2] *The Guide Book of the A.B.F.M.S.* (1918–19); *The Judson Centennial 1814–1914*, Historical Introduction.

though it was not until 1818 that the Conference instituted a "General Missionary Society" to embrace the District Societies that began in 1813.[1]

One more Society appeared before Waterloo closed the Napoleonic period. This was the first of the German Societies, with its headquarters at Basel in Switzerland. The earlier Danish-Halle Mission had had friends in South Germany, and the continuing missionary interest was much stimulated by events in England, notably by the establishment of the London Missionary Society.[2] The beginning of the new Society in 1815 was made, with characteristic German thoroughness, by the founding of a missionary training institution. This led to further interrelations, for to this training school the Church Missionary Society in particular was much indebted for its pioneers in Western Africa. The Basel Society's independent work in Africa began in 1827.[3]

Enough has been said within the limits of the war period to make clear that this missionary awakening was a direct expression of the evangelical movement. That it was fundamentally one, whether occurring in Great Britain or on the European or American continents is made plain by the interweaving of personal influence and action throughout the story. That so much should have been attempted and achieved amidst the turmoil and peril of international war is evidence of the deep devotion of these pioneers. The post-war period brought pressing problems of its own, yet the movement went on. It must suffice merely to chronicle the appearance of later Societies, always with the reminder that vital influences run back to evangelical sources, and that the mutual indebtedness already observed continues. In Scotland came the Church of Scotland Foreign Mission Committee (1824) and United Presbyterian Missions (1835); in the United States, the American Bible Society (1816), the Foreign Mission Board of the Methodist Episcopal Church (1819), the Foreign Missionary Society of the Protestant Episcopal Church (1820), and the Foreign Mission Board of the Presbyterian Church (1837); on the continent of Europe, the Berlin and the Paris Missionary Societies (1824),

---

[1] Findlay and Holdsworth, op. cit., I, 36–55, 60. The Methodist "Society" however, was not a self-constituted organization, for the initiative and control lay with the Conference, as, in Presbyterian polity, the Foreign Mission Committee is a function of the General Assembly.

[2] A special letter was addressed to the L.M.S. Directors by a "Select Committee" in Basel in 1798; it is printed in the Directors' Fourth Report (1798), 12–16. [3] G. Warneck, History of Protestant Missions, 123.

the Rhenish Missionary Society (1828), with the Swedish (1835), Leipzig (1836), Bremen (1836), and Norwegian (1842) Societies in their train—all these within a half-century of the first blazing of the trail.

Here at last were the necessary organizations through which the Christian devotion, fanned into a flame by the Evangelical Revival, could express its concern for the non-Christian world. They appeared at the moment in the history of Africa when the slave-trade was in process of being outlawed, and a generous impulse to make some reparation to her plundered peoples moved many hearts.[1] At the time the first Societies were organized there were two regions in Africa that in particular invited missionary enterprise: Sierra Leone and the Cape. It was at these two points that the first Protestant plantings were actually made. In due course they took root and flourished. From Sierra Leone the planting spread along the Guinea Coast, though the hope of striking into the interior of the continent from this vantage-ground was not realized. From the Cape the work extended east and north, until finally Livingstone thrust beyond the Zambezi and Central Africa lay at last unveiled.

(2) *Early Efforts in Sierra Leone.*

The significance to the philanthropists of the settlement at Sierra Leone was more than that of a home for stranded Negroes, or of a base for honourable commerce in the natural resources of Africa. It was regarded as a lamp in a dark place from which religious and civilizing influences might spread which should at last light up the continent. Thus the Directors of the Sierra Leone Company write that they "look forward with delight to that joyful period, when, by the influence of the Company's measures, and the efficacy of its example, the Continent of Africa shall have been rescued from her present state of darkness and misery, and shall exhibit a far different scene, of light and knowledge, and civilization and order, and peaceful industry, and domestic comfort".[2] Melville Horne, however, the Anglican clergyman who arrived as chaplain in 1792,[3] found

[1] "The number, already great, is daily increasing, of those who feel for the wrongs of Africa, and are eager to discover some mode of compensating to her the injuries she has so long been sustaining at our hands."—Postscript to the *Report of the Court of Directors of the Sierra Leone Company* (1792), 14.

[2] *Ibid.*, 15.

[3] Melville Horne had two predecessors: P. Frazer who was provided by Granville Sharp for his first party in 1787; and N. Gilbert, the first chaplain under the Company.—F. W. Butt-Thompson, *Sierra Leone in History and Tradition* (1926), 183.

himself disappointed in the opportunity presented. He had hoped to combine a missionary vocation to the local tribes with his duty as chaplain to the immigrant settlers. After fourteen months he returned to England with the conviction that he could not effect his purpose; he confessed with regret that beyond his chaplaincy duties he did nothing but "preach one single sermon by means of an interpreter". His chaplaincy duties involved the preaching of four or five sermons a week, but his heart lay elsewhere. However, he recommends the field for those who will forgo the comparative advantage of life in Freetown: "They must, I conceive, become inhabitants of the native villages, and as those villages seldom contain more than sixty or eighty adults, I should suppose, that, to effect the conversion of the natives, Missionaries must become itinerant, as well as stationary: so that they will be obliged to take the country as it is. Whether any Gentleman will come forward to countenance Missions there or whether Christian Ministers of any denomination will embark in the undertaking, time must determine."[1] Within the next decade five attempts were to be made, only the last of which was to succeed. But before proceeding to record these vicissitudes, there is another aspect of the religious life of the young settlement to be observed.

The Nova Scotia settlers brought across by Lieutenant Clarkson in 1792 claimed for the most part to be Christian. They had come under the influence of Christian preachers in the American colonies and in Nova Scotia. There were Baptists, Methodists and members of the Countess of Huntingdon's Connexion among them. They had their own Negro preachers, and on arrival at the settlement they each resumed their own religious life and practice, independently of any European supervision. English, as modified to their own use, was the language they employed. Clarkson recognized the limitations of these black preachers, but spoke with appreciation of their services.[2] Each denomination had its recognized leadership. David George was not only the principal minister of the

---

[1] Melville Horne, *Letters on Missions* (1794), iv. "I had gone to Sierra Leone", he writes, "with the hope of doing something towards the establishment of a Mission to the natives."

[2] Clarkson wrote in his diary, November 25, 1792: "Our black preachers require instruction. They have had their use in keeping the people together, and it has been principally through them, that I have had so much influence over the minds of the others. I am continually telling Mr. Horne that he could be more profitably employed in giving up a portion of his time to their instruction, than by going amongst the natives who do not understand English."
—Quoted in E. G. Ingham, *Sierra Leone after a Hundred Years* (1894), 146.

Baptists, but a man of considerable influence among the settlers in general. As Zachary Macaulay shows, he had his aberrations, but was on the whole loyal to the Company's administration. Macaulay refers to David George's people as "in general sober-minded and temperate men".[1]

The Methodists among the settlers were led by Moses Wilkinson, their principal Negro preacher. The first return in 1792 showed 223 members in Society. In the pages of Zachary Macaulay they appear as liable to religious extravagances, testing the validity of spiritual experience by dreams and visions, and lacking the discipline and pastoral oversight demanded by John Wesley for his Societies. They were extremely sensitive to any action which they interpreted as a veiled attack upon their religious liberty, yet were not equally eager to secure themselves from criticism of life and character. Macaulay complained to Wilkinson of "their uniform opposition to the establishment among themselves of the discipline required by the Methodist rules". More than once he expresses the hope that Dr. Coke or some Methodist preacher with authority should visit Sierra Leone to establish discipline among the Methodists there.[2]

The members of the Countess of Huntingdon's Connexion were led by a trio of Negro preachers: William Ash, John Ellis, and Cato Perkins. Two ministers of the Connexion who had been sent by the Countess as missionaries to North America, Mr. Fromage and Mr. Marant, were in Nova Scotia while the settlers were still resident there. Those who became converts through the work of these missionaries adhered to the practice of the Connexion on reaching Sierra Leone, though without white leadership. They took no steps, however, to establish relations with the Connexion in England. They were thus lost sight of, and it was not until 1825 that the home churches became aware of their existence. Meanwhile they seem to have maintained a vigorous Christian fellowship under Negro leadership. Cato Perkins was a man of some influence in the Nova Scotia community, being one of the two delegates who visited England in 1793 to lay the settlers' grievances before the Directors.[3]

The fact of Christian communities being thus transplanted

[1] Knutsford, *Life and Letters of Zachary Macaulay* (1900), 133, 137–8, 144–5.
[2] *Ibid.*, 49–50, 53–4, 60, 136, 143–7; Findlay and Holdsworth, *op. cit.*, IV, 76.
[3] *The Countess of Huntingdon's Connexion, Circular* No. 41 (Dec., 1847), 168; No. 42 (Jan., 1848), 169; *The Lady Selina Commemoration Meetings* (1941), 27; *Report of the Sierra Leone Company* (1794), 23–5.

to Sierra Leone and possessing their own chosen leaders might seem to presage a new day for the planting of Christianity in Africa. And indeed they were possessed of genuine religious sentiments and celebrated their first landing with a service of prayer and thanksgiving led by William Ash. A Meeting House was the first building they erected, where members of the three denominations joined in a daily "Praise-giving Service".[1] The initial misfortunes of the settlement, however, led to discontent and suspicion of the Company's intentions, among a people who had already suffered much in the frustration of their hopes both in the American colonies and in Nova Scotia. John Clarkson was aware of this attitude and refers to it more than once: "These people have delicate feelings, and just ideas of right and wrong, and as they have been ill-treated and deceived through life, they are very suspicious of the conduct of white people. . . ."[2] The effect was seen, not only in lamentable events in the political sphere when unworthy leadership of the settlers gained the ascendancy, but also in a suspicion of any approach in the religious sphere, when the Company's chaplain showed friendly interest in the development of their Christian life and witness.[3] What, we imagine, might have become an effective Christian community, a beacon light shining among pagan and Muslim tribes, a saving salt amid the rottenness of a slavery-ridden coast, in the event lent little lustre to the Christian name, little savour to African society. Perhaps the error lies in expecting too much of a few hundred people twice uprooted from their homes and deposited, amidst unexpected difficulties, in a settlement that demanded the utmost in active and loyal co-operation from all concerned to ensure such a success. More-over, it was not only the Negro Christian who failed to rise to the height of the opportunity. The story of the first missionary efforts from Europe, based on the settlement, is by no means a happy one.

The Baptists were the first among the new Societies to plan a mission to Africa. Sierra Leone and its neighbourhood became a natural selection, through the beneficial activity of the Sierra Leone Company and the known Christian character of its

---

[1] Butt-Thompson, *op. cit.*, 95–6, who says of these people: "They included some of the finest men the colony has ever known, Thomas Peters, David George, Moses Wilkinson, Boston King, Cato Perkins, John Ellis, and William Ash."

[2] Ingham, *op. cit.*, 71; cf. 42–3.

[3] Melville Horne and his successors in turn, Jones and Clarke, all experienced these rebuffs.—Knutsford, *op. cit.*, 49–50, 54, 60, 136–9.

Directors. Here was the one spot in Africa where the slave-trade was illegal, as stated in the constitution of the Company endorsed by Parliament. It was therefore an advantageous base for any missionary effort beyond. In April 1795 the Committee of the Baptist Missionary Society, encouraged by the published reports of the Sierra Leone Company, decided to attempt a mission to that part of Africa, and at the same meeting accepted Jacob Grigg for that service. Unwilling to send him without a companion, they later accepted the offer of James Rodway. These two young ministers were set apart for the work and reached Sierra Leone in December 1795, within a month from leaving England. They carried a letter of recommendation to the Baptists under the pastoral care of David George. Governor Dawes welcomed their coming and was generous in helping them to suitable locations. James Rodway was never able to take up his work effectively; he was so weakened by repeated attacks of malaria that after eight months the senior medical officer of the Company certified the necessity of his leaving the colony. Jacob Grigg fared more happily in the matter of health, but came to grief through neglecting his missionary vocation and actively interfering in local disputes. His excuse for returning to Freetown after a short residence at his station, Port Lokko, was that a member of David George's church, who had accompanied him for trade, had through his high prices made them both so unpopular as to defeat his missionary purpose in advance. In Freetown, however, he grew so meddlesome that Zachary Macaulay, who was now back as Governor, allowed him to choose either to return to England, or to resume his work at Port Lokko and not return to the colony without leave, or to go to America. He decided for the last. This was a heavy blow to the Committee. On investigation, they realized Macaulay's care for their interests and thanked him for it. The mission was not resumed.[1]

When Zachary Macaulay returned to Sierra Leone in 1796 he brought a missionary party with him. A few years before some officers of the Company had successfully completed an enterprising expedition into what is to-day French Guinea. Proceeding north to the Rio Nunez, they had then advanced

[1] *Periodical Accounts relative to the Baptist Missionary Society,* I (1800), 97–104, 239, 255–61, 306. There are letters from Jacob Grigg, and James Rodway, 241–55. Rodway received a warm tribute from the Baptists in Sierra Leone, *ibid.,* 256; and won the commendation of Macaulay.—Knutsford, *op. cit.,* 143. Butt-Thompson incorrectly speaks of "Mr. Rigg and Mr. Rodway" and implies they were both victims of the climate.—*Op. cit.,* 175.

inland some 200 miles to Labe, and another seventy-five brought
them to Teembo (? modern Tamba), the capital of a Fula
kingdom. They were impressed with the civilized society of
these Muslim peoples, and found them eager for direct relations
with the Company. Indeed, a Fula embassy returned with them
to Freetown. The suggestion that Europeans might settle in
the country, and the plough (which was unknown to them) be
introduced, was received with pleasure and promise of support.
Here was an opportunity which, if wisely used, might mean
much in forwarding the Company's object of introducing healing
influences into Africa, for Labe and Teembo were on the road
to the Niger and Timbuktu.[1] Zachary Macaulay had projected
a mission which was to enter this Fula kingdom. He secured
support among his friends and requested Dr. Coke to select
suitable men for the task.[2] These were secured among Methodist
mechanics and local preachers. They reached Freetown in
March 1796, and Macaulay made plans to accompany the missionary party to Teembo. But the women of the company were
so dismayed at the prospect before them, their husbands being
little better, that when the expedition was about to start they
all withdrew. The result was mortifying to Dr. Coke, and while
this was not officially a Methodist mission, Dr. Coke reported its
failure to the ensuing Methodist Conference, which thereupon
decided "that trial should be made in that part of Africa on the
proper missionary plan". More than a decade elapsed before this
could be done, but it then proved worthy of the Methodist name.[3]

Also in 1796 the Glasgow Missionary Society turned to Sierra
Leone where Henry Thornton promised the Company's co-
operation. In default of more suitable recruits Duncan Campbell,
a married man of forty, and Robert Henderson, a youth of
eighteen, were appointed as "missionary catechists". It is
claimed these were the first missionaries sent from Scotland
overseas. They set sail on a slaver on April 5, 1797. Macaulay
settled them in due course at Racon, some 100 miles up the
Sierra Leone River, and kept the Society informed of his

[1] A full account of this interesting expedition is given in the *Report of the
Sierra Leone Company* (1794), 134-43. The road from Labe to Timbuktu was
said to be open, and the journey to take four months. The hope that representatives of the Company might undertake it was not realized.

[2] Knutsford, *op. cit.*, 239; Findlay and Holdsworth, *op. cit.*, IV, 76.

[3] Knutsford, *op. cit.*, 116-18, 121-5, 130, 135. Macaulay reports of their
first arrival: "This morning there was nothing to be heard among the
Missionary ladies but doleful lamentations or bitter complaints. To their
astonishment Freetown resembled neither London nor Portsmouth; they
could find no pastrycooks' shops, nor any gingerbread to buy for their children.
Dr. Coke had deceived them; if this was Africa they would go no farther,

relations with them. In little more than a year Henderson had returned on health grounds, though he was otherwise unsuited to the work. Campbell proved unworthy, and after a sequence of unfortunate experiences eventually left Sierra Leone in 1801, becoming, it was feared, engaged in the slave-trade.[1]

The fourth attempt made at this time was a joint effort and appeared to start under the happiest auspices of missionary co-operation. The initiative was taken by the London Missionary Society. As soon as the pioneer mission to the South Seas had been despatched they turned their attention to Africa and decided, as the Baptists had done before them, that the activity of the Sierra Leone Company made that region especially attractive and that the report of the Fula kingdom indicated the specific field. A memoir on the subject, presented in October 1795, had been submitted to the criticism of Zachary Macaulay. Within two years the Glasgow and the Edinburgh Societies had joined in the undertaking, each supplying two men. But now the Fula kingdom was involved in war and the road to the country closed. Macaulay, however, assured the Societies that the men could be well employed in Freetown and neighbourhood, pending the opening of the Fula road once more.[2] The far-reaching purpose in view was clearly stated: "If it please God to give a successful entrance to his Gospel into this country, it may thence penetrate farther into the interior, even into the centre of that benighted, forsaken, degraded Continent."[3] Nevertheless the missionaries were warned at their departure that if the united mission to the Fula kingdom should not prove practicable, they might be stationed, at the discretion of Macaulay, in different localities.[4] The cordial relations existing

that they would not. Their husbands were silent; but their looks were sufficiently expressive of chagrin and disappointment."—*Ibid.*, 122. Macaulay might well have been apprehensive when one of ardent temper brandished his fist before a Mandingo merchant, denouncing Muhammad as a false prophet.

[1] *Glasgow Missionary Society, Quarterly Paper*, No. II (1828), 4–6; No. III (1829), 1–6. An illuminating letter from Macaulay is quoted.

[2] *Report of the Directors to the Members of the Missionary Society, 1796*, xix; *Ibid.*, *1797*, xxv–xxvi, xxvii.

[3] *Introductory Address to the Religious World*, prefixed to *A Sermon and Charge delivered at Surry-Chapel London, October 9, 1797, on the Occasion of the Designation of Two of the Six Missionaries to the Foulah Country, Africa*, (1797), vii. The same volume includes the General Instructions from the Directors, and a Farewell Letter. In the Instructions the missionaries are especially commended to Zachary Macaulay and Mr. Clark, the chaplain to the colony, for guidance.

[4] *Ibid.*, 40–2. Macaulay had suggested five possible locations, from the Rio Pongas (French Guinea) to Cape Mesurado (Liberia). Cf. *Report of the Sierra Leone Company* (1789), 55–6, where the same five centres are named as eligible missionary stations.

among the leaders of the three Societies were not, however, reflected among their representatives. On the eve of sailing one of their number preached a sermon that aroused bitter controversy; this reaching the ears of the London Directors, a fruitless attempt was made to get into touch with the ship at Falmouth. They anxiously awaited news from Sierra Leone: "At length it arrived; and we were grieved to hear that the spirit of discord had not subsided."[1] On their arrival Macaulay decided to station them in three pairs, according to their respective Societies, at widely separated stations. Henry Brunton and Peter Greig of the Edinburgh Society were placed on the Rio Pongas, some sixty miles north of Freetown; Peter Ferguson and Robert Graham of the Glasgow Society on the Banana Islands, some forty miles to the south, and Alexander Russell and George Cappe on the Bullom shore, across the estuary from Freetown. Once again the climate took its toll; in little more than six months half the party had died. Of the three survivors George Cappe was recalled as unfitted for the work; Henry Brunton, whom Macaulay found a worthy man, became colonial chaplain but before long was compelled by ill-health to retire; and Peter Greig met a violent death. When Brunton went to the colony as chaplain Greig continued in the Susu mission, where he had acquired a competent knowledge of the language and had won the affectionate regard of the people. He was murdered by itinerant Fula traders who seem to have coveted his personal belongings, and who succeeded in making good their escape before the crime was discovered. So ended the fourth attempt to establish a mission in this part of West Africa. As with the Baptists, so with the London and Scottish Societies, no steps were taken to resume the work.[2]

While these four efforts that failed were bitterly disappointing to their supporters at home, they were of value for the future in emphasizing the risks attaching to the malaria-ridden coast, and the great care and discrimination demanded in the selection of

[1] *The Report of the Directors, 1798,* 20–1.
[2] *Ibid.,* 1799, viii; *ibid., 1800,* 11; R. Lovett, *History of the London Missionary Society* (1899), I, 479–80; Knutsford, *op. cit.,* 182, 183, 209, 214; *Report of the Sierra Leone Company* (1798), 52–3; *ibid.* (1801), 21–2.
Brunton was in 1801 appointed to lead a pioneer mission sent by the Edinburgh Society, with the consent of the Russian Government, to the Tartar tribes of the Caspian. Here he rendered notable service, and so mastered Tartar-Turkish that he is said to have been regarded as a renegade Turk. His great work was a translation of the New Testament into Tartar-Turkish which he just lived to complete.—*Report of the Directors of the Edinburgh Missionary Society, 1802,* 35–6; *ibid., 1808,* 57–8; W. Canton, *op. cit.,* I, 179–80.

missionaries suited by Christian character for such pioneer work.

Before the next mission was launched another element had been added to the population of Sierra Leone by the arrival of the Maroons in September 1800. They had been removed from Jamaica to Nova Scotia after the Maroon war, but found the northern climate inhospitable, so were transferred by the British Government to Sierra Leone. They arrived just in time to assist the Sierra Leone authorities in dealing with the insurrection of the Nova Scotia settlers. They numbered some 550 men, women, and children. The Wesleyan Methodists in due course won many of them to Christianity.[1]

The end of the century thus found no mission established in West Africa, and the abolition cause at its lowest ebb in the House of Commons. The Sierra Leone Company, moreover, had faced one misfortune after another until the climax came with the settlers' armed revolt. The little group of Christian men who were promoting these good works were "pressed on every side, yet not straitened, perplexed, yet not unto despair". The Church Missionary Society, established at this very time, chose Sierra Leone and its neighbourhood to be its first field of action. Zachary Macaulay, now retired from the governorship of the colony, was a member of the Society's Committee and brought to its counsels not only his unrivalled knowledge of Sierra Leone and its environs, but the fruit of his painful experiences with earlier missionary ventures.[2]

The earlier attempt of the Edinburgh missionaries, Henry Brunton and the martyred Peter Greig, had directed the attention of the Society to the Susu country on the Rio Pongas, some one hundred miles north of Sierra Leone, coupled with the fact that several Susu boys were among those brought to England by Macaulay for education. Henry Brunton, who had already given some attention to the Susu language on the field, was commissioned by the Society to prepare suitable material in Susu for a mission to that country.[3]

[1] R. C. Dallas, *History of the Maroons* (1803), II, 283-9; *Report of the Sierra Leone Company* (1801), 16-17, 23-7; *The Countess of Huntingdon's Connexion Circular*, No. 42 (Jan., 1848), 169.

[2] Macaulay was attacked by some who resented the idea that a missionary, once commissioned from home, might prove unworthy overseas and require dismissal. Macaulay replied vigorously in support of the principle of proper discrimination in the selection of missionaries.—Knutsford, *op. cit.*, 237-41.

[3] At a Committee meeting in 1801, Brunton "produced a Susoo epitome of the Bible which he had prepared, and on his reading portions of it to two African boys who accompanied him, they readily translated it into English, to the great satisfaction of the Committee". Macaulay suggested Brunton as a possible missionary of the Society.—Hole, *op. cit.*, 63, 67-8.

The first missionaries of the Society came from Germany. One outcome on the Continent of the missionary awakening in England, and in particular of the establishment of the London Society, was the setting up of a Missionary Seminary in Berlin under a Lutheran minister, John Jaenicke.[1] The Church Missionary Society was hard pressed for men. No clergyman offered, no bishop was as yet willing to ordain men for the Society's service, and the proposal, in default of these sources of supply, to send out lay catechists did not mature.[2] The attention of the Committee having been directed to the Berlin Missionary Seminary, in December 1802 two of its students, Melchior Renner and Peter Hartwig, were accepted as missionary catechists with a view to appointment to the Susu country. They were brought to London and gave attention to English and Susu. After a return to Germany to receive Lutheran ordination, they were accepted in full capacity as missionaries in January 1804.[3] Travel to the field was now so difficult that passage in a slave-ship was actually sought, but not secured. They eventually reached Sierra Leone, travelling at first in convoy, on April 14, 1804. The first mission of the Church Missionary Society had begun.[4] The slave-trade was still legal and active, and missionaries had to accept this situation. Josiah Pratt, who gave the charge to the departing missionaries, said wise words on this point: "You will take all prudent occasions of weaning the Native Chiefs from this traffic, by depicting its criminality, the miseries which it occasions to Africa, and the obstacles which it opposes to a more profitable and generous intercourse with the European nations. But while you do this, you will cultivate kindness of spirit towards those persons who are connected with this trade. You will make all due allowances for their habits, their prejudices, and their views of interest. Let them never be met by you with reproaches and invectives, however debased you may find them in mind and manners. Let them never have to charge you with intriguing against them and thwarting their schemes; but let them feel that, though the silent influence of Christianity must, whenever truly felt, undermine the sources of their gain, yet in you, and in all under your influence, they meet with openness, simplicity, kindness, and brotherly love."[5]

[1] G. Warneck, op. cit., 122; Hole, op. cit., 81–3.
[2] Hole, op. cit., 63–8; Stock, op. cit., I, 73–4, 81.
[3] Hole, op. cit., 85, 91; Stock, op. cit., I, 83.   [4] Hole, op. cit., 91, 93–4.
[5] Stock, op. cit., I, 84–5. This admirably reflects Zachary Macaulay's own attitude during his difficult years of administration.

Two years passed, and the missionary party had not only not moved out of the colony but to the Committee's concern were not attempting to master Susu in readiness for their work. True, both missionaries were serving as chaplains, and after the murder of Peter Greig the authorities were reluctant to approve of an immediate advance, but work in the colony was not the purpose for which they had been sent out.[1] Here once more we meet disappointment and delay in the first years of the missionary undertaking. Whether this attempt might, like its predecessors, have also been abandoned had the slave-trade remained on its legal footing, we cannot say. It is at least the fact that not till the Abolition Act was passed did the missionaries reach their projected field on the Rio Pongas which had been a principal centre of the trade. By that time they had been reinforced.

Another change coincided with the passing of the Abolition Act. This was the surrender by the Sierra Leone Company of its governmental functions, and the transfer of the colony to the Crown.[2] Simultaneously there appeared the African Institution in April 1807, the object of which was to foster the development of legitimate trade and encourage the spread of education and civilization in Africa, though not itself becoming a trading corporation or competing in activity with missionary societies. While the Institution was under distinguished patronage, the core of energetic support came from the Clapham Sect with Zachary Macaulay as the indefatigable first secretary.[3] This combination of circumstances offered an opportunity no earlier missionary attempt in Sierra Leone and neighbourhood had enjoyed.

The reinforcement party of three missionaries, Nylander, Butscher, and Prasse, also from Berlin, took seven months from their first sailing in February 1806 to reach Sierra Leone.[4] In March 1808 the mission on the Rio Pongas began under Renner, Butscher and Prasse; Nylander remained as chaplain in Sierra Leone, and Hartwig had forsaken the work.[5] They soon mourned

[1] Hole, *op. cit.*, 128–30.
[2] The Act of Transfer, passed in August 1807, came into operation on January 1, 1808, the date when the Abolition Act also came into force on the African coast. The suggestion of the transfer had been made five years earlier, but the outbreak of war with France had caused delay.—*Report of the Sierra Leone Company* (1804), 44, 58.
[3] *Report of the Committee of the African Institution* (1807), 65–71.
[4] Eugene Stock relates the vicissitudes, *op. cit.*, I, 86.
[5] On Hartwig's defection, see Hole, *op. cit.*, 131 and n. 4; Stock, *op. cit.*, I, 88.

their first loss in the death of the much esteemed Prasse early in 1809. A second reinforcement arrived in 1811, Wilhelm and Klein, also from the Berlin Seminary, but having received some supplementary training in England. For the period 1808-12 the mission on the Rio Pongas remained the only work, and this was limited to schools for children. The landing at Sierra Leone of the cargoes of captured slave-ships had already begun, and the first liberated slaves committed to the care of the Society were six children handed over in June 1811 and conveyed to the Rio Pongas.[1] The instruction, however, was in English, for "the Susoos, it was said, would not be able to read in their own tongue for the next ten years, and there was no eagerness therefore to translate the Bible into Susoo".[2] It was disappointing to have no more than this to report eight years after the first missionaries had sailed: "The Rio Pongas was as yet a school, where the children were learning much English, the missionaries were picking up some Susoo. There was no church, no proper public worship, no itinerant preaching. Not a single Native under their care had been admitted to the Holy Communion. The Schoolroom was everything, and within its walls these ordained teachers, cramped and confined, were toiling on."[3] By 1812 there were reported 120 pupils in the schools, of whom some twenty were children of chiefs.[4]

During the next three years various developments of interest occurred. The first lay missionaries, again Germans but already resident in England as artisans, were sent out in 1812; these were to work for the objects set out by the African Institution, in seeking to encourage Africans to aspire to a civilized life.[5] An American Negro, reputed to know several African languages, was added to the educational staff in 1814.[6] The practice of redeeming Negro children now began to appeal to many donors, who exercised the privilege of selecting the names (usually of their relations and friends) to be given to the children. This practice was discontinued in 1813 as liable to be misunderstood and in fact to encourage the slave-trade.[7] During these years also, Nylander, relieved at his own request of his chaplaincy duties, started a work on the Bullom shore across the estuary north of Freetown. Here he applied himself to the study of

---

[1] The landing of cargoes at Sierra Leone was made possible by the appointment of a Court of Vice-Admiralty to sit there.—*Second Report of the African Institution* (1808), 22–3. The missionaries had actually received some liberated children before this date, redeemed by themselves.—Hole, *op. cit.*, 136.

[2] Hole, *op. cit.*, 137.   [3] *Ibid.*, 139.   [4] *Ibid.*, 224.
[5] *Ibid.*, 222.   [6] *Ibid.*, 465.   [7] *Ibid.*, 305, 365–6, 416–17, 466.

the language, and produced a grammar and vocabulary of Bullom, together with a translation of some chapters of St. Matthew.[1] These were all useful activities, but as the first decade of the Society's effort came to an end, another development occurred that profoundly affected the work of the mission. This was nothing less than a revival of the slave-trade.

The vigilant Directors of the African Institution had quickly realized that their more positive efforts to stimulate trade in the resources of Africa must for a time give way to a supreme concern for making enforcement of the law as effective as naval power and international understandings permitted. The Directors first advert to this in 1810, admitting that they had been "sanguine in hoping that ere this time something effectual would have been done, to limit the range of this destructive traffic, which has hitherto impeded the success of every attempt to do good to Africa".[2] The increased profits offered by the trade under the Abolition regime were considerable.[3] American and British traders sought to evade the law by ostensible sales of ships to foreign owners, enabling them to sail for the most part under the flag of Portugal or Spain. The cessation of the war with France threatened to aggravate seriously a situation already grave, for France claimed a five-year period before the trade should cease in her possessions, a period long enough to permit an alarming revival of the traffic from the region of the Senegal which the war had practically stopped. This prospect seriously affected the mission on the Rio Pongas, which could be expected to become once more an active centre of the trade; but more—a revival of the trade meant a deterioration in the total situation in which missionary work was being courageously attempted.[4] Meanwhile the continuing traffic meant continuous captures of slave cargoes and a large increase in the number of liberated Africans in Sierra Leone. By 1814 the number had reached 10,000, of whom a tenth were children. Colonel Maxwell, the Governor, urged upon the Society the

[1] Hole, op. cit., 210, 241, 465.

[2] Fourth Report of the African Institution (1810), 1.

[3] The acting Judge of the Vice-Admiralty Court at Sierra Leone declared in 1810: "I have had my hands pretty full of Admiralty business lately; but it appears to me that hardly any thing will put a stop to this abominable traffic. The profits are so extremely high, that if they save one cargo out of three, they will still make money."—Fifth Report of the African Institution (1811), 10.

[4] The C.M.S., indeed, held a Special General Meeting on July 18, 1814, at which a petition to both Houses of Parliament was adopted, to be presented by Lord Gambier, President of the Society, in the Lords, and by William Wilberforce, a Vice-President, in the Commons.—Hole, op. cit., 465-6.

opportunity awaiting it within the bounds of the colony.[1] It was the unexpected persistence of the slave-trade that was producing this entirely new situation—a population in Sierra Leone not of settlers from the New World but of native Africans recently torn from family and clan and deposited, friendless and destitute, on African soil indeed, but far from home. This determined the Society's policy in the post-war period.

In 1808 Sierra Leone received the attention of the Wesleyan Methodist Conference, but only to the effect that a preacher should be sent when a suitable person could be found. In 1811 George Warren, a Methodist minister, with three companions appointed as schoolmasters, sailed for the colony. Warren survived only eight months, the first Methodist casualty on the West African field. One of the schoolmasters was invalided, but Healey and Hirst held on devotedly until William Davies, Warren's successor, arrived in 1815. This second attempt of Dr. Coke's proved the beginning of a permanent work that not only developed strength in Sierra Leone, but later spread along the coast from the Gambia to the Niger.

(3) *Missionary Operations at the Cape.*

If the incidence of the slave-trade and the mounting popular support for the Abolition movement directed the searchlight of public interest upon Western Africa and focused it at Sierra Leone, developments in the Napoleonic wars also brought the Cape within the ambit of attention. When in 1795 the Batavian Republic was established in Holland as a client of the French Republic, England, already at war with France, became automatically at war with Holland. An expedition was thereupon fitted against the Cape to which, in September 1795, the Dutch garrison surrendered. By the Peace of Amiens in 1802 the territory was restored, but in the following year war was renewed between England and France, again involving the Batavian Republic. It was not, however, until 1806 that the English fleet arrived and for the second and last time the Cape passed from the Dutch. In the final settlement of 1814 the Cape was retained as part of a complicated agreement, virtually by right of purchase.[2] By contrast with Sierra Leone here was a territory colonized from Europe, with an admirable climate, and a continuous history of a century and a half.

The Dutch Reformed Church had, already on the eve of the

---

[1] Hole, *op. cit.*, 597.
[2] G. M. Theal, *History of South Africa since 1795* (1908), I, 219.

Napoleonic period, felt the impulse of the evangelical movement. A notable religious ambassador was Helperus Ritzema
van Lier who had himself passed through a spiritual experience
that proved transforming. He accepted an invitation to a
pastorate at the Cape in 1786, when twenty-two years of age.
He had already proved himself a brilliant student, and now
acquitted himself as a faithful minister of Christ. A circle of
Christian friends concerned for the spiritual welfare of slaves
and Hottentots was formed, and a missionary interest thus
kindled. He died in 1793 after seven years of devoted service.[1]
It is significant to find the Moravian Brethren write of him:
"We very much regret the loss of a most worthy and sincere
friend to the Mission among the Hottentots, by the decease of
the Rev. Mr. Van Lier, a faithful servant of Jesus Christ."[2]
Another Dutch minister of the same evangelical outlook was
Michiel Christaan Vos, South African born, who after studying
in Holland returned to the Cape in 1794, where his first sermon
was on the text: "Go ye into all the world and preach the gospel
to every creature." He courageously told Dutch masters and
mistresses that Hottentots and slaves would be included with
themselves in his ministry. Yet to his courage he added a
sincerity and tact that won the support of his parishioners, and
made possible the Christian instruction of many slaves and
servants. Du Plessis indeed hails him as "the man who above
all deserves the honour of being considered the pioneer of the
missionary spirit in South Africa".[3]

The Moravian Mission initiated by Schmidt was renewed half
a century later. The Moravian Bishop Reichel, calling at Cape
Town on his voyage from India in 1789, discussed the question
with van Lier, and on his return to Europe took steps to this
end. The Dutch East India Company consented, under conditions, to the Moravian proposal. In 1792 three Moravian
Brethren, Marsveld, Schwinn, and Kühnel, arrived in South
Africa and resumed the work on the site of their predecessor's
residence, using the very stones from his old dwelling for their
own. At their first meeting with nineteen Hottentots they
announced their purpose in coming: "To make known to them
the way of salvation, by faith in Jesus Christ." The living link
with George Schmidt was old Helena, then some eighty years
of age, whom Schmidt had baptized, and who paid several

[1] Du Plessis, *History of Christian Missions in South Africa* (1911), 61–4.
[2] *Periodical Accounts of the Missions of the Brethren*, I, 108.
[3] Du Plessis, *op. cit.*, 67–9.

visits to the Brethren: "She had still an old Dutch New Testament carefully kept, out of which another Hottentot woman, who had learned to read from her cousin, one of Brother Schmidt's scholars, used to read to her."[1]

With characteristic industry, the three Brethren had soon erected, with Hottentot co-operation, the necessary buildings for their work at Baviansкloof, had planted a garden, and opened a school. These were three musical missionaries, so they sang the gospel as well as preached it. Their emphasis on the story of the Passion moved the hearts of their hearers, and as men and women responded to that appeal a Christian community began to appear among the Hottentots. The first convert was baptized in July 1793; from that time the number grew. When in 1798 Lady Anne Barnard visited the settlement and attended evening prayers she was deeply impressed with the simplicity and reality of the worship: "I doubt much whether I should have entered St. Peter's at Rome, with the triple crown, with a more devout impression of the Deity and His presence than I felt in this little church of a few feet square, where the simple disciples of Christianity, dressed in the skins of animals, knew no purple or fine linen, no pride or hypocrisy. I felt as if I were creeping back seventeen hundred years, and heard from the rude and inspired lips of Evangelists the simple sacred words of wisdom and purity."[2] Such a picture, however, must not suggest that the work proceeded without difficulty, amidst benevolent neighbours. The authorities had received them with favour, but others were critical when not directly hostile—at least so the missionaries declared. The much-reported incident of the bell, presented to the mission by Cape Town friends and not allowed to be used on the representations of a Dutch minister, has been quoted as evidence of intolerance.[3] That there was bitter opposition on the part of a number of the Dutch colonists to any attempt to elevate the Hottentots is more than likely; that the prevailing attitude was one of distrust of this missionary enterprise is also intelligible. But these things added greatly to the strain under which the devoted men pursued their calling.[4] The culminating experience came on

[1] *Periodical Accounts*, I, 244–5; J. E. Hutton, *History of Moravian Missions* (1923), 266–9.

[2] *South Africa a Century Ago. Letters written from the Cape of Good Hope, 1791–1801*. By the Lady Anne Barnard (1901), 169.

[3] Du Plessis examines the story and rejects the reason alleged, *op. cit.*, 75. Hutton accepts Du Plessis' account and suggests an explanation, *op. cit.*, 273.

[4] Du Plessis has examined the charges of hostility laid against the colonists, and sought to assess their truth, *op. cit.*, 76, 423–5.

the eve of the British occupation in 1795, when a revolutionary party, under an Italian, Pisani by name, ordered the evacuation of Bavianskloof. The missionaries retired to Cape Town, but soon returned with official protection.[1] By 1798 more than 800 Hottentots were settled on the station, of whom a quarter were members of the Church. In this year a superintendent, Kohrhammer, arrived from Europe, and in 1800 a new chief, Christian Louis Rose. As all the workers by this time had their wives the staff now numbered ten. Meanwhile to meet the growing need a new church to seat 1,000 had been erected. When in 1803 a Dutch Governor once more took office, he personally inspected the work with great satisfaction. His suggestion that the name should become Genadendal (Vale of Grace) was adopted, and was in use from 1806.[2]

In 1804 the mission mourned its first loss by death, the superintendent Rose, the first of any mission to die at his post at the Cape. With the return of the British in 1806, the kindly Governor Janssens was succeeded by the Earl of Caledon who also proved a warm friend of the missionaries. Indeed, so impressed was he with the work at Genadendal that he urged them to establish a second such centre at Groene Kloof. This was undertaken in 1808 and the new station christened Mamre.[3] Genadendal retained pride of place, however, and in 1813 reported 1,157 persons on the station. In the twenty-one years of its existence, 700 Hottentots had been received into the membership of the Christian Church. Relations with neighbouring farmers had grown cordial, and numbers of these on occasion shared in the worship at the station. Kühnel had died in 1810, but Marsveld and Schwinn, now in their sixties, were alive to rejoice in the mission's coming of age.[4]

Second to none in its significance for the history of South Africa was the London Missionary Society. While the West Coast enterprise was occupying the Directors, the Cape was also engaging their attention. "The Cape of Good Hope", they reported in 1797, "appears among the most promising of our openings."[5] In the following year a mission to the Namaqua was determined upon. These were a division of the Hottentots living north and south of the Orange River. The offer of Dr. Vanderkemp was accepted for this service.[6]

---

[1] *Missions in South Africa* (1832), 56–60; Hutton, *op. cit.*, 274–5. Hutton's dates are incorrect. [2] G. M. Theal, *op. cit.*, I, 110.
[3] *Ibid.*, I, 170–1. [4] Du Plessis, *op. cit.*, 88–9.
[5] *Report of the Directors* (1797), xxvi. [6] *Ibid.*, (1798), 22–3.

Johannes Theodorus Vanderkemp was a remarkable man. Born at Rotterdam in 1747, the son of a Lutheran minister and professor of theology, he entered in due course the University of Leyden as a medical student, but before his course was completed, turned to a military career. Proud and self-willed, he freely pursued his sensual pleasures. Yet spiritual concerns would not be ignored, and even at this time he became a member of the Dutch Reformed Church on confession of faith. But his spiritual crisis had not yet come. Resigning his Army commission in 1780 after sixteen years' service, he married and proceeded to Edinburgh where he graduated as Doctor of Medicine. It was in 1791 that the tragedy occurred which changed his life. He was sailing with wife and child upon the river at Rotterdam, and in a sudden summer storm they both were drowned. For him God's chastisement, as he saw it, meant Divine salvation. When in 1795 news of the London Missionary Society reached Holland, he sent for the account of its proceedings. The upshot was his offer of personal service. He was accepted and received Presbyterian ordination as a minister of the Church of Scotland, a not unnatural step since the London Society enjoyed Presbyterian co-operation. On his return to Holland he was instrumental in the formation of the Netherlands Missionary Society, which began its work as a valuable auxiliary to the London Mission at the Cape. He also found a Dutch colleague, John Kicherer, already ordained, who was accepted for service by the London Society.[1]

That Dr. Vanderkemp was the man to lead the new mission to the Cape of Good Hope was clear. Though fifty years of age, he retained much of the physical resilience of youth, was an educated man with unusual experience of the world, as a Dutchman could meet Dutch officials and colonists on equal terms, and had undergone a spiritual discipline in the hard school of experience that made him single-hearted in the service of his Lord. His companions in the pioneer party were John Kicherer, his countryman, and the Englishmen, John Edmonds and William Edwards. After some difficulty passage for them was finally secured, and they sailed in the convict ship *Hillsborough*, bound for Botany Bay. Their missionary mettle was tested by this circumstance long before they reached the field.[2]

[1] A. D. Martin, *Doctor Vanderkemp* (n.d.), 11–60; R. Lovett, *History of the London Missionary Society* (1899), I, 481–7.
[2] See the vivid account in *Transactions of the Missionary Society*, II, 360–2, quoted in Lovett, *op. cit.*, I, 485–6.

After a voyage of more than three months they at last arrived at Cape Town on March 31, 1799. The Cape was then in British occupation. They were well received by the officials; and the Christian people of Cape Town, to whom a special letter had been addressed by the Directors of the London Society, gave them a cordial welcome. Thus as far as relations with the European community at headquarters were concerned, the beginning augured well.

The letter from the London Directors not only announced the objective of the mission party, commending its members to Christians at the Cape, but desired these to emulate their friends in the Netherlands, and unite for missionary enterprise, in their case among the heathen around them. The effect was to crystallize the general missionary interest in the formation of the first South African Missionary Society. This proved a valuable auxiliary to the London Society in the early years.[1]

The original intention to direct the pioneer mission to the Namaquas north of Cape Town in the neighbourhood of the Orange River had been modified by Dr. Vanderkemp's communication with the late Dutch Governor of the Cape. The scene of the mission was now to be Kaffirland, as the territory of the Bantu tribes beyond the eastern frontier of the colony was then called.[2] But while the missionary party were still at Cape Town an urgent appeal from three Bushman deputies in person led to a division of their forces. Vanderkemp with Edmonds proceeded eastwards as originally intended, while Kicherer and Edwards went north in response to this appeal. From these two journeys came many developments.

Vanderkemp and Edmonds reached Graaff Reinet near the eastern frontier at the end of June 1799, a month after leaving Cape Town and three months after landing in South Africa. The occasion was scarcely propitious for their purpose. The Xhosas, who were the Bantu people abutting on the colonial frontier, resented encroachment on their lands and had raided the colonists' herds from time to time. The third of these invasions of the frontier, known to history as "Kaffir Wars", was now in progress. Commandos of Dutch farmers had been called up in support of regular troops who were in the area. But General Dundas, the British Governor, was anxious for peace, and by September was himself on the frontier. The next month

[1] *The South African Society for Promoting the Extension of Christ's Kingdom*, April 1799. Du Plessis, *op. cit.*, 91–3.
[2] Fifth *Report of the Directors* (1799), ix.

hostilities officially ceased, but raiding continued and Dutch farmers retaliated intermittently.[1] Vanderkemp had been delayed by these events, but in late September had got through to the Xhosa chief Gaika. He eventually secured the chief's consent to remain, but his companion Edmonds was restive, hankering after a missionary career in India. At the end of the year Edmonds left for Bengal. Vanderkemp held on alone for another year, hoping against hope that some suitable centre for missionary work might be found among the Xhosas. An example of his encounters with Gaika was the following conversation on the pressing question of rain: "The king came to me, asking what law he must follow to obtain rain for his country? I said, that God had sufficient reason to keep his rain back from this country. Asking what these reasons were, I answered that the evils committed in his country were more than sufficient to account for it. He said, he knew not of any crimes committed under his dominion, and if I knew of them, I should mention them. I then represented to him the plunderings and excesses of some of his Captains against the Christians, to which he made no reply."[2] Two men, of a missionary party of reinforcement in 1800, were appointed to join Vanderkemp in his Xhosa mission, but the Government declined to authorize their going in view of the unsettled state of the frontier at the time. Vanderkemp had been slowly compelled to surrender the enterprise and on the last day of the year 1800 he withdrew, eventually settling for a time in Graaff Reinet. He did not again cross the frontier, but devoted his attention to the Hottentots within the colony.

Meanwhile Kicherer and Edwards, reinforced by a young Cape Dutchman, Cornelius Kramer, set out upon their pioneer journey northwards. The appeal to which they were responding had come about in the following way. Among the farmers on the northern frontier who had suffered much from Bushman depredations, was one Florus Fischer who, with other farmers, made a treaty with the Bushmen for future security, upon which Fischer solemnly appealed to Almighty God. This, together with his practice of family worship, led them to inquiries and finally to ask for a Christian teacher. It was Fischer who had taken these Bushman deputies to Cape Town.[3] It was at his farm the missionary party completed their preparations and he accompanied them on the final stage of their journey. After

[1] G. M. Theal, *op. cit.*, I, 49–55; E. A. Walker, *A History of South Africa* (1928), 120, 137–8. [2] Lovett, *op. cit.*, I, 492–3.
[3] R. Moffat, *Missionary Labours and Scenes in Southern Africa* (1842), 50.

leaving the last farmstead they travelled a week in desert country without meeting a human being, and finally reached the Zak River where they found some scattered Bushman settlements, near which they decided to make their centre. The curiosity of the Bushmen led them to visit shyly the new-comers, and gradually relations of confidence were established. Language was a problem, but fortunately there were available as interpreters a Hottentot and his wife who both knew Dutch and had lived in Bushman country. Kicherer thus describes the earliest mission activities in this situation: "Our days are spent in the following manner:—About the time of sun-rising we collect together for prayer, when we read the Scriptures and sing a hymn; then the elderly people depart, and the business of the school commences. We teach the younger people to spell and read Dutch. In the mean time our provision is prepared by a Boscheman girl. School being over, we proceed to our manual labour, such as gardening, building, etc. About noon we dine, and the afternoon passes away in the same occupations as the forenoon. Evening arriving, we conclude our day by prayer, singing hymns, and communicating, in the plainest manner we can, the knowledge of divine things."[1] This was the most isolated of stations. They were some 400 to 500 miles north-east of Cape Town, the journey to which under favourable conditions occupied three weeks. Edwards did not continue long, but Anderson, of the second missionary party arriving in 1800, joined Kicherer and Kramer. The ground was hard, but these pioneers persevered, and in 1801 Anderson reached the Orange River and founded a new station north of it, moving it lower down the river the following year. The successes attained, however, were not among the Bushmen, but Hottentots and Bastards (the name given by the Dutch to half-breeds later known as Griquas). "The Bushmen, with few exceptions, could never appreciate his (Kicherer's) object," wrote Robert Moffat, "but, as a people, continued to harass and impoverish those who remained attached to the objects of the missionary."[2] In 1803 Kicherer was called to Holland by family affairs. He took the occasion to introduce three of the Hottentot converts to sup-porters of the mission in Holland and England. They made a deep impression.[3] On his return to the Cape, where he then married a Dutch lady, he was desired by the Governor (then

[1] *Transactions of the Missionary Society*, II, 9, quoted in Lovett, *op. cit.*, I, 521–2.　　　　　　　　　　　　　　　　[2] Moffat, *op. cit.*, 51.
[3] Tenth *Report of the Directors* (1804), 6–8.

Dutch) to become pastor of the church at Graaff Reinet. This invitation he accepted, stipulating still to superintend the work at Zak River as far as occasional visits made it possible.[1] In the event, some of his Hottentot flock moved to the vicinity of Graaff Reinet, and in 1806 the mission at Zak River, left in charge of Mr. and Mrs. Vos and a devoted farmer Botma, who had sold his all for the mission, was abandoned. Vos wrote of it sadly: "This day we leave Zak River, the place which has cost us so many sighs, tears, and drops of sweat; that place in which we have laboured so many days and nights, for the salvation of immortal souls: the place which probably, before long, will become a heap of ruins."[2] This pioneer attempt to win the Bushmen, while it failed in its immediate objective, yet had a twofold result of great significance: it pointed the way to new peoples, and it trained individual converts who later became Christian leaders elsewhere. As Robert Moffat saw it: "Zak River became the finger-post to the Namaquas, Corannas, Griquas, and Bechuanas; for it was by means of that mission that these tribes and their condition became known to the Christian world." He also pays tribute to Hottentot and Bastard converts "who afterwards became the pillars of the Griqua mission; and from whose lips the writer has frequently heard with delight the records of by-gone years, when they listened to the voice of Kicherer, Anderson, and Kramer, at the Zak and Orange Rivers".[3] Arrangements were made by Kicherer for those Christian Hottentots who had been connected with the Zak River station to be placed in suitable employment in the neighbourhood of Graaff Reinet "in the most pious families, where they are likely to acquire useful habits of industry, and where it is stipulated that they shall enjoy the privilege of attending on the Lord's day, and on other suitable occasions, on the ministry of Mr. Kicherer", a plan the Directors approved, stating that they considered "this dispersed congregation as being yet in an affectionate connexion with the Society".[4]

Meanwhile work had been growing among the Korannas (a division of the Hottentots) on the Orange River, where Anderson and Kramer had been at work since 1801. Natural conditions were difficult and their hope of developing a settled community based on agriculture was frustrated by the meagre rainfall.

[1] Thirteenth *Report of the Directors* (1807), 10–11.
[2] R. Moffat, *op. cit.*, 52.   [3] *Ibid.*, 51–2.
[4] Fourteenth *Report of the Directors* (1808), 19.

With much self-denial they struggled on, and could report by 1806 that they sometimes had as many as 250 persons at a time to hear the gospel, which represented about a third of the available population, most of which attended in turn; some eighty-four were near enough to attend daily instruction and were taught to read (the missionaries were forbidden by the Cape Government to teach writing without special orders, despite the fact that they were beyond the limits of the Colony).[1] A Government commission that came into the neighbourhood was much impressed by the missionaries' work and reported in such favourable term that Anderson and his colleagues were granted facilities for supplies not previously enjoyed. Among other marks of favour, the ban on the teaching of writing was lifted.[2]

The year in which Zak River was relinquished as a station saw the advance into Great Namaqualand, north of the Orange River. In January 1806 that river was crossed by Christian and Abraham Albrecht and J. Sydenfaden, all new recruits from Holland. Previous contact with white men had proved so perilous that the Namaquas were far from seeking their society. The situation is vividly put in the reply of a Namaqua to an inquiry by Robert Moffat as to why he never visited the missionary station: "I have been taught from my infancy to look upon hat men (hat-wearers) as the robbers and murderers of the Namaquas. Our friends and parents have been robbed of their cattle, and shot by the hat-wearers."[3] Nevertheless the pioneers, in faith and hope, named their first temporary station Stille Hoop (Silent Hope), and the next one Blyde Uitkomst (Happy Deliverance).[4] The strong social sense that operates in African societies, particularly where, as here, there is constant exposure to peril from without, expressed itself in the reaction of a Namaqua chief: "Harmony must prevail; all the chiefs must have one heart and mind—for if I only accept it, I shall be murdered by the rest, and it will occasion a war."[4] Their settlement proved to be uncomfortably close to the residence of the noted Africaner whose name was sheer terror to Dutch colonist and neighbouring tribes alike. They therefore transferred their centre to Warm Bath, a hundred miles to the west. The people of Warm Bath became embroiled in a quarrel with Africaner,

---

[1] Thirteenth *Report of the Directors* (1807), 12–13.
[2] Sixteenth *Report of the Directors* (1810), ix.
[3] R. Moffat, *op. cit.*, 69.   [4] *Ibid.*, 72.
[4] Thirteenth *Report of the Directors* (1807), 15–16.

and Warm Bath was destroyed. The Namaqua mission was then moved to Pella, south of the Orange River, so called as the place of refuge.[1] Some 500 of the Warm Bath people accompanied the missionaries. The work prospered, and by 1815 more than fifty persons had been added to the Church, and six Griqua and Hottentot preachers recommended and received.[2]

Kicherer's colleagues at Zak River, Anderson and Kramer, finally moved in 1804 to Klaar Water (the later Griqua Town) north of the Orange River. Here "a select party though a mixed multitude", as Moffat calls them, settled down with the missionaries. By 1809 some 800 people resided at or near the station, among whom the missionaries worked, though they also cared for such Korannas and Bushmen around them as they could. Janz became a worthy colleague here. In 1814 an order from the Colonial Government had embarrassing results; it was a demand to send to the Cape twenty Griquas for the Cape regiment, though the Griquas lay ten days' journey beyond the boundary of the Colony. The order was not complied with, but since Anderson had hitherto been the personal link between the Griquas and the Cape Government, he came under suspicion and never recovered his former influence among them. The reactions of the Cape Government in its restrictions of London Society missionaries appear later.[3]

The response of Kicherer and Edwards to the Bushman chiefs' appeal had thus produced notable results by 1815 in pioneering outreach far beyond the northern frontier of the Colony. But what, meanwhile, of Dr. Vanderkemp, frustrated in Kaffirland, and now withdrawn within the eastern frontier to Graaff Reinet? Here he joined Read and Vanderlingen who had been sent out as his colleagues. Vanderlingen was called upon to take charge of the colonial church at Graaff Reinet, while Vanderkemp and Read devoted themselves to the service of the Hottentots. The opposition this produced among the Dutch colonists was sufficiently violent to determine Vanderkemp and Read to withdraw with the Hottentots already attached to them and constitute a settlement where they could attend school un- hindered, learn agriculture, and in other ways improve them- selves. The Commissioner of Graaff Reinet appreciated the

---

[1] Pella was a town east of the Jordan, to which the Christians of Jerusalem withdrew in A.D. 66, after the outbreak of the fatal war with Rome.

[2] Twenty-first *Report of the Directors* (1815), 20–2; Twenty-second *Report of the Directors* (1816), 27–8; R. Moffat, *op. cit.*, 82–91.

[3] J. Philip, *Researches in South Africa* (1828), II, 61–5; R. Moffat, *op. cit.*, 197–8.

missionaries' work and approved the scheme.[1] In November 1801 Governor Dundas authorized Vanderkemp to take up land for such a settlement, and in the following March this was done at Botha's Farm, near Algoa Bay. The principles on which the settlement was to be founded were stated by Vanderkemp in a letter to the Governor.[2] The settlement naturally became an asylum for such Hottentots as were oppressed and sought refuge there; this led to bitter opposition from those colonists who had no interest in Hottentot welfare. When in 1803 the Cape was once more in Dutch hands, Janssens visited Vanderkemp at Algoa Bay. While seemingly friendly to the missionaries' general purpose, he proposed certain restrictions that led Vanderkemp to write: "The Governor wished us to desist for the present from the instruction of the Hottentots in reading and writing, chiefly the latter; but I could not, however, with all the regard due to his rank and character, consent to a proposal so contrary to the apparent interest of Christ's kingdom, and so unworthy of the rights of a free nation, merely to stop the clamour of a number of ill-natured people."[3] The Governor consented, however, to the transfer of the settlement to a more favourable site, some seven miles north of Fort Frederick, and for this Vanderkemp chose the name Bethelsdorp, an institution destined to become the cause of bitter controversy.

One of the greatest handicaps to the free development of such an institution as Bethelsdorp was the demand for Hottentot labour made upon the missionaries by both colonists and officials. Vanderkemp's attitude to such demands was uncompromising. Asked for his grounds for refusal to send Hottentots who might be required by the local magistrate, he said: "That to apprehend men as prisoners, and force them to labour in the manner proposed, was no part of his duty." When asked whether he did not regard it as his duty to compel the Hottentots to labour, he answered: "No, sir; the Hottentots are recognized to be a free people, and the colonists have no more right to force them to labour in the way you propose, than you have to sell them as slaves." Asked whether he would refuse to accept Xhosas in the institution, and send such as might pretend to come for instruction as prisoners to the magistrate, his answer was: "Sir, my commission is to preach the gospel to every

[1] Eighth *Report of the Directors* (1802), 14–16.
[2] Quoted in J. Philip, *op. cit.*, I, 72–5.
[3] *Transactions of the Missionary Society*, II, 94, quoted in Lovett, *op. cit.*, I, 501.

creature, and I will preach the gospel to everyone who chooses to hear me. God has sent me, not to put chains upon the legs of Hottentots and Caffers, but to preach liberty to the captives, and the opening of the prison doors to them that are bound."[1]

Vanderkemp and Read finally made an appeal to the Governor in 1811 on behalf of oppressed Hottentots, as a result of which the various charges preferred against colonists for alleged crimes against Hottentots were brought before a Circuit Court in 1812. The charges deeply stirred the colonists, some fifty-eight of whom were placed on trial. A number were found guilty and punished. The effects were far-reaching; one historian sums it up from the colonists' side: "The irritation of the relatives and friends of those who were accused without sufficient cause was excessive; and this event, more than anything that preceded it, caused a lasting unfriendly feeling between the colonists and the missionaries of the London Society."[2]

Vanderkemp did not live to see the trial. He passed away on December 15, 1811, at the age of sixty-three. A devoted and intrepid missionary crusader, his name abides as the sturdy pioneer of the London Society in South Africa. So greatly were his services valued, that the Directors desired him to undertake a mission to China, but he replied with conviction: "I am convinced that God has called me to do his work in the place of my present residence, and that it is my duty to continue in that station till it shall please him to call me out of it as evidently as he called me into it."[3] Within two years, however, he was himself proposing to undertake a mission to Madagascar, a desire he seems to have cherished to the end.[4] It was his greatest glory to be the generous friend of the oppressed. He himself expended upwards of £1,000 of his personal property in the redemption of slaves.[5] Robert Moffat, in a wisely appreciative estimate, connects with this generosity to and sympathy with an oppressed people, Vanderkemp's action in marrying a Hottentot convert, a union so unsuitable that, says Moffat, it cast a gloom over his remaining years, and may even have accelerated his death.[6] Admitting his eccentricities and defects, his place in history is secure: "He was the first public defender of the rights of the Hottentot. . . . He counted not his own life

[1] J. Philip, op. cit., I, 125.
[2] G. M. Theal, South Africa (Story of the Nations, 7th ed., 1910), 146.
[3] Thirteenth Report of the Directors (1807), 9–10.
[4] Fifteenth Report of the Directors (1809), vii–viii.　　　　[5] Ibid., ix.
[6] R. Moffat, op. cit., 40. Read and Janz also married Christian Hottentot wives.

dear to himself; for when advised for his own safety to leave the Hottentots for a season, his reply was, 'If I knew that I should save my own life by leaving them, I should not fear to offer that life for the least child amongst them.' In this, though wanting in prudence, he displayed a magnanimity of soul which, in other circumstances, would have called forth the applause of a nation."[1]

On December 16, 1811, the day after Vanderkemp's death, he was appointed by the Directors in London General Superintendent of the work in South Africa, a step already for some time in contemplation. Read succeeded to the office for the time being. The new situation created by recent developments, together with the sudden deprivation of Vanderkemp's leadership, led the Directors to appoint as a deputation to visit South Africa and report on the work one of their own number, the Rev. John Campbell. Mr. Campbell was absent for two years (June 1812—May 1814), during which time he travelled extensively in South Africa. Coming as they do at the end of our period, his recommendations are best reported at the next stage of the South African story.

The close of the Napoleonic era finds Protestant missionary work permanently established in Africa at last. There are striking contrasts between the West and the South as mission fields: in the one, a hostile climate coupled with the deadly malaria, the ever-present background of the slave-trade, a reservoir of Muslim peoples in the interior, with trickling streams reaching the coast, and nothing of European residence beyond the coastline itself; in the other, a salubrious climate, a territory long colonized, with widely scattered farmsteads, providing a background of conservative colonial opinion not friendly to missionary effort among the useful Hottentots, and for those living on the frontiers the constant menace of marauding Bushmen on the north and Bantu on the east, who resented the increasing encroachment on their lands. Here were vast distances to be covered through semi-desert country by the pioneer missionaries who found themselves on their stations in the north perhaps a month's hard travel from the amenities of Cape Town. In the West the Church Missionary Society was the first to become firmly established; in the South, the London Mission was the pioneer of the new Societies. The Continent also made its contribution even in these early days. The

[1] R. Moffat, *op. cit.*, 41.

Church Missionary Society was at first entirely dependent upon German recruits from the Berlin Seminary, and the London Society also welcomed its share from the same source,[1] as well as receiving liberal support through the Netherlands Society in men and means. And all these beginnings were undertaken in time of international war.

These plantings were now to be watered and in due course to yield their increase.

[1] Eighth *Report of the Directors* (1802), 20; Tenth *Report* (1804), 8. Of twenty missionaries Campbell found in the direct service of the Society in South Africa in 1814, half came from German States.—Campbell, *Travels in South Africa* (1815), 393 (Appendix X).

CHAPTER II

SOUTH AFRICAN DEVELOPMENTS
1815–1840

THE quarter of a century that followed Waterloo was a momentous period in the history of South Africa both for colonial development and missionary enterprise. It saw the coming of the first British settlers, the securing to the Hottentots of their rights as free subjects, the emancipation of the slaves, closer relations with the Bantu tribes, and the Great Trek whereby thousands of Dutch colonists crossed the frontier and set up independent communities beyond. These happenings were so much the outcome of existing race relations and the effort to improve them, that missions are inextricably involved in the story. At the same time, existing missionary operations were extended both within and beyond the Colony, and new Societies arrived to share in the work. Wesleyan Methodists became actively engaged over a wide area, and with their characteristic evangelistic fervour and genius for organization, were soon second only to the London Mission itself. The Glasgow Society retrieved the disappointment it had shared with the London Mission in Sierra Leone, by a successful entry on the uneasy eastern frontier. The Paris and Rhenish Societies in due course found spheres in Basutoland and Namaqualand respectively, with which their names are indissolubly associated. The Berlin Society secured a foothold in what became the Orange Free State, and the American Board, after an abortive effort among the Matebele, established a permanent work with the Zulu tribes.

It is to be remembered that the contemporary picture in Europe was that of post-war lassitude, complicated by political and economic problems that almost led the godly to despair. Yet against such an unfavourable background the leaders of the British anti-slavery movement carried their campaign to a triumphant conclusion, and constituted the necessary group having political influence at home with whom the liberal leaders at the Cape could effectively join hands.

(1) *Missionary Progress, 1816–28.*

The political status of the Cape, left in suspense for the period of hostilities, had been finally determined in the general European settlement of 1814. England retained the Cape (and what is now British Guiana), and paid to the Dutch Government the sum of six millions sterling. Thus the Cape, held by right of conquest, was ceded by consent.[1] This involved no immediate change, for the second British occupation had already lasted six years. Dutch institutions and traditions had been respected and this facilitated the peaceful transition to British rule. In respect of religion in particular, the ordinance of 1804, published by the Dutch Commissioner-General, De Mist, continued in force. This declared that religious liberty should be enjoyed by all societies that promoted morality and worshipped an Almighty Being, thus giving equal civil rights to Protestants and Roman Catholics, Jews and Muslims. As the European residents of the country districts were at that time staunch supporters of the Dutch Reformed Church, it was only in Cape Town that this liberal policy had effect. At the same time the Dutch Reformed remained the State Church, with clergy appointed and paid by Government; and the express consent of the Governor was required for otherwise holding religious services or erecting a place of worship.[2] This control of religious affairs by the civil authority was not disputed by the missionaries in principle, though they might, and did, contest the equity of specific demands and decisions.

The two pioneer missions at the Cape had now reached the point where some independent survey of their work was demanded. This was undertaken for the Moravians by C. I. Latrobe, best known for his work as a musical composer and editor,[3] and for the London Mission by John Campbell. Both published their journals, which are contemporary records of value.[4] Latrobe confined himself to the actual Colony; Campbell on each occasion went far beyond its limits. The concern of the missions within the Colony was in the main with Hottentots and slaves; a few Bantu trickled into the settlements, but direct work among them was still beyond the eastern frontier.

Genadendal, some 120 miles east from Cape Town, remained the principal Moravian settlement at the Cape. At the time of

[1] The Convention with Holland was signed August 13, 1814. Details of the settlement are given in E. A. Walker, *A History of South Africa* (1928), 146, n. 1.
[2] Theal, *op. cit.*, I, 119–20; Walker, *op. cit.*, 143.   [3] *D.N.B.*, s.v.
[4] C. I. Latrobe, *Journal of a Visit to South Africa in 1815 and 1816* (1818); John Campbell, *Travels in Africa, undertaken at the Request of the Missionary Society* (3rd ed., 1815), and *Travels in South Africa, undertaken at the Request of the London Missionary Society: being a Narrative of a Second Journey in the Interior of that Country*, in two volumes (1822).

Latrobe's visit the village consisted of 256 cottages and huts, with a population of 1,276. A few Bantu, farming their own "Caffre-Kraal", had been permitted by Government to remain within the Hottentot settlement. With their accustomed atten-

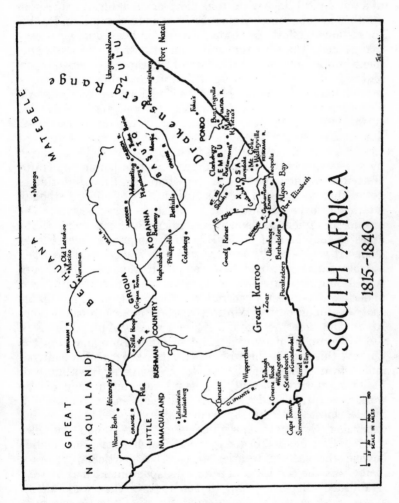

tion to the development of industry as part of Christian character training, the missionaries had established a cutlery and smithy where fourteen Hottentots were taught the trade. "Their busy hammers, files, and polishing-wheel", says Latrobe,

235

"made me often fancy myself living in a London street."[1] On his journey to the eastern frontier he found "Genadendal knives", as they were called, well known and valued, and one of the most acceptable presents he could offer a colonist. He speaks of a well-built bridge with stone piers, erected during his visit, as another instance of the effect of Christian principles in leading to sustained effort. Separate schools for boys and girls were maintained. The Christian tone and atmosphere of the settlement impressed him greatly. Two of the three pioneers of 1792, Marsveld and Schwinn, were still alive, and this continuity of service had been invaluable in the building up of the work. The community, however, was not without its stresses and strains due to earlier loyalties; clan rivalry expressed itself during Latrobe's visit by a request for a second Hottentot chief or "captain", but this was found on inquiry to be supported by one section only and to be urged "by a designing and crafty Hottentot in the village".[2] At the same time it is interesting to notice that the missionaries permitted the Hottentot method of interment to be continued at a Christian burial service.[3] The second Moravian settlement at Groenekloof lay some thirty miles to the north of Table Bay, and comprised several large farms. It was recently begun, being only seven years old when Latrobe paid his visit; here he found a Hottentot population of 300. A journey across the Colony to the eastern frontier was undertaken to select a centre for a third settlement. A suitable spot was found on the White River, a tributary of the Sunday River, and here the station of Enon was established in 1818, the Government making a grant of land. Though within the Colony, this was in the troubled frontier zone, and so suffered much from raids, which led to a temporary withdrawal. Following Latrobe's visit, a general superintendency of the work was established under Bishop Hans Peter Hallbeck, a Swede, whose leadership for twenty-three years led to impressive expansion. New stations were begun at Elim, some forty miles south of Genadendal, in 1824; and at Shiloh among the Tembus beyond the eastern frontier in 1828.[4] A particular work of mercy was the service of lepers. The Government had in 1817 established a leper asylum, Hemel-en-Aarde (Sky and Earth), a few miles south of Genadendal. In 1823 the Government requested the co-operation of the Moravians, and Peter Leitner

---

[1] Latrobe, op. cit., 397.   [2] Ibid., 154-7.   [3] Ibid., 129-30.
[4] Theal, op. cit., I, 257, 349; Walker, op. cit., 150-1; A. C. Thompson, Moravian Missions (1883), 398; Hutton, op. cit., 281, 289.

became chaplain and superintendent. Here he and his wife devoted themselves to the physical and spiritual care of the lepers. No treatment leading to disappearance of the symptoms was then known, and no case of cure was reported. There was spiritual responsiveness, however, and ninety-five converts were baptized.[1]

John Campbell's first visit to South Africa arose from the emergency created by the death of Dr. Vanderkemp.[2] His extensive travels not only covered the London Society's field of operations from Cape Town to Bethelsdorp, and from Griqua Town to Namaqualand, but also included an adventurous journey among the Bechuana tribes. At Bethelsdorp, upon which the complaints of the colonists were largely focused, he found the fault to lie in their own extravagant demand for labour rather than with the mission in withholding it.[3] Eighteen trades or occupations were being practised there, despite constant demands made upon the settlement by the Government and colonists for Hottentot labour.[4] Nevertheless he candidly admits that the appearance of the place was against it (it was customary to contrast it unfavourably with Genadendal): "Truth however obliges me to confess, that had the founder of Bethelsdorp (Dr. Vanderkemp) been more aware of the importance of civilization, there might at least have been more external appearance of it than there now is. He seems to have judged it necessary, rather to imitate the savage in appearance, than to induce the savage to imitate him—perhaps considering his conduct countenanced by what Paul says, of his becoming all things to all men, that he might gain some."[5] Campbell warmly approved of the purpose of the Institution as a refuge and training settlement for hard-pressed Hottentots, and two others were established in the Colony during his visit: Theopolis, sixty miles north-east of Bethelsdorp, upon which it drew for its first residents; and Hooge Kraal, 300 miles to the east of Cape Town. Theopolis, personally selected and named by Sir John Cradock, was in a situation far superior to Bethelsdorp.[6]

[1] Theal, *op. cit.*, I, 254–5; A. C. Thompson, *op. cit.*, 387–9; Hutton, *op. cit.*, 284–5.

[2] Campbell was nearly two years discharging his commission, June 1812 to May 1814.

[3] "The boors in this part of the colony are never satisfied unless they have twenty or thirty Hottentots running about them. When they happen to have fewer, they are full of complaints against Bethelsdorp."—Campbell, *Travels* (1815), 80–1.

[4] Of 223 men belonging to the Institution he found only 94 resident, 40 of whom were incapable of public service.—*Ibid.*, 84.   [5] *Ibid.*, 94–5.

[6] Campbell, *op. cit.*, 352; Twenty-first *Report of the Directors* (1815), 17–18.

At Hooge Kraal, occupied by a Hottentot "captain" with his dwindling people, Charles Pacalt, who started the Institution, died after five years of devoted labour. He had so commended his ministry to Hottentot and colonist alike, that the local request to rename the place Pacaltsdorp was granted by the Government.[1]

Beyond the Colony Campbell faced problems of a different character.[2] There were as yet no stations among the Bantu on the eastern frontier, but in the wide spaces of the north London Society missionaries had sought to establish settled stations among a sparse and wandering people. Griqua Town was the outpost north of the Orange River, some 700 miles from the Cape. If the missionaries here were free from direct Government control, so were the independent people whom they sought to serve. The missionaries were dependent on their goodwill, and could only secure improvement by consent. Campbell's constructive proposals were directed to assist a community slowly becoming civilized. As a contribution to civil government, magistrates were chosen for the town and its outposts, the two Griqua captains with the two missionaries being a court of appeal. A criminal code of fourteen articles was also drawn up by Campbell and agreed upon.[3] In the absence of a circulating medium, he suggested an application to the Missionary Society for a silver currency. A request by the Griquas for more missionaries led him to propose a missionary fund of their own. An Auxiliary Missionary Society was accordingly established, the first subscriptions (in default of a currency) being thirty pounds of "elephants' teeth", nine young bulls, four heifers, one ox, twenty-three sheep and five goats.[4] The total population at the time was 1,266. In the west Schmelen was deputed to explore possibilities in the Great Namaqua and Damara countries. He travelled north for seven weeks from Pella, sometimes in dismal wilderness not meeting a human being for two weeks together.

[1] Philip, *Researches in South Africa*, I, 237–43; Twenty-fifth *Report of the Directors* (1819), 66–7.

[2] For the first time in 1816 the Directors in their *Report* classify the stations as within and beyond the Colony.   [3] Campbell, *op. cit.*, 254–5.

[4] *Ibid.*, 255, 256; Twenty-second *Report of the Directors* (1816), 25. It was also on this occasion that the name Griqua first appeared. The people being a mixed race (Hottentot with Dutch blood) were known as Bastards. On Campbell proposing a change, they consulted among themselves, and "found the majority were descended from a person of the name of Griqua, and they resolved hereafter to be called Griquas". The reaction on their self-respect could not have been negligible.—Campbell, *op. cit.*, 252–3.

Prospects for expansion here were clearly unfavourable. Contact with an importunate Namaqua chief, however, led to Schmelen's settlement at Klip Fountain, two days' journey north of the Orange River. Here he soon had a school of 140 children, but was so remote from civilized supplies that in default of paper they learned to write with a reed on a sheepskin over which fine sand was spread—of sand there was enough![1] The real opening for future development in the north seemed to lie among the Bechuana tribes. They, too, lived in difficult semi-desert, with meagre rainfall the perennial problem. There were, however, peoples beyond them to the east and north-east beckoning on the pioneer; here therefore might be a stepping-stone to further advance. So at least Campbell seems to have thought when securing the promise of Mothibi of Lattakoo to receive missionaries. After two fruitless attempts to settle at Lattakoo, a third under James Read was successful, and in December 1816 the chief's consent to the missionaries' remaining was secured. The promise Campbell had obtained from him three years before proved decisive.[2] So was gained the foothold among the Bechuana where Robert Moffat won his missionary laurels, and from which David Livingstone began the probings east and north that eventually led to his breaking through into the unknown and lifting the veil from Central Africa. When on his second visit to the Cape Campbell visited this mission in 1820, he found a church with capacity for 400 persons, and a row of missionary houses attractively situated. New Lattakoo and Old, some fifty miles apart, he estimated to have 4,000 people each. Attendance of adults at church and children at school was regarded, however, as a favour done to the missionaries. Indeed, when a chief was suddenly found attending regularly they would begin to wonder whether it was their waggon or their plough he wished to borrow. At the time of this second visit the missionaries were in official favour, though under circumstances that would cause some minds misgiving. In a severe drought, when the rainmaker had failed, Mothibi had asked the missionaries to pray for rain. "Four weeks before our arrival", says Campbell, "they had appointed a weekly prayer-meeting, and it has providentially happened that there has been rain every week since the meeting commenced." One reform at least was

[1] Twenty-first *Report of the Directors* (1815), 20–1; Twenty-second *Report* (1816), 26.
[2] Twenty-third *Report of the Directors* (1817), 31–2; Twenty-fourth *Report* (1818), 32–3.

claimed; Mothibi now refrained from going on cattle-raiding commandos.[1] The motive of the chief in receiving missionaries was neither a thirst for the gospel nor a desire for education, but the protection that having white men as his friends might afford.[2]

Two of the most notable men in South African missionary history came to the country at this time, Robert Moffat and John Philip. John Philip was coadjutor with Campbell on his second visit, and remained, as had been intended, as General Superintendent of the London Mission. His work falls to be considered later in special relation to the Hottentot question. Robert Moffat arrived in South Africa in 1817. He was almost sent with John Williams to the South Seas, but one of the Directors, a canny Scot, considered "thae twa lads ower young to gang tegither".[3] He was twenty-one when he came to South Africa. He and a colleague were at first refused permission by the Government to proceed to Namaqualand, but after eight months the refusal was withdrawn. Moffat used the interval to learn Dutch. Eventually he reached his destination, Africaner's Kraal north of the Orange River. Africaner was a Hottentot chieftain, said to have a dash of European blood, dreaded by colonist and Hottentot alike. Campbell on his first visit had suggested that evidence of real Christian concern even for an enemy might win the heart of Africaner. He accordingly wrote him a conciliatory letter, accompanied with a present. At first no messenger would venture with it, but it eventually came into his hands, and was supported by a visit from the missionary Christian Albrecht. Africaner responded as Campbell had dared to hope, and even pleaded the latter's promise that a missionary would be sent. Ebner, transferred from Pella, was well received, and in due course had the reward of baptizing among others on confession of faith, first two sons of Africaner, and then Africaner himself.[4] Moffat soon won the complete confidence of the chief, and when he had to travel to Cape Town in 1819, proposed to take Africaner with him, despite the risk He vividly describes the sensation produced. The very Governor who had at first refused Moffat permission to proceed was now

[1] Campbell, *Travels in South Africa, a Second Journey* (1822), I, 65, 67, 72–5.
[2] Campbell was plainly told by other chiefs, expressing a desire for missionaries, that "Mothibi's having missionaries was a shield to his back". —*Ibid.*, II, 9.　　　　　　　　　　　[3] E. W. Smith, *Robert Moffat* (1925), 25.
[4] Twenty-second *Report of the Directors* (1816), 27–8; Twenty-third *Report* (1817), 34.

so impressed that he showed his goodwill by a present to Africaner of an excellent waggon, valued at eighty pounds sterling.[1]

Other events of some importance took place on this visit. Moffat and Mary Smith, who had come out to be his bride, were married. Campbell and Philip, who were in Cape Town at this time, proposed that Moffat should be transferred from Namaqualand to Bechuanaland. This was agreed, and Campbell and the Moffats travelled north together. They arrived at New Lattakoo in March 1820. After an interval at Griqua Town during which Moffat set in order affairs that had gone awry since Campbell's earlier reforms (for the Cape Government had again withheld permission for a time for Moffat to work in Bechuanaland), the Moffats returned to New Lattakoo and began that memorable service by the Kuruman River where they laboured for half a century. Though remote from civilized life with its interests, they had not long to wait for high excitement. Umsiligazi, in flight from Chaka, the Zulu despot, had fallen with the effect of a tornado upon the Bechuana tribes. In the resulting turmoil the Mantati, a horde of displaced people many thousands strong, swept down upon the Batlhapi under Mothibi, among whom the mission worked. With Griqua aid the attack was repulsed and the Mantati forced to retreat.[2] The part that Moffat played in this crisis—in giving the first warnings, in securing the indispensable Griqua allies, and in rallying the people—won for him at a stroke a place of supreme influence with the tribe. In 1824, the year following this deliverance, the mission was moved to a more favourable site, eight miles up the Kuruman River, where it remained.[3] It was here that Livingstone began his African career.

Another enterprise pioneered by the London Mission beyond the Colony at this time was among the Xhosas on the eastern frontier, where, before 1800, Dr. Vanderkemp had tried to get a foothold, but tried in vain. His colleagues had been forbidden by the Government to join him there, so he retired within the Colony. For fifteen years official discouragement of this mission continued, though the Xhosas themselves had sought a renewal of it. With the discovery, however, that frontier Boers in rebel-

[1] Moffat, *Missionary Labours* (1842), 173–9.
[2] Moffat, *Ibid.*, 340–70, gives a vivid narrative of the attack; E. W. Smith, *Robert Moffat*, 115–25, shows its relation to contemporary disturbances and its historical importance.
[3] About 100 miles to the west of the modern Vryberg on the "Cape to Cairo" line.—E. W. Smith, *op. cit.*, 131.

lion had made traffic with Xhosa chiefs to join them (who had nevertheless refused), the Colonial Government revised its attitude; an Englishman in touch with the border Bantu chiefs would be a political asset rather than a liability. The embargo was accordingly lifted, and in 1816 a missionary party crossed the Great Fish River, the then colonial boundary, and met leading chiefs in conference. Joseph Williams, who was designated for this work, was accompanied by James Read and Jan Tzatzoe of Bethelsdorp, the latter the son of a Xhosa chief. After an interview with Gaika, recognized as paramount by the Government, they selected a site by the Kat River, fifty to sixty miles beyond the Fish River and about fifteen from Gaika's Kraal. Here Joseph Williams settled with his wife and family in July 1816. Among the neighbouring Xhosas were scattered a number of the Ghonaqua tribe of Hottentots, refugees from the persecuting attentions of frontier colonists. A year later 138 persons were residing at the missionary settlement, the Sunday attendance at worship of 100 and on weekdays of ninety was encouraging; there were also fifty to sixty children in the school. Williams, however, was not long left in peace. Colonel Cuyler, the landdrost of Uitenhage, desired regular interchange of information about Xhosa thefts and complaints against colonists, but Williams resisted this attempt to treat him as a disguised Government agent with secular authority. In 1817 the Governor, Lord Charles Somerset, visited the frontier, when Colonel Cuyler accused Williams of harbouring runaway Hottentots: "His Lordship then said to me, 'I cannot allow you to receive and keep my people here, as Messrs. Read and Anderson do.' I replied, 'My Lord! I do not receive nor keep your people.' " Williams pointed out that if he were to attempt to exercise a secular authority in the way suggested "the natives would say that I was come to entrap them, instead of instructing them in the truths of Christianity". A certain Captain Sheridan of the Governor's staff gave, however, an encouraging word; he "took me by the hand and said. 'Mr. Williams, I wish you every success; and I doubt not but you will have it.' "[1] Williams devoted himself to his difficult task with unremitting zeal; exhausted prematurely by his labours, he died in August 1818.[2] The Colonial Government thereupon

[1] Mr. Thomas Sheridan, Colonial Paymaster at the Cape, and eldest son of the large-hearted Richard Brinsley Sheridan, M.P.

[2] Twenty-third *Report of the Directors* (1817), 26–7; Twenty-fourth *Report* (1818), 29; Twenty-fifth *Report* (1819), 72–3; Philip, *Researches*, II, 162–79; Macmillan, *Bantu, Boer and Briton* (1929), 8, n. 3; 59–60.

declined to authorize a successor from the London Mission, but instead appointed an agent of their own to establish an institution. This was John Brownlee who had formerly been in the service of the London Mission and later returned to it. He settled on the Chumie River in 1820 and was soon joined by a number who had been at the Kat River with Williams.[1] The delay in his settlement was due to the so-called "Fifth Kaffir War", starting in a quarrel between Gaika and his uncle Ndlambe. Gaika, as paramount recognized by the Government, appealed to Somerset for support, and the Governor gave it. But Ndlambe hit back and even besieged Grahamstown. When the war was over Gaika had perforce to submit to the moving east of the colonial frontier from the Great Fish River to the Keiskama River, the intervening territory being intended as a "no-man's land".

At this point a new missionary partner, the Glasgow Society, entered the field. William R. Thomson and John Bennie, sent out by that Society to the Cape, were despatched by the Government to join Brownlee in 1821. John Ross soon followed. Thomson shared Brownlee's status, but Bennie and Ross served as independent missionaries of the Glasgow Society. In 1824 these two commenced a new station some eight miles from the Chumie, and named it Lovedale, destined to become famous as an educational centre for the Bantu of the South.[2]

It was at this time also that the Wesleyan missionaries first appeared on the eastern frontier, though their arrival in the Colony took place at an earlier date. The initiative came from a Methodist soldier at the Cape, Sergeant J. Kendrick, who was himself active as class leader and preacher among the troops, and desired some guarantee of continuity for the work. His appeal led to Dr. Coke's leaving one man at the Cape when on his way to the East in 1813. The Governor, however, declined to grant the necessary authorization, so that after a few months this man, J. McKenny, followed his companions to Ceylon.[3] The next to arrive was Barnabas Shaw in 1816. He too applied to the Governor, though now with a letter from Earl Bathurst,[4] and he too was refused. "Having been refused the sanction of

[1] Philip, op. cit., II, 190–1, 193–9. Later missionary developments among the Bantu tribes were acknowledged by the Societies engaged to be in debt to Williams; they reaped where he had sown.

[2] Report of the Glasgow Missionary Society (1823), 8, 22; Report (1825), 8. Lovedale was so named in memory of Dr. Love, one of the secretaries of the Glasgow Society.—Report (1827), 8.

[3] Findlay and Holdsworth, op. cit., IV (1922), 239–41.

[4] Secretary of State for the Colonies from June 1812 to April 1827.

the governor," he wrote, "I was resolved what to do; and commenced *without it* on the following Sabbath. If his excellency was afraid of giving offence either to the Dutch ministers or the English chaplains, I had no occasion to fear either the one or the other."[1] H. Schmelen of the London Mission soon arrived in Cape Town with a dozen of his Namaquas, and Shaw sought him out. The account he heard of the need beyond the Orange River was a moving one, but he hesitated, for his wife was delicate, the expense would be heavy, and no such distant mission had been authorized by the home committee. Mrs. Shaw's word was decisive: "We will go with you, the Lord is opening our way to the heathen." To the Governor, who now wished to keep Shaw within the Colony and even offered him a Dutch pastorate, Shaw replied that had he wished to preach to Christians only he would have stayed in England. So it fell out that the Shaws joined Schmelen's party on their journey northward. Shortly after crossing the Oliphants River, they met a chief of Little Namaqualand travelling to Cape Town to seek a missionary. To the Shaws this was no chance encounter, but a divine direction to their field of labour. With high delight the chief and his people welcomed them at his home in the Kamiesberg. Here the first Wesleyan Methodist station in South Africa was begun at Leliefontein in October 1816.[2] Shaw soon discovered that, with a hunting people, the missionary must either become a wanderer himself or teach them agriculture. He chose the second, and set about the making of a plough. His success was spectacular; his first sowing produced over fifty-fold. "The Bible and the plough" was the missionary motto here, as it had been with the Moravian and London Missions elsewhere.[3] In June 1817 the first spiritual harvest was reaped with the baptism of seventeen adult converts and eleven children. The first communion service the following month was a solemn occasion. The story of the crucifixion, as many pioneers have testified, has a deeply moving effect on the hearts of untutored men; and Shaw said that on this occasion "many tears were shed at the remembrance of the Redeemer's agony and death". When, after ten years' service, the Shaws were called to Cape Town they left a prosperous settlement with a Christian fellowship

---

[1] Barnabas Shaw, *Memorials of Southern Africa* (1841), 60. Italics in original.   [2] *Ibid.*, 63, 68–71, 266.

[3] When James Read assisted in the founding of a Bushman mission at Rhinoster Fountain (the later Hephzibah) he said: "We take a plough with us. Let it be remembered that in Africa *the Bible and the plough go together*" (italics in original).—Twenty-third *Report of the Directors* (1817), 28.

of ninety-seven baptized adults.[1] Among several converts of
note were the brothers Peter and Jacob Links, who themselves
became missionaries, Peter in the Bechuana and Namaqua
countries, and Jacob to the Bushmen.[2] In 1824 the Governor
officially recognized the superintending missionary as the
secular authority of the settlement, with power to receive and
expel residents, to allot land for planting, and to control
erection of all buildings. This stripping of the chief of his powers
was announced to him directly by the field-cornet (a local
Dutch official) who was commissioned "to inform him that he
has no more power or influence amongst the people in giving
out land, etc., etc., but that this power and influence devolved
on the oldest, or superintending Missionary".[3] Granted that the
Governor's act was prompted by expediency, it is certainly
questionable how far such temporal power is a missionary asset,
even as a short-term policy.

The first Methodist interest in the Bechuana came through
the Namaqua mission. In 1818 some Namaquas of Leliefontein,
returning from a visit to Griqualand, brought a visitor who was
baptized during his stay. He had travelled among the Bechuana
tribes, and upon his baptism asked that a missionary might be
sent them. Not till 1821 was Barnabas Shaw able to send a man,
Stephen Kay, and even then he acted on his own initiative.
Some hesitancy on the part of Dr. Philip about the new
Wesleyan enterprise was due, not to any unwillingness to share
the Bechuana field, but to the youth and inexperience of Kay.
By a generous arrangement, however, Kay travelled with the
Moffats to Lattakoo and there became their guest to learn the
language and gain experience. When Stephen Broadbent
arrived in 1822 Kay withdrew to the Cape. In 1823 a station
was established among the Barolong, east of the London
Mission. It was engulfed by the Mantati invasion and destroyed.
A new station was established at Plaatberg, near the Modder
River, in 1826, where some 8,000 of the scattered Barolong were
soon gathered. Broadbent, though handicapped by ill-health,
sufficiently mastered the language to preach in it. He also
taught the people to sink wells successfully for a regular water
supply, and so deprived the chief of his prestige as official rain-
maker.[4]

[1] B. Shaw, op. cit., 83–5, 118–20.   [2] Ibid., 270–5; 280–7.
[3] Ibid., 109–10; Cheeseman, The Story of William Threlfall, 105, where is
reproduced in facsimile Shaw's own record, found in a book on the station.
[4] B. Shaw, op. cit., 250–3; Findlay and Holdsworth, op. cit., IV, 265–6.
Broadbent left a record of his pioneering venture in A Narrative of the First
Introduction of Christianity amongst the Barolong Tribes of Bechuanas (1865).

The most intensive development of the Wesleyan Society's work was on the eastern frontier of the Colony and in Bantuland beyond. This sprang directly from the coming of the English settlers in 1820. In the wake of the Napoleonic wars came economic depression in Britain with consequent social distress and discontent. One attempt to relieve the situation was the encouragement of emigration to Cape Colony. This also had in view the benefit to the Colony by the colonization of its eastern end at the Bantu border. The £50,000 voted by Parliament for the purpose enabled some 4,000 settlers to be selected from a crowd of applicants nearly twenty times as large. They were settled in the Zuurveld (renamed Albany), some 100 miles inland from Algoa Bay. The attractive features of the scheme were well advertised in advance; the drawbacks were discovered by painful experience. The areas allotted are said to have been inadequate, abnormal seasons were experienced, and roving Xhosa bands from over the border helped themselves to the settlers' cattle. Perhaps most important factor of all, many of these English settlers were artisans by training and mere tyros in agriculture. As a natural consequence there commenced a drift to the towns, Grahamstown and Port Elizabeth in particular gaining considerably from this movement.[1] "It was about five years after their arrival", says Theal, "before each one found himself in the sphere for which he was best adapted, and in another five years it began to be questioned whether a similar party had ever succeeded so well in any other country."[2] This was the first introduction into South Africa of a British community of any size. No longer were the British Government rulers of a wholly Dutch colony. The English language was introduced and began to spread, soon becoming the official language of the country.[3] The English element was used to political discussion as the stolid Dutch farmers had never been, and this introduced a new leaven into South African affairs. Of special significance was the prohibition of slavery in the Albany settlement.

Accompanying one party of settlers in 1820 in the capacity of chaplain was William Shaw, a young Wesleyan minister.[4] His first duty was to care for the religious needs of the colonists he accompanied, and as this involved itineracy over an area of

[1] Theal, *op. cit.*, I, 289–300; W. M. Macmillan, *The Cape Colour Question*, 109–21; Walker, *op. cit.*, 162–3.
[2] Theal, *South Africa* (Story of the Nations), 157.
[3] From 1825 for all official documents, and from 1828 in courts of law.
[4] He was no relation of Barnabas.

some 1,500 square miles without roads and bridges, the work made every demand that youthful energy and resolute endurance could satisfy.[1] While this was his first duty, he did not regard it as the whole, and wrote to the home committee during his first year: "With the exception of Lattakoo, which is far in the interior, there is not a single mission station between the place of my residence and the northern extremity of the Red Sea; nor any people professedly Christian, with the exception of those of Abyssinia." He formed the conception of a chain of Wesleyan stations stretching from the colonial border to Delagoa Bay.[2] William Shaw was no mere visionary, but a man of sound, practical sense, capable as an administrator, and with resolution to execute his plan, or at least to begin it. That this was in line with his original purpose in going to South Africa he himself affirms.[3] Barnabas Shaw wrote encouraging him in the enterprise. Mrs. Shaw's decisive "Let us go in the name of the Lord" finally clinched the matter.[4] In November 1823 William Shaw and his colleague William Shepstone (father of Sir Theophilus Shepstone) with their families set out on a prospecting tour beyond the Great Fish River. After visiting the mission station at Chumie sponsored by the Government, where they met the Xhosa chief Gaika and his son Makomo, they moved towards a strip of land along the coast under the chief Pato with whom they had already been in contact. Here a mission station was begun and named Wesleyville, the first Methodist mission in south-eastern Africa.[5] Shaw's influence with Pato and other chiefs was greatly strengthened at this time by a successful meeting between them and Government representatives which he had been desired to bring about[6]. Some fifteen miles beyond Wesleyville a second station was opened and named Mount Coke. By 1827 the time was ripe for

[1] B. Shaw, *op. cit.*, 230–4; Findlay and Holdsworth, *op. cit.*, IV, 248–52; W. Shaw, *The Story of My Mission among the British Settlers in South Eastern Africa* (New ed. 1872).

[2] W. B. Boyce, *Memoir of the Rev. William Shaw* (1874), 95.

[3] "From the time when I received my appointment to Southern Africa, as Chaplain or Minister to a party of British Settlers, my mind was filled with the idea that Divine Providence designed, after I had accomplished some preparatory work among the settlers who were located on the border of Kaffraria, that I should proceed beyond the colonial boundaries, and establish a Wesleyan Mission among the Kaffirs."—*Ibid.*, 94.   [4] *Ibid.*, 98–9, 101.

[5] The custom of giving European names to missionary settlements was in vogue at the time, but Shaw admits there were critics who urged the retention of African place names. Against these he defends the current practice.—*Ibid.*, 123–5.

[6] He gives a vivid narrative of the whole exciting experience.—*Ibid.*, 114–22.

further advance. W. J. Shrewsbury crossed the Kei River to the place of the chief Hintza, his interview with whom was not propitious. A visit from the landdrost of Albany to the chief, however, placed matters on a better footing, and Hintza agreed to receive the mission, to which the name Butterworth was given.[1] The first three links in the projected chain of Wesleyan stations were thus forged within five years. The first public baptism of converts took place at Wesleyville in 1825; as converts increased a system of quarterly baptismal services was introduced at each station. The chief Kama and his wife, a daughter of Gaika, were among the converts received by Shaw, who personally superintended the work from Wesleyville until 1830. By this time the number of stations had increased to six. The fourth was opened in Pondoland in 1829 and named Morley; here William Shepstone was appointed. Clarkbury, the fifth in the series, was established in 1830 among the Tembu; and the sixth, Buntingville, seventy miles north of the River Umtata, where W. B. Boyce was the pioneer. This was also among the Pondos. Thus within seven years Shaw had secured a chain of six stations (all named after Methodist worthies), extending south to north along the coastline for some 200 miles.[2]

An early Wesleyan attempt to establish work in Portuguese territory at Delagoa Bay did not succeed. William Threlfall was accepted for service in South Africa, though his passionate desire was for Madagascar. He reached Cape Town in 1822. After a year's service under William Shaw, the call came to Delagoa Bay. An English naval officer, the Hon. Captain Owen, R.N., who had a Christian concern for that region, offered a free passage on his frigate from Cape Town to any missionary who would go. Threlfall volunteered and in July 1823 was at his destination. But he was soon attacked by a malignant type of malaria, and after some months of severe suffering, left on a South Sea whaler. Cape Town was reached in distress after a tragic three weeks' voyage on which there were fifteen burials at sea of malaria victims. Threlfall survived, and proceeded to Barnabas Shaw's station in the Kamiesberg for convalescence. This story of malaria victims seems more in keeping with the West Coast than the South.[3] On recovering his health, Threlfall set out in 1825 with two of Shaw's African helpers, Jacob Links

[1] Original Manuscript Journal of the Rev. W. J. Shrewsbury, a summary of which is given in Francis Edwards, Ltd., Catalogue No. 645 (1940), 53.
[2] W. B. Boyce, *op. cit.*, 136–8. Findlay and Holdsworth, *op. cit.*, IV, 255–9.
[3] It is in keeping, however, with the earlier experience of the Portuguese in the valley of the Lower Zambezi.

and Johannes Jager, for Great Namaqualand, an expedition from which they never returned. They were murdered by their guide and his accomplices, the only apparent motive being covetousness of their few possessions.[1]

The Dutch Reformed Church and the Church of England during these years devoted themselves to the colonists and showed only a glimmering interest in missionary work among the African population. In 1824 the Dutch Reformed Church, at its first South African Synod, appointed a Committee on Missions, an earnest of activity to come. The Church of England had its first clergyman appointed for the civil population in 1811 for Cape Town and in 1813 for Simon's Town. It was in 1821, however, that William Wright, the first who can be called an Anglican missionary to South Africa, took up work under the Society for the Propagation of the Gospel. His pastoral work was also restricted to Europeans, but the schools he reorganized and extended served all races: English, Dutch, Malays, Negroes and Hottentots. He had no immediate successor. It was still to be many years before the Church of England was alive to the missionary task at the Cape.[2]

The Roman Catholics were also strangely slow in beginning work at the Cape. True, under the Dutch regime they were not tolerated, and although the ban was lifted by de Mist in 1805, when Roman public services were held for the first time in Cape Town, the clergymen concerned were required by the English to leave the following year. In 1818 was appointed the first Vicar Apostolic of the Cape of Good Hope and neighbouring islands, with headquarters at Mauritius. In 1819 permission for return was given, and from 1820 the Roman Church was able to carry on its work without further interruption. Its concern, however, was with its European parishioners.[3]

[1] B. Shaw, *op. cit.*, 329–45; T. Cheeseman, *The Story of William Threlfall, Missionary Martyr of Namaqualand*, with some account of Jacob Links and Johannes Jager who fell with him (1910).

[2] Theal, *op. cit.*, I, 210, 257; Walker, *op. cit.*, 150; Pascoe, *Two Hundred Years of the S.P.G.*, I, 269–70; II, 771.

[3] Theal, *op. cit.*, I, 120, 360–7; Walker, *loc. cit.*; Schmidlin, *Catholic Mission History*, 656. That Roman Catholics were among the Cape population at an early date is reported on the authority of the Jesuit Fathers who accompanied the embassy of Louis XIV to Siam in 1685. They called at the Cape where they found their co-religionists among both the free and the slave population, and of various nationalities: French, German, Portuguese, Spanish, Flemish and Indian. The Jesuits were not allowed to celebrate Mass on shore. They say: "We comforted them as best we could, and exhorted them to stand firm in the faith of Jesus Christ . . . to honour the holy Virgin as the one who could secure them grace to live the Christian life and to preserve them from heresy". —G. Tachard, *Voyage de Siam des Pères Jesuites* (1687), 72–3.

It is impossible to pursue this story of missionary beginnings at the Cape without realizing that a major factor in the situation was colonial policy towards the African peoples and the resultant attitude of the Government to the Missions. This was indeed a sinister background to all their endeavour, even threatening their continued existence if they were not conformable to official desires. As 1828 proved to be the year of crisis, it is appropriate to leave the general narrative at this point to review this particular issue. It was providential that the man matched for this time was in South Africa, Dr. John Philip, the Superintendent of the London Society's missions. His outstanding contribution to South African affairs as a missionary statesman must now be considered.

(2) Dr. Philip, the Hottentots, and the Bantu Tribes.[1]

Dr. John Philip, accompanying John Campbell on his second visit to South Africa in 1819, had engaged to stay for five years to set in order the affairs of the London Mission. He stayed over thirty, dying in South Africa in 1851. His congregation in Aberdeen were reluctant to release him, but the Directors were persistent, writing: "In so weighty a concern we dare not look to a man of ordinary make." They were rightly led. Philip proved the man for the hour. No history of this period in South Africa can fail to introduce him. Forty-four years of age when he came to the African scene, he had already had large experience of men, for he had started work at the age of eleven and was a works manager at twenty.[2] He too was a spiritual product of the Evangelical movement. The extent of his responsibilities in South Africa will be clear from the growth of the London Mission's work we have already chronicled. He itinerated regularly throughout this extensive field, and was constantly in correspondence with the stations of other Societies. "Few even of the Government officials", writes Macmillan, "had better

---

[1] Indispensable for this subject are W. M. Macmillan's studies of Philip and his policy: *The Cape Colour Question* (1927), and *Bantu, Boer and Briton* (1929). These are largely based on a study of the private papers of Dr. Philip, hitherto unused. In a disastrous fire at the University of the Witwatersrand in December 1931, these papers were destroyed, thus making these volumes doubly important as the only record of them. These researches have superseded all earlier work on the subject. D. K. Clinton, *The South African Melting-Pot, A Vindication of Missionary Policy, 1799–1836* (1937), offers a shorter study based on research into the extensive material in the archives of the London Missionary Society, and also taking note of Macmillan's researches.

[2] A post he only held for six months because he would not sanction or be privy to the conditions of child labour—an interesting forecast of his later crusade for oppressed African groups.—*Cape Colour Question*, 97–8.

opportunities of judging the problems of the country as a whole."[1]

Philip quickly realized that the twofold problem of land and labour lay behind the Government policy in its efforts to satisfy the demands of the colonists. First came the hunger for land with an ever-extending colonial population, pastoral rather than agricultural in interest; and then the demand for cheap labour to work the farms. Within the Colony the Hottentots had already lost their land, but their labour was now valuable, for, with the British Act of 1807 abolishing the slave-trade, the existing reservoir of slave labour was a steadily diminishing quantity. The Hottentots must therefore, although acknowledged to be a "free" people, be persuaded to undertake this service, and if reluctant, a little judicious pressure must be applied. As an example of the use of taxation for the purpose, there was the Proclamation of 1814, which levied *Opgaaf* tax only on Hottentots at the missionary Institutions, thus penalizing those who resided there rather than on European farms (which was in practice their only alternative). If within the Colony the Hottentot problem was a problem of labour, beyond its borders the problem was one of land, to some extent on the north, but especially on the east where lay the richest regions in the occupation of Bantu tribes. Here, with every extension of the colonial frontier, the farmers confidently expected the allocation of new lands. This pressure of the colonists for cheap labour and fresh land led to an official policy of expediency and injustice in the treatment of the African peoples that Philip was quick to detect, and to the rectification of which he forthwith devoted himself. Moreover, it was this policy of expediency that lay behind the restriction of missionary activities, which the Government often found inconvenient.

This is how Philip awoke to the real situation. In 1821 he passed to the acting Governor, Sir Rufane Donkin, with whom he was on intimate terms, papers sent him by James Read of Bethelsdorp of hard cases of Hottentots. These reflected on the local officials, the Governor made inquiry, was satisfied the charges could not be proved, and told Philip he had been deceived. Mortified by this, Philip sharply reprimanded Read, but later himself found at Bethelsdorp "letters in the handwriting of Colonel Cuyler containing the proofs of all the allegations

[1] *Cape Colour Question*, 105. "Usually at least every second year, till he was an old man of seventy, he went on long ox-waggon treks as far afield from his base at Cape Town as Kaffirland, Philippolis, and Kuruman" (Macmillan).

except one . . . I saw that I had in my hands not only the means
of vindicating the calumniated missionaries—including James
Read—but also the means of liberating the Hottentots from
their cruel bondage."[1] His attention was now concentrated
upon the principles involved in the whole policy, rather than on
individual hard cases. Among the severer disabilities from
which the Hottentots suffered was compulsory service, with a
pass system to restrict movement. Philip wrote of this: "All
Hottentots not in our Institutions at their commencement were
in a state of hopeless bondage; we had no access to them to
instruct them or preach to them without the permission of their
masters—they could not travel half a mile to hear us preach
without a written pass, without their being liable to be appre-
hended as vagabonds and subjected to severe punishments.
The whole Hottentot nation, with the above exception, were
compelled to be in service."[2] Again, the Hottentot, though
ostensibly a "free" person, suffered from an inferior status in
the eyes of the law. For example, in the Hottentot Proclamation
of 1809 provision was made for the "correction" of a Hottentot
bringing a false accusation against a master, but was silent on
the reverse possibility. "Did the omission take place", asks
Philip caustically, "on the same principle on which a celebrated
state of antiquity is said to have omitted enacting any law
against parricide, because they believed it was impossible that
such a crime could be committed?"[3]

Through his friend Sir Jahleel Brenton[4] who had offered his
help, Philip sent papers to England which came into the hands
of Wilberforce. " 'Why does not Dr. Philip appeal to the Colonial
Government?' Brenton was asked. 'My dear Mr. Wilberforce',
he replied, 'you are not aware of the state of things at the Cape.
It is with the Government that the oppression rests.' 'Meet me
to-morrow', said Wilberforce, 'with Mr. Buxton and Dr.
Lushington.' "[5] The result was a resolution moved by Wilberforce and carried to appoint Crown Commissioners to visit the
Cape, "to inquire into the state not only of the civil government
and legal administration of the Cape, but into the general
conditions of the slave and Hottentot populations." The Commissioners arrived in July 1823, and Philip was all alert to
secure relevant evidence to lay before them. He regarded the

[1] *Cape Colour Question*, 138.
[2] Quoted from *Journal of Philip's Tour*, 1832 (italics in original), *Ibid.*, 138.
[3] Clinton, *op. cit.*, 128–9.
[4] Naval Commissioner of the Cape of Good Hope till 1822.
[5] Philip to Mrs. Buxton, October 1834.—Macmillan, *op. cit.*, 185.

whole campaign on which he had embarked as an integral part of his missionary purpose.[1]

In January 1826 Philip was called to England by the Directors for consultation. It was September 1829 before he returned to the Cape. These were momentous years for his cause. Philip prepared an extensive memorial on the subject of the Hottentots which was submitted in the name of the Society to the Colonial Secretary. Close co-operation with T. Fowell Buxton, who had succeeded Wilberforce in the parliamentary leadership of the anti-slavery crusade, now developed. Philip contended that the Hottentot question was really part of the Emancipation issue: "All that is wanted for the Hottentots", he wrote to Buxton, "more correctly for the natives of South Africa, is liberty to bring their labour to the best market."[2]

Philip thus became associated with the Clapham Sect, who well knew from experience the value of direct appeal to the public. It seems to have been Zachary Macaulay who proposed that Philip should state his case by publication. The result was his *Researches in South Africa*, which appeared in April 1828. It was a book with a purpose, and it produced results, though of different kinds in London and Cape Town. The book reached the Colonial Office; Buxton was sent for, and told that he and Philip might draw up their motion, which would be a Cabinet question, on condition speeches were omitted. The offer was accepted, and on July 15, 1828, the House passed the Resolution which asked for publication of the reports of the 1823 Commissioners with Dr. Philip's evidence, and desired that "directions be given for effectually securing to all the natives of South Africa the same freedom and protection as are enjoyed by other free persons residing at the Cape, whether they be English or Dutch". The instructions immediately sent for this purpose proved unnecessary. A new Governor had promulgated an Ordinance (cited as Ordinance 50) "for improving the Condition of Hottentots and other Free Persons of Colour" which

[1] "I am at one object; the question is . . . in what way I can most certainly and effectually secure the emancipation of the poor Natives from their dreadful thraldom, the Missions from the oppressive system they are groaning under, and to give permanency to the cause of God in South Africa." (To Burder of the L.M.S., July 15, 1822).—Macmillan, *op. cit.*, 139.

"You will not think me extravagant when I express to you my firm conviction that the papers in question (exposing the 'system') are of much greater importance to the cause of God and of humanity than all that has been done in South Africa by all the missions from their commencement till now." (To Burder, Sept. 13, 1822.)—*Ibid.*, 185.

[2] July 1, 1828.—*Ibid.*, 216.

gave all that was required. The date was July 17, 1828, just two days after the Resolution of the House. All existing proclamations regulating the Hottentots were repealed, and their full rights on an equality with other subjects of the Colony expressly safeguarded. When the Ordinance reached England the Colonial Secretary asked Philip if he was satisfied. He replied that one thing was still needed: "The seal of the King in Council, without which Ministers must be aware that it would be of no value in the Colony, as it might otherwise be set aside by new enactments and leave us where we were." Philip gained his point.[1] The fight for the Hottentots was won. Yet the struggle was not altogether over. In 1834 a draft Ordinance on Vagrancy was prepared which purported to cover all classes, but was so drawn as to affect the landless Hottentots only. It was carried by the Legislative Council, but disallowed by Lord Aberdeen on the ground (among others) that it was in conflict with Ordinance 50.

Meanwhile the problem of the eastern frontier, and of the relations between the colonists and the Bantu tribes had become pressing. Again Philip unerringly analysed the frontier situation as essentially a question of land, and pleaded for a re-orientation of policy accordingly, but here he was not destined to succeed. Instead the tragedy of the Kaffir War of 1834–35 convulsed the frontier and left embittered colonists, distrustful chiefs and people, and a Colonial Government and Home Authority at variance with one another.

Philip, when on tour in 1832, was distressed by what he learned of the commando system on the eastern frontier, and predicted war if the oppression of the "nefarious system of commandos" continued.[2] To Philip's horror, another Commando

[1] Macmillan, *op. cit.* 218–19. Philip had in vain demanded this guarantee when a protecting ordinance was proposed in the Colony in 1822.—Walker, *op. cit.*, 159. His wisdom in the matter is illustrated by a parallel in recent history where what he feared has occurred. In 1930 a Native Lands Trust Ordinance was passed in Kenya Colony. Then came the discovery of gold in the Kavirondo Reserve, whereupon (in 1932) a Native Lands Trust Amendment Ordinance was passed, relaxing the conditions of the 1930 Ordinance, thus modifying what was in the nature of a public pledge to the African tribes. *The Times* wrote on the occasion: "It nearly happened that the reserves were made inalienable by Order in Council and closed to prospectors. . . . The Kenya ordinance was left as a local ordinance, with possibilities of amendment, on the explicit and declared understanding that, if land was to be taken away from the natives, they must receive equally extensive and not less valuable land somewhere else. That is the safeguard which is now in jeopardy."— January 4, 1933.

[2] "The pretence is the predatory habits of the Caffres, stealing the cattle of the colonists. Any lying Boer has only to go to a military post and say he

Ordinance was published in 1833 (though with special reference to the Bushmen on the northern frontier). He saw it as comprehending "the certain destruction of what remains of the whole of that unfortunate race of men within the reach of the Colonists."[1] The Colonial Secretary, however, was warned (Philip kept Buxton informed), and finally disallowed the Ordinance. Philip accurately diagnosed the frontier problem as one of social disorder, and so denounced the futility of seeking to resolve it by military methods; these would only inflame an already sensitive society. The essence of his treatment was to replace military officials by civil commissioners.[2]

In January 1834 Sir Benjamin D'Urban arrived at the Cape as Governor, with a special charge to concern himself with frontier policy. He was soon in consultation with Philip, though with a secretiveness which proved very unfortunate. When he proposed to visit the eastern frontier in September, and Philip suggested that he might go in advance to prepare the way, the proposal was "warmly embraced". Philip, however, was not publicly acknowledged as the Governor's agent, neither was Colonel Somerset, Commandant on the frontier, apprised of his mission. The fatal element in the situation, however, was the Governor's delay. He did not reach the frontier that year. Philip completed his tour, and had the Governor followed at the time agreed, great good might have come from Philip's contacts with the chiefs. As it was, disaster came. In December the "Sixth Kaffir War" began. In the old familiar round of

has lost so many cattle. A commando is immediately got up. No affidavit is required, no proof as to the number said to be stolen. . . . The first Caffre Cattle the commando comes to, upon the *spoor* of the cattle, are seized . . . If the Caffres resist they are shot dead upon the spot, as if they were dogs. On such *evidence* they have been declared to be a nation of thieves, robbed of their cattle, their only means of support, and from time to time of their country." (To Miss Priscilla Buxton, October 11, 1832. Italics in original.)—Macmillan, *Bantu, Boer and Briton*, 81.

[1] Clinton, *op. cit.*, 132. Philip had grounds for his presentiment from the London Mission's experience with Bushman stations. Tooverberg was opened as a Bushman station beyond the Colony north of Graaff Reinet in 1814, and Hephzibah two years later. Both were suppressed by the Government in 1818 on the ground that they were harbouring runaway farm servants. The sequel is significant. In 1820 Campbell found the Bushmen's Fountains occupied by Boers; about 1825 the colonial boundary was extended to include them, and in due course "Tooverberg has become the relatively important Dutch Church village of Colesberg".—Macmillan, *Cape Colour Question*, 130-2; Twenty-fifth *Report of the Directors* (1819), 74-5. Philip wrote from Tooverberg in 1825: "When Thornberg Institution was put down, it was without the limits of the Colony, and the Country is now peopled with Farmers a hundred and fifty miles beyond it."—Clinton, *op. cit.*, 120.

[2] Macmillan, *Bantu, Boer and Briton*, 102.

stolen cattle, colonists' complaints, and military reprisals, the Bantu now offered forcible resistance, and Somerset took drastic action. When D'Urban reached Grahamstown in January 1835 the eastern frontier was aflame and he was confronted with the trailing ruin of war. D'Urban's report that the outbreak had occurred entirely without warning was stoutly denied by Philip.[1] The war ran its course till May 1835, engulfing mission stations and causing acute distress to frontier farmers.

On May 10th D'Urban made his famous "May Proclamation", by which the colonial frontier was pushed forward to the Kei River, and the intervening territory annexed and named the Province of Queen Adelaide. The Bantu were described as "treacherous and irreclaimable savages", and they were declared "for ever expelled" from the annexed territory. But as they were still there, Macmillan's terse comment is apposite: "Sir Benjamin D'Urban was giving away the skin before he had caught his lion." On the following day occurred the tragedy of Hintza's death. Hintza, paramount chief of all the Xhosas, had come of his own free will to D'Urban to negotiate; when guiding troops to cattle that were to be restored, he made a dash for freedom, was shot and his body mutilated. The effect on Bantu opinion was lamentable.[2] Not less unhappy was the impression made when the news reached England.

Philip now stoutly contested the Governor's new policy; the mere pushing forward of the frontier was no solution; the problem was so to administer the frontier as to safeguard the rights of both colonists and tribes. This involved for the latter the security of their title to the land. Philip wrote to the London Missionary Society (June 28, 1835): "I wish it to be understood that I do not object to the extension of the colonial boundary to the Kei River, *provided the lands are secured to the Caffres* as has been the case in all our conquests in India."[3] The Colonial Secretary, Lord Glenelg,[4] left many months by D'Urban without further report, sent in December his famous despatch ordering

---

[1] "The irruption of the Kafirs has not come upon us without warning. The Government has been told for years that this crisis was unavoidable if the old system should be persisted in."—Macmillan, *op. cit*, 116.

[2] "According to frontier tradition it was a long time before chiefs would again willingly trust themselves to British officers . . . Moreover, among the natives the war of 1835 is known to this day as the 'War of Hintza'; though his share in or responsibility for the outbreak is only remote and indirect, its tragic denouement made him a hero."—*Ibid.*, 111–12.

[3] *Ibid.*, 125. Italics in original.

[4] Eldest son of Charles Grant of the Clapham Sect, and thus naturally in the tradition of the 'Philanthropists'.

the retrocession of the Province of Queen Adelaide, and the withdrawal of the frontier to its original line. The colonists, all for D'Urban and the policy of annexation, laid on Philip the responsibility for Lord Glenelg's reversal of it. Philip had written to Buxton in the previous January of the mounting opposition to himself: "The frontier colonists have long set their hearts upon Caffreland—they already calculate upon having it given them for sheep-farms and the general cry is 'blood! blood!' . . . we are told by the *Zuid Afrikaan* of yesterday that 'as for Dr. Philip and his crew, the inhabitants ought to extirpate them forthwith'. Here we have all the venom engendered by the Slave Question, the Hottentot Question, the Vagrant Act, and their fear of having their expectations with regard to Caffraria disappointed, concentrated and pouring out all its energies like the lava from the crater of an active volcano."[1]

Philip was supported in his stand by missionaries of the London and Glasgow Societies; others offered the Governor their felicitations. The Wesleyans presented D'Urban with a congratulatory address on the occasion.[2] Philip was far-sighted and statesmanlike in his persistent advocacy that the Bantu tribes on the frontier should have their land secure, as subsequent history has abundantly proved. *"I do not object"*, he wrote, *"to any of the countries beyond us becoming part of the Colony, provided the Natives have their lands secured to them and*

[1] Macmillan, *Bantu, Boer and Briton*, 119.
[2] "Justifying him for his proclamation of May 10 and the extermination of the Caffers."—Philip, quoted by Clinton, *op. cit.*, 140, n. 1. Philip used "exterminate" in the classical sense of "expel" (i.e. beyond the boundary), and so, deprive of land. Philip wrote to Buxton about the Wesleyan attitude, pointing out that "several leading Wesleyans were settled in European charges, shared the Albany panic, and 'knew nothing of the commando system which goaded the Caffres to desperation'".—Macmillan, *Bantu, Boer and Briton*, 122, n. 3. Not all, however, could be so excused. W. B. Boyce, a missionary in Bantuland, was a sharp critic of Philip, and after these events replaced him as D'Urban's confidential adviser. See W. B. Boyce, *Notes on South African Affairs* (1839), in which he rather impertinently criticizes Philip as an interloper in Kaffirland, expounds his own contribution to the Governor's policy, and offers an apologia for Wesleyan action. For a criticism of his calculations, see Macmillan, *op. cit.*, 242 n., who also quotes Colonel Smith's expression of disappointment with Boyce as "more full of dragooning our new subjects than a hundred soldiers"; "The Man of the Gospel is, after all, a worldly fellow."—*Ibid.*, 128. Philip regretted this division of the missionary body on an issue he felt so vital to future welfare. He remarked: "Lord Charles Somerset used to say if it were not for the religious people in England he would soon put us all down, but Sir B.'s thought does not extend so far, he thinks he is perfectly safe with the Wesleyan missionaries on his side."—Clinton, *op. cit.*, 148. William Shaw engaged in controversial correspondence with Philip defending the Wesleyan attitude, *A Defence of the Wesleyan Missionaries in South Africa* (1839).

are governed as the Hindus are . . . it is the system of extermination to which I am opposed."[1] D'Urban continued at his
post until Glenelg found further co-operation impossible and
secured his recall in 1837.

Meanwhile hard on the heels of the retrocession of the new
territory came one of the outstanding events of Cape history—
the Great Trek. Between 1836 and 1840 some 7,000 Dutch
farmers, it is said, crossed the Orange River, thus going beyond
the confines of the Colony, and settled in what eventually
became the Orange Free State; some crossed the Vaal to the
north; others went into what became Natal. British policy in
race questions was predominantly the issue that led to the
Boer withdrawal. This had been expressed in particular in three
directions. First, there was the success of Philip's policy in
securing the recognition of full Hottentot rights. This pleased
the humanitarians but alienated many Dutch colonists. This
cause, says Macmillan, is "admitted more and more to have
been the most important cause of the Trek itself".[2] Philip
reports a trekker as saying that "he must trek, that Dr. Philip
had spoiled the Hottentots, that he had got a law passed which
would oblige him to marry his daughter to a Hottentot, that he
would rather shoot her than see her so degraded, and that Dr.
Philip had taken all his slaves from him and that he wondered
at the mercy of God in suffering such a man to live."[3] Next
came the success of the Emancipation movement in England
with the Act of 1833 whereby it was enacted that slavery in Cape
Colony should cease on December 31, 1834. There were some
39,000 slaves at the Cape affected. This meant loss of property
to their masters, and the colonists felt a grievance in having
their claim to three million sterling compensation reduced to
some one and a quarter million. The method of payment seems
to have been unsatisfactory and to have produced further
discontent.[4] As Coupland discriminatingly observes of the
Dutch colonists: "It was not that they were wedded to slavery
as an institution; but they regarded its abolition as inspired,
like the previous measures, by the intolerable doctrine that
heathen blacks and Christian whites should be treated on a

---

[1] Letter of May 29, 1835.—Macmillan, *op. cit.*, 124. Italics in original.
[2] *Ibid.*, 194.   [3] *Ibid.*, 196, n.
[4] Coupland, *The British Anti-Slavery Movement* (1933), 149–50; Macmillan,
Cape Colour Question, 78–81. The charge sometimes made that a large part
of the compensation sum was never paid is incorrect. Of the amount awarded
only some £24,913 remained outstanding by June 1839.—Macmillan, *op. cit.*,
80, n. 1.

footing of equality."[1] The reversal of D'Urban's policy of annexation of the Bantu lands came as the last straw and the Great Trek began. With this movement away from the Colony the Dutch Reformed Church was not in sympathy.[2]

(3) *Vicissitudes of Missions*, 1829–40.

Against the definitely sombre political background of this period, the progress of missionary work was maintained, though not without strong courage and resolution. The year 1829 was a notable one. Robert Moffat then paid the first of his adventurous visits to Umsiligazi,[3] the powerful chief of the warrior Matebele. This chief, through a quarrel with Chaka, had fled north across the Vaal, and at the time of Moffat's visit occupied territory in the present Transvaal. The fame of the missionary settlement at Kuruman had reached Umsiligazi, and he wished to know the truth, so sent two of his *indunas* or councillors to inspect and report. They travelled down with white traders, but to return alone through country ravaged by the Matebele regiments would have been fatal. Moffat therefore determined to see them through the danger zone at least; twice he decided to return, having fulfilled this purpose, but his guests persuaded him to go on. At last they said that if, when he had come so far, they arrived before Umsiligazi without him, their lives would be forfeit, so he consented to complete the journey with them. He received a great welcome. "The land is before you; you are come to your son. You must sleep where you please", said the great chief. They had many talks. In one interview the chief, placing his left hand on Moffat's shoulder, and his right on his own breast, addressed him: "Machobane (the name of his father), I call you such because you have been my father. . . I cease not to wonder at the love of a stranger. . . . You fed me when I was hungry; you clothed me when I was naked; you carried me in your bosom." Upon Moffat replying he was unconscious of having done him any such service, the chief instantly pointed to the two ambassadors and said: "These are great men; 'Umbate is my right hand. When I sent them from my presence to see the land of the white men, I sent my ears, my eyes, my mouth; what they heard I heard, what they saw

[1] Coupland, *op. cit.*, 149; cf. Walker, *op. cit.*, 206–7.
[2] Walker, *op. cit.*, 214, 274; Macmillan, *Bantu, Boer and Briton*, 226, n. 2.
[3] Or Mosilikatse, as the name was pronounced by Basuto and Bechuana.
—E. W. Smith, *Robert Moffat* (1925), 115; Moffat, *Missionary Labours and Scenes in Southern Africa* (1842), 510, n.

I saw, and what they said it was Moselekatse who said it. You fed them and clothed them, and when they were to be slain, you were their shield. You did it unto me. You did it unto Moselekatse, the son of Machobane." When Moffat declined the praise titles which he says the chief profusely heaped upon him, and rather desired to be called teacher, he was asked, "Then shall I call you my father?" "Yes," rejoined Moffat, "but only on condition that you be an obedient son," a sally that vastly amused the despot and his nobles.[1] The personal influence Moffat secured over this Napoleon of the desert, as he calls him, was remarkable, and his confidence in Moffat seems to have been complete. On his arrival Moffat had been surprised to find his friends Mr. and Mrs. Archbell, of the Wesleyan mission to the Barolong, waiting to secure an audience, with a view to establishing a station. Umsiligazi, however, had declined to see them before Moffat arrived, and they eventually left unrewarded.[2] The doctrine of the resurrection of the dead the warrior king found disturbing, but the only power he feared was that of Chaka's successor, Dingaan.[3] In 1835 Moffat paid the second of four visits he made to the chief, and on this occasion secured his consent to the settlement of American missionaries among his people.[4]

The year 1829 saw the coming of the first Continental Societies to South Africa. The Paris Missionary Society, established in 1824, sent its first missionaries to South Africa. This was due to Dr. Philip's advice and encouragement. Indeed he paid a visit to Paris in January 1828 for the purpose of meeting the Committee, when he discovered their interest. He spoke of his hopes for the opening up of South Africa as a mission field when the purpose for which he was in England (the removal

---

[1] Moffat, *op. cit.*, 532, 537–8, 552. Moffat prepared a first draft of his report of this journey for the Directors of the London Missionary Society, but substituted another which is extant in the Society's archives. The one printed in Moffat's *Missionary Labours* is yet a third account. The text of the earliest version has now been published for the first time in *The Matabele Journals of Robert Moffat, 1829–60*, ed. J. P. R. Wallis (1945), I, 1–31, where the editor distinguishes the three versions. [2] Moffat, *op cit.*, 529–30, 536.

[3] "A few moments before I left him, I remarked that it was the duty of a wise father to instruct his son; and as he called me Machobane, I thought it right again to warn him, that if he did not cease from war, and restrain his lintuna (nobles) from perpetrating their secret and dreadful cruelties on the aborigines, he might expect that the eternal God would frown upon him, when the might of his power would soon be broken, and the bones of his warriors would mingle with those they had themselves scattered over his desolate dominions. To this solemn exhortation he only replied, 'Pray to your God to keep me from the power of Dingaan'."—*Ibid.*, 556–7.

[4] *Ibid.*, 583–4; *The Matabele Journals of Robert Moffat, 1829–60*, I, 36–130.

of Hottentot disabilities) was achieved.[1] The first three missionaries accompanied Dr. Philip on his return to the Cape in 1829:
Prosper Lemue, Isaac Bisseux and Samuel Rolland. Bisseux
settled with the Huguenot descendants near Wellington to
devote himself to the slaves. Lemue and Rolland moved north
to the Bechuana country, and first visited Robert Moffat at
Kuruman in July 1830. He advised them to begin work among
the Bahurutsi at Mosega, to the north-east of Kuruman. After
some language study Rolland proceeded to Mosega in May 1831.
He found the chief Mokatla friendly and chose a site for the
mission. This done, he returned to Kuruman, but as Dr. E. W.
Smith points out, it was a mistake to have made his arrangements without first securing the consent of Umsiligazi who
claimed the Bahurutsi as his people. In October Rolland again
set out for Mosega, but heard on the journey of Umsiligazi's
then uncertain temper (while he had practically destroyed a
commando of Griquas who had raided his cattle, he had on the
other hand been worsted by the Zulu Dingaan), and hence
thought it best to wait at Kuruman for the time being. A re-
assuring message having reached Moffat from Umsiligazi,
Rolland and Lemue, who had now been joined by Jean-Pierre
Pellissier, set out in February 1832 for Mosega once more. They
were warmly welcomed by Mokatla. Moffat had informed Umsiligazi of their plans. In due course Umsiligazi sent a message to
the missionaries at Mosega, saying he approved of their coming
and wished to see one of them in person. Pellissier was chosen to
pay the visit. Soon after Umsiligazi summoned all three to go to
him. The Bahurutsi believed this meant death and strenuously
opposed their going, though at the same time Mokatla said they
had better leave so as not to involve him and his people in
punitive measures. Under these circumstances the missionaries
decided to withdraw to Kuruman. Moffat, whom they met on
the road, offered to go with them to Umsiligazi, but the drivers
refused point-blank. Umsiligazi made a savage attack soon after
on the Bahurutsi and others, for aiding his enemies (so he
believed); in the course of it Mosega was left deserted. At Motito,
between this and Kuruman, the missionaries established a
station where remnants of the now dispersed Bahurutsi were
assembled.[2] Meanwhile a reinforcement consisting of Thomas
Arbousset, Eugène Casalis and the artisan Constant Gosselin had
arrived. Downcast by the news of the untoward events in the

---

[1] *Journal des Missions Evangéliques* (1828), 317–20.
[2] E. W. Smith, *The Life and Times of Daniel Lindley*, III, § 3.

Bechuana country, they were directed to the people of Moshesh where they found a new and fruitful field.[1] Moshesh with marked ability had secured his people in their "African Switzerland" astride and west of the Drakensberg, in exceedingly troublous times; this led to less fortunate groups attaching themselves to him until his Basuto became a people of consequence. In his mountain stronghold at Thaba Bosiu he had apparently been observant of the benefits of missionary work, and had heard of Moffat (not omitting his visit to Umsiligazi). At all events, when Philip was on tour in 1832, Moshesh sent an embassy with a thousand head of cattle to 'buy' a missionary from him. Koranna bandits secured the cattle, but the request was answered by the newly arrived French party turning to Basutoland.[2] They reached Thaba Bosiu in June 1833, where they were warmly welcomed and given liberty to settle where they would. In a valley some twenty-five miles distant they established their first station Moriah, the later Morija.[3] At about this time Philip transferred a Bushman station near the confluence of the Caledon and Orange Rivers to the Paris Society. Pellissier settled there, named it Bethulie and induced various refugee Batlhapi and Barolong to attach themselves to the station.[4] In 1835 Rolland, leaving the Lemues at Motito, established a new station on the Caledon: Beersheba, half-way between Morija and Bethulie. This station also grew from the attachment of refugee bands in that disturbed country. In 1837 Casalis left Morija to begin work in Thaba Bosiu itself. Here, thanks to the steady support of Moshesh, the work also prospered. In the same year yet another station, Mekuatling, was opened near the Caledon River among the Bataung, a vassal people of Moshesh.[5] Few missionary beginnings can have been more happily directed than this coming of the French missionaries to a hard-pressed but welcoming chief and people.

Also in the year 1829 a second Continental partner, the Rhenish Mission, began work at the Cape. Once again Dr. Philip was friendly coadjutor. He visited Germany for personal consultation, and the first four missionaries, Von Wurmb,

---

[1] J. Bianquis, *Les Origines de la Société des Missions Evangéliques de Paris,* III (1935), 350–1. Philip advised the Paris Society, after his visit to the eastern frontier in 1830, to avoid "Kafirland", on the ground that having suffered curtailments of territory, those chiefs who were without any fixed residence could neither promise to protect the missionaries nor settle at any one place where a station could be begun.—Macmillan, *op. cit.,* 75.   [2] *Ibid.,* 16.

[3] Their first arrival is vividly described by E. W. Smith in *The Mabilles of Basutoland* (1939), 27–8.   [4] Theal, *op. cit.,* I, 410.

[5] Du Plessis, *op. cit.,* 196; E. W. Smith, *op. cit.,* 29.

Leipoldt, Zahn and Lückhoff, sailed in his charge. Two of them were invited on arrival to minister to the slaves in Stellenbosch and Tulbagh, and this they accepted as their call to service. The others went farther afield on the road to Namaqualand, and in the District of Clanwilliam established Wupperthal in 1830 as a settlement for Hottentots, now fully at liberty to enter such an Institution. Some 200 Hottentots were soon received. In 1832 Ebenezer was begun as a station on the Oliphants River. Industrial work was prominent. For ten years there was little growth in the Christian fellowship, thirty-five baptisms being recorded. With 1840 came an advance into Namaqualand destined to become the Society's most successful field.[1]

A third Continental Society, the Berlin, entered the South African field in 1834, ten years after its origin. The party of five missionaries, the first to be sent overseas, found their field of service among the Korannas, a section of the Northern Hottentots, in what was to become the Orange Free State. Here they founded their station Bethany. But they were with a wandering rather than a settled people, and internal difficulties also hindered the progress of the work. Two withdrawals to other South African fields were followed by the dismissal of the remaining three on the arrival of a superintendent, Pehmöller, in 1837. One of those who withdrew, Gregorowski, served the South African Society at Zoar in the Cape, a station that later came under the Berlin Mission. A reinforcement of six missionaries arrived in 1836. One of these, C. F. Wuras, rescued the work at Bethany from its difficulties and led it to success. Another, J. L. Döhne, became the Berlin pioneer among the Xhosas. Kayser of the London Mission was the means of inducing him to settle in Gasela's territory, where the station Bethel was begun. A second station, Itemba, was founded in 1838. The work was hard and life was difficult under frontier conditions after the recent war.[2]

In 1835 the first of the American Societies appeared on the scene—the American Board of Commissioners for Foreign Missions. Once more it was Dr. Philip who was responsible for directing their attention to South Africa. John B. Purney, a student at Princeton Theological Seminary, had written to Dr. Philip on behalf of himself and others in March 1832, inquiring about missionary opportunities in Africa. Dr. Philip, with his

[1] Du Plessis, op. cit., 201–3; J. Richter, op. cit., 321–3.
[2] Du Plessis, op. cit., 212–16; J. Richter, op. cit., 324–5, 337.

large-hearted generosity, wrote a full reply, and suggested Zululand would be "a noble field for missionary labour", and commended it as a centre for American work. The American Board was prompted by this letter to choose South Africa as its second mission field. So it came about that a party of six missionaries with their wives set sail from Boston for the Cape in December 1834. They were Newton Adams, George Champion, Aldin Grout, Daniel Lindley, Henry Venable, and Alexander Wilson.[1] The party of six divided; three went north to Umsiligazi and three eastwards to Dingaan's country in Natal. It was to be a mission to the Zulus, in their two sections under Umsiligazi and Dingaan. Daniel Lindley, Alexander Wilson and Henry Venable were designated for the Matebele mission. They proceeded by way of Griqua Town (where they spent some months in language study) and Kuruman, to Mosega, the scene of the first French mission but now in Matebele occupation. Here they received Umsiligazi's permission to settle; this was in 1836. All seemed propitious when first came serious illness among the party (the imperfectly dried clay floors of the mission house they had built were mainly responsible), and then clashes between Boers and Matebele. It was under these circumstances that the final disaster occurred. One morning, in January 1837, the camp at Mosega was surprised by a Boer attack. The Great Trek had already begun, and parties of the emigrant farmers were moving into territory regarded by the Matebele as their own preserve. Clashes had already occurred, with a serious encounter in October 1836, when forty men and boys (among them was Paul Kruger) repelled 5,000 Matebele warriors, though with the loss of wagons and cattle. The attack on Mosega under Potgieter and Maritz was by way of reprisal. It was completely successful, for the Matebele warriors were on duty elsewhere, and the place was undefended. Cattle and wagons were recovered and the town fired. The American missionaries, who up to this point had held on despite every discouragement, decided that to remain would now be futile, and so withdrew with the emigrant farmers. So ended the mission to the Matebele and no attempt was made to renew it. The three missionaries joined their comrades in Natal.[2] Meanwhile Grout, Champion and Adams, who had been appointed to Dingaan's country, could not travel by land as

[1] E. W. Smith, *Life and Times of Daniel Lindley*, II, §§ 4–5.
[2] Theal, *op. cit.*, II, 287–8, 310; Du Plessis, *op. cit.*, 220–4; E. W. Smith, *op. cit.*, IV, §2.

the war of 1835 was in progress; it was thus the end of the year
before they reached Port Natal by sea. They waited on Dingaan
and received his permission to begin their work. Their first
station, some eight miles from Port Natal on the River Umlazi
(which supplied its name), was begun in February 1836. A
second at Ginani was opened in the same year. When their
colleagues from Mosega joined them in July 1837, two further
stations were started. Once again disaster overtook the missionaries and once again it resulted from conflict between the
emigrants and the Zulu tribes. Pieter Retief with a party of
emigrants decided to settle in Natal, and sought Dingaan's
consent. The chief's condition of recovery of cattle stolen from
him being fulfilled he purported to make the grant of land they
had desired. At a farewell session with the chief, which the
Boers had attended unarmed, Retief and his sixty or so companions were brutally murdered. A few hours later Venable
arrived to interview the chief, but on learning of the tragedy,
left as soon as prudence permitted and warned his colleagues,
who all withdrew to Port Natal. Lindley remained to report
events, but the others had left for Port Elizabeth when the
Zulu regiments, after various successes, swarmed into Port
Natal and stripped it of belongings. By December 1838 the
Boers had inflicted a decisive defeat on the Zulus and occupied
Dingaan's deserted capital. In June 1839 two of the six American
missionaries returned to Natal. Adams took up his work again
on the Umlazi; Lindley felt called to devote himself to the
pastoral care of the emigrant farmers, and became resident
clergyman at Pietermaritzburg, so named in memory of
Pieter Retief and Maritz, the two Boer leaders. He served
them for seven and a half years, and then returned to work
among the Zulus, surrendering an influential position to do so.[1]
Meanwhile the American Board temporarily discontinued the
undertaking, but Adams held on at his own charges, and a
Cape Town committee persuaded Grout to continue his work.[2]
When the Board decided to resume the mission large developments and encouraging successes awaited it.

One other Society, whose work proved to be only an episode,
has the Dingaan regime and the Retief tragedy as a grim background to its effort. The Church Missionary Society made its
one and only entry to South Africa at this time. The circumstances were these. Captain Allen F. Gardiner, R.N., conscious

[1] E. W. Smith. *op. cit.*, VI.
[2] Theal, *op. cit.*, II, 310, 314–20, 326, 347–8; Du Plessis, *op. cit.*, 224–30.

of a missionary call, determined to open the way for Christian work in Zululand. Reaching Port Natal in January 1835, in the course of the year he paid four visits to Dingaan with this purpose in view. He has left his own first-hand narrative of events.[1] It was not easy to convey the object of his visit, and delicate handling of the situation was necessary to avoid a curt refusal.[2] He stressed his purpose as being to teach "the Book", and so far prevailed on Dingaan as to be allowed to read from it: "I read in order a number of passages previously selected, as exhibiting the nature and penalty of sin, the power and omniscience of God, and the awful day of account when he will judge the world in righteousness. At the conclusion he asked several very pertinent questions, such as—'Where is God? How did He give His word? Who will be judged at the last day? What nations will appear? Will mine be there? Shall I live for ever if I learn His Word?' "[3] But this first visit yielded no result. Gardiner felt that suspicion of his purpose was explained by a story he heard later, of a disgruntled native interpreter from the coast in the time of Chaka, forecasting to that chief the coming of a white man in the guise of missionary who would be but the forerunner of many who would steal the country.[4] On his return to Port Natal in March he received a letter from the eight Europeans resident there, inviting him to commence a mission and promising their support. The invitation was accepted; Gardiner began holding services and started a small school. He named this mission centre Berea.[5] Three more visits were made to Dingaan that year, in the course of which the chief consented to the beginning of a mission. Gardiner named the station Culoola.[6] On his return to England he applied to the Church Missionary Society which accepted the two stations and responsibility for the Zulu Mission.[7] Francis Owen, a clergyman appointed by the Society, reached the field in company

---

[1] *Narrative of a Journey to the Zoolu Country in South Africa* (1836).

[2] Gardiner reports that Dingaan asked how the English King governed his people: "With so many decided proofs of despotism around, I considered this as rather a delicate question, and therefore avoided the circumstance of parliamentary interference altogether, by informing him that King William governed his people by means of his great men. He smiled and seemed evidently to regard even this as an inconvenient approximation to popular institutions."—*Ibid.*, 32.

[3] *Ibid.*, 33.   [4] *Ibid.*, 37–8.

[5] For the reason stated in Acts xvii, 11.—*Ibid.*, 77–81.

[6] In Zulu, to loose or set free.—*Ibid.*, 136–8, 179–80. Dingaan's final consent seems to have turned on Gardiner's returning to him from Port Natal four of his own escaped subjects, in accordance with treaty terms. This convinced him, apparently, of Gardiner's integrity.

[7] *Ibid.*, 409; Stock, *op. cit.*, I, 354–5.

with Gardiner in 1837, and took up his residence at Culoola, while Gardiner went to Berea in the double capacity of missionary and magistrate. Owen eventually prevailed upon Dingaan to permit him to reside at the capital, Umgungunhlovu, where he acted as private secretary to the chief.[1] He was an eye-witness from his hut of the treacherous murder of Retief and his men.[2] As soon as he could wisely do so, he took his leave of Dingaan, and with his party returned to Cape Colony. An attempt to work at Mosega was as unsuccessful as those of his French and American predecessors, and he eventually returned to England. Captain Gardiner had already left South Africa; he later won missionary fame as pioneer in Patagonia. The Church Missionary Society did not re-enter South Africa.[3]

That new Societies should have entered South Africa in such stormy times as we have noticed, and that existing work should not only have been maintained but its operations extended, is a tribute to the vitality of the missionary movement which was now well under way. Independent evidence of its progress is supplied by the Quaker, James Backhouse, who seems to have visited every mission station of every Society at work in South Africa from his arrival in June 1838 to his departure in December 1840.[4] He made individual reports on twenty-six stations of the London Mission (eighteen in Cape Colony; two in Kaffraria; three in Griqualand, counting the outstations of Griqua Town as one; two in Namaqualand; and Kuruman in the Bechuana country, from which the Moffats were absent on furlough in England); thirty-two of the Wesleyan Society (sixteen in Cape Colony, eight in Kaffraria, three in the Basuto, three in the Bechuana country and two in Great Namaqualand); six Moravian Stations (five in the Colony and one at Shiloh in Kaffraria); five of the Glasgow Society (all in Kaffraria); seven Paris Society centres (three each in Basutoland and the Bechuana country, and one at the Cape); six Rhenish Society stations (five at the Cape, and one jointly with the London

---

[1] The ostensible land agreement made with Retief was in Owen's hand.— Theal, *op. cit.*, II, 315, 332.

[2] Owen's account of the tragedy is recorded in his diary: Cory (ed.), *The Diary of the Rev. Francis Owen, M.A.* (1926), 107.

[3] Theal, *op. cit.*, II, 311, 319, 326, 482; Du Plessis, *op. cit.*, 237–41.

[4] James Backhouse, *A Narrative of a Visit to the Mauritius and South Africa* (1844). This includes the bulk of the material in *Extracts from the Journal of James Backhouse* (1840–41), with slight modifications. Backhouse, who was a minister of the Society of Friends, was accompanied by his friend G. W. Walker, and paid his visit with the authorization of the Society.

Mission in Namaqualand); and three of the Berlin Mission (one in Griqualand and two in Kaffraria). He also reported on thirteen centres of the Dutch Reformed Church in the Colony. This reveals the number of active centres of missionary work in the different areas to be as follows:

Cape Colony	45
Kaffraria	18
Griqualand	4
Basutoland	6
Bechuana country	7
Namaqualand	5

This grand total of eighty-five stations, all found in active operation, and ranging from such old-established settlements as Genadendal and Bethelsdorp to the latest pioneer stations, is eloquent of the extent of Christian effort among the African population.

To clothe with a little flesh and blood the skeleton of a mere statistical summary, some typical features may be added. The work done by the London Mission in elevating the Hottentots impressed Backhouse greatly; thus at Philipton on the Kat River, where he met the now aged James Read, he remarks: "It was pleasant to see an air of comfort and independence in the Hottentots, who are truly free here. . . . Many of the half-naked degraded Hottentots had been raised to a state nearly equal to that of the labouring classes in England, and in some respects superior; certainly above that often found in the manufacturing districts. They were dressed like decent, plain people of that class; and in the sixteen schools of the Kat River district, which are about half supported by the people themselves, and conducted by native youths, they had about 1,200 scholars, and an attendance of about 1,000."[1]

In Kaffirland Backhouse found only two Wesleyan stations that had not been destroyed in the war of 1834–35, Clarkbury and Buntingville, the former preserved by the care of a chief, and the latter by the courageous loyalty of Richard and Ann Tainton, who remained at their post, despite the remonstrances of their friends. They were cut off from all communication with the Colony for eighteen months. As a result Tainton gained great influence with the chief Faku and succeeded in preventing local wars. He was also able to get the chief to give up ritual murder, practised for the sake of his invulnerability in war.

[1] Backhouse, *Narrative*, 185–6.

That a couple who had acquired such personal influence should be removed, according to the Methodist system of itineracy, seemed to Backhouse sheer folly, and he is not sparing of his criticism.[1] He also felt that at the Wesleyan stations, though not at these alone, education was scarcely given its rightful place as a missionary activity. When he met William Shaw and others in friendly conference, and raised this point, they agreed with his judgment, but replied "that the claims upon them to extend Christian instruction beyond their field of labour were so great that they were cramped for want of means to carry out this primary object, and they could not consequently give the attention they wished to secondary ones."[2]

That there were devoted ministers to be found in the Dutch Reformed Church, with a concern for African welfare ahead of their people, Backhouse also bore witness. True, many of these were Scotsmen. At Graaff Reinet he met the saintly Andrew Murray, and found that in his church the Dutch people and the coloured met together for public worship, though they sat apart. At Colesberg (the earlier Tooverberg of the London Mission) he found Thomas Reid, another Scot, as minister. The Dutch people did not object to united worship with the coloured, "but when their minister attempted to collect the Hottentots, and others of that class daily, in this building, to instruct them, the Dutch would not suffer it. . . . The Minister, however, was not to be diverted from his purpose or duty . . . he told the Dutch that if they would not suffer him to teach the Coloured People in the 'Kerk', they should find him some other place; to this they consented."[3]

The theological and ecclesiastical variety represented by the Societies engaged—Calvinist Presbyterian and Arminian Methodist, Free Church Independent and State Church Lutheran—would make it surprising if there were no sectarian rivalry as the work went forward. To this matter Backhouse and Walker refer in the course of some "Observations" they addressed to all Christian workers in South Africa: "We should fail in the discharge of a duty, did we shrink from adverting to a subject that has occasionally excited our regret. Very generally, we have found our Missionary Friends pleased with their own fields of labour, but in some instances disposed to speak slightingly of the fields occupied by others. We think this

[1] Backhouse, *Narrative*, 280–2.
[2] *Ibid.*, 285, 302.
[3] *Ibid.*, 344, 486–7.

is of hurtful tendency, and needs to be guarded against . . . there is need for all, but particularly for Missionaries, to have their minds habitually clothed with this charity or love so that no one may regard with an unworthy Jealousy, or despise another, whether connected with the same, or with a different religious body."[1]

That the Christian message must be offered to a people in the mother tongue is a basic principle of modern missions. How fared it at the Cape? For the Hottentots within the Colony—and often enough for the Bushmen—Dutch was assumed to be the satisfactory medium. In such a centre as Griqua Town there was a good case for it. But when contact was made with Bantu tribes on the east and north the language question became more pressing. Often enough there was contentment with interpreters, but there were language students as well. W. B. Boyce was the first to discover the principle of the so-called alliterative concord characteristic of the Bantu language family, whereby a prefix reappears before every word in agreement with the noun. Boyce published the first Xhosa Grammar in 1834.[2] James Archbell prepared the first Sechuana Grammar three years later.[3] J. H. Schmelen (assisted by his first wife, who was a Hottentot) translated the New Testament into Hottentot, and also prepared a hymn book in that language.[4] But the classical instance is that of Robert Moffat who in 1827 isolated himself for two months from all European society, so that he could hear nothing but Sechuana. He returned able to preach to the people in their mother tongue. Steady work at translation followed, so that by 1840 the New Testament in Sechuana saw the light.[5] This was a service to more than the London Mission, for Wesleyans at Thaba Nchu and French missionaries at Motito were equally beneficiaries. The unit of the language area is rarely identical with the denominational field.

The language, however, was but the medium. What of the message itself? How was it presented by these early missionaries? Here our material is too slender to admit of an easy

---

[1] Backhouse and Walker, *Observations submitted in brotherly love to the missionaries and other Gospel labourers in South Africa* (1840), 13–14.
[2] *A Grammar of the Kafir Language* (Grahamstown, 1834, 54 pages), in which he acknowledges his obligations to Theophilus Shepstone. With revision, it passed through three editions by 1863.
[3] *A Grammar of the Bechuana Language* (Grahamstown, 1837, xxii, 82 pages).
[4] Backhouse, *op. cit.*, 532. [5] E. W. Smith, *Robert Moffat*, 168–85.

characterization. That the substance of their preaching was provided by the great themes of the Evangelical Revival may be safely assumed. The appeal was a personal one, emphasizing human accountability before God, the dread tribunal all must face at the resurrection, and the deliverance available for all by faith in Christ who gave Himself for man's redemption. The moral demands of Christianity were insistently presented, and African customs that appeared to conflict with these were unhesitatingly denounced. We are possessed of several reports of personal conversations on these matters with eminent chiefs of the period, when attention was naturally directed to subjects in which their personal responsibility was concerned, notably in attacks upon their neighbours and the easy taking of human life. Vanderkemp declared to Gaika that the drought he lamented was sufficiently accounted for by the action of his people.[1] Moffat has placed on record his religious conversations with Umsiligazi: "I told him I was a teacher from God, who was the creator of all things and the governor among the nations. . . . I explained to him the nature and extent of divine government, a particular and retributive providence even among those like the Matabele, who knew not God. . . . The next conversation I had with him I explained to him the first principles of our religion, man in his natural state, asserting his immortality, the redemption of the soul by the death of Christ, the resurrection of the dead and the state of rewards and punishments beyond death. The last two particulars particularly arrested his attention. He would stare at me to see if I maintained my gravity."[2] Captain Gardiner similarly, when asked by Dingaan to read to him from the Bible, selected passages to exhibit the nature and penalty of human sin, the Divine attributes, and the final judgment.[3] That these specific occasions make clear the tenor of the message generally declared it is reasonable to assume: human sin, Divine grace, and the judgment to come were the dominant themes. Little seems to have been known of African religious ideas to enable the missionaries to present the message in terms congenial to the African mind. Nevertheless the direct appeal to conscience was not without effect, and the deep concern for the welfare of their African hearers both in this world and the next, which faithful missionaries showed, won its own measure of response.

[1] Lovett, *op. cit.*, I, 492-3.
[2] *The Matabele Journals of Robert Moffat*, I, 15-16.
[3] Gardiner, *Narrative*, 33.

The Protestant monopoly of the South African field was not to remain unchallenged. A step significant of developments to come was taken in 1837 when the Roman Church set up a Vicariate Apostolic of the Cape of Good Hope separate from Mauritius.[1]

The Malay population of Cape Town were Muslim, and by the time of Lord Charles Somerset they possessed two mosques.[2] In 1824 W. Elliot, with experience of work among Muslims and knowledge of Arabic, was appointed by the South African Society to work among the Malays of Cape Town, but with no result that could be seen.[3] Of fifty copies of the Malay New Testament supplied by the British and Foreign Bible Society in 1824, he had by 1829 sold only thirteen, while practically all he had given away had been returned by order of the *Imams*. Yet, add the L.M.S. Directors: "Their own priests are too successful in making proselytes from among the slaves. . . . The number of these proselytes is supposed to be not a little increased by the zeal displayed by the more respectable Mohammedans in furthering the manumission of this description of converts to their faith."[4] Thus once again the brotherhood of Islam has advanced the frontiers of that faith.

We reach the year 1840 with much in the South African scene for which Christians could give thanks, and not a little to cause disquiet. Moreover, the heart of the continent to the north was still unknown. Splendid as the advance had been, Kuruman the outpost still lay 300 miles below the tropics and 700 from the Zambezi. But the halt was temporary only. In 1840 David Livingstone sailed for Africa.

[1] By an Ordinance of 1830 Roman Catholics at the Cape were already declared to possess full civil rights.—Theal, *op. cit.*, I, 307.
[2] *Ibid.*, I, 119. [3] *Ibid.*, I, 350.
[4] Thirty-sixth *Report of the Directors of the London Missionary Society* (1830), 73; Du Plessis, *op. cit.*, 98.

CHAPTER 12

WEST AFRICAN HOPES
1815–1840

In West Africa the twenty-five years following Waterloo were a period of progress, but not at the pace or in the direction that had been anticipated. It was a period of almost over-whelming difficulty. As the missionary staff increased so did the casualties at a most alarming rate; indeed, at times the mortality was so serious as to threaten the very continuity of missionary work. But the ranks were reinforced again, and the challenge of the fever-ridden coast taken up, though three generations had yet to pass before protection based on scientific knowledge could be given.

But the difficulties did not only spring from nature; they also came from man. The slave-trade was far from dying. French participation had been eliminated during the war, and it was hoped that after 1815 France would not resume it, but it was 1831 before effective action was taken by her Government. Spain and Portugal came more slowly into line in making a paper prohibition genuinely effective. In 1815 Portugal and in 1817 Spain agreed to restrict their share in the trade to the southern hemisphere.[1] But as no measures were attempted to enforce the law, the trade went on. It was 1835 when the first of two necessary measures was accepted by Spain under British pressure. The Portuguese, under whose flag slavers of any nation could and did still prosecute the traffic, proved more obdurate when desired to enter into a treaty with Britain for effectual suppression. Palmerston thereupon took the drastic step in 1839 of securing an Act of Parliament authorizing British cruisers to seize any Portuguese vessel (or vessel of no nationality) found equipped for the trade. But the United States still resisted reciprocal right of search[2] so that two months after the passing of the Act of 1839 against Portugal, the British Ambassador at Washington is found declaring that

[1] Portugal was encouraged to this action by a remission of a debt of £450,000 together with a gift of £300,000; Spain received a gift of £400,000, all from the British taxpayer.—Coupland, *The British Anti-Slavery Movement*, 159–60.

[2] The United States had abolished the trade for its own nationals in 1807, and in 1819 had authorized the use of the Navy for the purpose. But in practice this meant little. Reciprocal right of search was nearly conceded in 1822-24, when first the President, and then the Senate, declined it.—*Ibid.*, 167–8.

"Spanish, Portuguese and Brazilian slave-traders, with out-laws and pirates of all nations, are now flocking under cover of the American flag".[1] While this long-drawn-out fight to suppress the foreign slave-trade was in progress the traffic not only continued but increased. Captain Maclean, the able Governor of Cape Coast Castle, estimated from his own careful observation that in 1834 (admittedly a peak year) more than 140,000 slaves were carried off from the Bights of Benin and Biafra alone. He wrote in 1838: "I can state as a *fact*, that there are at this moment on the coast 200 slave-vessels, all under Portuguese colours."[2] Buxton's assertion in 1839 that "upwards of 150,000 human beings are annually conveyed from Africa, across the Atlantic, and sold as slaves", was not wide of the mark, and indicated a volume of traffic exceeding anything reached in the eighteenth century.[3] But British pressure was not relaxed; in the 'forties, it is estimated, about one-sixth of the British Navy was engaged in hunting the slavers, at an annual cost to Britain of some £750,000. And the hearts of the naval men were in the business: "In officers and men alike the Trade inspired a burning hate. It was scarcely ever mentioned in dispatches without some violent epithet— this 'abominable', 'infamous', 'diabolical', 'traffic in human flesh'. Captains of the old school felt themselves to be fighting God's battle with the Devil."[4] Captured cargoes deposited at Sierra Leone, after adjudication by the Court of Vice-Admiralty there, steadily increased until service to liberated slaves represented the major missionary opportunity.

Roman Catholic activity in West Africa during this period was slight. In Senegambia the difficulties of climate were considerable; in 1817 the prefect at St. Louis had to retire, and five years later the prefect at Gorée. The Sisters of Cluny valiantly established a settlement in 1819.[5] Sierra Leone was visited by priests from Portugal, and in 1823 the foundress of the Sisters of St. Joseph came to the Colony.[6] The Capuchins were finally expelled from the Portuguese Congo in 1838.[7] In Angola it has been generously estimated that there were some

---

[1] Mathieson, *Great Britain and the Slave Trade, 1839–1865* (1929), 27.
[2] T. Fowell Buxton, *The Slave Trade and its Remedy* (1840), 47–8. Italics in original.
[3] *Ibid.*, 15; Coupland, *op. cit.*, 173. Mathieson subjects Buxton's figures to some criticism.—*Op. cit.*, 37–8.　　　　[4] Coupland, *op. cit.*, 161–2.
[5] Schmidlin, *op. cit.*, 650.　　　　[6] *Ibid.*, 652.
[7] Van Wing, *Études Bakongo* (1921), 72–3.

700,000 Roman Catholics but with only eight to ten priests.[1] The missionary progress that has to be recorded is therefore to all intents and purposes a Protestant achievement.

(1) *Missionary Service to Liberated Slaves.*

In the early days of the Sierra Leone Company the absence of slavery and the presence of the settlers' Christian churches led distressed sailors to speak of the colony as "this Christian Country".[2] But with the accession of pagan Negroes in their thousands a new situation arose. It has been estimated that up to the end of 1825 alone, nearly 18,000 liberated Africans entered the colony.[3] This presented the Government with a major social problem and the missions were encouraged to co-operate with them in solving it. The Church Missionary Society, with its work already begun, was naturally called upon to play the major part.

In 1815 this Society decided the time had come to take stock of the situation in Sierra Leone. It was over ten years since the first two missionaries had gone to West Africa, and out of twenty-six men and women who had sailed, sixteen had died, and only two had visited England.[4] Edward Bickersteth, a Norwich solicitor, was invited to undertake this responsible task of visitation and review. He accepted the call, received ordination and sailed for Sierra Leone in 1816. Dr. Stock says of this important step. "Bickersteth's visit was greatly blessed of God. It corrected many evils; it initiated many new plans; it gave a fresh impetus to the whole work; it proved the real starting-point of the permanent Sierra Leone Mission."[5] Bickersteth was in no doubt about Christian missionary priorities; evangelism must come first. "This is your first, your great work," he told the missionaries who had neglected it; "everything else must be subordinate to this."[6] While he did not propose the closing down of the Rio Pongas mission (a step soon necessitated, however, by the disposition of the chiefs), he was deeply impressed with the large opportunity presented by the liberated Africans and saw this clearly as the great work to which the Society was called within the Colony. The able Governor, Sir Charles McCarthy (whose length of service,

---

[1] Schmidlin, *op. cit.*, 648–9 and n. 15 and 16.
[2] Fifth *Report of the Sierra Leone Company* (1798), 2–3.
[3] C. P. Lucas, *Historical Geography of the British Colonies*, III (2nd ed., 1900), 189.
[4] Stock, *History of the Church Missionary Society* (1899), I, 159, 160.
[5] *Ibid.*, 160.
[6] *Ibid.*, 161.

from 1814 to 1823, was a record) made appropriate recommendations to Bathurst, the Colonial Secretary. In three years from 1816 nine villages for liberated Africans were formed and graced with English names—Gloucester, Leopold, Bathurst, Charlotte, Wellington, Waterloo, Hastings, York and Kent. In 1817 the Colony was divided into twelve parishes, each to have a minister and a schoolmaster.[1] The Society was to provide the personnel while Government would largely find the funds. The problem of staffing was insuperably difficult, both through dearth of suitable candidates and fatalities from fever, but in the five years to 1822 seventeen men were sent out by the Society.

Among the schoolmasters who went out at this time were two of German origin but recruited in England, Johnson and Düring. Both received ordination from their Lutheran brethren in Sierra Leone, and both rendered conspicuous service to the liberated Africans. William Augustine Bernard Johnson hailed from Hanover; at the time of his offer he had worked two years with a sugar-refiner in London. He and his wife were accepted as schoolmaster and schoolmistress for Sierra Leone and sailed in 1816. They were appointed by Bickersteth to Hogbrook, a freed-slave village, later called Regent's Town. Johnson was oppressed by his first contact with the place: "There are a very few of these people who can speak broken English, the greatest part have lately arrived from slave-vessels, and are in the most deplorable condition, chiefly afflicted with the dropsical complaint. To describe the misery of Regent's Town would indeed be impossible. Oh, may the Lord hold me up, and I shall be safe under these difficulties which are apparently before me." He was not only schoolmaster but also superintendent of the community for the Government and in charge of stores from which clothing was supplied and rations allowed for a limited period to the liberated Africans. There had been sad neglect, however, and he found some of the people in a state of starvation. The register of the community was also in hopeless confusion.[2] Difficulties even greater than he foresaw lay before him, but so high was his conception of his missionary vocation and so humble his view of his own ability to fulfil it, that in his reliance on a power not his own he won a clearness of aim and a tenacity

[1] J. J. Crooks, *A Short History of Sierra Leone* (1900), 70.
[2] *A Memoir of the Rev. W. A. B. Johnson* (1852), 27–8. This record draws liberally on Johnson's own journals and includes much correspondence with the missionary secretaries. Johnson's story has been abbreviated in A. T. Pierson, *Seven Years in Sierra Leone* (1897).

of purpose that overcame all obstacles. He proved in himself the paradox of the Pauline experience: "When I am weak, then am I strong."[1] In the seven short years of his service he saw a spiritual and moral transformation in his liberated African community.

Johnson's first concern was the spiritual welfare of his people, and to this all else was subordinate. He satisfied Bickersteth's demand that evangelism be the first priority. Four months after his arrival came his first encouragement: "One evening a shingle maker followed me out of the church, and desired to speak to me. I was in some measure cast down, thinking that he wished to speak to me for clothing. However, with astonishment, I found that he was in deep distress about the state of his soul. He said that one evening he had heard me ask the congregation if anyone had spent five minutes in prayer that day to Jesus, or the past day, week, month, or ever? He was so struck with it, and could not answer the question for himself." More came the following week, and removed from Johnson's humble mind all doubt of his missionary vocation: "I went and related the circumstances to Mr. Butscher at Leicester Mountain, and begged him to come and baptize them, which he did. Twenty-one adults, one boy and three infants, captured negroes, were baptized." By January 1817 he reported forty-one communicants.[2] The Society's Secretaries soon became aware of his rare quality and proposed that he should receive Lutheran ordination from his German colleagues. In March 1817 this was done.

The rapid growth in the membership of the church was not due to easy admission. Johnson had standards which he would not relax. Inquirers, accepted as catechumens, were received in the presence of the communicant members, who were desired to watch over them and report on the sincerity of their intentions as observable in their conduct. Thus the period of preparation became a responsibility of the whole church. Catechumens remained some four to five months under instruction, according to the progress made. Johnson himself and African helpers instructed them twice a week. The rite of baptism was preceded by a public questioning before the whole congregation.[3] He declined to baptize without previous instruction, and only received for this purpose those who had an evident spiritual concern. This careful policy brought him

[1] II Corinthians, xii. 10.
[2] *Memoir*, 37-8.
[3] *Ibid.*, 227, 260, 288-9.

into collision with McCarthy. He reports in his journal for May 13, 1818: "His Excellency the Governor came here to-day. He led the conversation while we were in the garden to baptism. He wished I would baptize more people. I told him that I could not, unless God first baptized their hearts. He said that the reason so many were baptized on the day of Pentecost was that the Apostles despised none. I replied that they were pricked in the heart, and that I was willing to baptize all that were thus pricked in the heart. He thought baptism an act of civilization, and that it was our duty to make them all Christians. He spoke in great warmth about these things, and I endeavoured to show him through Scripture passages, the contrary. He gave it up at last; calling me and the Society a set of fanatics."[1] With all their confidence in Johnson, the Secretaries began to wonder whether he was not pitching his standard too high, and wrote him: "The Committee have been disposed to think, from the Governor's representations, that you may have been rather too slow to baptize, making all due allowance for his not having our views and feelings."[2] Yet even so, in 1823 Regent's Town held pride of place with 410 communicants out of a total of 603 for the eight communities of liberated slaves under the Society.[3]

Education was steadily promoted at Regent's Town. Johnson had begun his work as schoolmaster, and introduced Bell's system of education.[4] His return to the Governor in June 1817,

---

[1] *Memoir*, 94. McCarthy returned to the attack at the end of the year. "The Governor ... said a great deal about baptizing all the people, which I refused. He said much about its necessity, but I kept to the word of God. He said that the Apostles, on Pentecost day, baptized 3,000 at once. I replied that they were pricked in their heart, and as *many as believed* were baptized ... He could not answer to this, but said that he would write to the Archbishop of Canterbury concerning the matter ... and would send those refused to Mr.———, the Wesleyan minister, to be baptized: for he thought Mr. ———'s baptism as good as ours."—*Ibid.*, 125–6. Italics in original.

[2] *Ibid.*, 151. [3] *Ibid.*, 380.

[4] Andrew Bell (1753–1832) developed at Madras a system of mutual instruction by the scholars which enabled great progress to be made with slender resources of teaching staff. Joseph Lancaster (1778–1838) founded the Lancasterian system of education independently on similar lines. His work was at first encouraged by royal patronage, and issued in the British and Foreign School Society, whence the so-called "British Schools". Zachary Macaulay, at first in sympathetic contact with Lancaster, came to feel that an education based "on general Christian principles" was so vague as to leave the door open to Deism and irreligion. He and others therefore promoted the National Society for the Education of the Poor in the Principles of the Church of England (hence the "National Schools"), and Dr. Bell became their educational director. Bell's system thus became identified with the Church of England and Lancaster and the "British system" with the Free Churches.—

after his first year, showed in the day school 172 boys and 87 girls, and in the night school 99 men and boys learning trades, and 28 women, a total of 386.[1] His last return for March 1823 showed a total of 1,079, and reported 710 persons who could read. It was also encouraging to have almost as many girls at school as boys (230 to 251).[2] It is rather startling to find him requesting Latin books in 1821 for students in the seminary, but about two years later he reported that "teaching the present seminarists Latin is inexpedient; they are too far advanced in years".[3] However we may now criticize such an inclusion, it at least signified a desire to share the best in education with the least privileged.

If evangelism was the first concern, and an education aiming at general literacy the second, general social welfare was not neglected. "We have now", Johnson reported in 1817, "masons, bricklayers, carpenters, shinglemakers, sawyers, smiths, tailors and brickmakers. We have made about 16,000 bricks, and have as many ready to be burnt."[4] A Benefit Society was established among the communicant members, each paying a halfpenny a week and being entitled to support when sick or distressed.[5] The road to Freetown travelled inconveniently up hill and down dale in one section; Johnson surveyed a better route and had a new road engineered, for which a Government report paid him this tribute: "This road is two rods wide throughout, and solid and level to a degree not easily attainable in a country like this. . . . The combination of Mr. Johnson's skill and ability with the bodily strength and hearty zeal of his people, produced such rapidity of execution that the task was completed in considerably less than one month, although the extent is full two miles."[6]

Though the improvement among the liberated Africans at Regent's Town was spectacular it was not isolated. Johnson's friend at Gloucester, H. Düring, also had remarkable success, and all the villages in the Society's care received public testimony. Thus Johnson reported in 1822 that he and his missionary colleagues went as usual to Freetown to attend the Quarter

---

Knutsford, *Life and Letters of Zachary Macaulay*, 302–4 and n. 1. Thus we find the British system introduced into South Africa under the London Mission.—Twenty-second *Report of the Directors of the L.M.S.* (1816), 19; Thirty-first *Report* (1825), 123; Thirty-third *Report* (1827), 88. The British system was also used by the Wesleyan Methodists in Sierra Leone.—*Special Report of the African Institution* (1815), 123–4. It was natural that Bell's system should be favoured by the Church Missionary Society.

[1] *Memoir*, 56.   [2] *Ibid.*, 393.   [3] *Ibid.*, 272, 350.
[4] *Ibid.*, 51.   [5] *Ibid.*, 100.   [6] *Ibid.*, 132.

Sessions, which was required of them as village superintendents: "His Honour, the Chief Justice, observed that ten years ago, when the population of the colony was only 4,000, there were forty cases on the calendar for trial, and now the population was 16,000, there were only six cases on the calendar; and he congratulated the magistrates and the grand jury on the moral improvement of the colony. It was remarkable that there was not a single case from any of the villages under the superintendence of a missionary or schoolmaster." The missionaries were then dismissed, well pleased, as having no further reason to attend.[1] The Commodore of the West African Squadron gave his testimony from personal observation: "I visited all the black towns and villages, attended the public schools and other establishments; and I have never witnessed in any population more contentment and happiness."[2] From time to time throughout the years fresh accessions of captured Negroes arrived that had to be absorbed into the new society that was being raised. It might be that lost relations would then discover each other, and this made the task of assimilation a little easier. Thus in May 1821 Johnson was informed by the chief superintendent of captured Negroes that a vessel had been brought in with 238 slaves whom it was proposed to send to Regent's Town; would he go to Freetown to receive them. He received 217, the others having to be sent to hospital: "I was obliged to have them surrounded by our people, and marched so out of Freetown, as the soldiers of the Fort were on the look-out to get some of them for wives. . . . I cannot describe the scenes which occurred when we arrived at Regent's Town. I have seen many negroes landed, but never beheld such an affecting sight . . . many of our people recognized their friends and relatives, and there was a general cry, 'Oh, massa, my sister!' 'My brother!' 'My sister!' 'My countryman!' 'My countrywoman!' etc. . . . The poor creatures being faint—just taken out of the hold of a slave-vessel and unconscious of what had befallen them—did not know whether they should laugh or cry when they beheld the countenances of those whom they had supposed long dead, but now saw clothed and clean, and perhaps with healthy children in their arms."[3] Sixty-eight boys and sixty-one girls were placed in the residential schools, while the adults were distributed among the people.

---

[1] *Memoir*, 369.   [2] Stock, *op. cit.*, I, 167.
[3] *Memoir*, 296–8. The details of liberation procedure at a later date are supplied in F. H. Rankin, *The White Man's Grave: A Visit to Sierra Leone in 1834* (1836), II, 102–16.

Such progress as Johnson, Düring and others were thus able to record would have been notable had the human problem been the only one that faced them. But we must be again reminded that all this time a grim battle with disease was being waged. Johnson himself had frequent bouts of fever, and was sorely afflicted with ophthalmia. His wife was invalided home. In 1823, while on his journey home to see her (she was not long expected to survive), a fatal attack of malaria seized him, and he was buried at sea. Great was the lamentation in Regent's Town at the loss of their spiritual guide. This was a dark year. Düring was laid low by malaria, and was hurried on board a ship to save his life, but the ship was lost at sea. In that same year seven new schoolmasters and five wives came out; six died that year, and ten were dead within eighteen months. And still the work went on.[1]

In 1827 a development of importance in education occurred. At the time the new parishes were formed a central residential school was established, called the Christian Institution. It was located near Freetown, on Leicester Mountain. This had not realized the hopes set upon it, and in 1827 Fourah Bay College was set up in its stead. A Basel man, C. L. F. Hänsel, was its first head. It opened with six students, the first name being that of Samuel Adjai Crowther. He had been rescued from a slave ship and brought to Sierra Leone five years before, and baptized in 1825. He was destined to achieve fame as Negro bishop of the Niger, and to be for his generation a symbol of Africa's redemption. Fourah Bay was to become affiliated, half a century later, to the University of Durham, thus enabling African students to read for British degrees in their homeland.

The Wesleyan Methodists prosecuted their work steadily during this period, though also at a heavy cost in lives. William Davies, who had been appointed successor to the pioneer George Warren, arrived in 1815. Within the year he had buried his wife. Butscher, now colonial chaplain, gave him hospitality for a time. Davies reports the friendly relationship between himself and the Lutheran clergyman and their people: "When I administer the Sacrament in our chapel, I give the bread and he the wine; and once in the quarter all our people go to church, and he gives the bread and I the wine." Davies suffered repeatedly from malaria and in 1818, the year after his friend Butscher died, returned home with the colleague who

[1] Stock, *op. cit.*, I, 169.

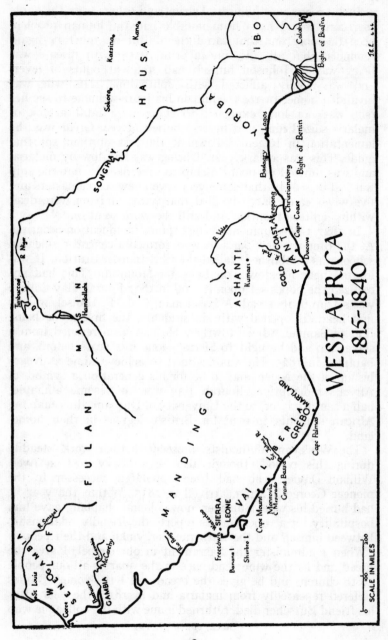

WEST AFRICA
1815-1840

had joined him and had also buried his wife on the field. Two more men were appointed, one was alive after six months. This was Baker who managed to hold on and in 1821 could report a church roll of 470 members. And so the workers come and go—and die.[1]

The British possession of the Gambia, some 500 miles to the north of Sierra Leone, came to have more importance after the Napoleonic wars. With the restoration of the Senegal and Gorée (off Dakar) to France, British merchants who had resided there removed to St. Mary's Island in the estuary of the Gambia where the then dilapidated Fort James had been built in the seventeenth century. Their new settlement was named Bathurst by McCarthy, under whose administration at Sierra Leone the Gambia now came. The neighbouring tribes—Mandingo, Jolof and Fulani—were Muslim, for this was the western fringe of the region ruled by Ghana, Mali and Songhay centuries before. This Colony also was being used for liberated Africans, so here too was a field with possibilities of fruitful missionary work. It was McCarthy who first proposed to the Wesleyan Methodists that they should take it up, though the station he recommended lay 100 miles up the river at Tentabar. The proposal was welcomed, John Morgan was appointed, and in 1821 reached his field. He has left a vivid and detailed narrative that presents the missionary situation as he knew it.[2] The settlement of the mission at Tentabar not proving feasible, Morgan made overtures to a ruler on the south bank of the river, and secured a site at Mandinari in the chieftainship of Kombo. Here he was joined for a time by Baker. It was some nine miles from St. Mary's with which there was direct communication by water. But it was work among a Muslim people; Morgan laboured on for two years without a sign of success.[3] "Mohammedans seemed to be shielded against Christianity," he wrote, "as perfectly as the crocodiles in the river were against the spear and the bullet. Preaching and school-teaching were alike unsuccessful. The young men manifested great aptitude for learning; and persons further advanced in life readily attended; but in a few days they inquired how much they were to be paid for attendance. When informed that they had put the boot on the wrong leg, and that they should rather have asked how much they were expected

[1] Findlay and Holdsworth, op. cit., IV, 77–80. Also W. C. Barclay, Early American Methodism, II, 1950, 58.

[2] John Morgan, Reminiscences of the Founding of a Christian Mission on the Gambia (1864).

[3] Ibid., 20–4.

to pay—though nothing was desired of them—they at once broke up the school. To the preaching they generally refused to listen, unless 'the missionaries would say, 'Mohammed is good'."[1] Mandinari had its mosque, and he found Muslims literate in Arabic; some of the Jolofs wrote the language in beautiful characters. The Koran in Arabic was the only book to be found and that was scarce, copies fetching a high price. He found his preaching countered by the Muslim teaching they had already received: "Christ was acknowledged as a greater prophet than Moses, but inferior to Mohammed. Some of the people had heard of the crucifixion, but regarded it as a cheat on the part of Christ. One of them, having heard the Missionary speak of the great atoning sacrifice, said 'That was a clever trick, was it not?' 'A trick! what do you mean by that?' 'Why, you know Jesus was never crucified.' 'Who was it then?' 'Rabmag.' 'Who was Rabmag?' 'A man who stood behind the cross; and when Jesus was being dragged to the cross, he stepped forward, and Jesus slipped away: so the soldiers crucified Rabmag, thinking it was Jesus. Afterwards Jesus came forward again, and said he was risen from the dead'."[2]

His failure in making the slightest impression led Morgan to devote himself to those who were responsive, the liberated Africans at St. Mary's with whom he and his colleagues from time to time had maintained contact. The little group of Christians had remained faithful and with these as a nucleus he prosecuted the work until he could report a church of thirty-five Negro members. He started a school, devoting six hours a day to it himself; in the evening there were classes for the slaves. These made such progress that in six months they began to read the Bible. When going on tree-felling expeditions for their masters, they were as careful to pack their Bibles as their axes. When he sought school material from Sierra Leone, both Bell's and Lancaster's equipment were sent him, and the cards and sheets of the rival systems were both employed![3] About 250 miles up the Gambia lay McCarthy's Island; when in 1823 the Commandant at St. Mary's sailed up the river

[1] Morgan, op. cit., (1864), 46.

[2] Ibid., 74-5. It is interesting to find that this Muslim doctrine of the crucifixion had reached the Atlantic coast of the Sudan. The Koran asserts that Jesus was not crucified but does not name the substitute (Sura iv. 155-6). There were various traditions on this point. Cf. Rodwell's translation of the Koran (Everyman ed.) 427, n. 2; E. M. Wherry, Commentary on the Quran (1896), II, 21-2; D. B. Macdonald, Aspects of Islam (1911), 245, 248-9.

[3] Ibid., 56-8.

thirty miles beyond this island to the Bara-Kunda Falls to select a commercial settlement, Morgan accompanied him with a view to missionary extension also. A site on McCarthy's Island was granted, but the hope of developing it was denied him. He retired from the field in 1825. Ten years later there was appointed to the Gambia R. M. Macbrair who had seen experience in Egypt and Malta and possessed a knowledge of Arabic. His commission was to translate the Scriptures into Mandingo and Fulani. His work suffered many interruptions, but on his return to England in 1836 he published (thanks to the Bible Society) a Mandingo version of St. Matthew, and also a grammar of the language.[1] In that year the Methodist membership on the Gambia had reached 535, and the schools had 230 on the roll. The later growth of the Church has been almost entirely among the liberated Africans and their descendants.

The year 1837 was a black one in the annals of the Gambia. In that year an exceptionally heavy mortality from yellow fever occurred, while Sierra Leone suffered at the same time from the epidemic. The European staff of the Wesleyan missions on the Coast was all but extinguished, with one man each surviving on the Gambia and in Sierra Leone while the Gold Coast was left quite denuded the same year. Recruits soon filled some of the vacant places.[2]

In 1821 the Society of Friends had a proposal placed before it to initiate a "Mission of Instruction to the Negroes on the Gambia". The object in view was education of Africans through the medium of their own vernaculars and by means of African teachers and the translation into these vernaculars of portions of Scripture. The Meeting for Sufferings, before which the proposal came from their Committee on the total Abolition of the Slave Trade, deferred decision for three months and then declined the proposal.[3] To four Friends, however, this was a

---

[1] Findlay and Holdsworth, op. cit., IV, 129–30; Thirty-fourth Report of the British and Foreign Bible Society (1838), xci.

[2] Findlay and Davey in Transactions of the Royal Society of Tropical Medicine and Hygiene, XXIX, 672, refer to this epidemic of 1837 and regard it as the first identification of yellow fever in the Gambia, though some accounts from the eighteenth century appear to point to the disease as already on the Coast. Hirsch, in his Handbook of Historical and Geographical Pathology (1883), records the 1837 outbreak in Sierra Leone, contemporary authorities being McDiarmad in London Medical Gazette, XXI (1837), 444, and Ferguson, Ibid., XXIV (1839), 839. I am indebted for this information to Dr. G. Macdonald, Director of the Ross Institute of Tropical Hygiene.

[3] H. T. Hodgkin, Friends beyond Seas (1916), 24–5, n., where the text of the Minute is given.

compelling concern. They determined to act on their own initiative; Hannah Kilham, Richard Smith, Ann and John Thompson sailed to the Coast in 1823. The following year the two women were back in England, the only survivors.

Hannah Kilham was a remarkable woman. Her husband, Alexander Kilham, was the founder of the Methodist New Connexion, the first Methodist secession after John Wesley's death. She was early left a widow and in due course found a congenial religious fellowship among Friends. Social service in Ireland and among the poor of London occupied her for a time, but the welfare of Africa became the overriding concern of her life. It took an interesting direction: she became convinced that the neglect of the African vernaculars was a fatal mistake. Anxious to experiment with a simple system of orthography for these vernaculars, she secured the services of two Jolofs from a ship in the docks, and proceeded with her purpose. One of her convictions was that to begin with a limited vocabulary was best.[1] Experience was gained on three visits to West Africa. The first, in 1823, was to the Gambia, when she reports never feeling more at home than when treading the African shore. It was determined to open school in Bathurst, where the chaplain was friendly and offered the use of his premises. There was to be a session for children in the mornings and one for liberated Africans (or "king's boys", as liberated by King George) in the evenings: "This was just what I could have desired—to have an opening for some usefulness towards the re-captured negroes, and to have a school for the Jaloof language."[2] The schools were started but conditions were not propitious. This visit to the coast lasted only six months. It was three years before the next was paid at the end of 1827, but this time severe attacks of malaria compelled an early return after only ten weeks in Sierra Leone. The object of this second visit she stated as: "First, the obtaining of an outline of the principal languages spoken by the liberated Africans and others in the colony, so as, by taking down in writing, in an easy and distinct orthography, the numerals and some of the leading words, to identify as far as may be practicable the dialects of the different tribes,—to form an idea of the number of distinct languages spoken in

[1] S. Biller, *Memoir of Hannah Kilham* (1837), 116, 125-6, 132-3. Her proposal is an interesting parallel to Basic English and other modern developments based on limited vocabularies.

[2] The language known as Jolof in the Gambia and Wolof in Senegal is one of the most important in West Africa. Dr. Ida Ward offers a short phonetic study in *Africa*, XII (1939), 320-34.

Sierra Leone, and to consider what prospect there might be of proceeding to reduce those of most importance to a written form: also to prepare such an outline for elementary instruction in each language, as might introduce the pupils in the liberated African schools to a better knowledge of English than they at present possess."[1] In pursuance of this purpose thirty distinct dialects were taken down on this visit. The third visit, from which she did not return, was her longest on the coast. She arrived at Sierra Leone in December 1830, and this time established a school in the village of Charlotte with the Governor's cordial approval. Her method evidently worked in practice, for when the Governor later paid the school a visit, one of his officers remarked of the scholars that they were "the most intelligent company of liberated African children he had ever seen".[2] Weakened by severe attacks of malaria, she nevertheless paid a much desired visit to Liberia in 1832, and was buried at sea on the return voyage to Freetown. Her actual contribution in missionary service on the field was slight; her conception of the use of the vernacular in missionary work was far-reaching. She was impatient of the teaching of the liberated Africans in English only. On her first visit she wrote: "It appears to me now more desirable than ever that the system of teaching even the liberated Africans should, in the first instance, be through their own language."[3] On the last visit she realized how hard it would be to establish such a revolutionary policy: "I hear still the old sound of 'This colony is an English colony, and for our own people we do not need the native languages.' The manner in which English is understood and spoken here is grievous. I believe the people singing hymns often remember but very few of the words given out in two lines, and either use other words, or sing a part of the tune without words, and this I apprehend arises from their not knowing enough of the meaning of what they hear to enable them to understand."[4] The same desire for English to oust the vernacular she found on the Gambia.[5] One wish was prophetic: "How rejoiced should I be to see a college for the African languages; and . . . I cannot but hope that there will be such an institution"—a strange forecast, in its day, of the School of Oriental and African Studies.[6] Hers was a lone adventure; her endeavour to stir up Friends to work out these ideas did not succeed. It was a full generation before S. W. Koelle, encouraged to linguistic research by Henry

[1] S. Biller, *op. cit.*, 326–7.   [2] *Ibid.*, 395.   [3] *Ibid.*, 213.
[4] *Ibid.*, 379.   [5] *Ibid.*, 260.   [6] *Ibid.*, 403.

Venn, produced his *Polyglotta Africana* which would have rejoiced the heart of Hannah Kilham. It consisted of a comparative vocabulary of 300 words and phrases in 150 languages and dialects. But the year was 1853.[1]

Meanwhile the Bible Society supplied West Africa with the Scriptures as liberally as the existing versions permitted and its means would allow. From 1835 to 1841 nearly 7,000 copies were sent out of which some 5,500 went to Sierra Leone, with another 500 for the Gambia.[2] In 1817 Bickersteth had formed in Sierra Leone an Auxiliary to the Bible Society; 2,000 attended its anniversary meeting in 1840.

There were those who found a missionary vocation in Sierra Leone as district managers of groups of liberated African villages, though they were not in the service of a missionary society. The position was poorly paid, and by contrast with higher ranking officials the disparity was truly startling. The three members of the Mixed Commission Court for the adjudication of slavers received respectively £3,000, £2,000 and £1,000, with a pension, after eight years' service, of half the salary. District managers received from £100 to £150 (£200 was the occasional maximum), were without pension, and liable to dismissal at the whim of the Governor. The former had about one slaver a month to deal with (at least when Alexander visited Sierra Leone in the 'thirties), while the district managers carried continuous and often harrying responsibility.[3] Yet men there were both from the ranks of missionaries and naval officers, who found in this form of service to liberated Africans a satisfying destiny. That educated men could be found who would devote themselves to this service in such isolation from polite society and with such paucity of reward amazed at least one discriminating observer: "The rare sight of a library well stocked with classical, French, German, and English literature (a sight rare indeed even in the capital), only made the marvel more marvellous that a European of cultivated mind could be induced to accept exile in a place almost hermetically sealed to intercourse with men of congenial habits, and apart from all that is literary,

[1] Stock, *op. cit.*, II, 102.
[2] W. Canton, *op. cit.*, II, 294. These are said to have been "in various languages", but as the copies provided for the Niger Expedition of 1841 were in Arabic and Hebrew, it does not follow that African vernaculars were earlier to the fore. The principal demand in Sierra Leone was for Scriptures in English, for the schools and those liberated Africans who could read.
[3] F. H. Rankin, *op. cit.*, I, 338–9; J. E. Alexander, *Narrative of a Voyage of Observation among the Colonies of Western Africa in 1835* (1837), I, 94, 119–20.

social, or improving. I believe that the same philanthropic zeal for the amelioration of his fellow-men, which led this gentleman to the shores of Africa, has detained him there."[1] It is to such unselfish men, both inside and outside missionary ranks, that humanly speaking the cleansing of the African scene and the steady development of her peoples are mainly due.

At the close of our period the Church Missionary Society reported 1,500 communicants in Sierra Leone with a regular attendance at public worship of 5,500 more. The fifty schools had 6,000 pupils on their rolls. The Wesleyan membership was approaching some 2,000 members, with 1,500 at their schools; their membership included many of the original settler population, and these were still, as earlier, resentful of church discipline.[2] To complicate the situation they showed anything but brotherly love to liberated Africans, whom they despised as their inferiors. "Pride", says Rankin who knew them in 1834, "has been their worst enemy; resting upon the remembrance of what they once were, and displaying itself in contempt for the Maroons and Liberated, now in almost all respects their equals."[3] The Maroons were mainly in Wesleyan membership, but they too were uneasy partners. At one period a rupture over the Maroon chapel in Freetown "ended by the Superintendent marching out, after a closing 'sermon from the text: 'Behold, your house is left unto you desolate'."[4] The Church Missionary Society, not having secured these elements in its membership, was thereby delivered from such embarrassments.

It was in 1825 that the Countess of Huntingdon's Connexion became aware of a Christian community bearing its name in Sierra Leone. In that year the Address to the Conference reported the receiving of a letter from a Negro minister, John Ellis, whose congregation bore the name: A Religious Society in the Connexion of the Countess of Huntingdon. Ellis was one of the three leaders of this Society who arrived with the first settlers. A proposal was made for a minister of the Connexion to visit Sierra Leone, but apparently it was not acted upon.[5] Contact was next renewed, as far as the records go, in 1839 when two members of the Sierra Leone Society came to London

---

[1] F. H. Rankin, *op. cit.*, II, 15–16.
[2] Stock, *op. cit.*, I, 336. In 1837 the Wesleyan figures for Sierra Leone were 1,337 members and 1,134 scholars in the schools.—Findlay and Holdsworth, *op. cit.*, IV, 87.   [3] Rankin, *op. cit.*, I, 98.
[4] Findlay and Holdsworth, *op. cit.*, IV, 86.
[5] *The Countess of Huntingdon's Connexion Circular*, No. 19 (February 1846), 183.

and reported on their religious activities. A letter received later in the year told of the death of John Ellis, then ninety years of age, and gave their membership as 879 on five stations in the Colony. Three ministers, Anthony Elliott, Scipio Wright, and James Strapnell, signed the letter. This proved the beginning of a steady, if irregular, correspondence.[1]

The hope of the promoters of the Settlement at Sierra Leone fifty years before, that it might be the base from which healing influences would flow through stricken Africa, had not been realized. Yet in a manner they did not anticipate this hope was now to be renewed. Some of the more enterprising among the liberated Africans, men of the Yoruba tribe, decided on a trading expedition to the coast of their homeland, a thousand miles eastward along the Guinea coast. They bought a small slaver, significantly renamed her the *Wilberforce*, and set out. At Badagry they traded their goods for produce, and set sail for Sierra Leone. Thus began a commerce between Sierra Leone and Yorubaland that was to result in a return of bands of Sierra Leone Christians to their ancestral home.[2] Sierra Leone began to reach beyond herself at last. Those who laboured on her soil were sowing for a wider harvest.

(2) *The American Colonization of Liberia.*

The success of the British Settlement for free Negroes in Sierra Leone led to similar action being taken in the United States, though the motives that prompted it were scarcely the same. In December 1816 at a meeting in Washington of those interested, there was founded the American Colonization Society. It was formally constituted on January 1st, 1817, with Bushrod Washington, a nephew of George Washington, as its first President. Its full title as stated in the constitution ran: The American Society for Colonizing the Free People of Color of the United States. This fairly stated its object. It was exclusively directed to removing from the States Negroes already free. As one of its later supporters put it: "Free blacks are a greater nuisance than even slaves themselves." The twelve managers of the Society were all slave-owners.[3] True, there were those who sincerely wanted to alleviate the lot of the free Negro and who thought return to the African homeland the happiest answer to their question. But motives were as

---

[1] *The Lady Selina: Commemoration Meetings* (1941), 27.
[2] Stock, *op. cit.*, I, 456–7; Findlay and Holdsworth, *op. cit.*, IV, 88.
[3] F. Starr, *Liberia* (1913), 52–3.

mixed as the Society's supporters were varied in their attitude to the Negro. The Society was on anything but cordial terms with the Abolition Societies in the United States.

The first practical step was taken in 1818 when Samuel J. Mills and Ebenezer Burgess were sent to the West Coast to seek a suitable location for the proposed settlement.[1] They came to Sierra Leone and under the guidance of John Kizell visited Sherbro Island lying some thirty miles south of the Sierra Leone Peninsula. Kizell, who hailed originally from that part of the coast and who was one of the 1792 settlers, had himself, it is said, established a settlement on Sherbro Island and was acting as Christian leader of it.[2] The commission were satisfied, and took this proposal back to the Society. Mills died on the return voyage.

In 1820 the first party of free Negroes, eighty-eight in number, set out under the leadership of three white Americans: Samuel Bacon, a minister, John P. Blankson, and Dr. S. Crozer. They attempted to found their colony on Sherbro Island; a virulent fever decimated the party, the three leaders died and a quarter of the colonists. The sixty-six survivors thereupon took ship for Sierra Leone. In 1821 a second party from the States with four white leaders joined them; these were Ephraim Bacon (brother of Samuel), J. B. Winn, J. R. Andrus, and Christian Wiltberger. Bacon and Andrus were clergymen of the Episcopal Church.[3] The leaders were soon in touch with W. A. B. Johnson, and wisely sought his advice about their settlement. He indicated the unsuitability of Sherbro Island on various grounds, and advised them to go farther along the coast: "I have pointed out two places to them—Cape Mesurado, and St. John's River, Bassa Country. I believe that at both those places there is good anchorage for large vessels, and they are both about 400 miles from this colony and thus remove all prejudice."[4] They took.

---

[1] Mills was one of the four signatories to the Andover students' letter that prompted the founding of the American Board in 1810.—*First Ten Reports of A.B.C.F.M.*, 10.   [2] Starr, *op. cit.*, 55–6.

[3] On the authority of W. A. B. Johnson of Sierra Leone, who also reported an interesting link between the C.M.S. and the States: "One of them (Mr. Andrus) showed me a letter from Mr. Pratt, and I was much pleased that that letter had proved effectual to the formation of a Church Missionary Society in America."—*Memoir*, 274–5.

[4] *Ibid.*, 275. With reference to Johnson's last point, it has to be remembered that the Sierra Leone settlers from Nova Scotia had fought on the British side in the War of Independence, not so very far in the past, while the Negroes now seeking a settlement had for the most part favoured the American cause. To a British captain who offered help in time of difficulty at Cape Mesurado, if he were given ground for running up a flag, Elijah Johnson, then the Negro

his advice and sailed down the coast to prospect. Johnson generously loaned them as interpreters his two African lieutenants, W. Davis and Tamba, who knew well both the coast and the chiefs. Thus once again we find a generous sharing of experience and resources, the Church Missionary Society making its contribution to this American enterprise at a vital moment in its inception. The final decision was given for Cape Mesurado.[1] Wiltberger was now left as sole leader—his companions were dead or invalided—but was soon joined by Dr. Eli Ayres. Captain Stockton, who commanded the brig that brought over the party in 1821, co-operated with them in securing land at Cape Mesurado from the chiefs. In December 1821 the land was ceded in return for some goods paid immediately, and a further instalment to come.[2] Early in 1822 the colonists arrived, only to find that the act of the chiefs in signing the contract had been repudiated by their people. The colonists were only able to take possession of a low-lying (and therefore unhealthy) islet in the lagoon, about a quarter of a mile in length. Ayres proposed a return to Sierra Leone; Wiltberger voted to remain and was supported by a colonist who was soon to become a leader of repute, Elijah Johnson. Ayres and Wiltberger, victims of fever, were invalided home, and Johnson was left in command. He acted with courage, and left the unhealthy islet for the high ground of Cape Mesurado, where Monrovia was later to stand. After a few months a party of fifty-three fresh colonists arrived from the States, with a white leader, Jehudi Ashmun. Ashmun proved the real founder of Liberia. For a critical six years he guided the fortunes of the little settlement of free Negroes, and left it well established. He is said to have just decided for missionary work when the Colonization Society was in need of a suitable man to direct the enterprise. He offered his services and was appointed. On arrival he found

leader, is said to have replied in refusing: "We want no flagstaff put up here that will cost us more to get it down than it will to whip the natives."—Starr, *op. cit.*, 65.

[1] Johnson was surprised they did not select Grand Bassa (*Memoir*, 321), but the reason is said to have been an outbreak of fever there that laid three of the leaders low.—H. H. Johnston, *Liberia* (1906), I, 128.

[2] The goods paid at the time were: "Six muskets, one small barrel of powder, six iron bars, ten iron pots, one barrel of beads, two casks of tobacco, three looking-glasses, four umbrellas, three walking-sticks, one box of soap, one barrel of rum, four hats, three pairs of shoes, six pieces of blue baft, three pieces of white calico."—H. H. Johnston, *op. cit.*, I, 129. A similar list represented the deferred payment. As Johnston remarks, the chiefs probably had no intention of handing over freehold rights in land. They may well have thought they were getting the better of the bargain.

the settlement virtually beleaguered. Tribal neighbours were hostile, the rainy season was in full swing, and there were only thirty-five men and boys capable of bearing arms. In little more than a month Mrs. Ashmun died. Three months later Ashmun himself was down with desperate fever and for two months was battling for life. But in the interval a fierce onslaught upon the settlement had been repelled. Cuban slave-traders in the neighbourhood resented the coming of the settlers as a threat to their lucrative traffic, and accordingly they saw that the tribes were kept supplied for the fight. The arrival of a British schooner, the *Prince Regent,* brought relief in the course of a second attack. Major Laing, the well-known traveller, was on board and offered his services to secure an understanding. He was successful, and peace was restored between colonists and chiefs. A young midshipman, Gordon, stayed with eleven of his men to safeguard the settlement, but in a month he and eight of the men had died from fever. His memory is said to be still cherished by Liberians. Ashmun found 1823 a difficult year, what with hostile slave-trading chiefs without and disloyal intriguers within. The following year 105 further colonists arrived, together with a special envoy, Robert Gurley, who was commissioned to prepare a constitution for the settlement. Meanwhile General Harper proposed the name Liberia for the country and Monrovia for its capital. These names and the provisional constitution were ratified the same year by the Government of the United States. There was now more opportunity of peaceful development, and Ashmun seized it, adding to the lands of the settlement by treaty, and seeking to encourage agriculture. Ashmun had throughout suffered from ill-health; he was invalided home in 1828, and the same year died at New Haven, Connecticut. Before his death he persuaded the Society to allow the colonists a measure of control in electing all but the two senior officials. The population was now 1,200.[1]

Other American organizations now contributed their quota to the new venture. In 1831 the Maryland Colonization Society, established four years earlier, sent out thirty-one colonists under a white leader, Dr. Hall, to establish a settlement where liquor would be prohibited and agriculture be the regular occupation. The earlier colonists at Monrovia were not co-operative. When therefore Dr. Hall returned in 1833 with a second party of twenty-eight, they all migrated down the coast to Cape Palmas where they established "Maryland in Africa".

[1] Starr, *op. cit.*, 60–8; H. H. Johnston, *op. cit.*, I, 132–50.

Also in 1833 came the settlement Edina[1] on the banks of the St. John's River, near Grand Bassa, one of the sites originally proposed by Johnson of Regent's Town. Another centre was established from Pennsylvania, on the St. John's River. In 1835 a Quaker organization, the Pennsylvania Young Men's Society, took up the venture and sent out 126 Negro colonists, all trained artisans. This settlement was also established on temperance principles. Yet again, in 1838, the Mississippi Colonization Society contributed its quota to "Mississippi in Africa". The total population of American origin was now 2,281. A new constitution was prepared and all settlements but Maryland in Africa were included in the new Commonwealth of Liberia.[2]

The new Negro element thus introduced to this part of Africa did not mix with the old. As the chequered career of the first settlement has shown, there was active hostility between the two. There were thus two distinct sections to this potential mission field: the American newcomers already aware of civilized standards and demands, and the African tribes with a primary interest in trade, the slave-trade for preference, but trade with liquor in it. American missions were naturally attracted to Liberia as British had been to Sierra Leone. Five American Societies began work in this period, and one from the continent of Europe.

The Baptist Board of Foreign Missions for the United States adopted as their missionaries two Negroes who sailed with Ashmun in 1822, Lott Carey and Collin Teague. Both had been members of the Baptist Church at Richmond, Virginia, and both were ministers. "The Board has afforded them some assistance," it reports, "but it is expected that they will, in a good degree, support themselves." Lott Carey had been a slave and had purchased his freedom in 1813. He was an able leader and became Ashmun's chief lieutenant, being left in command on his departure. He seems to have pursued faithfully his missionary vocation, "active in church work, interested in school affairs, instructing the recaptured Africans, aiding in the care of the sick and suffering".[3] He died in 1828.

[1] Edina from Edinburgh; Starr says Edinburgh in Scotland, "citizens of which had contributed liberally to the American Colonization Society."— *Op. cit.*, 74. Johnston says: "Either Edinburgh in Pennsylvania or Edinburgh in Mississippi."—*Op. cit.*, I, 154, n.

[2] Starr, *op. cit.*, 73–4, 77; H. H. Johnston, *op. cit.*, I, 152–7.

[3] *American Missionary Register*, I (1820–21), 293; II (1821–22), 55; Starr, *op. cit.*, 68–9; H. H. Johnston, *op. cit.*, I, 135.

The Basel Mission had long supplied from its training school missionaries for other Societies. It now commenced its own work overseas, and Liberia, despite the obvious difficulties of the West Coast, was the first choice. The fact that Basel men had served the Church Missionary Society in Sierra Leone had prepared the Committee in some respects for such a field. In 1825 they got into touch with Ashmun, and he replied, encouraging them to proceed, and painting a rather rosy picture of the situation. Careful preparations were made; three candidates came to England to perfect their English. The British and Foreign Bible Society provided 200 copies of the Scriptures in English, Danish, German, French, and Arabic.[1] The five pioneers reached Monrovia in 1828—J. C. S. Handt, C. G. Hegele, J. F. Sessing, G. A. Kissling, and H. H. Wulff. They arrived with high hopes of their mission, but were speedily disillusioned. Soon after their landing Ashmun was invalided, never to return. The promised support of the Christian colonists they found illusory: the Baptists proved exclusive, and the Methodists over-exuberant to suit their religious standards. They found little in common with the American Negroes. But there were the pagan tribes. One man found an entry among the Bassa, and another with the Vai, but living was hard and the climate took its toll. Wulff died, others were invalided, and within the year Kissling alone remained. For twelve months he held on single-handed. Then Sessing returned, and with him J. Bührer, H. Graner, and R. Dietschi. But tragedy speedily overtook them. They arrived early in 1830; in March Dietschi and Bührer died of fever, and Graner in May. In the following year Sessing withdrew to Sierra Leone in the service of the Church Missionary Society, and urged Kissling to join him. The latter left the field four months later. The mission was at an end, and by the decision of the Committee was not to be resumed. The one tangible result to chronicle was the baptism of the first Bassa convert in Sierra Leone by the name of Jakob von Brunn.[2]

In 1833, when Maryland in Africa was established, American Roman Catholics had their interest aroused in the enterprise. Catholic Negroes were included among the Maryland settlers and this secured the attention of the Second Provincial Council of Baltimore. This Council, meeting in 1833, gave the new mission into the charge of the Jesuits.[3]

[1] Canton, *op. cit.*, II, 31.
[2] W. Schlatter, *Geschichte der Basler Mission* (1916), III, 9–16.
[3] Schmidlin, *op. cit.*, 649 and n. 22.

5ʌ.

Also in 1833, two years after the withdrawal of the Basel Mission, the Methodist Episcopal Church of the States entered Liberia. This was its first overseas mission.[1] Melville B. Cox, the pioneer, landed in March 1833, and died the following July. A second party consisting of Spaulding and Wright with their wives and Miss Sophronia Farrington, arrived on New Year's Day, 1834. The Wrights were dead in three months. Spaulding determined to abandon the mission but Miss Farrington, though laid low by malaria, declined to go with him: "I can never see this mission abandoned. I can die here, but I will never return until the mission is established." To his warning, "The board will probably cut you off if you do not go", she countered, "I will stay and trust the Lord". To the staunch loyalty of this first woman missionary of the Methodist Episcopal Church was due the continuance of the mission when to others it was a forlorn hope. Her heroic courage made its own appeal and brought relief. John Seys volunteered for the post and arrived towards the end of 1834. After five months he was back in the States pleading the cause of the mission; in another three he was out again, taking his wife and younger children. Before the end of that year (1835) his son was dead. Again he returned to America, his wife heroically remaining to hold the fort. For the third time he sailed for Africa, in October 1836, with a white minister, S. Chase, and a Negro lay preacher. But shortly before he sailed a letter was received at the office of the Board. It was from Mrs. Ann Wilkins who had been moved by Seys' appeals and said: "A sister who has a little money at command gives that little cheerfully, and is willing to give her life as a female teacher if she is wanted." She was wanted, and wanted badly. She was appointed, she sailed, and gave twenty years of self-denying service. The turning-point had been reached. The mission was now secure.[2]

The Presbyterian Church in America had as its pioneer John B. Pinney, who came to prospect the field in 1833. The following year Dr. Mechlin, a physician who had been appointed agent in control of the settlement in 1829, returned to the United States, and Pinney was called to succeed him. Starr commends his efficient if brief period of control: "He attempted to give agriculture its proper position as the fundamental interest of

[1] T. B. Neely, *The Methodist Episcopal Church and its Foreign Missions*, (1923), 71.
[2] *The Missionary Review*, IV (1881), 267–9, based on J. M. Reid, *Missions and Missionary Society of the Methodist Episcopal Church*.

the community; he purchased fertile lands in the interior for cultivation; he emphasized the claims of Liberia to lands lying behind Cape Mount; he adjusted difficulties between the Congoes and Eboes, recaptured Africans; had he remained long in office, he might perhaps have accomplished much."[1] He left for the States in 1834, but was back before long with reinforcement for the mission—Laird, Cloud, Finley and Temple a Negro. In four months the only survivors were Pinney and Finley; Cloud and the Lairds were dead and Temple had withdrawn. Pinney and his companion then left for the States, but in 1839 he was back again with three more helpers. These were all victims of the climate and Pinney now retired from the field.[2]

In 1833 yet another American Society started in Liberia—the American Board. John Leighton Wilson and Stephen R. Wyncoop were sent out in that year, going with a party under the Colonization Society of Maryland; though eight years earlier the Board had determined to seek the first opportunity of beginning work in West Africa. About 1829 a Negro Presbyterian minister was actually appointed "a missionary of the Board to the native tribes within the colony of Liberia". He proceeded to Liberia, but not as the Board's representative.[3] Wilson decided on a site at Cape Palmas, in "Maryland in Africa", where the first station of the Board was established in 1834, and gave seven years' service. The local tribe was Grebo; he reduced their language and started on translation into it. Colleagues fell around him. There were great difficulties, arising from the continual tension between the Negro colonists and the African tribes; the colonists did not welcome African converts. The Board therefore decided to transfer the mission to Gaboon.[4]

In 1835 the Baptist Board of the States, whose work began with Negro ministers in 1822, sent their first white missionaries to Liberia, Crocker and Mylne, but the field was abandoned after twenty years.[5]

The Protestant Episcopal Church of America, whose Foreign Mission Board was set up in 1820, began work in Liberia in 1836. In March of that year James M. Thompson, a Negro, started a mission school at Mount Vaughan with seven scholars.[6]

[1] Starr, *op. cit.*, 75.   [2] Du Plessis, *Evangelization of Pagan Africa*, 99.
[3] *Memorial Volume of the First Fifty Years of the A.B.C.F.M.* (1861), 235–6.
[4] Du Plessis, *op. cit.*, 101–3; E. W. Smith, *Life and Times of Daniel Lindley*, II, §4, VII, §5.   [5] Du Plessis, *op. cit.*, 96.
[6] *The Spirit of Missions* (1913), quoted in Starr, *op. cit.*, 241. Johnston slips in giving the date as 1830.—*Op. cit.*, I, 374.

White reinforcements were soon sent, and by 1839 the staff consisted of Thomas S. Savage, Lancelot B. Minor, and John Payne, ordained men, with E. S. Byron and G. A. Perkins lay helpers. Savage, Payne, and Perkins were married, so that the mission staff then consisted of eight persons. Savage, the leader of the mission, was also a qualified physician.[1] Thompson had died in 1838 and was buried at Mount Vaughan. By his own request, as a witness to the Christian hope, his bearers wore white cloths and white scarves round their hats.[2] Dr. Savage was an energetic leader and in 1837 undertook a tour of twenty towns. He reported on it: "The section embraced by this tour constitutes nearly one-third of a semicircle (having the Mission for its centre), which contains a population not less, I should think, than 60,000 souls who would to-day gladly receive sixty Christian teachers."[3] Dr. Savage found the adults difficult of access, but the children to present an immediate opportunity. Remembering that his contact had been in the main with the coast native who was demoralized by liquor and the slave-trade, it is not a surprise to read his experience: "I have never yet found an adult in whose conduct there appeared the slightest influence of conscience. But again, what is a consoling fact under our discouragements, I have found their children teachable, and susceptible of a good moral influence—and here, under God, lies our hope of immediate usefulness."[4] The jealousy of the coast people proved the greatest obstacle to the extension of the mission. They were unwilling that its benefits should be shared with the interior tribes, who would then be less under their influence. It is interesting to find Dr. Savage promoting the use of quinine as a specific against malaria.[5] Yet they were not without their casualties. Liberia has remained the only African field of the Church.

The Methodist Protestant Church of the States constituted its Board of Missions in 1834, and attempted its first overseas work in 1837 by sending a Negro missionary to Liberia, and apparently Negro colonists with him. We are told, however, that "the project proved a failure from the fact that none but

---

[1] *The Spirit of Missions*, IV (1839), 268. [2] *Ibid.*, 186.
[3] *Ibid.*, 184. [4] *Ibid.*, 112.
[5] " . . . found myself under an attack of the intermittent fever . . . inadvertently left behind my almost specific, 'Sulphate of Quinine.' " "Quinine ought to be sent every six months. My experience is that with a proper dose of the article, upon the approach of the premonitory symptoms, a paroxysm will surely be prevented."—*Ibid.*, 146, 362. In this he was distinctly a pioneer.

white men were then allowed the privilege of franchise in the
Methodist Protestant Church".[1]

The story of twenty years of valiant effort is a sad one.
Perhaps too much was expected too soon. In Sierra Leone it
was full twenty years from the start before a Society was able
to maintain itself, and thirty before its real work could be said
to have begun; and this, with more favourable conditions of
political stability and more countenance and support from the
home authority than Liberia enjoyed. But the story of the
devoted service of pioneers stands imperishable in missionary
annals; American and German graves attest its truth.

(3) Christianity on the Gold Coast.

In the first half of the century the Danes still held their Gold
Coast territory with Christiansborg their principal fort. In 1826
the Danish Governor, Major de Richelieu, was in Denmark on
leave after two to three years' service. On first going out he had
found the religious life of the colony at a low ebb, the church
was empty, and no chaplain had appeared for fifteen years. He
saw to it that public worship was resumed, conducting it himself; he established a school, and himself taught in it; he even
baptized 150 scholars. The people besought him on leaving to
bring them back a minister. Rönne, who represented the
interests of the Basel Mission in Denmark, took the occasion
to raise with the Crown Prince (a former pupil of his) the
question of a mission on the Gold Coast in these more favourable
circumstances, indicating that the Basel Mission would be
prepared to support it if official sanction were given. The
suggestion reached the King, and he warmly approved, re-
marking that it was appropriate a new mission should begin
on Danish soil when they were celebrating the thousandth
anniversary of the baptism of Harald, the first Christian
Danish king.

Under such propitious circumstances the Basel Committee
decided to initiate a mission on the Gold Coast under Danish
auspices. This raised the question of the relation of their
missionaries to the State Church. The Gold Coast territory was
within the jurisdiction of the Bishop of Zeeland. Bishop Münter,
when approached, expressed his approval on condition that
the missionaries were ordained by him and subject to his
authority. This the Basel Committee saw no reason to contest,
as it was their policy not to encourage independent Christian

[1] *The Missionary Review*, II (1879), 352.

groups, but to link them up with the Church of the country. Indeed, they regarded themselves at that time as but preparing the way for a Danish mission. Four missionaries were accordingly selected to be the pioneer band: K. F. Salbach, J. G. Schmidt, G. Holzwarth, and J. P. Henke. Part of their training was taken in Copenhagen where they studied Danish. They landed at Christiansborg in December 1828. They were soon actively engaged among the people, two of them moving eastwards along the coast. But calamity was near: in August 1829 Holzwarth, Salbach, and Schmidt were all taken ill and died the same month. Henke was overwhelmed, but bravely plodded on. The moral decadence and spiritual insensibility of European and African alike in the coast settlements deeply distressed him. He reported that he continued to deliver his Christian message in the hope that some seed sown might find favourable soil, though all appearances were to the contrary. In great loneliness of soul he toiled on faithfully for two more years. In October 1831, in his last letter to Basel, he admitted his strength was exhausted; on the twenty-second of November 1831 he died in loneliness, without a friend to give him care and comfort at the end. Within three years the pioneer party of the mission were in their graves.

Six months before Henke wrote his last letter home, three students at the Basel Training School had offered themselves for Gold Coast service. They were P. P. Jäger, Andreas Riis, and C. F. Heinze. Jäger and Riis were ordained for the service; Heinze held a medical qualification. In March 1832 the three men were at Christiansborg. In six weeks Heinze, the doctor, was dead; in July, Jäger was buried; in September, Riis's life was despaired of, but thanks to a Negro doctor, he was given treatment that pulled him through. Once again there was one lonely survivor. For three years, subject to the ecclesiastical authority of the Danish chaplain at Christiansborg, Riis was kept on the actual coast, sorely against his will. But with a new chaplain he was given freedom, and moved up to the high land of the Akwapim Mountains. In May 1835, with Lutterodt, a Danish merchant, he entered Akropong. This transfer proved a turning-point in the mission. Vicissitudes still lay ahead, but better health was enjoyed on the highlands than on the low-lying coast, the sphere of work in an African tribe offered more hope than the sophisticated and demoralized population of a coast town, and the new centre was on the way to Kumasi which was destined to become the objective of the mission. In

1837 Riis had the joy of receiving two colleagues, J. Mürdter and A. Stanger. With them came Anna Wolters, his bride-to-be, the first woman missionary to go inland. Prospects were bright at last. And then, in December, Stanger died of fever. A year later Mürdter also died. Riis and his wife were now alone. Riis explored the country east and west. In 1838 in company with Mürdter he had gone east to the Volta region; in 1839 he travelled westwards. His last visit was to Kumasi where he was detained by the king from December 29, 1839, to January 12, 1840. He sought an interview but failed to secure it. His report to the Basel Committee, which he met in 1840, was that the time to enter Ashanti was not yet. But the Committee was now faced with the question of the whole future of the mission. Twelve years had gone by; nine men had been sent out, and one survived. Of baptized converts there was not one. Must the sore experience in Liberia become a precedent, and the mission to the Gold Coast be abandoned too? The question was a hard one when men were few and other fields showed better promise of success. But the price already paid had given the Basel Mission a solemn claim upon that field. Riis was willing to return. They resolved to carry on, but with a change of policy. A vital decision had been made.[1]

In 1818 the British and Foreign Bible Society received an interesting gift. It was gold dust, sent by officers of the African Company of Merchants on the Gold Coast. The value was £103 14s.[2] This may be taken as reasonably good evidence that the Society's Bibles were then on this coast. A few years later we find critical events turning on the use that was made of them. When the African Company came to an end in 1821 the Gold Coast forts were placed under the Government of Sierra Leone, and these, together with the Gambia, became the West Africa Settlements, with Sir Charles McCarthy of Sierra Leone the Governor of the whole. One of his first acts was to establish a school at Cape Coast Castle where young Africans of ability could be trained for eventual service in the administration. An African, Joseph Smith, was in charge of it. Smith was a sincere Christian with an implicit faith in the Word of God. He, therefore, on his own initiative, included Bible readings in his curriculum, but they were readings "without note or comment." The closing words of the Book of Revelation seem to have impressed him deeply.[3] Among the students he taught was one

[1] W. Schlatter, op. cit., III, 19–31.
[2] Canton, op. cit., II, 30–1.
[3] Revelation 22: 18–19.

of unusual ability and alertness of mind, William de Graft. Of the few copies of the Bible Smith possessed, he gave him one. Through his reading of it De Graft became a Christian. But as compared with Smith, he was a Christian with a difference; he insisted on understanding what he read. To Smith this evidently smelled of heresy, and two parties appeared among the Christian students. De Graft called his company "A Meeting or Society for Promoting Christian Knowledge"; the first meeting was on October 1st, 1831. They were systematic in their Bible reading, and stated their purpose in these words: "That, as the Word of God is the best rule a Christian ought to observe, it is herein avoided framing other rules to enforce good conduct; but that the Holy Scriptures must be carefully studied, through which, by the help of the Holy Spirit and faith in Jesus Christ, our minds will be enlightened, and find the way to eternal life." The names of the first members of the band have been preserved: George Blankson, John Sam, Henry Brew, John Smith, Brown, Neizer, Aggrey, Sackey Kwobina Mensa, and Insaidu. From what Joseph Smith came to hear of their doings, he was gravely disturbed. At last he reported to Governor Maclean what he regarded as a dangerous movement. The Governor, almost certainly misunderstanding the significance of the charge, imposed a heavy fine and had De Graft and John Sam imprisoned until it was paid. This meant an end to any prospect of the Government service for which they were training, but they remained unmoved. Indeed, their conduct when in prison, reminiscent of the days of the Acts of the Apostles,[1] so impressed their fellow-prisoners that one at least, an African trader, became a Christian and later a distinguished leader in the Church. The Governor seems to have relented, and the prisoners were released.[2]

De Graft settled in Dixcove along the coast. His band of students in Cape Coast asked him to get them more Bibles. He had heard of Captain Potter, known to be a Christian, and decided to ask him to secure the Bibles. Potter was impressed, not only by De Graft, but by members of the Cape Coast Bible band whom he also met. He decided to bring out more than Bibles if he could. Potter was a Wesleyan Methodist, so naturally sought the help of the Missionary Committee of his own Church. He offered to take out at his own expense any missionary the

---

[1] *Acts* 16:25.
[2] A. E. Southon, *Gold Coast Methodism* (1934), 24–31. The author has drawn upon original correspondence from contemporaries for his record. Cf. 55.

Committee might appoint. The generous offer was accepted. Thus it came about that the Wesleyan Methodists were granted this exceptional opportunity.

Joseph Dunwell was appointed and sailed with Captain Potter on October 17, 1834. He landed at Cape Coast on New Year's Day, 1835. Only half the year was out when he was carried off by fever, but in that short six months he had done much. He had discovered and reconciled the two Bible bands and their leaders. De Graft was an invaluable lieutenant, and Joseph Smith became Dunwell's interpreter and, we are told, his closest friend. But more: two Ashanti princes, under the terms of an agreement between Governor Maclean and the king of Ashanti, were to come to England to be educated. While they were waiting at Cape Coast, Dunwell sought them out; they accepted the Christian faith before they sailed.[1] It was two years before a successor came; then H. O. Wrigley and his wife arrived, to be followed in 1837 by P. Harrop who also was married. The Harrops survived three weeks only, and Mrs. Wrigley, exhausted by her service to them, soon died also. H. O. Wrigley was the sole survivor, but in ten months he too had died. Governor Maclean committed his body to the ground as he had done that of Dunwell, for there was no missionary left.[2] The year 1837 was a tragic one for the little fellowship of African believers.

The next appointment was unusual: Thomas Birch Freeman was the son of a Negro father and an English mother. His own complexion is said to have been so light that he constantly passed for a European on the Coast. His offer of service had been made when the sad news of the first deaths of 1837 reached England. He was accepted, ordained, and sent out to be Wrigley's colleague. Wrigley had died while the Freemans were still at sea: it was on landing at Cape Coast they first received the news.[3] In January 1838 Freeman reached that ill-reputed coast where he was to give outstanding service, not only in its length (he achieved the amazing record of fifty-two years on the coast), but also by its quality. His is a prominent name on the African roll of honour.[4] He was soon bereaved. A month

[1] Southon, *op. cit.*, 34–7.
[2] Findlay and Holdsworth, *op. cit.*, IV, 153.
[3] F. D. Walker, *Thomas Birch Freeman* (1929), 11–22. The standard life based on original materials.
[4] His biographer can say of him: "My fairly exhaustive researches have shown Freeman to be an even greater man than I had previously supposed. I regard him as one of the outstanding pioneers of modern missionary enterprise."—*Ibid.*, 8.

after his arrival he suffered from a violent fever; his wife nursed him till she, too, was prostrated and succumbed. She had been six weeks in Africa. Freeman was stricken but undaunted: "I stand in the deadly breach", he wrote, "with humble confidence that God will long spare my life."[1] The first year he spent in supervision of the Christian communities already formed (for under Dunwell and Wrigley, despite the shortness of the time, the work had grown), and in visiting neighbouring chiefs and people. An unfailing tact and courtesy, deeply appreciated by Africans and of which he proved to be a master, greatly commended him to these discriminating peoples. But Freeman was of too active and imaginative a nature to be content with settled work alone. The kingdom of Ashanti was near at hand, as distances in Africa are measured, and to Ashanti he decided he must go.

War between the Fanti peoples of the coast and the Ashanti under the hegemony of Kumasi had been the order of the day until 1826. McCarthy had had to face an Ashanti invasion in 1823; in it he lost his life, and the victorious Ashanti advanced on Cape Coast Castle. They withdrew to gather strength for a fresh invasion, and advanced again in 1826, only to be decisively defeated. In 1831 a tripartite treaty was signed between the Ashanti and the English and their African allies. By this the Ashanti relinquished their claim over the Fanti peoples. This was how the situation stood when Freeman had arrived.[2] He has fortunately left a journal of his visit, addressed to the Secretaries of the Wesleyan Missionary Society.[3] He set out on January 30, 1839. He made friendly contact with villages as he passed through them, and observed the unfailing demand of etiquette in Africa that a stranger must first see the chief. A week of such travel brought him to the River Prah, boundary of the Ashanti kingdom.[4] At Kwisa, the first town, he was detained by the chief Korinchi who, as keeper of the gate, was anxious lest an unwanted intruder should pass on to Kumasi. During the interval of enforced waiting, he found a Sunday service which he held attended by Christian Fanti from Cape Coast who were trading in Ashanti. So does the African trader travel, and if a true Christian, witness to his faith.[5] It was the 27th of March before his journey was resumed. On the 1st of

[1] Walker, op. cit., 39–41.
[2] C. P. Lucas, op. cit., III, 118–19.
[3] J. Beecham, Journal of Two Visits to the Kingdom of Ashanti by the Rev. Thomas B. Freeman. (2nd ed. 1843).   [4] Ibid., 17.   [5] Ibid., 27.

April he was permitted to enter the capital, Kumasi. An imposing pageant of the might and glory of Ashanti had been arranged to impress him. He found the king and chiefs seated on "wooden chairs" (the Ashanti stools) beneath splendid umbrellas, some of which were generous enough in size to shade a dozen persons at a time: "I was occupied for half an hour in walking slowly through the midst of this immense assembly, touching my hat and waving my hand, except before the King, in whose presence I of course stood for a moment uncovered. I then took my seat at a distance, accompanied by my people and several respectable Fanti traders, who are staying in the town . . . many of the chiefs passed me in succession . . . then came the officers of the King's household. . . . The display of gold which I witnessed as His Majesty passed was astonishing. After the King, followed other chiefs, and lastly the main body of the troops. This immense procession occupied an hour and a half in passing me. . . . I suppose the number of persons which I saw collected together exceeded forty thousand. . . . The wrists of some of the Chiefs were so heavily laden with golden ornaments that they rested their arms on the shoulders of some of their attendants. The appearance of this procession was exceedingly grand and imposing. The contrast between the people themselves, and their large umbrellas, seventy in number, and of various colours, which they waved up and down in the air, together with the dark green foliage of the large Banyan-trees, under and among which they passed, formed a scene of that novel and extraordinary character, which I feel unable to describe."[1] In due course he had an interview with the king, and explained the object of his visit. The reply to his request to be allowed to preach and teach in the kingdom was, however, deferred. He waited some days, but the season was advancing, so he proposed to take his leave. To this the king agreed, sending Freeman a parting gift of gold dust and a slave, together with the message: "His Majesty knows that you cannot stop longer, on account of the rains; and as the thing which you have mentioned to him requires much consideration, he cannot answer you in so short a time: but if you will come up again, or send a messenger, after the rains are over, he will be prepared to answer you."[2] Freeman left Kumasi on the 15th of April and reached Cape Coast again on the 23rd. A pioneer journey of outstanding significance for future missionary developments had been happily completed.

[1] J. Beecham, op. cit., 46-8. [2] Ibid., 62.

Although no definite word had yet been given, it is clear the king liked Freeman, and that good personal relationships had been established.

And as this story of Gold Coast beginnings started with Fanti Christians, so it must close with one. There lived in Kumasi, as British representative appointed by Governor Maclean, James Hayford, a Fanti. He had become a member of the Wesleyan Church in 1836. By his integrity of character he acquired considerable influence with the Ashanti king. And more: he bore his Christian witness in Kumasi by holding services for worship which visiting Fanti or local Ashanti were welcome to attend. And one of the Christian Fanti traders, Freeman found, had secured an Ashanti convert, and in default of other means, had himself baptized him.[1]

Governor Maclean wrote to the Committee, underlining the significance of Freeman's visit: "I hope and trust that the Wesleyan Missionary Committee will be satisfied that there is such an opening as will justify them in pushing the advantage gained by your indefatigable zeal. I will almost go so far as to say that if they have the means a serious responsibility will rest upon them and upon Christian England if so glorious an opening into interior Africa, if so rich a harvest, be neglected. But I hope better things."[2]

(4) Movements in Muslim Lands.

Meanwhile north of Ashanti profound changes had been taking place. There were in this same period movements in the Muslim lands of which some brief notice must now be given. It was in the Western Sudan that the most significant of these movements occurred; the agents were the Fulani (as the Fulas are called in Nigeria), a people whose racial origin is still a puzzle; and the result, the revival of Islam with some extension over peoples pagan hitherto. Usuman dan Fodio was the Fulani leader who carried through a political and religious revolution in the states that now constitute the emirates of Northern Nigeria. He was born in 1754; the year of his "Flight" from a chief he had offended, 1804. He then preached a Holy War in the region between the Niger and Lake Chad. The title born earlier by the Askias of Songhay—Sarkin Musulmi (Chief of the Muslims)—was bestowed upon him, and he set out on his career of conquest. "Shehu (Usumu) was himself", says

[1] Southon, op. cit., 54–5, 61.
[2] Findlay and Holdsworth, op. cit., IV, 155.

Meek, "a fervid Muslim to the point of fanaticism. He was a good scholar and linguist, and was thus in every way a suitable person to initiate a Holy War. But he had laid his plans long before his flight . . . and, viewed in the light of other Fulani revolutions in the Sudan, it must be admitted that the ultimate aim of this one in Nigeria was the foundation of a Muhammadan theocracy. The movement was at once national and religious."[1] Despite stubborn opposition, there were early successes for Fulani arms; Katsina was taken in 1805, and in the same year Kano fell. The tide surged on towards Lake Chad until met by determined and effective resistance in Bornu. This was not on religious grounds (for the Sheikh was an ardent Muslim), but on grounds of national security.[2] In 1810 Sokoto was built as the new capital of the Fulani empire, and to Sultans of Sokoto until the twentieth century belonged the right of appointing Emirs to the subject Hausa states. Usuman's son Belo, who had built Sokoto, succeeded him in 1817. He was the reigning Sultan visited by the explorers Denham, Clapperton and Oudney in 1821.

A similar movement farther west led to more conversions to Islam. The Fulani, Seku Hamadu Bari, conquered Masina; here he built a capital in 1810 and called it Hamdallahi (Praise to Allah). Another was al-Hadj Omar who made the pilgrimage to Mecca in 1820, was granted the title of Caliph for a people of the Sudan, and started in 1838 a career of religious and military conquest that lasted for a quarter of a century. If therefore the Western Sudan was likely before this to have proved a difficult missionary field, it was much more so now. "It was in the eighteenth and nineteenth centuries", says Delafosse, "that Islam made most progress in the Western Sudan, and a progress more marked than it had ever made since the Almoravid period."[3]

In North Africa a movement of a different order was taking place.[4] In 1830 France was in Algiers. The piracy supported from this base had disturbed all nations using those seas. International action had not been sufficiently effective to

[1] C. K. Meek, *Northern Nigeria* (1925), I, 98–9.
[2] "El-Kanemi, sheikh of Bornu . . . accused the Fulani of grasping at empire under the guise of a religious reformation."—*Ibid.*, 99.
[3] M. Delafosse in *Ency. Islam*, IV, 496; A. Werner in *Ency. Islam*, III, 1079–80. For the resistance of Bornu, see G. Yver in *Ency. Islam*, I, 752–3.
[4] It will be convenient at this point to include some reference to contemporary developments in North Africa and Egypt together with Abyssinia, although this takes us across the continent.

suppress it. For France there was combined a motive of colonial ambition with one of security for the freedom of the seas, though the occasion was a rebuff to her ambassador. But France was soon to discover that to conquer Algiers was not to possess Algeria; the geographical contour determines that, as the Romans had discovered in their day. It was many years before the interior was occupied in more than name, and the proud Berber tribes at last submitted to an alien Christian rule. North Africa was now being once more brought into the full orbit of the Mediterranean world. The strength of the Roman Catholic hold on France presented an opportunity for that Church in this connexion that it was not slow to seize. The opportunity for Protestants, from this very fact, was not equally promising. The Paris Missionary Society did indeed toy with the idea of making an entry in the 'thirties. Eugène Casalis and Thomas Arbousset, on reaching Paris for their missionary training, were put to the study of Arabic and the Koran. But this was before long discontinued; they were informed their designation was to be the Cape, not the new dependency of France in the land of the vanished Church.[1]

The Bible Society, however, was pressing its claims and taking steady but effective steps to use the opportunity. In 1819 Dr. Pinkerton, visiting the Mediterranean lands for the Society, had "strongly urged the extension of their operations to the States of Barbary, and it was agreed to open correspondence with friends in Tangier, Tunis and Tripoli".[2] Copies of the Scriptures were from time to time distributed in North Africa, and it is interesting evidence of the journey into the interior these might make that in 1824 some were said to have found their way to Fezzan, Bornu and similar destinations.[3] The year 1832, however, after the coming of the French, marked the beginning of more vigorous work. Four years later it was reported that in that period some 5,000 copies of the Scriptures had been put into circulation in Algiers, Tunis and Tripoli, despite Muslim and Roman opposition; up to 1839 it was 5,000 more. But most significant of all: in 1830 a Berber version of the Gospels (and of Genesis) was at last produced for the Berber tribes.[4] The case of Egypt was a

[1] J. Bianquis, Les Origines de la Société des Missions Evangéliques de Paris (1935), III, 326–7. [2] W. Canton, op. cit., II, 3.
[3] Twentieth Report of the British and Foreign Bible Society (1824), lix.
[4] W. Canton, op. cit., II, 27, cf. 276. "A small edition of the Gospel of St. Luke was printed in 1833 . . . but more than half a century elapsed before the bulk of the New Testament appeared in the language from which so much had been expected".

special one, with the surviving Coptic Church to care for. Copies of the Scriptures in various languages were sent to Egypt, but the particular gesture of friendship to the Coptic Church was an edition of the Coptic Gospels with an Arabic version, these languages in parallel columns. The Coptic text had been prepared by the patriarch himself. The edition was issued in 1829.[1]

In 1825 the Church Missionary Society sent a company of five missionaries to Egypt. They were all men from Basel: Samuel Gobat, Christian Kugler, J. R. T. Lieder, Theodor Müller, and W. Krusé. The policy was to revitalize as far as possible the ancient Oriental Churches; the Coptic Church in Egypt and the Church of Abyssinia were two of these, and to them the present action was directed. Gobat and Kugler, it was hoped, would move on to Abyssinia as they perceived opportunity. Lieder was the outstanding worker of the group in Egypt. The Coptic patriarch and priests were not unfriendly. The missionaries even penetrated up the Nile into the ancient Nubia. The distribution of Christian literature was a principal activity, and a beginning was made with education. A boarding school for boys, begun in Cairo, developed later into a Theological College for the Coptic clergy. Muslims were also included within the mission's scope.[2]

It was not till February 1830 that Gobat was able to enter Abyssinia, and even then his stay was brief; he left in February 1833. His Journal recounting his experiences includes conversations with Abyssinian ecclesiastics and accounts of their practices.[3] Kugler and Aichinger, who had accompanied him from Egypt, remained for some months in Tigré where Kugler set himself to learn the dialect. The party carried Scripture versions in both Ethiopic, the ancient tongue, and Amharic, the vernacular. The amount Gobat could carry when he went forward alone was small—sixty copies of the Four Gospels, and some copies of Acts and Romans. He spent some time in Gondar the capital, and thus expressed his feelings on leaving: "It is not without mingled emotions of joy and grief that I quit this city; in which, for the first time in my life, I have felt myself a Missionary. If I may judge of Abyssinia from its capital, our Mission may expect happy results from its labours; for there is, in many, a hungering and thirsting for the Word of God, such as I have never found elsewhere. . . . The grand aim

[1] W. Canton, op. cit., II, 26.   [2] Stock, op. cit., I, 350-1.
[3] S. Gobat, Journal of a Three Years' Residence in Abyssinia (1834).

of Evangelical Missions in this country should be to multiply copies of the Bible, and to instruct the people in the Holy Scriptures."[1] Kugler, who had died in the country in 1830, was succeeded by C. W. Isenberg; C. H. Blumhardt and J. L. Krapf followed in 1837. In 1839 Isenberg and Krapf undertook a joint expedition to Shoa, with the Galla tribes beyond as a further objective. Isenberg prepared literature in Amharic, and Krapf did the same for Galla. Thus a striking beginning was made in this new enterprise of the Church in an ancient Christian land.[2]

We reach the year 1840 in West Africa with some measure of encouragement for those engaged in the Christian mission. A secure foothold had now been won at Sierra Leone, while in the Gambia to the north and Liberia to the south of it, continuous work was at least being maintained. After many vicissitudes a brighter day for Christian work was appearing on the Gold Coast. The successful result of much devoted work in exploration, from Mungo Park in 1795 to the brothers Lander in 1830, had at last traced the course of the mighty Niger to the sea. A new arterial highway to the heart of the continent seemed open in the West. Preparations were made to exploit it in the interests of Christianity and civilization, and to deal the slave-trade its final blow by encouraging Africa to develop her own resources. At last the happy issue of a delivered Africa for which philanthropists and missionaries had toiled seemed near. These hopes were expressed by an American missionary secretary on the designation of the Board's first missionary to Africa in 1833: "Having made a successful beginning among the tribes of the coast, around the colonies, we shall, as our labourers increase and the roads are opened, advance into the interior with our permanent establishments. . . . Our European brethren of different denominations, whose line of march already extends across the continent on the south, will advance from that quarter; the English Episcopal missions will advance from the Mountains of Abyssinia, and our brethren from the same denomination at Sierra Leone, and those of various names at Liberia, will move with us from the west; and our children may hear of the meeting of these upon some central mountain, to celebrate in lofty praise Africa's redemption."[3]

[1] S. Gobat, *op. cit.*, 262–3.
[2] *Journals of the Rev. Messrs. Isenberg and Krapf, Missionaries of the Church Missionary Society* (1843), v–x.
[3] *Memorial Volume of the A.B.C.F.M.*, 239–40.

But this was not yet to be. Tragic days lay just ahead. The failure of the Niger Expedition of 1841 brought high hopes crashing to the ground. Yet the vision of an opened continent was not cherished in vain. In 1841 David Livingstone arrived in Africa.

INDEX

313